101 618 508 1

This book provides a comprehensive guide to Spain's major political and economic institutions analysing their role, structure and functions, as well as their relationship to each other. Set against the background of Spain's consolidation as a young democratic nation and increasingly important contribution to EU affairs, the book examines the 1978 Constitution; the Monarchy of Juan Carlos I; the Parliament; central, regional and local government; political parties; trade unions; public sector enterprises; business and professional organisations; financial institutions; and the judiciary. While most chapters reflect Spain's now well advanced adaptation to life within the European Union, chapter 15 also looks in detail at the country's representation in EU institutions, as well as the activities of EU-oriented institutions within Spain itself. This is a new expanded, revised and updated edition of the authors' *Spain: a guide to political and economic institutions*, first published in 1987.

D0492360

Institutions of modern Spain

Institutions of modern Spain

A political and economic guide

MICHAEL T. NEWTON

with

PETER J. DONAGHY

CAMBRIDGE
UNIVERSITY PRESS

Published by the Press Syndicate of the University of Cambridge
The Pitt Building, Trumpington Street, Cambridge CB2 1RP
40 West 20th Street, New York, NY 10011-4211, USA
10 Stamford Road, Oakleigh, Melbourne 3166, Australia

Institutions of modern Spain: a political and economic guide (first published 1997) succeeds and replaces
Spain: a guide to political and economic institutions (0 521 30032 0 hardback; 0 521 317347 paperback)
first published in 1987, of which it is an updated and expanded edition.

Printed in Great Britain at the University Press, Cambridge

A catalogue record for this book is available from the British Library

Library of Congress cataloging in publication data

Newton, Michael T., 1942–
Institutions of modern Spain: a political and economic guide /
Michael T. Newton (with Peter J. Donaghy). – New expanded, rev. and
updated ed.
p.   cm.
"'Institutions of modern Spain: a political and economic guide'
(first published 1997) succeeds and replaces 'Spain: a guide to
political and economic institutions' . . . first published in 1987, of
which it is an update and expanded edition."
Includes bibliographical references and index.
ISBN 0 521 57348 3. – ISBN 0 521 57508 7 (pbk)
1. Spain – Politics and government – 1975–   2. Decentralization in
government – Spain.   3. Regionalism – Spain.   4. Local government –
– Spain.   5. Government business enterprises – Spain.   6. Political
parties – Spain.   7. Trade associations – Spain.   8. Financial
institutions – Spain.   I. Donaghy, P. J. Spain.   II. Title.
JN8210.N48   1997
320.946–dc20   96-2353   CIP

ISBN 0 521 57348 3 hardback
ISBN 0 521 57508 7 paperback

For Rosie, Sally and Paul
and in memory of Denise Soria

Contents

Figures

Tables

Preface to the second edition

The first edition of this work was published in 1987. At that time, the Franco dictatorship was still a relatively recent experience in the minds of many Spaniards; it was still arguably appropriate to refer to Spain's 'fragile' democracy. Now a whole generation has emerged which remembers nothing of the Franco regime, and since 1986 Spain has matured into one more stable democracy within the framework of the European Union (EU). At last the country has shaken off its one-time image of a backward and isolated Latin nation dominated by the army and the Church; no longer can it be said that Spain has no relevance to the mainstream of European and world affairs. Indeed, in recent years, in parts of Latin America and elsewhere in the developing world, Spain's relatively smooth transition from dictatorship to democracy has been seen as a model for achieving peaceful political change. On the other hand, the curve of economic development has been subject to greater instability, and Spain has only recently begun to recover after suffering severely during the world recession of the early 1990s. Spain's levels of unemployment, for example, have consistently been the highest in the European Union. None the less, many countries which still suffer the kind of backwardness experienced by Spain not many decades ago will envy the standard of living now enjoyed by the majority of the Spanish people.

Clearly Europe in general, and the European Union in particular, has been right at the heart of Spain's 'quiet revolution', providing a broad framework for economic activity, support for democracy and a goal to strive for in terms of socio–economic development and trans-national co-operation. The impact of EU membership on Spain's laws, institutions and way of thinking has been considerable, and in general terms the Spanish people have welcomed their country's growing integration with their European neighbours. Since joining the European Union in January 1986, they have already participated in three Euro-elections and many Spanish professionals have held high office in European institutions, including the presidency of the European Parliament. For two half-year periods, the most recent from July to December 1995 Spain, in turn with other member countries, has held the presidency of the European Union. The European dimension is indeed a very significant factor in the Spain of today; chapter 15 therefore attempts to reflect the extent of Spanish institutional integration in the European Union.

Undoubtedly, a major influence on Spanish institutions, as well as on the wider political and economic scene, has been the substantial devolution of power from the centre to the seventeen newly-created autonomous communities or *comunidades autónomas*. When the first edition went to press, this process was in its infancy. A key element of this edition will therefore be an examination of the impact of decentralisation within what is (uniquely in Europe) an open-ended, evolving relationship between central and regional centres of decision-making. In this context, the current move to reform the composition and functions of the Senate, involving the first major reform of the 1978 Constitution, will receive due attention.

Another key issue pervading Spanish public life has been the increasingly important role which the country has been assuming on the world stage. Such changes spring partly from Spain's membership of NATO (since 1982), partly from her special relationship with the Arab World, partly from her long-standing cultural and personal ties with many countries of Latin America and partly from her new role within the European Union itself. As examples of this new, pro-active world role, one can cite Spain's participation in the UN peace-keeping forces in El Salvador, Cambodia and Bosnia, her involvement in the 1990 Gulf War and her hosting of the crucial first Middle East Peace Conference in November 1991. Off the political stage, Spain has gained greater international appreciation through her hosting of such prestigious events as the Barcelona Olympics of July–August 1992.

Apart from chapter 15 on Europe, the next most obvious new feature of this edition is the inclusion of an additional chapter devoted to the judiciary (chapter 14). With hindsight, this crucial sector of the country's institutional structure should perhaps have been included in the first edition; there is little doubt that within any constitutional system the judiciary plays a major role, and indeed the esteem in which it is or is not held provides a useful barometer of the health of the democratic system.

Attention is drawn to the comment made in the Preface of the first edition concerning the gender of office holders. It cannot be overstressed that the use of the masculine form is not meant in any way to imply that women do not or cannot occupy important posts of responsibility within the institutions described. On the contrary, as is shown in chapter 1, there has been a substantial improvement over the last decade in the position of women in this respect. Indeed, this is clearly reflected in the now common use of alternative noun forms such as *presidenta*, *ministra*, *consejera*, *directora*, *jefa* and others.

As stated in the Preface to the first edition, while each chapter is free-standing, a number of common threads link many of the institutions concerned; thus, to help the reader in making these connections, a substantial number of cross-references have been inserted in the body of the text. These refer to the numbered section and sub-section headings. In the Index of institutions and office holders (pp. 356–79), references are to these same sections rather than to page numbers.

An important point that readers should note is that, although it has not been thought appropriate to include references in the body of the text, a detailed, up-to-date Select Bibliography appears at the end of the book after the Appendix. The publications quoted, which include both books and articles in learned journals, in both English and Spanish, are organised according to chapter. A number of general critical works are also cited.

In the years that have passed since the first edition was published, interest in Spanish affairs has if anything accelerated, thus fully justifying the need for a follow-up. Not only have business men and women, as well as politicians, become increasingly involved with this still relative newcomer to the European Union but, as a result of the impetus given to language and related nation studies by the challenge of the Single Market, many more students, particularly at university and college level, have been given the opportunity to learn the Spanish language and study the country's political and business environment. Indeed, a significant percentage of students on these 'Europeanised' courses are able to spend periods of up to twelve months studying and/or working in other countries of Europe, including Spain. Moreover, to the already substantial number of university and college courses in the United States offering Hispanic studies, many others have been added in recent years to accommodate the growing interest among professors and students in the language, culture and institutions of the country whose mother tongue is the second language of the United States. Hence the growing need, on both sides of the Atlantic, for an up-to-date volume on the principal political and economic institutions of Spain.

Finally, I would like to express my gratitude to the University of Northumbria at Newcastle (UNN) for allowing me a sabbatical semester from February to July 1995, as well as a generous travel grant, to enable me to carry out the research necessary to write this new edition. Moreover, I am especially indebted to the co-author of the first edition, Peter Donaghy, who as Acting Head of Modern Languages at the time gave such sympathetic support to my application for assistance. I very much regret that, because of very heavy research and other commitments, he has been unable to be as deeply involved as in the first edition. However, I am very grateful to him not only for finding time to update chapters 12 and 13, but also for giving me the inestimable benefits of professional advice and personal encouragement. Grateful thanks are also due to my friend and colleague, David Kaufman, who has often given invaluable technical advice. Last but by no means least, I would like to extend my warmest thanks to David Crook, Seph Nesbit and David Marshall, three excellent technicians in the Department of Modern Languages at UNN; without their infinite patience and expertise, the word-processed version of this edition would surely never have seen the light of day.

Michael T. Newton
Newcastle upon Tyne

Preface to the first edition

Since the death of Franco, on 20 November 1975, Spain has undergone substantial transformation. This is reflected in the way in which many of the political and economic institutions which characterised nearly forty years of Francoism have been either swept away or modified along democratic lines.

Largely as a result of these changes, the world in general, and Europe in particular, has focused increasing attention on Spanish affairs. Spain is once more regarded as 'respectable'. Former barriers to international relations have been gradually removed as the country, for several years now a member of the Council of Europe and NATO, establishes herself as a member of the EEC. While post-Franco Spain saw intrinsic value in democratising her many outdated institutions, the determination to secure integration with Europe injected an extra dimension of urgency into the task of modernising the country's political and economic structures.

Thus, it appears an appropriate time to publish a reference work which describes and examines the political and economic institutions of post-Franco Spain, something which, we believe, has not been attempted before, at least in English. We expect that this publication will be of value and interest to all those who need to be informed about the new institutional framework of contemporary Spain. On the one hand, it is hoped that the book will appeal to the increasing number of industrialists, bankers and investors who see the potential of the country within its new EEC context and who require a reference guide to current institutions and official bodies. On the other hand, it should provide essential background reading for students on the increasing number of A-level, polytechnic and university courses which are oriented towards Spanish contemporary affairs.

We would like to stress that in two senses this work should be regarded as only an introduction to the subject of Spain's political and economic institutions. In the first place, only the major institutions figure here since clearly a work of this nature could not hope to encompass the thousands of bodies and organisations which function at various levels of public life. Second, given that a minimum number of these institutions must be examined if anything like an authentic and representative picture of official Spain is to emerge, it has not been possible to provide more than an introductory and basically descriptive study. However, we trust that we have provided the groundwork for the further study and analysis of the major institutions of post-Franco Spain. Nevertheless, through our examination of these institutions some opinion is bound to emerge, if only incidentally, in spite of the fact that our basic aim is not to evaluate the success or otherwise of Spain's new institutional arrangements.

Although each chapter contains some reference to the historical evolution of the institutions studied therein, we have felt it appropriate to provide an overall context and background against which the institutions can be viewed. Hence chapter 1 is devoted to a brief outline of political and economic developments since 1939. Chapter 2 examines the 1978 Constitution which provides both the theoretical framework for the new state and the principles that should govern its institutions in the post-Franco era. Chapters 3, 4 and 5 look at the major political institutions at national level, while chapter 6 is concerned with both political and economic aspects of public administration. Chapters 7 and 8 are devoted to regional and local institutions respectively and chapters 9 and 10 outline national and regional level organisations of political and trade union participation. Finally, chapters 11, 12 and 13 introduce a wide range of important public and private enterprises as well as financial institutions.

Each of the above chapters is, to a certain extent, free-standing. However, it will be seen that a number of common threads unite many of the institutions concerned; for example, the consequences of reform in one area are often felt in others. To aid the reader in making these connections, a number of cross-references have been supplied wherever possible. Inevitably, because of the interlocking nature of many institutions, a certain amount of overlapping and repetition has occurred; it is hoped that this will help rather than hinder the reader by reinforcing his perception of their interdependence.

Since institutions, like the society that gives birth to them, are never static, it is possible that some (it is to be hoped, minor) changes will have occurred between the writing of these pages and their publication. Any work that attempts to reflect contemporary realities is bound to run this risk. Nevertheless, unless the country experiences a major political catastrophe, it is likely that, notwithstanding minor modifications that changes of government may well bring, the basic institutional structures described in these chapters are likely to remain largely unchanged for some time to come.

In order to facilitate the maximum accessibility to the institutions, an index has been provided. This index includes not only the names in Spanish of the institutions referred to in the text, but in many cases the Spanish acronyms, since many of these organisations are better known by these than by their full titles. As far as the text is concerned, readers need to recognise the names of institutions in their original Spanish form; however, where appropriate and when it is felt that it is not misleading to do so, English translations have been supplied.

In view of the range of areas and topics considered in this volume, it would be a daunting task to provide a fully comprehensive bibliography. Thus, we have included only a select bibliography which in our opinion contains some of the key works necessary both to provide more detailed historical background and to go beyond this introduction to a critical assessment of the institutions and their role in public life.

We would like to make it clear that in all references to office holders, the use of the masculine form is not meant to imply any favouritism towards the male sex, any more than it is intended, at least in theory, in the Spanish Constitution and other documents which, following an age-old convention, use the masculine form in a neutral sense and do not thereby imply any discrimination.

To thank individually all those who have helped us over a longer period of time would be an impossible task. We are indebted to several Hispanist colleagues in the UK as well as a number of most helpful experts in Spain working both inside and outside the institutions which we have studied. We are extremely grateful to all concerned. We would like to stress that the viewpoints which we have expressed here are, in the final analysis, our responsibility alone.

Finally, we would like to thank our colleagues at Newcastle Polytechnic for their valuable suggestions, our students on the BA (Honours) course in modern languages and economic/political studies, whose questions prompted the need for such a publication and, most of all, our wives and families without whose support, patience and understanding its completion would have been impossible.

Peter J. Donaghy
Michael T. Newton
Newcastle upon Tyne

Acknowledgements

Grateful thanks are due to the following who kindly provided interviews and in most cases also supplied vital primary source material:

Antonio Abad Martínez, Technical Adviser, Subdirectorate General of International Relations, Ministry of Health and Consumer Affairs, Madrid

Ramón Abaroa, Head of Office of General Secretary for European Union, Ministry of Foreign Affairs, Madrid

Ramón Alises Romero, Head of Press Department, TENEO, Ministry of Industry and Energy, Madrid

Juan Ignacio Alvarez Gortari, Minister Plenipotenciary, Permanent Representation of Spain, Brussels

Manual Alvarez Núñez, Technical Adviser, IMAC, Ministry of Labour and Social Security, Madrid

María Jesús Aramburu del Río, IU Euro-MP, Euro party spokesperson for Committee of Culture, Education, Young People's Affairs and the Media, European Parliament, Brussels

Carlos Báez Evertsz, Assistant Director General for the Press, Social Relations and Documentation, Ministry of Justice and Home Affairs, Madrid

Enrique Barón Crespo, PSOE Euro-MP, leader of first PSOE delegation to European Community, former president of European Parliament, Brussels

José Luis Benavides del Río, Registrar, Central Mercantile Registry, Madrid

Francisco Borges, Department of Organisation, UGT, Madrid

Oscar Carrilero, International Relations and Foreign Policy Committee, CC.OO, Madrid

Alfonso Díez Torres, Counsellor, Spanish Permanent Representation, Brussels

Claro José Fernández-Carnicero González, Director of International Relations, Congress of Deputies, Madrid

Francisco Fernández Fábregas, Director General, DG for Relations with European Parliament and with Economic and Social Committee, and for Institutional, Budgetary and Staffing Affairs, Council of Ministers, Brussels

Camilo Fernández Marín, Head of Legal Affairs, *Diputación Provincial*, Málaga

Francisco Fonseca Morillo, Adviser to the Director General, IGC Task Force, European Commission, Brussels

Carlos García de Cortázar y Nebreda, Assistant Director General, Technical General Secretariat, Ministry of Labour and Social Security, Madrid

José-María Gil-Robles Gil-Delgado, PP Euro–MP, Vice-president of European Parliament, Brussels

Salvador García Llanos, Executive Adviser to Minister, Department of Communication, Ministry for Public Administration, Madrid

José María García-Perrote Escartín, Head of Media Relations Department, Repsol, Madrid

Ana González, Adviser, Technical General Secretariat, Ministry of Labour and Social Security, Madrid

Mari-Angeles González, Assistant Director General for Bilateral Co-operation, Ministry for Public Administration, Madrid

Miguel González Zamora, Assistant Secretary for International Relations, CC.OO, Madrid

Guillermo Gortázar, PP Euro–MP, Congress of Deputies, Madrid

Antonio Hidalgo López, Technical General Secretary, *Consejería de Cultura, Junta de Andalucía*, Seville

Juan Fernando López Aguilar, Director of the Office of the Minister, Minister for Public Administration, Madrid

Angel Losada Fernández, Assistant Director of Technical International Bodies and Development, Ministry of Foreign Affairs, Madrid

José Sánchez Maldonado, Professor of Public Finance, University of Málaga, Málaga

Juan Márquez, Clerk to the Council, *Diputación Provincial*, Málaga

Ignacio Martínez, Correspondent, *Canal Sur*, Brussels

Anna Melich, Head of Unit, Monitoring of Public Opinion Trends, European Commission, Brussels

Carmen de Paz, Department of International Relations, CC.OO, Madrid

Arturo Pérez, Assistant Director General of International Relations, Ministry of Health and Consumer Affairs, Madrid

Cristina Pérez Cantó, Head of Press Department, Secretary of State for the European Union, Ministry of Foreign Affairs, Madrid

Diana Rodríguez García, Head of Department of Company Information, Central Mercantile Registry, Madrid

Rafael Salas Gallego, Head of Division of Administration and Tourism Promotion, *Consejería de Industria, Comercio y Turismo (Delegación Privincial)*, Málaga

Jorge Sanz Oliva, Department of Economy, Prime Minister's Office, Madrid

José Luis Sardina García, Central Documentation Services, PSOE, Madrid

Miguel del Val Alonso, General Secretary, Directorate General for State Assets, Ministry of Economy and Finance, Madrid

Asunción Valdés Nicolau, Head of Public Relations, Royal Household, Palacio de la Zarzuela, Madrid

Agustín Zurita Pinilla, Head of Press Relations, General Council of the Judiciary, Madrid

Very special thanks are due to the following who went out of their way to be helpful in many different ways over a long period of time:

Juan Antonio González Mestre, Department of Tourism, *Ayuntamiento*, Málaga

Alun Jones, Research Assistant, European Parliament, Brussels

Juan Antonio Lacomba Abellán, Professor of Contemporary History, University of Málaga

Coralie Pearson, Senior Translator, Press and Information Office, British Embassy, Madrid

Graham Shields, Librarian for Modern Languages, University of Northumbria, Newcastle upon Tyne

Part 1: Chronological résumé of Spanish history since 1939

Dictatorship of General Franco (1939–75)

1939–45	Second World War; Spain neutral
1947	Succession Law
1953 August	*Concordat* signed with Vatican
September	Military and economic agreements signed with United States
1955	Spain admitted to UN
1956	Spain admitted to ILO
1957	Appointment of more liberal cabinet
1958	Spain admitted to IMF and IBRD
1959	Stabilisation Plan
1961	Spain admitted to OECD
1962	Spain requests associate membership of EEC
1964	First of three Development Plans
1967	Organic Law of the State
1969	Juan Carlos named heir to Franco
1970	Preferential Trade Agreement with EEC
1973 June	Luis Carrero Blanco appointed prime minister
December	Carrero Blanco assassinated by ETA
1974	Carlos Arias Navarro appointed prime minister
1975	Death of General Franco (20 November)

Spain since 1975

1975 November	Juan Carlos crowned King of Spain
December	Arias Navarro re-appointed prime minister
1976 July	Adolfo Suárez appointed prime minister
November	*Cortes* aproves Political Reform Law
1977 June	First democratic elections; victory for UCD; Suárez elected prime minister
July	Spain requests full membership of EEC
October	Moncloa Pacts; Spain admitted to Council of Europe
1978	New Constitution approved

1979 March	Second democratic elections; victory for UCD; Suárez re-elected prime minister
October	Basque and Catalan statutes of autonomy approved
1981 January	Resignation of Adolfo Suárez
February	Attempted *coup* via seizure of *Cortes*; Leopoldo Calvo Sotelo elected prime minister
1982 May	Spain admitted to NATO
October	Third democratic elections; victory for PSOE; Felipe González Márquez elected prime minister
1985 February	Reopening of frontier with Gibraltar
June	Treaty of Accession to EC signed in Madrid
1986 January	Spain admitted to EC
February	Spain signs Single European Act (SEA)
March	Referendum confirms Spanish membership of NATO
June	Fourth democratic elections; victory for PSOE; Felipe González re-elected prime minister

Spain since 1986

1987 June	First European elections held in Spain; won by PSOE
1988	Official divorce between PSOE and UGT
December	General strike
1989 June	Second European elections; won by PSOE
October	Fifth democratic elections; victory for PSOE (loss of overall majority); Felipe González re-elected prime minister
1991 November	First Middle East Peace Conference held in Madrid
1992 January– December	Madrid designated Cultural Capital of Europe
February	Spain signs Treaty of Maastricht; Government, PSOE and PP sign new Autonomy Agreements
1992 April– October	Universal Exhibition (Expo) held in Seville; Commemoration of discovery of America
July– August	Olympic games held in Barcelona
1993 April	Death of Don Juan, Count of Barcelona, father of King Juan Carlos and former Pretender to the throne of Spain
June	Sixth democratic elections; victory for PSOE (greatly reduced number of seats); Felipe González re-elected prime minister
1994 January	General strike
June	Third European elections; won by PP
1995 March	Marriage of Infanta Elena; first royal wedding in Spain since 1906
June	Tenth anniversary of Spanish signing of Accession Treaty
1996 March	Seventh democratic elections; José María Aznar elected prime minister

Chapter 1

Introduction

1.1 Political and economic background

Franco's death in 1975 marked a watershed in contemporary Spanish history. Since then, Spain has witnessed the dismantling of his dictatorial regime and the gradual establishment of democracy. The first free elections since 1936 were held on 15 June 1977 and on 28 December 1978 a new Constitution came into effect, paving the way for the creation of a completely new political structure, as well as more democratic political and economic institutions.

1.1.1 Democratic tradition in Spain

It is sometimes forgotten that, in spite of her propensity for authoritarian regimes, Spain has a long, albeit turbulent, democratic history stretching back to 1812, when the first constitution was drawn up. Although weak in comparison with the forces of reaction, a democratic tradition, founded by the liberal politicians of the early nineteenth century, survived the vicissitudes of authoritarian rule and, prior to the post-Franco period, expressed itself first in the short-lived First (Federal) Republic of 1873–4 and later in the Second Republic of 1931–36. In fact, the Republican Constitution of 1931, far more progressive than anything that had preceded it in Spain, presented an important landmark in the development of the Spanish democratic tradition. It was the first Spanish constitution, for example, to grant universal suffrage to the whole adult population; it was the first to consider that the regions of Spain, traditionally a source of friction, might constitute self-governing entities within the Spanish state; it was the first to tackle seriously the problem of agrarian reform; and it was the first to embark on an ambitious programme of state education. It was also the first constitution not to accept the special position of the Catholic Church *vis-à-vis* the state; and, indeed, in attempting to separate the Church and the state, the Republican government succeeded in alienating large sectors of the population which subsequently gave their support to Franco's attempted *coup d'état*. Both in its positive and negative features, the 1931 Constitution proved to be an example and a starting point for the constitution drafters of 1978 who, after a forty-year interruption, embarked on the task of providing Spain with a new framework for democracy.

1.1.2 Spain, 1939–59

Following his victory in the Civil War of 1936–39, General Franco set about demolishing the progressive political structure and the institutions established under the ill-fated Second Republic, replacing them with structures that reflected his own authoritarian instincts. The dictator's so-called constitution, the seven Fundamental Laws (*Leyes Fundamentales*) represented a complete rejection of the ideals that lay behind the 1931 Constitution. In particular, Franco turned the clock back regarding the crucial issue of the relations between the executive and the legislature, ensuring that the one-chamber Parliament or *Cortes* was to be no more than a rubber-stamp body to which the executive was not accountable. Moreover, Republican legislation on the Church, education, regional autonomy and land distribution was annulled. The Church regained its privileged relationship with the state, including its traditionally dominant role in education. The regions were once more subjected to a repressive centralism. Property expropriated by the state during the Republic, both land and industrial enterprises, was restored to former owners, who were henceforth to benefit from state paternalism. Most significantly, whereas the 1931 Constitution stressed liberty, Franco's basic laws laid emphasis on unity. In the cause of unity, the traditional separation of powers was rejected, all political organisations apart from Franco's all-embracing National Movement (*Movimiento Nacional*) were outlawed, all trade union groupings, with the exception of the state-run *sindicatos*, were abolished, and many basic civil rights were denied. For a period of nearly forty years, rigid centralist control of both the political structure and the economy was imposed. The effects of this regime still persist to some extent in the Spain of the 1990s.

Once the basic political apparatus of Francoism was established, the regime could concentrate on the resuscitation of the war-ravaged economy. Partly inspired by Fascist ideology and partly imposed by sheer economic necessity, as a result of being ostracised by the victorious allied powers, Spain embarked on a course of economic autarky or self-sufficiency. This policy was most obvious during the 1940s and 1950s, a period characterised by protectionism, economic nationalism and state intervention. Responding to the needs of a war-torn economy that was short of raw materials and energy, in 1941 Franco created the National Institute for Industry (*Instituto Nacional de Industria/INI*), a state holding company, the original objectives of which were to strengthen defence industries and to promote economic viability in sectors where private interests could not or were not willing to do so (9.4.2.2). INI in turn spawned a whole series of public sector enterprises where, for a long time, senior posts were the prerogative of political appointees or retired military personnel. In addition, numerous semi-autonomous bodies were established to administer particular services at the behest of the regime.

While the fragile economy of the nineteenth century had been boosted by foreign investment, this was not the case for a long time in the post-Civil War period. US-backed Marshall Aid programmes, which did so much to restore other war-damaged economies, were not forthcoming for Spain, which furthermore had to suffer an economic boycott by nations distrustful of this former ally of Hitler and Mussolini. The government had to increase the national debt at the expense of its own citizens and companies had to mortgage their boardrooms to the banking sector.

Labour was in no position to resist the inflationary pressures which suppressed workers' livelihoods. From its inception, the Franco regime was determined to bring the whole apparatus of labour organisation under state control. The free trade unions of the Republican era were outlawed and replaced by a single vertical system encompassing both management and labour. Strikes were made illegal and wages were strictly regulated by the Ministry of Labour (*Ministerio de Trabajo*).

By the late 1950s, it had become plain that autarky had failed and that Spain was on the verge of bankruptcy. The new 'technocratic' and outward-looking cabinet, which had strong links with the influential lay Catholic organisation, the Opus Dei, realised that the only solution lay in a break with the economic (though not the political) policies of the past. This was facilitated by the fact that, gradually during the 1950s, Spain had gained admittance to a number of international organisations, ranging from the UN to the IMF. It was, in fact, with the help of IMF officials that an austerity programme was drawn up to bring the economy more onto an even keel and to enable Spain to embark upon normal multilateral trade. The subsequent Stabilisation Plan (*Plan de Estabilización*) of 1959 was accompanied by measures designed to liberalise foreign investment.

1.1.3 Spain, 1959–75

During the second half of the Franco era, only minor steps were taken to modify the monolithic political edifice that had been erected in 1939. Such steps responded to the regime's new-found interest of the early 1960s in integration with Europe, a concept unthinkable in the xenophobic days of the late 1940s and 1950s. In its clumsy and unconvincing attempts to present a more respectable image to its European neighbours, the regime allowed a small group of so-called 'family MPs' to be elected in a semi-democratic way, accepted the need for religious toleration, approved a new press law, which substantially reduced the use of prior censorship, introduced a limited form of collective bargaining into industrial relations, and made minor cultural concessions to the regions. However, none of this tampering with the facade impressed either the EEC or the opposition groups which, in spite of the continuing repression, were growing more vocal and confident in their demands for change.

The economy, meanwhile, began to take off: the economic boom enjoyed by Spain's EEC neighbours and other Western economies exerted a considerable influence. Foreign investment, under the terms of very liberal legislation, flowed into Spain at ever-increasing rates, bringing with it much-needed technology and know-how. The surplus labour created by the shakeout resulting from the 1959 Stabilisation Plan was able to find an outlet in the prosperous industrial areas of Northern Europe. Workers, officially encouraged by the Spanish Emigration

Table 1.1 *Distribution of working population, by sector, 1950–94*

	1950	1960	1970	1980	1985	1990	1992	1994
Agriculture and fishing	48.8	41.7	29.0	19.1	16.7	11.8	10.1	9.5
Industry and construction	26.1	30.0	34.8	35.9	32.2	33.4	32.4	30.1
Services	25.1	28.3	36.2	44.5	51.1	54.8	57.5	60.4
Total	100	100	100	100	100	100	100	100

Sources: Banco Bilbao Vizcaya/Instituto Nacional de Estadística (INE) (various years).

Institute (*Instituto Español de Emigración/IEE*), sent back remittances which made a further contribution to Spain's balance of payments surplus. Other workers migrated from the land only as far as the larger cities of Spain itself, and came to constitute the new industrial proletariat as the country's own industries, including motor-manufacturing, petro-chemicals and textiles, began to prosper.

One industry that made spectacular progress was tourism. Spain's more affluent neighbours sought areas where they could enjoy their increased leisure possibilities. Between 1960 and 1994, the number of tourists rose from 6 million to over 60 million. This brought enormous benefits to the balance of payments and to allied industries, such as construction. However, the consequent misallocation of resources, the infrastructural pressures and environmental problems which resulted are still very much in evidence today, although governments of recent times have at last begun to put much-needed reforms in place.

The rapid economic growth of the 1960s and early 1970s was such as to merit the use of the term 'economic miracle' and to place Spain in second position behind Japan in terms of growth in gross national product (GNP). This period saw the final transformation of Spain into an industrialised, as opposed to an agricultural, economy and this was reflected, for example, in the movement of labour from agriculture to industry and services, a development that has continued unabated over recent decades (table 1.1).

There is no doubt that, in global terms, the performance of the Spanish economy between 1960 and 1973 was impressive, and in overall terms Spain moved into the league of the top ten industrial nations of the West, a position that has generally been maintained since that time. However, the price for this progress was high in several respects. Firstly, Spaniards in the 1970s were still often deprived of basic civil and political rights; secondly, the migrations of the 1960s involved untold personal hardship for thousands of families, and the pressures on the services of the rapidly expanding urban sprawls were enormous; thirdly, the benefits of economic growth were not shared equally either between the regions or between social classes: great disparities in *per capita* income levels remain prevalent even today; and, fourthly, industry was cushioned by high protective tariffs which concealed considerable inefficiency, and immune sectors suffered from an excessive proliferation of small firms. In addition, as a result of the oil crisis and consequent economic recession in the mid-1970s, even before Franco's death, the economy had begun to flag. Emigrants returning from a western Europe which was also forced to lay off much of its workforce only fuelled the growing unemployment and added to the accumulation of social and infrastructural problems. Thus, economically, the circumstances in which Spain made her second attempt in the twentieth century to implant a democratic regime were not auspicious.

1.1.4 Spain, 1975–86

Since the death of General Franco in 1975 and the restoration of the Spanish monarchy in the person of King Juan Carlos, a remarkable transformation has taken place. Between 1976 and 1978, against a background of potential political instability and economic crisis, Spain made considerable progress towards the establishment of new democratic institutions based on the twin principles of modernisation and decentralisation. Some tentative steps were taken between December 1975 and July 1976 to liberalise the political structures during the premiership of Carlos Arias Navarro, Franco's last prime minister, reluctantly re-appointed by King Juan Carlos. However, these pseudo-reforms did not satisfy the accelerating pressures for substantial change. The pace of change quickened under his successor, Adolfo Suárez, a more open-minded former Franco minister, whose appointment was secured by the king; the new premier's Political Reform Law (*Ley para la Reforma Política*), approved in the autumn of 1976, paved the way for a genuine restoration of democracy, promising Spain's first genuine elections for forty years on 15 June 1977. In these historic elections, Suárez, with his newly formed Union of the Democratic Centre (*Unión de Centro Democrático / UCD*) won a clear victory over his nearest rivals, the Spanish Socialist Workers' Party (*Partido Socialista Obrero Español / PSOE*), led by Felipe González. However, the elections represented only the first step on the long road to a complete restoration of democratic processes and institutions, to achieve which a new constitutional framework was required. Thus the newly elected Parliament (*Cortes*) saw its main task as the drafting of Spain's first democratic constitution since 1931. Significantly, all the major parties represented in Parliament, including the UCD, the PSOE, the Conservative Popular Alliance (*Alianza Popular / AP*), the Communist Party of Spain (*Partido Comunista de España / PCE*) and Basque and Catalan Nationalists, participated in this historic process, which culminated in December 1978 with the publication of the new Constitution. The general elections of 1979, again won by the UCD, were the first to be held under this Constitution.

During the period 1976–78, the emphasis was so much on political change that economic reform tended to be neglected, although it has to be recognised that the priority given to tax legislation in 1977 (involving a much-needed rise in direct taxation, as well as an attempt to cut down tax evasion) was an important first step in economic reform. Moreover, the Moncloa Pacts (*Pactos de la Moncloa*) of that year, which constituted a statement of broad economic and political objectives, represented an encouraging willingness to co-operate in economic affairs on the part of the major political parties, who were all signatories to the document. However, the deterioration of the economic situation between 1976 and 1981, by which time both inflation and unemployment had soared to over 20 per cent, plus the escalation of Basque-inspired terrorism, soon dampened the euphoria that had accompanied the restoration of democracy and provided ammunition for frustrated reactionary generals to indulge in sabre-rattling and in the more serious attempted *coup* of 23 February 1981, when a detachment of civil guards under Lieutenant-Colonel Antonio Molina stormed the *Cortes*. The *desencanto*, or disillusion, which had characterised the years 1978–81 was suddenly dissipated by this coup, which galvanised wide sectors of the population into demonstrating in favour of democracy and the new Constitution. A further healthy sign was the level of moderation and willingness to compromise shown by the major political parties and the trade unions, the members of which showed considerable restraint in sacrificing personal and sectoral advancement in the interests of the consolidation of democracy.

The reaction of the outside world, and of western Europe in particular, to the process of reform in Spain was generally very positive. The first sign that Europe recognised the new direction the country was taking came in October 1977 when Spain was admitted to the Council of Europe. Three months earlier, the Spanish foreign minister, following the elections of June 1977, had formally presented Spain's application for full membership of the European Community (EC), to which she had previously been linked only by a very modest commercial agreement known as the Preferential Trade Agreement (PTA) signed in 1970. Both western Europe and the United States, which had established military bases on Spanish soil in 1953, were now anxious to integrate Spain more closely into the defence programmes of the Atlantic Alliance. This process culminated, in May 1982, with the UCD government of Leopoldo Calvo Sotelo (who became leader of the party following Suárez's resignation in January 1981), securing the approval of the Spanish Parliament for Spain's entry into NATO. At that time, the move was strongly opposed by Felipe González and the PSOE, who argued that the government had a moral obligation to consult the people in a referendum before taking such a momentous decision, promising that, once elected, they would hold such a referendum and abide by its result.

Moderation seemed to be the key-note of the Socialist government first elected in October 1982 and re-elected on three subsequent occasions (1986, 1989 and 1993). Rather than radically alter the direction of policy, the socialists under Felipe González tended to build on the reforms of their predecessors. Working closely with the constitutional monarchy of Juan Carlos, the government strove to consolidate the country's new system of decentralised government and administration based on autonomous regional institutions. It accepted the realities of its role within the Western Alliance, eventually urging the electorate to vote for continued membership of NATO in the long-delayed referendum held in March 1986. It also grasped the nettle of industrial restructuring as a prerequisite for efficient operation in the framework of the European Community. Politically there were major successes, not the least of which was the ability to convince the armed forces to agree to structural change and to accept a purely military, non-political role within the new democratic Spain. On the negative side, however, in spite of some limited successes, the government was still not able to resolve the continuing problem of terrorism committed by the Basque separatist organisation, ETA. Economically some progress was made, notably in the gradual reduction of inflation to tolerable levels and in the improvement of the balance of payments situation; however, unemployment continued to rise and during this period remained stubbornly over 20 per cent, an overall figure that in fact disguised even higher levels in some of the poorer rural parts of central and southern Spain.

Spain's path to membership of the European Community was long and arduous. The negotiations which began in 1979 faltered on many occasions and it took until January 1986 to convert Spain's long-cherished aspiration into a reality. However, ultimately this wait probably benefited the country since it permitted some measure of harmonisation to take place in advance of entry and a number of important institutional reforms to be carried out in the economic sphere, in addition to the major shift that occurred in the political system. Nevertheless, EC (now EU) membership, at that time seen by all the major parties and the majority of the population as politically desirable, involved considerable economic risks, as well as long-term opportunities, for a country whose economy had for decades been protected by the state. However, Spain had political and cultural as well as economic reasons for wanting to 'come in from the wilderness', and clearly saw integration with Europe as a way of consolidating its new democracy and protecting its then still fragile political and economic institutions.

1.1.5 Spain since 1986

During the last decade, the second since the death of Franco, Spanish democracy has been consolidated, and Spain has entered the fold of 'normal' Western nations, experiencing similar problems to her partners within the European Union and entertaining similar aspirations. Remarkably, the man who became prime minister in 1982, Felipe González, remained at the helm of the nation's affairs until the general election of March 1996, when he was narrowly defeated by the PP. During that period, he had rivalled the British Conservative Party and the CDU in Germany by winning four consecutive general elections. While the PSOE won outright victories over the Conservative AP in 1982 and 1986, its declining (albeit substantial) share of the popular vote meant that, after the 1993 election, the ruling party was forced to do a deal with the Catalan nationalist party, the CiU (*Convergència i Unió*), in order to stay in power. Conversely, the revamped AP, now known as the PP (*Partido Popular*), after 1990 steadily gained ground on the socialists under its youthful leader, José María Aznar, culminating in its electoral triumph of 3 March 1993. Aznar in fact first defeated the PSOE in the European elections of June 1994 and consolidated his position in the regional and local elections of May 1995 when the PSOE experienced a serious and progressive haemorrhage of its traditional urban vote.

On the credit side, Felipe González and his Socialist administrations can claim a number of successes on both the home and the international fronts. There is little doubt that, during the last decade, democracy has been strengthened in Spain, that its institutions have been seen to function adequately, if not perfectly, and that the process of integration into the structures of the European Union has been relatively smooth (chapter 15). In this, the Spanish government was, at least until quite recently, aided by the generally consistent support (and, indeed, in many cases enthusiasm) for Europe expressed both among the political classes and at the grass-roots' level (15.2.1). Perhaps paradoxically, while this increasing involvement with supranational institutions has been evolving, the country has also witnessed the consolidation of decentralisation to the autonomous communities, first established in the early 1980s. A process that was in its infancy a decade ago has now been further developed; not only have effective political elites (quite powerful in certain cases) grown up at regional level, providing channels for local talent and energies, but substantially more powers and resources have now been devolved to the regions – though by no means to the extent or at the rate at which the more powerful regional governments, for example those of the Basque Country and Catalonia, might have wished (chapter 7).

On the economic front, Spain has followed a very erratic course during this period, swinging between the mini-boom years of the mid- and late 1980s, when the growth rate was the highest in the European Union, to the traumatic recession of the early 1990s when unemployment and firm closure figures registered record levels. While the private sector has borne the brunt of these changes, the public sector has been, on the whole, better protected and, indeed, thanks to generous levels of investment from the structural funds of the European Union (notably the European Regional Development Fund/ERDF), central and regional government plans to transform once and for all Spain's backward infrastructure have barely been affected. The substantial improvements in this field, particularly in road and rail communications, but also in the rapid adoption of information technology, have not gone unnoticed by the increasing number of foreign companies investing in Spain. An overall statistical picture of the evolution of the Spanish economy over the last five years is given in table 1.2.

On the debit side, the governments of Felipe González had to sustain the combined pressures of a steadily diminishing parliamentary presence, continued internal feuding (chapter 10), growing social unrest (as manifested in the general strikes of 1988 and 1994, see chapter 11), the problems of an economy very sensitive to external pressures, and an alarming succession of financial, security and corruption scandals involving individuals who were highly placed in some of the major institutions of government and state. The latter included the governor of the Bank of Spain, Mariano Rubio, and the first civilian director of the Civil Guard, Luis Roldán, both accused of abusing their positions to make vast personal fortunes. More sinister was the recent revelation (in the summer of 1995) that the Centre for Defence Information (*Centro Superior de Información de la Defensa/CESID*) had, for over a decade, been tapping the phones of high-placed individuals of the state,

Table 1.2 *Basic economic statistics, 1990–95*

	1990	1991	1992	1993	1994	1995[a]
GDP	3.6	2.4	0.8	−1.0	2.3	3.1
Public debt	43.6	44.5	47.3	54.5	60.0	62.6
Public deficit	3.9	5.0	4.2	7.5	6.6	6.0
Inflation	6.7	5.9	5.9	4.6	4.2	4.9
Interest rate	14.7	12.4	12.2	10.2	7.6	9.3
Unemployment	16.2	16.4	18.2	21.8	24.1	22.1

Notes:
[a] Latest part-year figures as at July 1995.
Sources: Instituto Nacional de Estadística (INE) and Eurostat (various years).

including the king himself. However undoubtedly the most serious case, related to Spain's most intractable problem (i.e. Basque terrorism in the form of ETA) is the widely held belief that the government itself, through the security department of the Ministry of Home Affairs (*Ministerio del Interior*) was directly involved in the sponsorship of the illegal and violent activities of the far right-wing *Grupos Anti-terroristas de Liberación* (*GAL*); in the early 1980s, this organisation was responsible, in addition to numerous acts of wounding and kidnapping, for the assassination of at least 26 alleged members of ETA. Throughout 1995, the prime minister, supported until September of the year by the Catalan leader, Jordi Pujol, resisted all pressure to stand down and to call for a general election, as demanded by all other opposition groups. Less easy to resist, however, were pressures to persuade him that he should give evidence before the Supreme Court (14.5.1) which in the summer of 1995 declared itself competent to investigate the GAL affair and the alleged involvement of the premier. In April 1996, however, the Court absolved the former premier from direct involvement in the GAL affair – though critics continue to allege that, at the very least, he showed extreme incompetence if he was unaware of the illegal activities in which high ranking civil servants (and even some of his ministers in all probability) were engaged.

Postscript

Following the general election of March 1996, Spanish politics entered a new and uncertain phase. The narrow nature of José María Aznar's election win (table 10.3b), in spite of polls predicting an outright triumph, meant that the new premier-elect was forced, much against his instincts, to seek support from nationalist groups in the Congress, in particular from the very Catalan party, the CiU, which until September 1995, had been propping up the ailing administration of Felipe González. Not surprisingly the wily Catalan President, Jordi Pujol, has used this bargaining position to great advantage, winning a number of concessions for the regions (including a commitment by Aznar to allow them to share in 30 per cent of personal income tax generated locally) which will benefit Catalonia in particular.

The new premier, sworn in on 5 May 1996, seems to have undergone something of a 'conversion' in terms of his attitude to the regions, making a virtue out of the necessity of collaborating with nationalists/regionalists and committing himself to a 'new deal' approach to the relationship between central and regional institutions. At the top of Aznar's agenda, however, is preparation of the Spanish economy to meet the Maastricht convergence criteria required for entry into Economic and Monetary Union (EMU). While, in general, economic policy is not likely to differ substantially from that followed by successive PSOE administrations, Aznar, with the full backing of his nationalist/regional supporters in Parliament, has demonstrated his firm commitment to tight stewardship by announcing some stern austerity measures combined with deep cuts in the number of top civil servants. However, the single party government recently formed, being in such a dependent position, cannot count on being in office for the next four years. Meanwhile, the PSOE, after a defeat so narrow that it was almost regarded as a triumph, finds itself in the happy position of contemplating the premier's difficulties in forming and keeping a government together, while knowing that Felipe González, according to the latest opinion polls (May 1996), is still a more popular leader than José María Aznar.

1.2 Institutions

1.2.1 Nature of institutions

Note: Since the first draft of this new edition was submitted to the publishers (September 1995), a major change has occurred in the political life of the country, namely the general election of March 1996 which, for the first time in fourteen years, returned the Right to power in Spain (1.1.5). Since its formation in May this year, the government of Aznar has taken a number of steps which are bound to have far-reaching consequences for the institutional framework of the country, particularly at the level of national institutions, which the PP is committed to pruning in a radical way. At the time of going to press, this incipient process is far from complete and is likely to take several weeks to finalise. Thus, although every effort has been made to ensure that the book is as up to date as possible, it is inevitable that in certain areas events will have raced ahead of the author's ability to record them.

Any work on institutions must inevitably involve a rigorous selection among the myriad official and unofficial, private and public bodies, to be found in any modern country. This work aims to provide an introduction to Spain's major political, judicial and economic institutions in order to furnish the reader with a basic guide to how the country works and which are the principal sources of power. An alternative title considered by the author was 'The powers that be in Spain', thus suggesting a selection among those institutions which exercise a degree of control over aspects of public life in the country, being either *de facto* powers or important pressure groups which have a significant influence on decisions made by the latter.

1.2.2 'Official' and 'unofficial' institutions

In democratic countries like Spain, one must make a clear distinction between those institutions whose existence is 'obligatory' or 'official' and those of a 'voluntary' or 'unofficial' nature. The first group includes the organs of state, the government and administration at all levels, as well as those bodies which depend on or are allied to them. Following an examination of the Constitution in chapter 2, such official bodies are examined in chapters 3–8 and 14. Chapter 3 deals with the monarchy, the particular form of headship of state (always obligatory) that has been applied in Spain since the death of Franco. The second group, 'unofficial' institutions, comprises political parties and trade unions (dealt with respectively in chapters 10 and 11), as well as a whole range of institutions established on the initiative of individuals or groups. In fact, under the 1978 Constitution, parties and unions, for historical reasons, enjoy semi-official status, a situation that does not normally obtain in other democratic countries (10.2). This group, which also includes all private sector enterprises whether in the commercial, industrial, financial or service sectors, is covered in chapters 10–13. Chapter 15, devoted to Spain's integration into the complex network of EU institutions, constitutes something of an exception in that it examines a wide range of bodies both in Spain and Europe related to European affairs, both official and unofficial. Table 1.3 lists the whole range of official and unofficial institutions studied in this volume.

1.2.3 'State public sector'

Within the group of official institutions, further distinctions need to be made. To a large extent, these constitute what might be called the state public sector (*sector público estatal*), which in Spain has much wider connotations than it has in the United Kingdom where a rather restricted economic definition has tended to be applied. The major components of this sector are shown in figure 1.1.

The first group in figure 1.1 comprises the highest ranking state bodies to which explicit reference is made in the Constitution and include:

- The Crown (*Corona*) (chapter 3)
- Parliament (*Cortes Generales*) (chapter 4)
- Ombudsman (*Defensor del Pueblo*) (chapter 2)
- Constitutional Court (*Tribunal Constitucional*) (chapter 2)
- General Council of the Judiciary (*Consejo General del Poder Judicial*) (chapter 14)
- Audit Tribunal (*Tribunal de Cuentas*) (chapter 9)

In fact, the term 'constitutional bodies' was only coined with hindsight, as recently as 1982 and does not appear in the Constitution itself. It should be noted that the ombudsman and the Audit Tribunal in a sense occupy a slightly lower hierarchical order, since they are dependent on the *Cortes*. Bodies envisaged in the Constitution,

Table 1.3 *Major Spanish institutions, 1995*

Official bodies at national level

Constitutional bodies (1)[a]	Central state administration (2)	Institutional administration (1, 6, 9)	Social security (6)	State enterprises (9)	Public financial institutions (13)
Constitutional Court (2)	Central government (5)	Autonomous administrative bodies (6)	Management entities (6)	Public law entities (9)	Bank of Spain (13)
The Crown (3)	Central administration (ministries) (6)	Autonomous commercial, industrial and financial bodies (9)	Common services (6)	Trading enterprises (9)	National Securities Market Commission (13)
Parliament (4)	Consultative bodies (5)				Spanish Banking Corporation (13)
Audit Tribunal (9)	• Council of State (5)				
Ombudsman (2)	• Economic and Social Council (5)				
General Council of the Judiciary (14)	• Directorate. General of State Legal Service (5)				

Official regional and local bodies

Regional institutions (7, 9)	Local institutions (8, 9)	

Regional level (7)	*Municipal level (8)*	*Provincial level (8)*
Government (7)		
Administration (7)	Administration (8)	Administration (8)
Autonomous administrative bodies (7)	Autonomous administrative bodies (8)	Autonomous administrative bodies (8)
Autonomous commercial bodies (9)		
Public law entities (9)	Public enterprises (9)	Public enterprises (9)
Trading enterprises (9)	Trading enterprises (9)	–

Non-official bodies/private sector

Political (10)[a]	Labour (11)	Business (12)	Financial (13)	Insurance (13)
Political parties • National parties (PSOE/PP/IU)	Trade unions • National unions (UGT/CC.OO/ USO/CSI–CSIF)	SA companies SL companies	Private banks Credit companies	Private companies
• Regional parties (CiU/PNV/ HB/CC)	• Regional unions (ELA–STV/CIG)	Partnerships	Insurance companies	
		Co-operatives	Investment institutions Pension funds	
		Employers' associations		

Notes:
[a] Figure in brackets refer to chapter numbers.
Sources: Various, including *El Sector Público Estatal*, Ministerio de Economía y Hacienda (1992).

Figure 1.1 *Composition of state public sector, 1992*

though not in fact defined as 'constitutional bodies', are the Council of State (*Consejo de Estado*) and the Economic and Social Council (*Consejo Económico y Social/CES*), which, as consultative bodies for the government and administration of the State (in the case of the Council of State, the highest body of this kind), are examined in chapter 5. The Directorate General of the State Legal Service (*Dirección General del Servicio Jurídico del Estado*) enjoys a similar status, and is also studied in chapter 5.

The second group in figure 1.1 comprises the ministries (*ministerios*) or ministerial departments (*departamentos ministeriales*), which will be dealt with in chapter 6. The third group refers to the administration of health, social security and social services, key parts of which make up the largest component of state expenditure (at both national and regional levels) within the system of public administration. The fourth group is what has been termed 'the institutional administration of the state'; this covers a wide range of autonomous bodies (*organismos autónomos*) which are part of state administration, each depending on a particular ministry, but enjoying a certain degree of administrative and financial autonomy. These may be of an administrative nature or related to commercial, industrial or financial activities. The fifth group refers to state enterprises (*sociedades estatales*) which are wholly or partly owned by the state and which may contribute to the services or the commercial/industrial sectors of the economy. The last two of these groups of institutions are dealt with in chapter 9.

Finally, a word of caution. The categorisation of institutions is notoriously difficult and even experts in the Spanish case seem to differ over the criteria to be used. For example, the above classification is based largely on administrative, hierarchical criteria, though a classification based on budgetary and financial considerations would produce a slightly different picture. Moreover, as the process of transferring more and more powers to the autonomous communities is likely to continue well into the future and as Spain proceeds with greater legal and institutional integration into the European Union, it is very probable that further attempts will be made to refine the classifications and definitions currently in force.

Table 1.4 *Women in central government and administration, comparative percentage, 1982 and 1993*

Year	Members of cabinet	Secretaries of state	Under-secretaries of state	Director generals	Civil governors/ government delegates
1982	5.56	0	0	1.44	6.45
1993	16.67	14.29	5.36	13.82	9.09

Source: Cambio 16 (19 December 1994).

In terms of the human resources within the institutions described in this work, a significant change since the first edition concerns the position of women at the higher levels of power. As can be seen in table 1.4, within central government and administration, they made substantial advances between 1983 and 1993. Although only four currently occupy a place in the cabinet (one more than in the last government of Felipe González), the number in the junior departmental posts has risen quite dramatically in the last decade. This, however, represents only 16.6 per cent of the total number of government posts, comparable to the 15.7 per cent of women deputies in the Congress (4.3.1). On the other hand, as will be seen in 15.3.2.2, Spanish Euro-MPs comprise a significantly higher proportion of women. Where women seem to have made the most spectacular progress is in the judiciary where they now constitute close to 50 per cent of judges (*jueces* not *magistrados*, see chapter 14, p. 288) and one woman, Milagros García Crespo, has been appointed president of the Audit Tribunal (9.9.3). In general the new government of José María Aznar has tended to adopt a more positive approach in this respect than his predecessor, appointing a greater number of women as junior ministers and as heads of important state-run institutions: Mónica Ridruejo, for example, is now in charge of *Radiotelevisión Española (RTVE)*. In general, however, it has to be recognised that women (not one of whom has so far become a political party leader) have not yet reached a point where they can exert a crucial influence on policy at national level.

Chapter 2

The Constitution of 1978

2.1 Introduction

With its 169 articles, the 1978 Constitution represents one of the longest in Spanish constitutional history, taking longer to draw up than any previous constitution. It was drafted and approved by both Houses of Parliament (*Cortes Generales*), the Lower House or Congress of Deputies (*Congreso de los Diputados*) (4.3.1) and the Upper House or Senate (*Senado*) (4.3.2). During the sixteen months of its gestation, it passed through an unprecedented number of committees and, in the course of its approval, over one thousand amendments were tabled; no previous constitution had been subjected to such searching scrutiny.

The 1978 Constitution started life in the Committee of Constitutional Affairs and Public Liberties (*Comisión de Asuntos Constitucionales y Libertades Públicas*) consisting of thirty-six members of the Congress drawn from the major parties represented in Parliament in proportion to their strength in the Lower House. The Committee appointed a seven-man working party with a similar composition, whose task was to draw up the original draft of the Constitution. The draft was passed to the Constitutional Committee of the Congress (*Comisión Constitucional del Congreso*) before being submitted for approval to the full Congress. Subsequently it was considered by the Constitutional Committee of the Senate (*Comisión Constitucional del Senado*) prior to being approved by the full Senate. In the final stage of the process, the draft was scrutinised by a joint committee of both Houses of Parliament before being approved in a full joint session of both Houses on 31 October 1978 (table 2.1). Finally, on 6 December of the same year, the final text was submitted to the direct vote of the Spanish people in a referendum (table 2.2). Following ratification by the people, the new Constitution was signed and promulgated by King Juan Carlos in an historic gathering of both Houses of Parliament held in the Congress building on 28 December 1978. The following day the Constitution was published in the *Official State Gazette* (*Boletín Oficial del Estado/BOE*).

At each stage of its approval, the new Constitution was supported by large majorities, thus lending conviction to the commonly expressed belief that it was a Constitution 'of all the people for all the people'. As shown in table 2.1, the Congress approved the document by 326 votes to six with fourteen abstentions (mainly Basque Nationalists), while the Senate did so by 226 for, five against and only eight abstentions. In total, therefore, 551 members of Parliament out of a possible 589, approxi-

Table 2.1 *Approval of Constitution in Parliament, October 1978*

	'Yes' votes	'No' votes	Abstentions
Congress	326	6	14
Senate	226	5	8
Both Houses	551	11	22

Source: El País (October 1978).

Table 2.2 *Approval of Constitution in national referendum, December 1978*

	'Yes' votes	'No' votes	Blanks	Void
Number of votes	15,782,639	1,423,184	636,095	135,193
Percentage of votes	87.79	7.90	3.53	0.75
Percentage of total electorate	59.40	5.30	2.39	0.50

Source: El País (December 1978).

mately 94 per cent, gave their support to the document which, it was hoped, would formally end the transition from dictatorship to democracy. In the referendum campaign which followed, of the parliamentary parties, only the Basque Nationalist Party (*Partido Nacionalista Vasco / PNV*) urged voters to abstain or register a negative vote, although several small, generally extremist, non-parliamentary parties like the extreme right *Fuerza Nueva* and the Republican Left of Catalonia (*Esquerra Republicana de Catalunya*) (10.4.6), also recommended rejection. In the event, when Spaniards went to the polls on 6 December 1978, the Constitution was approved by 87.8 per cent of those who voted. Whilst the percentage of abstentions, 32 per cent in Spain as a whole and 56 per cent in parts of the Basque Country, gave the government and the major opposition parties some cause for concern, nonetheless the Spanish people seemed to have voted convincingly, if not overwhelmingly, to open a new democratic chapter in the country's history (table 2.2).

In political circles and the press, the Constitution was hailed as a triumph for common sense and compromise, the tangible results of months of consensus politics. The need for consensus in fact derived from three main causes. Firstly, no single party was in a strong enough position to achieve a satisfactory solution by itself; Franco's heirs and the opposition needed each other to overcome the impasse created by the dictator's death. Secondly, the victors in the 1977 elections, the UCD led by Adolfo Suárez, did not have an overall majority in Parliament. Thirdly, there was a tendency among all parties to gravitate towards the centre of the political spectrum, either to disguise their past associations with *franquismo* or to demonstrate a commitment towards the vote-catching concept of moderation.

Consensus certainly produced positive results, and the document can be regarded as a symbolic reconciliation of the two Spains divided, first by the Civil War, and then by the policies of the Franco regime. However, it has to be recognised that, to a large extent, this consensus was not an agreement among equals: not only did the government negotiate from a position of strength, making full use of the bureaucratic machinery of the previous regime, but certain issues like the role of the monarchy, the Church and the armed forces were not open to serious negotiation and simply had to be accepted by the parties of the Left, in particular the PSOE. Other negative features of the process were the fact that certain sections of the Constitution are contradictory, reflecting the conflicting attitudes of Left and Right towards such issues as the role of the state within the economy; and some are ambiguous, like parts of the protracted section on regional autonomy. Most objective commentators agree that, while the end might have justified the means, many cracks were papered over during the functioning of consensus and many agreements were reached not in the committee rooms of the *Cortes* but behind closed doors in party offices or Madrid restaurants.

2.2 Structure

The 1978 Constitution is divided into eleven major sections (*títulos*), including the introductory section or *título preliminar* which lays down the guiding principles which regulate the functioning of the new Spanish state and Spanish society. Section I enumerates a whole range of civil, political and socio–economic rights. The remaining nine sections deal with the division of the powers of the state, the nature and functions of the different institutions of the state and the territorial organisations of the country. Section II examines the role of the monarchy, laying particular stress on its role *vis-à-vis* the Constitution and the question of the succession. Section III outlines the composition, functions and powers of both Houses of Parliament. Section IV deals with the organisation of the government and public administration, while sections V and VI respectively refer to the relationship between the government, the legislature and the judicial authorities. Section VII breaks new ground in Spanish constitutional history by laying down the basic principles by which the economy shall be run. Section VIII concerns the territorial organisation of the state and thus the whole question of the relationship between central government and the regions of Spain. Section IX outlines the composition and competencies of the Constitutional Court and Section X the processes by which the Constitution may be reformed. It is worthy of note that, compared to its predecessors, the 1978 Constitution devotes much more attention to such key aspects as rights (forty-six articles), the legislature, which embodies popular sovereignty (thirty-one articles) and the rights of the regions of Spain *vis-à-vis* the state (twenty-three articles).

2.3 Basic principles and provisions

The more idealistic clauses of the Constitution are contained in the introductory section. Article 1.1, for instance, proclaims that Spain is a 'social and democratic state based on the rule of law' and that 'national sovereignty resides in the people from whom all powers derive'. Article 2, while referring to the 'indissoluble unity of the Spanish nation' recognises and guarantees the 'right of the nationalities and regions of Spain to autonomy' (chapter 7). Article 3 recognises regional languages as co-official in the regions concerned alongside Castilian, the official language of the Spanish state. It is interesting to note that on two occasions the Constitution refers to the concept of 'political pluralism' (articles 1 and 2) and in this context both political parties and trade unions, the internal structures and functioning of which are to adhere to democratic practices, are expressly recognised (chapters 10 and 11). Article 9.1 affirms that both citizens and the authorities are subject to the Constitution and to the law in general. Article 9.2 puts an obligation on the public authorities to create the conditions in which the freedom and equality of the individual and groups can be genuine and effective, and to remove obstacles to the full participation of all citizens in the political, economic, social and cultural life of the country. Though not inserted in this outline of general principles, there is no doubt that the concept of decentralisation enshrined in article 103, referring to the government and civil service, was also a major guiding principle.

Two major provisions refer to Spain's major socio–political institutions, the armed forces and the Catholic Church, often referred to by contemporary politicians and commentators as the *de facto* powers (*poderes fácticos*). These institutions, as is well known, have played such a dominant role in the political and constitutional history of Spain that their interests have always, to some extent at least, had to be accommodated and their role clearly defined. Even the Constitution of 1978 had to take them into account, and indeed tried to ensure that, unlike the case in 1931, they were not alienated to the point where they could become forces of dissension and opposition.

2.3.1 The armed forces (*fuerzas armadas/FFAA*)

Article 8 of the Constitution states that the role of the armed forces is 'to safeguard the sovereignty and independence of Spain, defend its territorial integrity and the constitutional order'. On the face of it, this wording does not seem to differ significantly from that of Franco's 1967 Organic Law of the State. Traditionally suspicious of all moves towards a weakening of central control, the armed forces have once again been granted the role of safeguarding 'the territorial integrity' of the country, a direct allusion to the possible attempt of any region of Spain to secede. Moreover, article 2 of the Organic Law on National Defence and Military Organisation (*Ley Orgánica de Defensa Nacional y Organización Militar*) of 1980, makes it clear that one of the aspects of national defence, in which the armed forces are obviously involved, is guaranteeing 'the unity of Spain'. The opening sentence of this article reads: 'National defence is the deployment, integration and co-ordination of all the moral and material energies of the nation in the face of any form of aggression, and all Spaniards must participate in the achievement of this objective.'

Article 8 also stresses that the ultimate responsibility for national defence lies not with the armed forces but with the popularly elected government. Furthermore, since the new arrangements for territorial organisation are enshrined in the Constitution (Section VIII) the armed forces' obligation to safeguard 'the constitutional order' must extend to the protection of this new status quo. While no written document could prevent army intervention in the last resort, and the proclivity of at least certain sections of the military to contemplate intervention was clearly demonstrated in February 1981, it is now clear that in the 1990s the Spanish military is prepared to work with the politicians to protect the country's still relatively new democracy.

2.3.2 The Church (*Iglesia*)

Unlike the armed forces, the Church would seem to play only a minor role within the new Constitution, especially when we consider the importance Franco attached to it in his Fundamental Laws (1.1.2). However, unlike the 1931 Constitution, which effectively paved the way for the establishment of a completely secular state and thus provoked the conservative elements of Spanish society, the 1978 document merely states in article 16 that there will be complete religious freedom and that there will be no state religion. However, article 16.3 goes on to say that 'the public authorities shall take into account the religious beliefs of Spanish society and shall maintain consequent links of co-operation with the Catholic Church and other faiths'. While in theory this prepared the way for a gradual move towards the separation of Church and state – involving, for example, the eventual financial independence of the former – the Church, which has basically accepted the new order, has in practice retained much of its influence, not least within the education system. Moreover, under both UCD and PSOE governments, the Church has not been averse to lending both moral and material support to groups protesting against government policies on education, divorce and abortion. Statistics show, however, that over the years society has become increasingly secularised, and it is highly unlikely that the Church will again be the predominant factor that it has been in the past.

2.4 Fundamental rights within the Constitution

By far the longest section of the Constitution deals with fundamental rights and the obligation of the state to uphold and guarantee these rights, except in the most exceptional circumstances. It is worthy of note that article 10 declares that such rights shall conform to those listed in the Universal Declaration of Human Rights. Following a now classical categorisation, three types of rights can be identified: basic human or civil rights; political rights; and socio–economic rights. The latter involve some positive action on the part of the state to benefit the public.

2.4.1 Civil rights

The most basic rights enumerated are:

2.4.1.1 Right to life (derecho a la vida) and right to personal physical integrity (derecho a la integridad física)

For the first time in Spanish constitutional history, the death penalty is expressly abolished 'except for those offences covered by military law in times of war' (article 15).

2.4.1.2 Right to equality (derecho a la igualdad)

This refers above all to equality before the law, irrespective of differences of birth, race, sex, religion or belief (article 14). This general affirmation is reinforced by more specific references in later provisions of the Constitution: for example, article 32.1 insists on the equality of partners in a marriage and article 35.1 upholds the ideal of equal opportunities in the workplace for both sexes.

2.4.1.3 Right to freedom (derecho a la libertad) and right to security (derecho a la seguridad)

This includes the protection of *habeas corpus* under which no person can be detained by the authorities for longer than seventy-two hours without being set free or handed over to the judicial authorities. Similarly any detainee has the right to be informed of his rights and the reasons for detention as well as the right not to make a statement without the presence of a lawyer (article 17).

2.4.1.4 Right of effective access to the courts (derecho al efectivo acceso a los tribunales)

This is guaranteed in article 24, which, among other safeguards, includes the right of the accused to be defended in court and to have access to a solicitor while in detention. An accused person is not obliged to plead guilty; indeed innocence is assumed until guilt is proved. Article 9.3, significantly situated in the introductory section of the Constitution, expressly forbids the application of retroactive legislation. Another 'progressive' clause in the Constitution (article 25.2) states that convicted offenders should not be obliged to undergo hard labour and that prison regimes should be geared towards rehabilitation and re-education.

2.4.1.5 Right to private property (derecho a la propiedad privada)

This right, plus the associated right of inheritance, is enshrined in article 33, which affirms that a citizen can only be deprived of property 'for a justified cause of public utility or social interest' and then only with appropriate compensation.

2.4.1.6 Right to free enterprise (derecho a la libertad de empresa)

Article 38 recognises this within the framework of the market economy and, where appropriate, of national planning.

2.4.1.7 Right to religious liberty (derecho a la libertad religiosa)

This right is enshrined in article 16, which links this freedom with that of ideological freedom and guarantees to protect the religious activities of either individuals or groups. No one shall be obliged to reveal his or her religion or ideology. Moreover, as already stated above, no particular religion shall enjoy state protection. Closely linked to this freedom is that of the right to conscientious objection (*derecho a la objeción de conciencia*) (article 30). Objectors are now given the option of undertaking social work deemed equivalent to military service.

2.4.1.8 Right to honour (derecho al honor) and right to privacy (derecho a la intimidad)

Article 18 recognises a series of rights linked to the theme of personal and family privacy: for example, article 18.1 2 recognises a limitation of entry to property except where, in very exceptional circumstances, a judicial warrant is granted to the police; article 18.1 3 guarantees secrecy of correspondence and, indeed, of all communications, including the telephone, with the same exceptions.

2.4.1.9 Right to freedom of abode (derecho a la libre elección de domicilio) and right to free movement (derecho a la libre circulación)

Entry to and exit from the country cannot be denied for political or ideological reasons, except when a state of exception or siege has been declared (4.6.3.2).

2.4.2 Political rights

The major political rights to be protected are:

2.4.2.1 Right to freedom of expression (derecho a la libre expresión de ideas)

The Constitution recognises and protects the right 'to express and disseminate freely thoughts, ideas and opinions by word, in writing or any other means of reproduction' (article 20.1). Article 20.1 also recognises rights to production and creation in the fields of literature, art, science and technology. Article 20.2 expressly forbids any form of prior censorship, something that was widely practised during the greater part of the Franco regime. Article 20.3 3, in a highly significant statement, ensures that the means of communication belonging to the state or other public entities shall be subject to parliamentary control and that access to the same shall be guaranteed to all social and political groups, 'respecting the pluralism of society and the various languages of Spain'.

2.4.2.2 Right of assembly (derecho de reunión) and right to demonstrate (derecho de manifestación)

Article 21.1 recognises the right of assembly provided it is peaceful and does not involve the use of firearms. Assemblies in public places or demonstrations require the permission of the authorities but can only be forbidden when there is a serious risk to public order or to the safety of people or property (article 21.2 2).

2.4.2.3 Right of association (derecho de asociación)

This has particular relevance to political parties and workers' organisations and trade unions, which, over the last century in Spain, as well as in other European countries, have waged an often one-sided battle to have these rights recognised (11.1). Following forty years of illegality for any organisation that did not conform in its aims and ideology to the narrow concepts enshrined in Franco's National Movement (1.1.2), article 22 recognises the right of association for all organisations, except those whose objectives include activities declared to be of a criminal nature. Secret or paramilitary organisations are banned.

2.4.2.4 Right of participation (derecho de participación)

Article 23 recognises two ways in which the citizen has a right to participate in public affairs: firstly, he has a right to vote (derecho de sufragio activo), as well as a right (in most cases) to stand for election (derecho de sufragio pasivo); secondly, all citizens have the right to compete on equal terms for access to public office.

2.4.2.5 Right to initiate legislation (derecho de iniciativa legislativa)

Article 87 recognises the possibility that legislation can emanate directly from the will of the citizenry, provided that at least half a million signatures are obtained and that the proposal does not refer to taxation, international affairs or the prerogative of pardon (4.7.2).

2.4.2.6 Right of petition (derecho de petición)

Article 29.1 recognises the right of citizens to make an individual or collective petition in writing to the government although, in the case of the armed forces and police forces subject to military discipline, this can only be done on an individual basis.

2.4.2.7 Right of union association (derecho de asociación sindical)

In spite of the existence of the all-embracing right of association granted in article 22, the constitution-drafters, perhaps not surprisingly after forty years' suppression of union activity, deemed it essential to provide specific protection for the trade unions. Article 28 includes the right to found a trade union, the right to join the union of one's choice, the right of unions to form confederations and found international organisations. At the same time, no citizen is bound to join a trade union (11.2).

2.4.2.8 Right to strike (derecho de huelga)

This right is expressly recognised in article 28; the only limit to its use is the need to protect the essential services of the community (11.2).

2.4.3 Socio–economic rights

Since the Constitution defines Spain as a social, as well as democratic, state governed by the rule of law, it is not surprising that it should recognise a series of social and economic rights of the type found in the most advanced European constitutions. It is precisely in this area that the constitution-makers have projected the most progressive image of the new Spain. To a large extent, the rights that are here recognised, many of which did not appear in previous constitutions, are an extension of the civil rights already listed. The majority of them require positive, often financial, action on the part of the state. The major rights in this category are:

2.4.3.1 Right to work (derecho al trabajo)

Article 35 links the right to work with the duty of work, the right to the free selection of one's profession or job, the right to promotion through work, the right to a remuneration that is sufficient to cover one's needs and those of one's family, and the right of women to equal treatment to men in all the above respects.

2.4.3.2 Right to collective bargaining (derecho a la negociación colectiva laboral)

Article 37.1, recognises the right of representatives of labour and management to negotiate collective agreements, and ensures the binding nature of such agreements (11.3.1.3).

2.4.3.3 Right to adopt collective conflict measures (derecho a adoptar medidas de conflicto colectivo)

Article 37.1 recognises the rights of both workers and employers to adopt collective conflict measures, provided that they conform with the necessary guarantees to ensure the continued running of essential public services.

2.4.3.4 Right to education (derecho a la educación)

This right is recognised in article 27, which also upholds the freedom to choose the type of education and school one wishes. The authorities guarantee the rights of parents to acquire for their children the religious and moral education that accords with their own convictions (article 27.3). The authorities also undertake to provide a general programme of education for all citizens, with the participation of all those affected in decision-making, and to create new centres of learning. Significantly, however, article 27.6 recognises the right of individuals and groups to found centres of learning. This is of particular interest to the Catholic Church, whose religious orders control most of the private schools in Spain, the private sector providing education for around 35 per cent of the 6–14 age group and over 30 per cent of secondary education.

Also of interest to the Church is the fact that, albeit couched in vague terms, the Constitution endorses the obligation of the state to continue giving grants to private schools. Between 1983 and 1984, the Socialist minister of education came under frequent attack from the Church for demanding more control over private institutions in exchange for continuing financial support from the state. Changes in this sphere were contained in the Law on the Right to Education (*Ley del Derecho a la Educación/LODE*) approved by Parliament in 1984.

2.4.4 Principles guiding economic and social policy

Closely linked to the rights referred to in 2.4.3 are a series of socio–economic commitments on the part of the state, which in practice amount to an extension of these rights. These include:

2.4.4.1 Protection of the family (protección a la familia)

In particular, both the state and parents have obligations to protect children, whether or not born in wedlock (article 39).

2.4.4.2 Protection of health (protección a la salud)

Article 45 ascribes a fundamental role to the state in relation to the organisation and protection of health care and welfare. The same article refers to the authorities' role in promoting physical education, sport and the adequate use of leisure time.

2.4.4.3 Protection of the elderly (protección a la tercera edad)

Article 50 guarantees that all senior citizens shall enjoy economic self-sufficiency, with adequate pensions that are periodically updated in line with the cost of living. The social services are to pay particular attention to their needs in housing, health, culture and leisure.

2.4.4.4 Protection of the right to decent housing (protección del derecho a una vivienda digna)

The authorities are stated to be under an obligation to provide all citizens with adequate housing and to provide necessary conditions, backed up by the appropriate legislation, to make this possible. Land use will be controlled to avoid speculation (article 47).

2.4.4.5 Protection of the right to work and satisfactory working conditions (protección del derecho al trabajo y de unas condiciones laborales satisfactorias)

In this regard, the state undertakes to pursue policies that ensure economic stability and full employment, as well as professional training and retraining. In this regard, article 40 obliges the state to protect the safety and health of the citizen at the place of work, to place a limit on the working day and to provide adequate holidays. The social security system will be maintained to protect citizens' financial position, and this will include unemployment benefit *(seguro de desempleo)* (article 41). Article 42 offers to safeguard the social and economic rights of emigrant workers abroad and to facilitate their re-integration at work on their return to Spain.

2.4.4.6 Protection of the handicapped (protección a los minusválidos)

Article 49 obliges the state to provide for the adequate treatment, care and rehabilitation of all types of handicapped people, ensuring that they are not deprived of the basic rights which apply to all citizens.

2.4.4.7 Protection of the environment (protección del medio ambiente)

According to article 45, all Spaniards have the right to enjoy an adequate environment and they are also under an obligation to conserve it. Severe penalties are envisaged for those who damage the environment. It is worth noting that this article is the result of growing pressure from environmental and ecological groups that, in parallel with counterparts in the rest of Europe, are gaining in strength in Spain.

2.4.5 Theory and practice

Needless to say, even in the most advanced and developed democratic system, difficulties are often expressed in translating constitutional ideals into everyday realities. In the case of Spain, which emerged only relatively recently from a dictatorial regime where civil and political liberties were constantly denied, this task seems to have been particularly difficult and recent governments have not always set the best of examples in regard to respect for the law (1.1.5). As far as socio–economic rights are concerned, whatever obligations theoretically bind the authorities, in the final analysis their protection and consolidation must depend on the success of the economic policies pursued by successive governments. In the short term at least, such goals may be considered utopian. A court ruling may be sufficient to ensure that a woman has the right to equal treatment to a man either in marriage or in terms of job opportunities, but only an increase in the overall economic prosperity of the country, coupled with the will of central and regional governments to distribute fairly their resources, will ensure improvement in such vital areas as education, health and housing that in the past were severely neglected.

2.5 Constitutional Court (*Tribunal Constitucional*)

The Constitutional Court, envisaged in section IX of the Constitution, is the supreme interpreter of the Constitution and a theoretically impartial body which has the final say in the settling of appeals arising from legislation that emanates from the Constitution. Its powers, composition and role are spelled out in the Organic Law of the Constitutional Court of 3 October 1979. All other constitutional bodies (1.1 and 1.3) are subject to its control and there is no appeal against its decisions.

2.5.1 Composition and organisation

The Constitutional Court consists of twelve members formally appointed by the king; of these, four are elected by the Congress by a majority of three-fifths of its members, four by the Senate by a similar majority, two by the government and two by the General Council of the Judiciary (*Consejo General del Poder Judicial*) (14.4.2). The members or magistrates (*magistrados*) of the Court must be jurists of recognised competence, with at least fifteen years' experience in the legal profession; in practice, they will have occupied top level posts such as magistrates, public prosecutors, university professors and high-ranking civil servants in the judicial area. They are appointed for a period of nine years; in order to ensure continuity, a third of their number are replaced every three years. No member of the Court can simultaneously be a public representative, i.e. as ombudsman (2.6), national or regional deputy, a member of the government or any branch of public administration, an office holder in a political party or trade union; neither can he or she practise privately in the legal profession. All members are expected to be independent and permanent in the exercise of their duties (article 159). The Court itself elects a president, appointed for three years, from among its members by secret ballot prior to formal appointment by the king. He is assisted in his duties by a vice-president and a general secretary.

The court meets either in plenary session (*pleno*) or in one of two divisions (*salas*) to which work can and often is delegated. There is no practical distinction between the activities of the two divisions, nor indeed between these and the plenum. Each consists of six magistrates designated by the plenum; the first is chaired by the president of the court and the second by the vice-president.

2.5.2 Powers

According to article 161 of the Constitution, the Court has jurisdiction throughout the national territory. Its judgements (*sentencias*) may be sought in the following cases:

2.5.2.1 Appeals against unconstitutional laws (recursos de anticonstitucionalidad)

These can be made in the case of statutes of autonomy, organic laws, ordinary laws of the national or regional parliaments, international treaties and the standing orders of the Congress or Senate (4.4.3). Such appeals can be initiated by the prime minister, the ombudsman, or a group of no fewer than 50 deputies (4.3.1) or senators (4.3.2). The October 1979 Law in fact makes a distinction between *recursos de anticonstitucionalidad* and *cuestiones de anticonstitucionalidad*; in the case of the latter, the initiative is taken by a judge or a court.

In the course of the early 1980s, there developed a distinct type of appeal known as the *recurso previo de anticonstitucionalidad*, by which doubts were cast on the constitutionality of legislation *prior* to completion of the legislative process. In 1984 the predominantly Socialist members of the court agreed to eliminate this practice, in the conviction that it hindered and distorted the legislative process. The PP, however, is committed in its programme for government to a reversal of the present situation.

2.5.2.2 Constitutional conflicts (conflictos constitucionales)

These concern disputes relating to the division of responsibilities between the state and the autonomous communities or between constitutional bodies, such as the *Cortes* (chapter 4) and the General Council of the Judiciary (14.4.2).

2.5.2.3 Government challenges to autonomous community regulations

In this category of appeals, the central government may challenge the constitutionality of regulations and rules emanating from any body of the autonomous communities provided that the challenge is made within two months of the latter being published; in such cases, legislation is suspended for a maximum of five months while the Court decides whether to ratify or lift the suspension.

2.5.2.4 Appeals for constitutional protection (recursos de amparo constitucional)

These can be lodged when fundamental rights or freedoms have been allegedly violated by the state, the autonomous communities or other official bodies or authorities. Such appeals can be presented by individuals or legal bodies, as well as the ombudsman or the Department of the Attorney General of the State (14.4.3), but only when the process of appealing to lower courts has been exhausted.

2.5.2.5 Appeals for electoral protection (recursos de amparo electoral)

Article 49 of the General Electoral Law of June 1985 initiated this additional appeal against decisions of electoral boards (*juntas electorales*) regarding the exclusion of candidates from electoral lists. In the first instance, appeals are made to ordinary courts.

One of the first and most publicised appeals to the Constitutional Court was initiated in 1981 by the autonomous communities of the Basque Country and Catalonia which claimed that certain Articles of the controversial Law on the Harmonisation of the Autonomy Process (*Ley Orgánica de Armonización del Proceso Autonómico/LOAPA*) contravened the Constitution (7.4 and 7.7.5). In fact, the Court, to the great embarrassment of the government, found in favour of the autonomous communities, thus leaving a dangerous constitutional void in August 1983. Other appeals, presented under both the *recurso de anticonstitucionalidad* and under the *recurso de amparo constitucional* were filed by the right-wing AP during the first period of Socialist government between 1982 and 1986, when the latter was trying to push through legislation relating to education and abortion. In all cases, the appeals were rejected. In subsequent years, a large part of the appeals heard by the Court have concerned disputes between central and regional governments, though in recent years there has been a significant decline in such conflicts (7.8.4.3).

There is no doubt that, over the last decade and a half, the Constitutional Court has played a vital part in consolidating democracy in Spain, helping to reinforce the rule of law, and in the process has enhanced respect for the Constitution. It has certainly been extremely active, pronouncing judgements in no less than 4,274 cases in 1993. Sadly, like other institutions of state, it has not been entirely free from political controversy, relating in particular to nominations for membership. Even when there is agreement between the major parties over nominations, problems can arise if a magistrate has some link, however indirect, with a delicate political issue. For example, following the appointment as a member of the distinguished jurist Manuel Jiménez de Parga in April 1995, other jurists opined that, because of his already expressed views on the case and because his son was a lawyer acting for the former minister of home affairs being investigated in the GAL affair (1.1.5), he would have to abstain in the case of the appeal (*recurso de amparo constitucional*) submitted by two leading accused in the case – an appeal that at the time was being considered by the Court.

2.6 Ombudsman (*defensor del pueblo*)

The ombudsman (in Spanish literally 'defender of the people') is a post envisaged in article 54 of the Constitution. This independent figure is designated by both Houses of Parliament and his role is to defend the rights enshrined in section I of the Constitution, monitoring the activities of all branches of public administration and reporting to both Houses of Parliament. He is appointed for a period of five years.

The role of the ombudsman was set out in an Organic Law of April 1981 (4.7.1.1). This law permits him to watch over the activities of ministers, administrative authorities, civil servants and persons working for any branch of public administration. All public authorities are obliged to assist him in his investigations, giving him preference over other claimants on their time. One of his main duties is to present to Parliament an annual report (*informe anual*), in which are detailed all the complaints (*quejas*) submitted to him, the responses adopted and any investigations carried out in the process of arriving at decisions. Both Houses of Parliament are obliged to debate these reports. Like the Constitutional Court, the Office of the Ombudsman (*Oficina del Defensor del Pueblo*) has been extremely busy in recent times, dealing with no less than 23,372 complaints in 1993.

In practice this post was left unfilled throughout the period when the centre-right (UCD) was in power; however, after the 1982 elections, when the Socialist Party (PSOE) came to power, Parliament voted to appoint to this prestigious office a jurist of international repute and former Christian-Democrat leader, Joaquín Ruiz-Giménez. The current ombudsman, equally prestigious, is Fernando Alvarez de Miranda, the president of the first democratic Congress in the post-Franco era and a key figure in the transition to democracy.

It is worth noting that in recent years there has been a trend to appoint similar figures at the level of the autonomous community with the title of parliamentary commissioner (*comisionado parlamentario*). Six regions currently have such a person who, while acting totally independently from Madrid, in fact is obliged by law to co-ordinate his activities with the *defensor del pueblo*.

2.7 Constitutional reform

The initiative for reform of the Constitution may come from the government, the Congress, the Senate or the autonomous communities (article 166). Proposals for constitutional reform must be approved by a three-fifths majority in each House of Parliament. If there is a disagreement between the Houses, a joint committee (*comisión mixta*), composed of an equal number of deputies and senators, will draft a text which will again be put to the vote of the Congress and the Senate. If this procedure fails, the text can be approved by a two-thirds majority of the Congress, provided that an overall majority of the Senate has already approved it. Following approval in the *Cortes*, the reform may be put to a national referendum to be ratified, provided that fifteen deputies or senators request it within fifteen days of the reform being approved in the *Cortes* (article 167).

According to article 168, if the proposed reform refers to a total revision of the Constitution or to a partial reform that affects the introductory section or the first part of section I or the whole of section II, the proposal has to be approved by two-thirds of each House. This is followed by the dissolution of Parliament. Following elections, the newly elected Parliament must ratify the original decision by a two-thirds majority in each House. Subsequently, the reform must be put to a national referendum for final ratification.

No initiative for constitutional reform can be taken while the country is at war or when a state of alarm, exception or siege is in force (article 116). It need hardly be emphasised that, in the face of such stringent requirements, it is very unlikely that the country will witness a plethora of proposals for constitutional reform; indeed the constitution-drafters and numerous parliamentary committees, having spent a considerable amount of time agreeing on the final text of the Constitution, have clearly set out to discourage all but the most determined reformers.

Since 1978, in fact, there has only been one such reform, indeed a very minor one. This occurred on 27 August 1992 when the words '*y pasivo*' were inserted into article 13.2 of the Constitution to enable foreign nationals resident in Spain not only to vote but to stand as candidates in municipal elections. Because bilateral reciprocal agreements with certain countries (including the United Kingdom) had not been signed by the time, at the first opportunity for this provision to be enacted, in the municipal elections of May 1995, few countries were able to take advantage of this change (8.3.2.1).

There is clearly likely to be a second (more major) reform when the committee currently debating changes to the composition and role of the Senate (4.3.2) eventually submits its findings and firm proposals are put before Parliament.

2.8 Comment

The 1978 Constitution undoubtedly paved the way for a radical transformation of the nature of the Spanish state which it attempted simultaneously to democratise and decentralise. The many ways in which these changes have affected Spain's institutions, as well as its political and economic life in general, are examined in the chapters that follow. Suffice it to say at this point that not only did Spain's constitution-drafters reinstate the concept of a democratic state based on the rule of law (*estado democrático de derecho*), the corner-stone of which is the new parliamentary monarchy, but they laid the foundations for a complete restructuring of the state in which regional institutions were to share responsibilities with their counterparts in Madrid. The Constitution, of course, represented only the first step in the long and complex process of creating a whole new political structure and a new set of institutions. On to this basic framework, politicians had to graft a web of detailed legislation which, over time, would enable administrators to translate the theory of this new democratic state into practical reality.

While the Constitution itself has so far stood the test of time, and is unlikely to undergo any substantial reform in the foreseeable future, some of the so-called 'constitutional bodies' have given a certain cause for concern. While in general the work of the Constitutional Court, for example, has been much praised among political scientists and students of constitutional affairs, who have extolled its contribution to the process of democratic consolidation, concern has also been expressed about the politicisation of appointments and about the fact that this over-worked institution has on many occasions appeared to act in the place of an ineffective Upper Chamber (4.3.2).

Chapter 3

The monarchy

3.1 Introduction

Prior to the restoration of the Bourbon monarchy in 1975, the last King of Spain was Alfonso XIII, who effectively ruled from 1902 to 1931. Following a period of political unrest, during which the monarchy fell into increasing disrepute and the political tide turned strongly in favour of republicanism, Alfonso fled the country in April 1931 'to save the country from civil war'. Until after the Civil War of 1936–39, the Spanish royal family was to remain in exile in Italy. Shortly before his death in 1941, Alfonso abdicated in favour of his son Don Juan, Count of Barcelona, who was to live in exile in Portugal up to and beyond the end of the Franco era (figure 3.1).

3.2 Monarchical restoration

On 22 November 1975, two days after the death of General Franco, Juan Carlos de Borbón y Borbón, son of Don Juan and grandson of Alfonso XIII, was proclaimed King of Spain. In a simple ceremony, the new monarch was sworn in by the president of the *Cortes*; on this occasion, as in 1969, Juan Carlos pledged to uphold Franco's Fundamental Laws, which include the Succession Law (3.2.1.1) and the Organic Law of the State (3.2.1.2).

Since Juan Carlos had been appointed successor to the headship of state by a widely hated dictator and since in November 1975 his father, Don Juan, had not renounced his dynastic rights, it is worth asking what legitimate authority, if any, the new monarch had for ascending the long-vacant throne of Spain. This question is very pertinent when we consider that not only had Juan Carlos' acceptance of the succession led to a certain friction between father and son, but the majority of Spaniards at that time were at best indifferent and at worst hostile to the idea of a monarchy, particularly if it meant, as Franco no doubt intended, a continuation of Francoism in a more respectable guise.

Thus, prior to examining its nature, role and functions, it would seem appropriate to examine the process by which the monarchy was restored in the person of Juan Carlos and, in so doing, attempt to examine its possible sources, if any, of legitimacy.

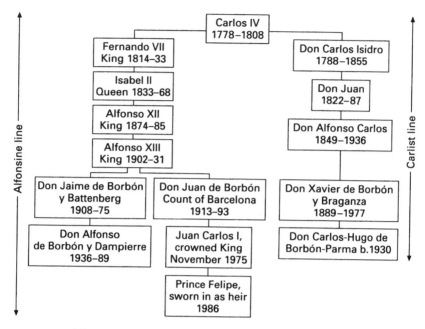

Figure 3.1 *Genealogical table of the Spanish monarchy, 1995*

3.2.1 Constitutional legitimacy

3.2.1.1 Succession Law (Ley de Sucesión)

Between 1939 and 1947, the form of the new Spanish state that emerged from the Civil War was left an open question. However, in 1947, whether to appease monarchist opinion in Spain or to convey a more democratic image abroad, Franco issued the Succession Law which, while conferring on himself for life the powers of regent, envisaged the eventual restoration of the monarchy. No particular pretender was nominated at that time; it was not even clear whether Franco intended to select his successor from the Alfonsine or the Carlist line of Bourbons (figure 3.1), since followers of both were represented in his cabinets and other institutions of government. The only conditions laid down for the future monarch were that he should be male, Spanish, Catholic and over thirty years of age (article 9). It is interesting to note that article 11 refers to an *instauración*, not a *restauración* of the monarchy, stressing, as Franco did in speeches of the time, that this was not to be a continuation of the traditional (that is, constitutional) monarchy, but a new monarchy rooted in the uprising of 18 July 1936 – the day when Franco launched his so-called crusade against the Second Republic. This concept was reiterated in 1969 when Franco presented Juan Carlos to the *Cortes* as his successor.

3.2.1.2 Organic Law of the State (Ley Orgánica del Estado)

The monarchical form of the state was confirmed in two later fundamental laws, namely the Law of Principles of the National Movement (*Ley de Principios del Movimiento Nacional*) issued by Franco in 1958 and the Organic Law of the State, promulgated in 1967. The latter, which like the Succession Law was submitted to a carefully controlled national referendum, outlined the function and powers of the head of state and other national institutions. In theory, the limitations placed on the powers of the former were to apply to Franco as well as to his successor, still at that time unknown, but in practice the dictator retained reserve powers dating back to 1938 and 1939 which allowed him, whenever he deemed fit, to rule in a dictatorial way without consulting his cabinet. The powers conferred on the future head of state were still considerable, however, extending to the realms of the executive, legislature, judiciary and the armed forces. There were to be no concessions to liberal concepts such as accountability and the separation of powers. In reality, the Organic Law envisaged a kind of executive monarchy, very different from the constitutional monarchies of western Europe or pre-republican Spain. Thus, any successor to Franco would enjoy very considerable constitutional powers.

3.2.1.3 Nomination of Juan Carlos

Preferring to keep his options open and to play off competing groups against each other, Franco delayed the nomination of his successor for as long as possible. For many years the odds had been in favour of Juan Carlos who, following a meeting between Franco and Don Juan, had been educated in Spain since the age of ten and had served in all three armed services and several ministries. Moreover, especially after his marriage to Princess Sofía of Greece in 1962, he had appeared increasingly with Franco in public and it appeared that he was being groomed for the succession in spite of the dictator's known antagonism towards Don Juan. However, other claimants did exist in the form of Juan Carlos' late cousin, Alfonso Borbón y Dampierre, at the time married to Franco's own grand-daughter, and Carlos-Hugo de Borbón-Parma, the Carlist pretender, by this stage a less favoured claimant. At all events, in line with predictions, on 22 July 1969 Franco proposed Juan Carlos to the *Cortes* as his intended successor; the proposal was approved by 491 votes to nineteen with nine abstentions. Subsequently, Juan Carlos was to be known as Prince of Spain (not Prince of Asturias, the traditional title of the heir to the throne) and his wife as Princess. Thereafter, *los Príncipes* appeared more frequently in public with Franco, and assumed the role of ambassadors-extraordinary to several foreign countries.

It should be stressed, however, that, even after this nomination, Franco could have implemented article 13 of the Succession Law, which allowed him to revoke this decision and to nominate an alternative successor; the possible justifications for such a revocation were either a demonstrated incapacity to govern or 'blatant deviation from the fundamental principles of the state'. No doubt, if at that time Juan

Carlos had expressed the sort of democratic sentiments that he was later to embrace, Franco would have had no hesitation in invoking this provision.

3.2.2 Dynastic legitimacy

With his nomination of Juan Carlos in preference to his father Don Juan, Franco had appeared deliberately to sever all connections between his monarchy and that of pre-republican days, which in numerous speeches he had associated with allegedly decadent liberal democracy and the party system. This was sufficient reason for many monarchist supporters to rally to the cause of Don Juan whose liberal and democratic leanings were well known. Indeed, while he was living in exile in Portugal, Don Juan's Privy Council was composed of a wide range of democratic liberal opinion from conservatives and ex-Francoists like José-María de Areilza to socialists like Raúl Morodo. Though the Pretender remained in close contact with his son, the latter's apparently passive acceptance of all the dictator's instructions met with a certain amount of paternal disapproval, not least his acceptance of the succession in 1969. It was only in May 1977, a month before the first democratic elections were held, that Don Juan publicly renounced his claim to the throne.

However, it has to be recognised that during the Franco era Don Juan's supporters were few in number. Opponents of Franco tended to identify democracy not with the restoration of the monarchy but, if anything, with republicanism. Hence Juan Carlos' link with the traditional monarchy, as far as the general public was concerned, offered little more source of legitimacy than his adoption by the Franco regime. One might indeed argue that his acceptance of the succession, apparently against his father's wish, effectively debarred him morally, if not legally, from claiming to be the legitimate heir of the traditional monarchy.

3.2.3 Earned legitimacy

On Franco's death, a crisis of legitimacy occurred for the Spanish monarchy, caught as it was between three rival groups: those who wished to use it as a means to perpetuate Francoism; the reformists (*reformistas*) who wanted to employ it as a protective umbrella for the operation of a smooth transition from dictatorship to democracy; and those (the *rupturistas*) who were at the outset totally opposed to the monarchy, considering that not only was it discredited for historical reasons, but that Juan Carlos' apparently close identification with the Franco regime disqualified him from holding office. The fact that the monarchy has now survived for two decades would seem to bear testimony to the ability of Juan Carlos to tread a carefully chosen path among these conflicting groups. His manner of doing so in fact conferred on him a third and much more durable form of legitimacy – one that he has earned by his commitment to democracy.

An examination of the king's role in the transition properly belongs to works of political history, hence reference here will be made to his role only in so far as his actions implied changes to the institutions of the new state. In this context, Juan

Carlos' outstanding contribution, apart from his unequivocal support, if not inspiration, for the fundamental reform process initiated by Adolfo Suárez (1976–81) was his determination to divest himself of the substantial powers conferred upon him by Franco and to rule as a constitutional monarch within the framework of the new democratic order. Although, at the time of the attempted military coup of February 1981, Juan Carlos exercised a kind of political power, this could surely be justified in terms of his evident concern for the survival of democracy; in any case, the king subsequently made it clear to both the military and the politicians that he never again wanted to have to intervene so directly in the political arena.

3.3 Monarchical form of the state

According to article 1.3 of the 1978 Constitution, 'the political form of the state is the parliamentary monarchy'. The significance of this is that under the new order the king is not sovereign; sovereignty is exercised by the people, whose will is expressed through their democratically elected representatives in Parliament. It is very significant that the above clause follows article 1.2, which states that 'national sovereignty resides in the Spanish people from whom all the powers of the state derive'. Thus, since the king is not sovereign, it is not correct to talk of a monarchical state; the overriding characteristic of the Spanish state, as described in article 1.1, is that it is 'a social and democratic state based on the rule of law'. This is a vitally important consideration because it embodies the concept that parliamentary democracy emanates from the will of the people and not from that of the monarch. Neither would it be correct to refer to the monarchy as Spain's form of government for, in constitutional law and historically, this would imply that the king was the titular head of the executive or government which, as we shall see, is far from the case. Basically, the nature of the Spanish state is a parliamentary democracy organised in such a way that currently its head of state is a hereditary and constitutional monarch.

3.4 Role and functions of the monarch

These are outlined in article 56 of the Constitution, where it is possible to distinguish three types of function. In the first place, as head of state (*jefe del estado*), he is its supreme representative and this is most obviously manifested in the area of international relations; moreover, he is the symbol of its unity, acknowledged as head of state by all the autonomous communities; furthermore, he is the symbol of continuity, enhanced by the hereditary principle of succession (3.7). Secondly, the king has the responsibility of ensuring that the institutions of the state run smoothly; where necessary he is required to exercise an arbitrating or restraining influence in pursuit of this goal. Thirdly, the Constitution confers on him a limited number of specific functions which enable him to carry out effectively the above roles. It cannot be over-emphasised, however, that the monarch has no powers outside the Constitution. These different functions will now be examined separately.

3.4.1 Symbolic functions

The first of these concerns international relations. Although the monarch has no power constitutionally to direct foreign affairs, which are the responsibility of the government, he nevertheless plays a vital role as chief representative of the state both at home and abroad. In a sense, his most important function is that of communication with other countries and their leaders; through his numerous journeys abroad and his contacts with visiting foreign leaders, Juan Carlos has often served a valuable purpose in preparing the ground for later links, both commercial and political, forged by the Spanish government. In recent years, the king has given a strong lead in his unequivocal support for Spain's membership of the European Union. Indeed, for his efforts to promote European understanding, he was awarded the prestigious Charlemagne Prize in 1982. Another major preoccupation has been his concern to promote and strengthen links with the Latin American countries; in this context Juan Carlos has been a major protagonist of the annual conference of the heads of state and government of Latin America, the first of which was held in Guadalajara, Mexico, in 1992.

The extent of the king's involvement in the international field is reflected by the fact that in 1994 alone Juan Carlos and Queen Sofía made no less than eleven official visits abroad and received visits from as many as nineteen heads of state, including Boris Yeltsin of Russia and F. W. de Clerk of South Africa. It is interesting to note that, while all official royal business is conducted in the Royal Palace (*Palacio Real* or *Palacio del Oriente*), the traditional home of Spanish monarchs, Juan Carlos and his family live in relatively modest surroundings in the mansion of *La Zarzuela*, just outside Madrid.

The king's responsibilities in the international field also include: accrediting Spanish ambassadors and other diplomatic representatives of the country and receiving the credentials of resident ambassadors and diplomats (article 63.1); indicating the consent of the state to international treaties and agreements in accordance with the Constitution (article 63.2); and declaring war and peace, following approval by the *Cortes* (article 63.2).

In relation to Parliament, an important symbolic function is the speech which he makes every four years or so following elections. Unlike the Queen's speech every year to the British Parliament, this speech is not a presentation of the government's future programme, but simply a speech of welcome to the members of the new Parliament – part of the official opening ceremony.

With regard to the judiciary, article 117 of the Constitution lays down that the judges administer justice in the name of the king; clearly this is a purely formal and symbolic attribute. The same article makes it clear that justice emanates from the people and that the judges are independent and subject only to the law (14.2). None the less, the association of the crown (*la corona*) with the judiciary helps to stress its impartiality and imbue it with an aura of traditional dignity.

One of the king's major functions as head of state is to make various civil and military appointments, as well as to award special honours and distinctions (article 62f).

It should be stressed, however, that the government has the right to control both the civil and military administration (5.5.2) and that the king's role is limited to the act of ratifying appointments already made by the government. The only exception to this is outlined in article 65.2, referring to the king's right freely to select the staff for his civil and military households (3.6.2).

The king is normally invited to act as honorary patron of such august societies as the eight royal academies, which all belong automatically to the Cervantes Institute (*Instituto Cervantes*) which during the early 1990s opened several international offices, including three in the United Kingdom. This is, of course, only a symbolic function, yet it has its importance in demonstrating the support of the crown, and therefore the state, for the highest level of cultural and scientific endeavour (article 62j).

Finally, but by no means least in importance, article 62h confers on the monarch the title of commander-in-chief of the armed forces (*mando supremo de las fuerzas armadas*) (2.3.1). This title is commonly assumed by heads of state, and certainly in the Spanish case does not imply any special constitutional relationship between the head of state and the armed forces; the monarch can make no decisions with regard to the latter, which are in any case ultimately under the control of the government. On the other hand, as we have already seen, in practice this particular monarch has clearly exercised considerable influence over the military in his determination to consolidate democracy. Juan Carlos has always remained in regular contact with the armed forces, and uses the annual military celebration of the *Pascua Militar* on 6 January both to reiterate his approval of their endeavours and, on occasion, to remind them of their duty to uphold the Constitution.

3.4.2 Moderating functions

This function involves the collaboration of the monarch with the organs of the state to ensure that extremist or arbitrary tendencies are avoided which might threaten the proper functioning of the system. To a large extent, these functions are carried out in relation both to the legislative and the executive power and, as with most of the other functions of the king, they are subject to limitations and controls which reduce their practical significance to a minimum.

With regard to the legislature, the king requires the backing of either the government or the head of government in order to perform the following functions:

3.4.2.1 To call elections to Parliament

Article 62b grants this 'power' to the king 'in the terms envisaged in the Constitution' meaning, in practice, that when Parliament has run its normal course or when the government decides to call an election (4.5.1). At all events he must, on the advice of the prime minister, call elections between thirty and sixty days following the dissolution of Parliament.

3.4.2.2 To summon and dissolve Parliament

Article 62b refers to the king's responsibility to summon and dissolve Parliament, again 'in the terms envisaged in the Constitution'. Article 68.6 lays down that he must summon the Congress within twenty-five days following elections. With regard to the dissolution, the Constitution distinguishes four possible scenarios: (i) when the maximum four-year mandate has expired; (ii) when the Congress, within the two-month period following elections, fails to give its support in a vote of confidence to the candidate for the premiership (4.6.3.4); (iii) when the *Cortes*, by a two-thirds majority in each House, approves a proposal for a total or partial revision of the Constitution; and (iv) when the prime minister proposes a dissolution of Parliament, for whatever reason.

It should be stressed that in none of the above cases are we dealing with a power of discretion granted to the monarch; at no time can the king prevent the dissolution of the *Cortes*. The only person to exercise this prerogative is the prime minister of the day.

3.4.2.3 To sanction and promulgate laws

Article 62a grants the monarch the right to sanction and promulgate laws that have already been approved either by Parliament or by the Council of Ministers. With his signature, the king is confirming that all the formal requirements for approval of any given law have been met, and he can only withhold his signature, something which in practice is barely conceivable, if such requirements have not been fulfilled. In a sense, this function bears comparison with others which we have included in the section on symbolic functions. It need hardly be said that the king has no legislative power; as we shall see in 4.6, this belongs almost exclusively to the *Cortes*.

With regard to the executive, the 'powers' of the monarch are similarliy limited. These include the following:

3.4.2.4 To terminate a premiership

The monarch has the right to terminate the functions of the prime minister according to article 62d, which in practice means the acceptance, for whatever reason, of the resignation of the latter. In no circumstances does he have the authority under the Constitution to dismiss him or oblige him to resign (5.2.2).

3.4.2.5 To appoint and dismiss ministers

Article 62f grants the king responsibility with regard to government ministers; here his role is essentially that of a rubber-stamp since the basic decisions are taken by the prime minister (5.4.1). Article 52.1 of the Constitution also accords him the responsibility of appointing the presidents of the seventeen autonomous communities (7.6.2).

3.4.2.6 To issue cabinet decrees

According to article 62f the monarch must issue and make arrangements for the publication of decrees agreed in the Council of Ministers (4.7.1.6–8).

3.4.2.7 To attend meetings of the council of ministers

Article 62g, as well as allowing the king to be informed about matters of state, also grants him the right to attend sessions of the Council of Ministers (5.5) when he should consider it appropriate, but only on the request of the prime minister.

3.4.3 Arbitrating functions

The only area where the king may possibly exercise some residual discretionary powers concerns the proposal of a candidate to head the government, either following elections or following the resignation of an existing premier. In normal circumstances, this 'power' is very restricted: following consultations with party leaders, the monarch automatically calls on the leader of the majority party in the Congress to head the next government, and provided that the latter obtains the required vote of confidence from that House, the king appoints him and swears him in. If, following an indecisive election, no obvious candidate emerges, the arbitrating role of the king might well assume more importance. However, it must be stressed that the king has no executive power as such, only a certain moral authority and influence which, of course, has no constitutional basis.

3.5 Limitations to role

As has already been shown, none of the functions of the monarch outlined above grant him any independent decision-making powers within the judicial, executive or legislative institutions of the state. Juan Carlos is a constitutional monarch in the full sense of the term, having no reserve powers outside the Constitution.

One of the major constitutional devices for limiting the monarchy is the use of the endorsement (*refrendo*). By means of this device, no official document is issued solely with the signature of the king but must be countersigned by either the prime minister or by one of his ministers. In the case of the recommendation and appointment of the premier or the dissolution of the *Cortes*, such documents must be endorsed by the president of the Congress (article 64a). In a sense, it is the king who is countersigning or endorsing the document and the others referred to who exercise the real power.

3.6 Privileges

3.6.1 Royal endorsement and immunity

In fact the *refrendo* is a kind of monarchical privilege as well as a limitation on the king's power. Since the Constitution states that 'those who endorse the acts of the king are responsible for them', the king is absolved of all responsibility for them. In this way, the monarchy is spared the risk of becoming politically involved and associated with unpopular legislation.

This basic constitutional concept is repeated in article 56.3, which also states that the monarch is inviolable. This does not mean, however, that he stands outside the criminal law, for if he were to commit a criminal offence, article 59 would come into force; this envisages the possibility of the king, for whatever reason, being found unfit to rule by the joint Houses of Parliament. It should be stressed that only the *Cortes* can act as a court in the case of any offences allegedly committed by the king.

3.6.2 Royal Household (*Casa Real*)

Two further privileges which the monarch enjoys refer to the royal family and household. Article 65.1 enables the king to receive a global sum from the state budget for the maintenance of his family and household, a sum which he has the right to distribute as he wishes. He enjoys a similar and rare freedom to appoint and dismiss the members of his civil and military households. The king or his senior staff also have the right to seek advice or support from any government department and to request any documents or papers which may be useful in helping them to carry out their official duties.

As can be seen in figure 3.2, the Royal Household, whose structure is laid down in the royal decree of 6 May 1988, consists of four major departments, three of which are of a military nature, all under the control of the head of the royal household (*jefe de la casa real*), who is usually a personal friend of the king and a person of recognised stature. His second-in-command is the general secretary (*secretario general*) who is responsible for co-ordinating all the services of the household and also acts as its head of personnel. One of his major tasks is to prepare an annual report on the progress, cost and performance of the seven areas under his direct control. It is important to distinguish the Military Household (*Cuarto Militar*) and the Royal Guard (*Guardia Real*), which perform such honorary duties as providing a palace guard and escort duties, from the security service, whose members are drawn from the Ministry of Defence and who are responsible for the personal safety of the king and the royal family.

In order to allow him to carry out all his official obligations, Parliament votes each year a fixed sum for the king (for 1995 it was 956 million pesetas) from the general state budgets (4.7.3.1). It is worth noting that, unlike certain European monarchies, the Spanish royal family have very little private wealth; the four royal residences, including their regular residence of *La Zarzuela*, all belong to the state. It should

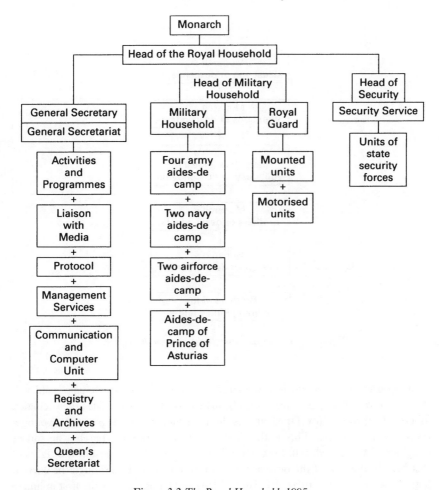

Figure 3.2 *The Royal Household, 1995*

also be noted that the king pays taxes in exactly the same way as other Spanish citizens.

3.7 Succession and regency

In the constitutional, if not the political, sense Juan Carlos' position as head of state and monarch, rooted in Franco's fundamental laws, has been ratified and legitimised in the 1978 Constitution which, by converting the king's role into a constitutional one, is able to designate him as 'the legitimate heir of the historic dynasty' (article 57.1). At the same time, the succession is attached to his heirs in a traditional and hereditary monarchy.

As far as the order of succession is concerned, article 57.1 states that a male heir

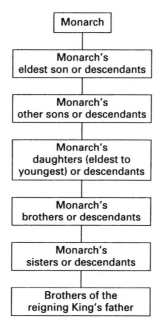

Figure 3.3 *Line of succession to the Spanish throne, 1995*

is always preferred to a female of the same generation, even if the female is older. If the heir to the throne dies prematurely, his eldest child, first males then females, inherits the throne. Only if the heir dies childless does the throne pass to his younger brother(s) or sister(s). This is the theory of representation whereby the son or daughter of an heir who dies prematurely is considered to represent the rights of that heir. In the case of the present royal family, for example, although the current heir, Prince Felipe, has two elder sisters, Elena and Cristina, he is the first in line to the throne; one of them could succeed to the throne only if Felipe died childless. Under this system, therefore, unlike that obtaining under Franco's Fundamental Laws, which forbade a female monarch, females can accede to the throne. It is clear, however, that males enjoy a privileged position with regard to the succession. The main reason for its adoption in 1978 is that it is in line with a Spanish tradition dating back to the fourteenth century. The line of succession is shown in figure 3.3.

The heir to the throne from birth enjoys the traditional title of Prince of Asturias (article 57.2). On attaining the age of majority (eighteen), which Prince Felipe did on 30 January 1986, he must take the same oath as taken by a monarch on ascending the throne, that is, faithfully to carry out his functions, to observe and ensure the observance of the Constitution and the laws, and respect the rights of citizens as well as those of the autonomous communities. He must also take the oath of loyalty to the king. These oaths also apply to a regent or regents on taking office (article 61.2).

If all legal lines of succession are extinguished, the joint Houses of Parliament, according to article 57.3, 'will provide for the succession to the throne in the form most suitable for the interests of Spain'. It is interesting to note that no particular type of majority is referred to in this vitally important constitutional matter (4.6.1).

One important principle and advantage of the traditional monarchy is the provision of continuity even at the time of a monarch's death. Constitutionally, the state can never be without a head because at the moment of such a death the heir automatically becomes king; it is not required that he should previously be sworn in before he assumes office. Nor is there a problem even if the heir is still below the age of majority: although it may take some time for the regency to take effect, the heir is still recognised as the monarch and titular head of state. Thus, unless the last heir to the throne dies childless, a highly unlikely circumstance, there can never be a vacuum in the headship of state.

There are two possible scenarios for the establishment of a regency in Spain and these are spelled out in article 59. First, as indicated above, if the heir to the throne should not have attained the age of majority; and, second, if the king should be declared unfit to rule by the joint *Cortes*. In the first case, the regency would be assumed by the father, mother or the next adult in line of succession. In the second case the heir himself would automatically assume the regency; if he were still not of age, the order outlined above would be followed until the heir became of age. If no clear candidate for the regency were available, the joint *Cortes* would have the right to appoint a regent. The latter would have to be Spanish and would have to have attained the age of majority; in this case the regency could consist of one, two or more persons. It should be stressed that a regency is always provisional and all its functions and acts are carried out in the name of the king. Normally, too, any regency would have a fixed time-span, for example, until the heir had attained the age of majority.

3.8 Comment

It is ironic that, prior to the 1978 Constitution, Juan Carlos used the wide powers bequeathed to him by Franco to steer the country away from dictatorship and towards democracy. He used these powers partly to encourage the new political establishment to draw up a Constitution under which he himself would be divested of his executive authority and would become a constitutional monarch with very few powers. In doing so, Juan Carlos earned for himself the kind of moral authority which, it is probable, no successor could hope to obtain. At the same time, for the foreseeable future, unless his heirs prove to be extremely incompetent, it would seem that the monarchy as an institution is likely to benefit from this authority and from the popular legitimacy which the actions of Juan Carlos have conferred upon it. Indeed, recent surveys have consistently indicated a much higher level of popular support for this institution than all other institutions of state, and the king's personal standing has been consistently higher than that of all political leaders. This may be related, at least in part, to the apparent ability of the monarch (and, indeed, the royal family as a whole) to combine the 'common touch' with the necessary dignity and ceremony of official occasions, exemplified in recent times at the state funeral in Madrid for the king's father in April 1993 and the wedding in Seville of the Infanta Elena in March 1995. While taking great care not to become embroiled in party politics, Juan Carlos has not, on the other hand, shied away from making strong pronouncements on issues which he would regard as matters of state, such as the condemnation of terrorism (and, indeed, extremist nationalism), the need to give real support to the developing countries of Latin America and the desirability of forging even stronger links within the European Union. The king's most recent opportunity to develop the latter theme came on 10 June 1995, the tenth anniversary of Spain's signing of the Treaty of Accession to the European Communities (15.1).

Chapter 4

Parliament

4.1 Introduction

From 1939 to 1977, Spain was endowed with a one-chamber legislature known as the *Cortes*. Franco, profoundly hostile to the legislative systems of liberal democracies, swept away the democratically elected single-chamber Parliament of the Second Republic, and imposed what amounted to a rubber-stamp chamber packed with his own nominees and supporters.

Although a modest attempt was made in the the Organic Law of 1967 to introduce a more democratic element, offering the voter an opportunity to elect 108 so-called 'family MPs', the result meant little change to the existing system. On the one hand, these comprised no more than a fifth of the membership of the House and, in any case, candidates were carefully screened by the officials of the regime to ensure that only approved figures were allowed to stand. On the other hand, in terms of its mode of functioning, the *Cortes* was subjected to constant interference from the executive; debates were rarely held, ministers were not obliged to appear on request before the House, and certain issues such as foreign policy and public order were not deemed to be part of its remit.

4.2 The legislature today

The above situation, however, changed dramatically in October 1976 when, in an historic decision, the Franco *Cortes* signed what amounted to its own death-warrant by approving Adolfo Suárez's Political Reform Law (1.1.4). This paved the way for fully democratic elections, and envisaged, pending the drafting of a new constitution, the establishment of a bicameral Parliament with a Congress of Deputies and a Senate. These far-reaching reforms were later to be enshrined in the Constitution of 1978.

In accordance with the principles of liberal democracy, post-Franco Spain implicitly, if not explicitly, recognised in the Constitution a separation of powers between the legislature, the executive and the judiciary. Following the guidelines of the Political Reform Law, the Constitution (sections III and V) outlines the nature, composition and functions of the new legislature as well as its relationship to the executive and the other institutions of the state. Article 2 makes it clear that 'national sovereignty resides with the Spanish people, from whom all the powers of the state derive'. This sovereignty is expressed through the *Cortes*, whose elected members are the trustees and representatives of the will of the people. Parliament is the supreme institution of the state and, as we have already seen, even the monarchy, quite deliberately defined as a 'parliamentary monarchy', is in the last resort subject to its will (3.3).

4.3 Basic structure of Parliament

The term *Cortes* has come to refer to the national Parliament, whether expressed through one or two Houses or chambers (*cámaras*). In the course of this chapter, it will be seen that, while certain functions are carried out separately by each chamber, a number of important functions, mainly related to the monarchy, are exercised by both Houses, in which capacity they are known as the *Cortes Generales* or joint Houses of Parliament.

Like many European democracies, Spain has established a bicameral Parliament consisting of a Lower House (*Cámara Baja*) or Congress and an Upper House (*Cámara Alta*) or Senate. As in the United Kingdom, for example, the lower house has precedence in most matters, including legislative affairs, and this is represented symbolically by the fact that the president of the Congress (4.3.1) presides over sessions of the *Cortes Generales*. The individuality of the two chambers, however, is emphasised by the fact that they occupy separate premises in Madrid: the Congress assembles in the *Palacio del Congreso*, while the Senate meets in the *Palacio del Senado*.

4.3.1 Congress of Deputies (*Congreso de los Diputados*)

According to article 68 of the Constitution, the Congress consists of a minimum of 300 and a maximum of 400 deputies (*diputados*). In fact, the June 1985 General Electoral Law (*Ley Orgánica de Régimen Electoral General/LOREG*) established that 350 should be the norm. As in the case of the Senate (4.3.2), elections are held through universal, free, direct, equal and secret suffrage, and both males and females over the age of eighteen are eligible to vote. Unlike what occurs with the Senate, however, votes are cast, not for individual candidates, but for a party list in which candidates appear in a ranking order fixed in advance by the parties concerned. The constituency for elections to the Congress is the province (figure 4.1). Article 68.3 establishes a system of proportional representation for allocating seats to the fifty-two provinces (fifty mainland provinces plus Ceuta and Melilla) (7.3.5), and the details of this are spelt out in article 162 of the 1985 Law. Article 163 of the same law specifies the details of the method by which votes are distributed among candidates in each province: this is the D'Hondt system, which is also used in regional and local elections. This system is commonly accepted to favour large parties and less populated, often more conservative, rural areas. The life-span of the Congress is a maximum of four years, after which elections must be called. In any event, the term of office of a deputy ends when Parliament is dissolved by the head of state (3.4.2.2).

Figure 4.1 *Electoral constituencies: the provinces of Spain, 1995*

4.3.2 Senate (*Senado*)

Basically, the Senate is what article 69 of the Constitution calls 'the chamber of territorial representation', which claims to represent the interests of the country's newly formed autonomous communities (chapter 7). In fact, this is only partly the case. A number of senators (*senadores*) are indeed elected from among the members of the regional assemblies through a system which reflects both the population size of the regions and the political composition of their assemblies. However, the vast majority of senators, 208 out of a total of 256 in 1993 are elected from the provinces which, as with the Congress, provides the normal electoral constituency. Since, in fact, the Constitution makes no reference to the constituency for the Senate (7.9), a reform in this area would be relatively easy. Each province elects four senators, with each elector casting only three votes, in a first-past-the-post or majority system, which makes no allowance for the enormous variations in population between sparsely populated areas like Soria and Teruel and enormous urban conurbations like Madrid and Barcelona. Generally speaking, this system favours the conservative rural areas and for that reason was vigorously defended by the right in the constitutional debates. However, in 1982 and 1986, this bias did not prevent the Socialists from winning twice as many seats in the Senate as their main rivals, the Popular Alliance.

In September 1994, however, opening a three-day historic debate in the Senate on the autonomous regions, attended by all but one of the regional presidents, Felipe González, while stressing that neither the unity of the state nor its decentralised model were in question, proposed that there should be a reform of the Constitution (2.7) to allow for the establishment of an Upper House that more genuinely reflected its designation as the 'chamber of territorial representation'. Although the reform process is still at an early stage (7.9), one well supported proposal is that the Senate would include many more representatives elected from the regional chambers and there would be a corresponding decrease in the number of senators directly elected from the provinces. Many political leaders also believe that the Upper House should be given exclusive powers to debate matters relating to the autonomous communities.

4.3.3 Members of Parliament (*parlamentarios*)

Parlamentarios is the umbrella term used in Spanish to refer to both deputies and senators, whose rights and duties are laid down in both the Constitution and the standing orders (*reglamentos*) of the Congress and Senate, which were first published in 1982, but may soon be subject to a major revision. They detail all matters relating to the internal organisation of each House. Although the statutes of the deputies and senators are spelled out separately in these documents, their rights and duties are substantially the same, as suggested in articles 70 and 71 of the Constitution.

4.3.3.1 Prerogatives and rights

Like MPs in most democratic countries, Spanish deputies and senators enjoy a major privilege known as immunity (*inviolabilidad*). This is manifested in two ways. Firstly, during their term of office, and even after it has expired, they are not liable in respect of verbal opinions expressed in the performance of their parliamentary duties. Secondly, during their term of office, they can only be arrested if caught in the act of committing a crime and, in any case, they cannot be indicted or prosecuted without the previous authorisation of the *Cortes*. To obtain the latter, the court concerned must seek an injunction (*suplicatorio*) from the House concerned within a fixed period of time before proceedings can commence. The most recent recourse to this measure came in 1995 concerning a former minister of home affairs and deputy, José Barrionuevo, allegedly implicated in the establishment of the GAL (1.1.5).

Parliamentarians are not bound by any compulsory mandate; their votes are personal, and they are not obliged to vote in accordance with previous instructions emanating from individuals or groups. In practice, of course, most deputies and senators vote in line with party instructions.

They have the right to attend and vote at all plenary sittings of Parliament and all committees of which they are members. Deputies are allowed to attend any committee without the right to vote, although this is not stated in the case of senators.

All have a right not only to a fixed salary, annually reviewed, but allowances (*dietas*) for all expenses incurred in the exercise of their duty. Senators may travel free on agreed systems of public transport. Each House agrees to adopt the social security payments made by former employers in order to safeguard their health, pension and other rights while members of Parliament.

Deputies have the right to demand from any branch of public administration data or information that might be useful to them in the exercise of their duties. Interestingly, this right does not seem to be accorded to senators, although the latter may request the minutes and documents emanating from any body within the House.

4.3.3.2 Restrictions and duties

Parliamentarians are not allowed to be members of both Houses of Parliament at the same time; neither is it lawful to occupy a seat simultaneously in the Congress and a regional assembly. Presumably, senators are allowed to sit in the latter, however, since nothing is stated to the contrary.

According to article 70, the following are not allowed to stand for Parliament: members of the Constitutional Court, high-ranking civil servants, the ombudsman, practising judges and public prosecutors, professional soldiers and other military personnel, active members of the police and security forces, and members of electoral boards.

All parliamentarians not only have the right but also the obligation to attend plenary sittings of the appropriate House and the committees of which they are members. Senators may incur a financial penalty following consistent failure to attend.

Parliamentarians must respect article 79.3 of the Constitution which states that votes are personal and cannot be delegated. There is no pairing system like the one that operates in the House of Commons in the United Kingdom.

All parliamentarians are required to make a public statement before a notary (*notario*) of their assets and of any activities which provide them with an income. Deputies and senators have two months and four months respectively to make such statements following their election to the House.

In the autumn of 1993, the government bill to amend sections of the General Electoral Law (in particular articles 157 and 159) which refer to extra-parliamentary employment and remuneration was received by a storm of protest, especially from a group of Socialist senators.

4.4 Internal organisation

According to article 72 of the Constitution, each House is free to draw up standing orders or rules of procedure (*reglamentos*) governing its own internal organisation and mode of functioning, including its own budget and the establishment of offices to administer such affairs.

4.4.1 President

The president (or speaker) of the Congress (*presidente del Congreso*) and the president of the Senate (*presidente del Senado*) are elected by secret vote in their respective chambers and require either an overall majority of the House (first ballot) or the highest number of votes in a 'run-off' between the top two candidates (second ballot). The presidents have several functions in common. Basically, their main task is to supervise the everyday running of the House, both inside and outside the debating chamber. Within the chamber, they and their presiding councils (4.4.2) are responsible for drawing up the legislative agenda in consultation with the board of party spokesmen (4.4.6) and for exercising discipline within the House. As we shall see later, there are rigorous regulations controlling procedures in each House and the president is empowered to take strong disciplinary action against members who contravene the regulations and practices of the House.

In addition the president of the Congress performs several special constitutional functions. For example, article 99 of the Constitution implies that he must be consulted or at least informed before elections are called and the decree convening elections must have his countersignature. According to the same Article, it is through the president of the Congress that the king proposes a candidate for the premiership.

The presidents are assisted by vice-presidents (*vicepresidentes*), four in the case of the Congress and two in the case of the Senate, who are elected by the same procedure as the president. In order of hierarchy, they stand in for the president as and when needed. In addition, the presidents are supported by secretaries (*secretarios*), four in each House; one of their major tasks is to supervise and authorise the minutes (*actas*) of the plenary sessions of the Presiding Council (4.4.2) and the Board of Party Spokesmen (4.4.6) and another is to help the president ensure that debating and voting procedures are properly carried out. Both the vice-presidents and the secretaries are drawn from the major political groupings represented in each chamber in proportion to their strength in each chamber.

4.4.2 Presiding Council (*Mesa*)

The presiding council or bureau is elected at the constituent meeting of the Congress and Senate following elections. It includes the president, vice-presidents and secretaries of each House. In each case, the council is responsible for the overall management and organisation of the work of the House, in this context, one of its main functions is to establish conventions of procedure within the House, draw up the order of business of the plenary sittings and committees and co-ordinate the activities of the various bodies established within the House. Other tasks are: (i) to prepare a draft budget; (ii) to supervise and control its administration; and (iii) to present an annual report on its implementation to the full House. The Council is also entrusted with the task of evaluating all parliamentary papers and documents in accordance with the standing orders and to rule on their admissibility.

To assist it in the above functions, each Presiding Council can call on a team of special legal advisers or *letrados*. These non-political figures are lawyers trained in every aspect of parliamentary procedure, who play a vital technical role in the day-to-day running of each Chamber. Their main function is to supervise and author-ise, with the approval of the president of the House, the minutes of plenary meetings of the Congress or Senate and their respective presiding councils and boards of party spokesmen (4.4.6). During full meetings of each House, they assist the president in ensuring the smooth running of debates and voting. In their work, they are advised and guided by the chief legal adviser (*letrado mayor*) in the case of the Congress and the general secretarial adviser (*letrado secretario general*) in the case of the Senate. The first of these also acts as the senior legal adviser to the Joint Houses of Parliament (*letrado mayor de las Cortes Generales*).

4.4.3 General Secretariat (*Secretaría General*)

These bodies, established under the standing orders of each House, basically repre-sent the bureaucracies of the Congress and the Senate. The Secretariat is composed of secretaries (not to be confused with those on the Presiding Council), who, like the *letrados*, are non-political experts. The major functions of the Secretariat are to provide all the bodies operating within the House, particularly the committees, with legal, technical and administrative assistance. Each of the two secretariats is headed by a general secretary (*secretario general*) who, in addition to the above functions, is specifically responsible for the registration and distribution of documents, protocol, the diffusion of information, and relations with the media. The make-up of the Congress Secretariat is shown in table 4.1.

4.4.4 Standing Council (*Diputación Permanente*)

The other major body within each House is the Standing Council which consists of the president of the House and at least twenty-one members. These are elected at the constituent meeting of the House in proportion to the membership of the par-liamentary groups (4.4.5) from among the members of the latter. Apart from the president, the Council consists of two vice-presidents and two secretaries, elected from among the members of the Council; these are not to be confused with their counterparts in the Presiding Council. The main purpose of the Council is to provide continuity between sessions of Parliament, including the period after Parliament has been dissolved and before a new Parliament has been elected and convened. Each Council has the right to request an extraordinary sitting of Parliament. One of the major functions of the Standing Council of the Congress is to approve or reject decree-laws which are submitted to it by the Council of Ministers and to act in the name of the House as a whole. If the Congress is not sitting, the Council is also empowered to act in its name regarding the declaration of states of alarm, exception and siege (4.6.3.2.).

Table 4.1 *Composition of General Secretariat of the Congress, 1996*

Function	Name in Spanish
Research and documentation	*Estudios y documentación*
Technical and parliamentary assistance	*Asistencia técnico-parlamentaria*
Parliamentary relations	*Relaciones parlamentarias*
Internal organisation	*Gobierno interior*
Economic affairs	*Asuntos económicos*
Audit department	*Intervención*
Computing department	*Informática*
Committees	*Comisiones*

Source: Boletín Oficial de las Cortes Generales (April 1996).

4.4.5 Parliamentary groups (*grupos parlamentarios*)

From the political point of view, these are the most important bodies within each House. They are the organs through which the bulk of parliamentary business, and certainly the work of full sittings of the House and committees, is conducted. In general, each group consists of the deputies or senators within the House belonging to one political party or coalition. In the case of the Congress, each group must in theory contain a minimum of fifteen deputies, although provision is made for a smaller group of no less than five deputies representing one or more parties, provided that together they represent 15 per cent of the votes in the constituencies in which they have put up a candidate. (In fact, following the 1993 election an agreement was reached to allow the Canary Islands Coalition (CC) (10.4.8), with only four deputies, to form a separate group.) All remaining deputies must join the Mixed Group (*Grupo Mixto*). In the case of the Senate, each group must contain at least ten senators; if the membership falls below six, the group must be dissolved until the end of that session of Parliament. Following the 1996 elections, the configuration of parliamentary groups in each House is as shown in table 4.2.

From several points of view the composition of the above groups has various important implications: (i) members of Parliament are elected to serve on parliamentary committees, composed in strict proportion to the political structure of each House (4.5.4); (ii) the size of the parliamentary groups also governs the length of time granted for speeches, questions, and so on, as well as the order in which they are called to speak; and (iii) in both the Senate and the Congress the members are seated according to the group to which they belong.

Figure 4.2 shows how, in 1995, the debating chamber of the Congress, often referred to as the *hemiciclo* because of its semi-circular shape, was divided to accommodate the various parliamentary groups.

4.4.6 Board of Party Spokesmen (*Junta de Portavoces*)

Each parliamentary group elects a spokesman (*portavoz*) to represent its interests in its dealings with the President and the administration of the House. The various

Table 4.2 *Political division of Parliament: parliamentary groups, 1996*

Congress		Senate	
Name of group	No. of members	Name of group	No. of members
Popular group	156	Popular group	133
(*Grupo popular*)			
Socialist group	141	Socialist Group	96
(*Grupo Socialista*)			
United Left group	21		–
(*Grupo Izquierda*			
Unida/IU)			
Catalan group	16	Catalán group	11
(*Grupo catalán*)		(CiU)	
Basque group	5	Basque group	6
(*Grupo vasco*)			
Canary group	4		–
(*Grupo Coalición*			
Canaria/CC)			
Mixed group	7	Mixed group[b]	10
(*Grupo mixto*)[a]			
Total	350		256[c]

Notes:
[a] This includes one member from EA (10.4.2), one member from ERC (10.4.6), one member from UV (10.4.11), two members from BNG (10.4.9) and two members from HB (10.4.3) who traditionally do not take up their seats.
[b] This includes two members from IU (10.3.2), one member from EA, one member from UV and five members from small local groupings from the Balearics and the Canaries
[c] Forty-nine of these members are appointed from the regional assemblies on the basis of one per region plus one for every million inhabitants (4.3.2 and 7.6.1).
Source: Boletín Oficial de las Cortes Generales (April 1996).

spokesmen, together with the president of the House, who chairs their meetings, constitute the Board of Party Spokesmen. The meetings of the Congress Board must be attended by at least one vice-president, one of the secretaries of the House and the general secretary. Until recently, it was also customary for the deputy premier (5.3) to attend. The composition of the Senate Board is similar; in addition, its meetings may be attended by a representative of the government.

The main functions of the Board in each House, in collaboration with the Presiding Council, are: to fix the dates for the start and end of parliamentary sessions; to agree on the agendas for plenary and committee meetings of the Houses; and to suggest means of ensuring the smooth operation of debates and other aspects of parliamentary activity. The boards normally meet once a week on Tuesdays prior to full sittings of the *Cortes* (4.5.3).

4.5 Procedures

In addition to the internal organisation of the Houses of Parliament, the standing orders lay down detailed procedures regarding the way in which each House oper-

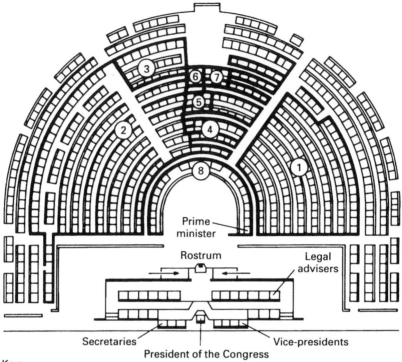

Prime minister

Rostrum

Legal advisers

Secretaries

Vice-presidents

President of the Congress

Key:

1. Popular group (156)[a]   5. Basque group (5)
2. Socialist group (141)   6. Canary group (4)
3. United Left group (21)   7. Mixed group (7)
4. Catalan group (16)   8. Government benches[b]

[a] The numbers in brackets represent the number of members in the group in July 1996.

[b] The government benches are known as the *banco azul,* blue seats, clearly distinguishable from the red ones occupied by other deputies and officers of the Congress.

Figure 4.2 *Debating chamber of the Congress*

ates from day to day in the fulfilment of its various tasks. Although there are slight differences here between the Congress and the Senate, they are not great enough to warrant separate treatment for each.

4.5.1 Summoning and dissolution

As we have already seen (3.4.2.2), one of the king's prerogatives is to summon and dissolve Parliament. In reality, of course, as will be seen in 5.2.4, it is the prime minister who decides to dissolve Parliament and call elections; the monarch's role is merely symbolic. A point worth noting at this juncture is that Houses must be dissolved and convened simultaneously, although it may well be a government defeat (for example, a confidence vote) in the Congress that leads directly to a dissolution.

4.5.2 Parliamentary sessions

Article 73 states that the Houses of Parliament convene in ordinary session twice a year, between September and December and between February and June. In between these sessions, however, as we have seen, a parliamentary presence is maintained through the Standing Council (4.4.4), and the two respective bureaucracies, of course, continue to function. Article 73 also goes on to admit the possibility of calling an extraordinary session of both Houses of Parliament at the request of the government, the Standing Council or an overall majority of the members of either House. Such extraordinary sessions must address themselves to a specific agenda, and Parliament must be adjourned once this has been completed.

4.5.3 Plenary sittings (*plenos*)

Article 75.1 of the Constitution makes it clear that Parliament operates in both plenary sittings and committees. In recent years, plenary sittings of both Houses have tended to take place on Tuesday and Wednesday afternoons and all day Thursday during three weeks of any month, although this pattern can vary depending on the amount of business to be transacted. Plenary sittings are convened by the president of each House, either on his own initiative or at the request of at least two parliamentary groups or a fifth of the members of the House concerned. Sittings of the Senate are not supposed to last more than five hours, though no maximum is laid down for the Congress, where in practice sittings tend to be much longer.

As we have seen, agendas for plenary sittings are fixed by the president in consultation with the Board of Party Spokesmen, However, at least in the case of the Congress, the government has the right to insert in the agenda a matter which it considers deserves priority treatment. Likewise, on the initiative of the government or a parliamentary group, the Board can have an urgent matter included at any time, even without the normal statutory criteria having been met. Moreover, a full sitting of the House can agree to change the order of the agenda, either on the recommendation of the president or on the request of two parliamentary groups or a fifth of the total membership of the House concerned.

With respect to debates, all reports, information and documents relating to the topic to be debated must be circulated to all members of the House at least forty-eight hours before the debate, unless the Presiding Council has agreed a different arrangement. In the course of the debate, no member is allowed to speak without having first requested and obtained the permission of the president. However, a speaker, who may intervene from his seat or from the rostrum (*tribuna*), has the right to speak without interruption. Without prejudice to the overall rights of the president to control procedure, the members of the government present in the Congress may request the right to speak at any time.

Table 4.3 *Standing committees of the Congress, 1996*

Committee	Name in Spanish
Legislative committees	
Constitutional committee	*Comisión constitucional*
Foreign affairs	*Asuntos exteriores*
Justice and home affairs	*Justicia e interior*
Defence	*Defensa*
Education and culture	*Educación y cultura*
Health and consumer affairs	*Sanidad y consumo*
Economy, commerce and finance	*Economía, comercio y hacienda*
Budgets	*Presupuestos*
Agriculture, stock-breeding and fishing	*Agricultura, ganadería y pesca*
Industry, energy and tourism	*Industria, energía y turismo*
Infrastructure and environment	*Infraestructuras y medio ambiente*
Social and employment policy	*Política social y de empleo*
Public administration system	*Régimen de las administraciones públicas*
Non-legislative committees	
Internal administration	*Reglamento*
Statute of the Deputies	*Estatuto de los Diputados*
Petitions	*Peticiones*

Source: Boletín Oficial de las Cortes Generales (April 1996).

As stated earlier, the procedure of these sittings is rigidly controlled by the president who, with the aid of sophisticated electronic equipment, can determine the length of time allotted to each speaker, which will depend on the parliamentary group to which he belongs. This applies whether the task in hand is the questioning of the premier or a debate on a parliamentary bill. Speakers who abuse these limitations and ignore two warnings will have their microphones disconnected, and may be subject to disciplinary action by the president and his Presiding Council.

4.5.4 Parliamentary committees (*comisiones parlamentarias*)

The bulk of parliamentary work is done through various types of committee, most of which consist exclusively of the members of each House, although some, the joint committees (*comisiones mixtas*), include both deputies and senators. Committees are either standing (*permanentes*) or *ad hoc* (*no-permanentes*). The majority of the committees in both Houses are in fact legislative standing committees (*comisiones permanentes legislativas*). In addition, each House has created several non-legislative permanent committees (*comisiones permanentes no-legislativas*). In addition, each House has exercised its right, under article 76 of the Constitution, to set up ad hoc committees; in the case of the Congress, these are known as committees of investigation or enquiry (*comisiones de investigación o encuesta*). Tables 4.3 and 4.4 show the standing committees, both legislative and non-legislative, of both Houses, and table 4.5 highlights the five joint committees which, as can be seen, include the all-impor-

Table 4.4 *Standing committees of the Senate, 1996*

Committee	Name in Spanish
Legislative committees	
Constitutional committee	*Comisión constitucional*
Agriculture and fishing	*Agricultura y pesca*
Foreign affairs	*Asuntos exteriores*
General committee of the autonomous communities	*Comisión general de las Comunidades Autónomas*
Defence	*Defensa*
Economy and finance	*Economía y hacienda*
Education and culture	*Educación y cultura*
Industry, commerce and tourism	*Industria, comercio y turismo*
Justice	*Justicia*
Public works, environment, transport and communications	*Obras públicas, medio ambiente, transportes y comunicaciones*
Prime Minister's Office and home affairs	*Presidencia del Gobierno e interior*
Budgets	*Presupuestos*
Health and social affairs	*Sanidad y seguridad social*
Labour and social security	*Trabajo y seguridad social*
Home affairs and civil service	*Interior y función pública*
Non-legislative committees	
Internal administration	*Reglamento*
Petitions	*Peticiones*
Ineligibilities	*Incompatabilidades*
Injunctions	*Suplicatorios*
Latin American Affairs	*Asuntos Iberoamericanos*

Source: Boletín Oficial de las Cortes Generales (April 1996).

Table 4.5 *Joint committees of the Congress and Senate, 1996*

Committee	Name in Spanish
Scientific research and technological development	*Investigación científica y desarrollo tecnológico*
Study of drug-related problems	*El estudio del problema de la droga*
The rights of women	*Los derechos de la mujer*
The European Union (15.4.1)	*La Unión Europea*
Liaison with the Ombudsman (2.6)	*Relaciones con el Defensor del Pueblo*
Liaison with the Audit Tribunal (9.9.3)	*Relaciones con el Tribunal de Cuentas*

Source: Boletín Oficial de las Cortes Generales (February 1995).

tant Joint Committee for the European Union (*Comisión Mixta para la Unión Europea*) (15.4.1).

According to the standing orders of each House, the number and composition of each committee is decided by the Presiding Council concerned following consultations with the Board of Party Spokesmen. Each parliamentary group is represented

Table 4.6 *Composition of legislative committees of the Congress, 1996*

Parliamentary group	No. of members
Popular group (PP)	17
Socialist group (PSOE)	14
Catalán group (CiU)	4
United Left group (IU–IC)	3
Basque group (PNV)	1
Canary Coalition group (CC)	1
Mixed group	1
Total	41

Source: Own elaboration, based on *Boletín Oficial de las Cortes Generales* (April 1996).

in proportion to its numerical strength in the chamber. For example, following the 1996 elections, it was agreed that the main Congress committees would have forty-one members; each parliamentary group would be allocated a minimum of one member plus additional members relative to their parliamentary strength. This produced the composition shown in table 4.6.

The Senate committees, most of which have a maximum of twenty-five members, have a similar composition, calculated according to the relative strength of each party. The size of certain committees, usually non-legislative committees, is laid down in the appropriate standing orders. Members of the government are allowed to attend and speak at all committees, but are not allowed to vote unless they happen to be members. At its first meeting, every committee must elect a presiding council composed of a chairman, two vice-chairmen and two secretaries. Meetings are called by the chairman, on the request of two parliamentary groups or a fifth of the members of the committee concerned.

The major function of the legislative committees is to examine, amend and approve legislation, most of which emanates from the Council of Ministers or the ministries. As can be seen in tables 4.3 and 4.4, the purpose of the non-legislative committees is quite distinct, and relates to either the internal affairs of the House concerned or liaison with outside bodies and organisations. Over and above all these committees, which are of a permanent nature, each House can create ad hoc committees to deal with specific problems as and when they arise. These must be disbanded once their work is completed, and in any case at the end of the legislative period in question. These may be Congress, Senate or joint committees. Currently, there are four of these in the Congress and three in the Senate, including the one reluctantly set up by the government in the Senate to look into the GAL affair (1.1.5).

In addition to the above 'internal' committees, the Spanish Parliament has established so-called interparliamentary delegations (*delegaciones interparlamentarias*), whose role is to receive their counterparts from parliaments overseas and undertake visits to a country or group of countries abroad. There are two of these in the

Congress; one is the Spain–France Friendship Group (*Grupo de Amistad España–Francia*) and the other is the Spain–Portugal Friendship Group (*Grupo de Amistad España–Portugal*). Additionally, there are five such committees whose members are drawn from the Congress and the Senate. These delegations are linked to various geographical areas or international institutions, including the all-important delegation to the European Union (15.3.2) and others to the Council of Europe (15.3.9.1), the Western European Union (WEU) (15.3.9.2), and NATO. All these delegations are of a permanent nature.

4.5.5 Working parties (*ponencias*)

These groups are set up by the committees to prepare documents and material for the meetings of the latter and of the Standing Council of each House. The number of members in each case is much smaller than that of the committees themselves but reflects the same balance of political groups.

4.5.6 Voting procedures

In order for plenary sittings and committees to adopt valid agreements, there must be a quorum of members present, that is, half the total membership plus one. Agreements must normally be approved by a simple majority of those present.

Both Houses of Parliament have agreed on a more or less common pattern of voting procedures. These are as follows:

4.5.6.1 Normal voting procedure

The commonest form of this occurs when, following a debate, members are called upon to stand up in a certain order: first those who approve the motion, then those who disapprove and finally those who abstain. Votes are counted by the secretaries. Alternatively, voting can be done by an electronic system which allows individual votes as well as totals to be displayed.

4.5.6.2 Roll-call voting (*votación pública por llamamiento*)

Under this system, members' names are read out in alphabetical order beginning with one name drawn at random by a secretary and they must answer 'yes' or 'no' or 'abstain'. Voting on the investiture of the prime minister, motions of censure and votes of confidence are always conducted by this method. It can at any time be requested by two parliamentary groups or one-fifth of the deputies or committee members.

4.5.6.3 Secret voting (*votación secreta*)

This can be carried out by one of two methods: either by an electronic system which displays only the final results of the voting, or by the use of ballot papers (*papeletas*).

4.5.7 Public, media and publicity

Plenary sittings of both Houses of Parliament are open to the public and the media. In the case of the former, entry to the public galleries can be secured either by invitation or by queueing. Committee meetings of the Congress and Senate are not, however, open to the public but, unless a secret session has been decreed by the Presiding Council concerned, the media may have access to them, as well as to plenary sessions of Parliament.

Transcriptions of the proceedings of both Houses are published in a document known as the *Diario de sesiones*. Draft laws at different stages of approval are published in the Official Cortes Gazette (*Boletín Oficial de las Cortes Generales*), while only fully approved Acts of Parliament, along with other decrees and ministerial orders and so on, are published in the *Official State Gazette* (*Boletín Oficial del Estado/BOE*).

All plenary sittings of both Houses are recorded on tape for the parliamentary archives, but only certain important sessions of the Congress, such as the opening of Parliament, investitures, censure motions, and high profile political debates are broadcast on radio or televised.

4.6 Functions and powers

In article 66 of the Constitution, it is stated that the major functions of the *Cortes* are: 'to exercise the legislative power of the state, to approve the state budgets, to control the actions of the government and to exercise the other powers vested in them by the Constitution'. The latter refer, among other things, to three non-legislative areas mentioned in article 74.2 of the Constitution: (i) the approval of certain international agreements and treaties; (ii) agreements of co-operation between autonomous communities; and (iii) the allocation of resources to the latter through the Inter-regional Compensation Fund (7.5.3.4). Each House shares in these responsibilities in the parallel but separate exercise of its powers. Prior to examining these, however, some consideration needs to be given to the specific functions of the *Cortes Generales* when, on only rare occasions, they meet in joint session.

4.6.1 Joint sessions

The two Houses of the Spanish Parliament meet in joint session in accordance with certain requirements laid down in section II of the Constitution which refers to the monarchy. Some of its functions in this context are merely ceremonial: for instance, the *Cortes* must assemble jointly on the occasion of the inauguration of the king, and heir to the throne or the regent. In December 1978, King Juan Carlos I made what was possibly a unique appearance for such a purpose before the joint Houses of Parliament (*Cortes Generales*) when he signed the new Constitution.

Joint sessions are also held for the following, non-legislative purposes: (i) to approve the appointment of a regent (article 59.3) following agreement that all the legal lines of royal succession have been extinguished (article 57.3); (ii) to agree on the monarch's incapacity to rule and thereby set the succession procedure in motion (article 59.3); and (iii) to authorise the king to declare a state of war or peace (article 63.3).

As we have already observed, such joint sessions are chaired by the president of the Congress, and indeed it is in the *Palacio del Congreso* that such sessions take place.

4.6.2 Shared functions

Apart from the major, legislative function, both Houses of Parliament share responsibility for exercising parallel power in the following areas:

4.6.2.1 Constitutional matters

They can require the Constitutional Court to decide whether a treaty contains elements contrary to the Constitution (article 95).

Having obtained the signatures of fifty deputies or senators, the *Cortes Generales* can present an appeal against unconstitutional laws (article 162) (2.5.2.1); they must approve by a three-fifths majority in each House all constitutional reform bills (article 167). A tenth of the members of either House can request that a constitutional reform bill be submitted to a national referendum (article 167.3). This may be enacted when the Senate (4.3.2) is reformed, as seems very likely (7.9).

4.6.2.2 Regional matters

As already indicated above (4.6), both Houses of Parliament must approve agreements of co-operation (*acuerdos de cooperación*) between autonomous communities (article 145). They must also decide on the criteria for and the allocation of grants to the autonomous communities through the Inter-regional Compensation Fund (article 158.2 and 7.5.3.4). In both the above cases, if agreement between the two Houses cannot be reached, a joint committee with equal Congress–Senate membership is set up to find a formula for resolving the issue; if the amended text is not approved in both Houses by a simple majority, the Congress then has the right to decide the issue by an overall majority.

Both Houses may decide, by an overall majority in each case, that there is a need to draw up legislation to harmonise laws affecting the autonomous communities. This power was first used in 1981 when the UCD and the PSOE agreed the approval of four laws to harmonise the autonomy process (7.8.4.2) and more recently in 1992 when the government, the PSOE and the PP signed the Autonomy Agreements (*Acuerdos Autonómicos*) (7.7.5.2), paving the way for more powers to be granted to the so-called 'slow-route' autonomous regions.

4.6.2.3 Appointments

The two Houses of Parliament share responsibility for the periodic nomination of high-ranking officials in certain constitutional bodies. Each House can nominate ten members of the General Council of the Judiciary (14.4.2) and four members of the Constitutional Court (2.5). In addition, they elect, by a separate vote in each House, the ombudsman (2.6).

4.6.3 Specific powers of the Congress

These refer to the relationship of the Congress to the government and constitute part of the Lower House's powers of control over the government, thus conferring on it important political authority.

4.6.3.1 Ratification of decree-laws

Either through the full House or the standing committee, the Congress must ratify or reject decree-laws adopted by the government within a period of thirty days (article 86).

4.6.3.2 States of alarm, exception and siege (estados de alarma, excepción y de sitio)

The Congress is obliged to authorise the extension of a state of alarm and the declaration of a state of exception. By an overall majority, it can authorise a state of siege (article 116).

4.6.3.3 Treasonable offences

The Congress carries the heavy responsibility, should circumstances demand it, of having to accuse the prime minister, or his ministers, of treason, or of any other offence against the security of the state, obliging them to face criminal proceedings (article 102).

4.6.3.4 Prime minister

The Congress also enjoys a unique and vitally important role related to the appointment and dismissal of the premier (5.2.1 and 5.2.2). As laid down in article 99.2, the latter must submit himself to a vote of investiture (*voto de investidura*) in the Congress before he can formally be sworn in by the king as prime minister. As we shall see in 5.2.1, in the first vote an overall majority is required, although in succeeding rounds of voting, a simple majority will suffice.

At any time, a premier can seek from the House a vote of confidence (*voto de confianza*) in his leadership and programme, in which case a simple majority is required; failure to achieve this will normally result in the dissolution of both Houses of Parliament and the calling of elections (article 112).

In accordance with article 113, the Congress is also the protagonist of a censure motion (*moción de censura*). In order to succeed, the motion must be approved by an overall majority of the House and its text has to contain the name of the opposition's candidate for the premiership; if the motion is carried, that candidate automatically becomes prime minister without elections having to be called.

4.6.4 Specific powers of the Senate

The only power which the Constitution grants exclusively to the Senate, without any involvement on the part of the Congress, concerns the autonomous communities. Article 155.1 states categorically that if a community fails to fulfil the obligations placed on it by the Constitution or other laws, the government, following the approval by an overall majority of the Senate, is empowered to force such a community to comply with its obligations and to take steps to protect the general interest. As we have already seen (4.5.4), through the special monitoring committee, the Senate has been given a special role in overseeing the activities of the Inter-regional Compensation Fund (7.5.3.4).

4.7 Legislative function

Quite clearly this is by far the most important function of any democratic Parliament and is no less the case with the Spanish *Cortes*.

4.7.1 Hierarchy of laws

A simplified résumé of the hierarchy of laws and regulations at present operating in Spain is presented in diagrammatic form in table 4.7. Naturally, at the apex of this structure, we find the Constitution which, as we saw in chapter 2, provides the basic principles which must inspire and inform all subsequent legislation and regulations. The major laws will now be considered in descending order of importance. At the outset, it should be stressed that, at the level of the autonomous community, ordinary laws are of the same hierarchical level as those of the state, just as directives issuing from a department of regional government have the same force at regional level as those emanating from a ministry in Madrid.

4.7.1.1 Organic laws (leyes orgánicas)

Modelled on the French Constitution of 1958, these highest-ranking laws enjoy a status mid-way between the Constitution and ordinary laws. They can only be approved by the *Cortes*. The approval, modification or repeal of these laws requires an overall majority of the Congress in a final vote on the complete text of a bill (article 81.2), although no type of majority is specified for the Senate, from which

Table 4.7 *Hierarchy of laws and regulations, 1995*

Constitution

Laws
Organic laws of the state
(including Statutes of Autonomy)
Ordinary laws of the state
Basic laws
Royal legislative decrees
Framework laws
Basic legislation
Royal decree laws
Legislative decrees

Regulations
Royal decrees
Orders of the delegated committees of the government (5.6)
Ministerial orders
Circulars and regulations of the central administration

Source: Own elaboration.

one assumes that a simple majority will suffice. Article 81.1 makes it clear that organic laws are required in the following fields of legislation: the development of fundamental rights and public liberties; electoral arrangements; statutes of autonomy; and 'others envisaged in the Constitution'.

In fact the latter cover a wide range of areas, including: the royal succession (article 57); international treaties (article 93); the Council of State (article 107); states of alarm, exception and siege (article 116); the creation of regional police forces (article 149); the transfer and delegation of powers to the autonomous communities (article 150); and the Constitutional Court (article 165). Between October 1979 and December 1992, no less than 122 organic laws were approved, including the seventeen required to approve the statutes of autonomy of the new autonomous regions (7.5.1), and the one of 28 December 1992 to authorise Spain's ratification of the Treaty of Maastricht (15.2). A point to stress about the organic laws is that in no circumstances are they to be delegated to other authorities, since the areas which they encompass are considered to be of special national interest.

4.7.1.2 Ordinary laws (leyes ordinarias)

These constitute the bulk of laws passed by ordinary procedure either at the national or regional level. At the national level, they must be approved by both Houses of Parliament before they can be put on the statute book. At both levels, bills of ordinary laws must normally be examined in both plenary session and committee; in the final vote, a simple majority of both Houses of Parliament is required before such bills become law.

Since these are the most common type of law, it is these that will be used in 4.7.3 below to examine some of the details of the legislative process.

4.7.1.3 Basic laws (leyes de base)

These are of the same rank as ordinary laws. By means of such laws, the *Cortes* can delegate legislative power to the government in specific fields. According to article 82 of the Constitution, such laws must spell out in broad terms the purpose and scope of the legislation to be delegated, as well as the principles and criteria which must govern them. Such delegation must be granted to the government in an express manner, identifying concrete items and specifying the time-scale of the process; in fact, once the government has published its legislation on the subject, its jurisdiction expires. The government is not permitted to sub-delegate this power to any other bodies. Similar in function and rank to the *leyes de base* are the royal legislative decrees (*reales decretos legislativos*).

4.7.1.4 Framework laws (leyes marco)

These laws are of similar rank to ordinary laws. As a kind of basic law, they outline the objectives and principles underlining legislation on matters which the state is willing to delegate or transfer to the autonomous communities (7.7.3.1).

4.7.1.5 Basic legislation (legislación básica)

Basic legislation is comparable to the framework laws and refers to areas of competence shared between the state and the autonomous communities (7.7.2).

4.7.1.6 Royal decree-laws (reales decretos-leyes)

According to article 86 of the Constitution, as we have already seen in 4.6.3.1, the government is empowered, 'in situations of extraordinary and urgent necessity', to issue temporary legislative provisions (*disposiciones legislativas provisionales*), which take the form of royal decree-laws sometimes known simply as decree-laws. These must not refer to the basic institutions of the state, the rights, duties and liberties of citizens referred to in section I of the Constitution (2.4), the political system of the autonomous communities, or the provisions of electoral law. Such decrees, which are applicable across the whole nation, must be submitted to the Congress for ratification within thirty days. The full House or the Standing Council must debate the decree and decide whether to process it as a law using the emergency procedure referred to in 4.5.3.

4.7.1.7 Legislative decrees (decretos legislativos)

This is legislation issued by the government when exercising delegated law-making authority, following authorisation via the basic laws referred to in 4.7.1.3. Such decrees have the force of law and they are known as *normas con rango de ley*.

4.7.1.8 Royal decrees (reales decretos)

Within the hierarchy of regulations emanating from national or regional government departments, these are of the highest rank. Because of the importance attaching to them, they must be signed by the minister of the presidency and countersigned by the king. Such royal decrees, not to be confused with royal decree-laws, were used frequently between the early 1980s and the mid-1990s to transfer or delegate very specific powers to the autonomous communities following the previous approval of framework laws.

4.7.1.9 Other regulations

As can be seen in table 4.7, after the royal decrees, the highest-ranking regulations are the orders (órdenes) emanating from the delegated committees of the government (5.6). These are followed by the ministerial orders (órdenes ministeriales) issued by the ministries in Madrid, which are of equal rank to the resolutions (resoluciones) of regional ministries. At the lower end of the hierarchy are the circulars (circulares) and instructions (instrucciones), issued by either national or regional ministries.

4.7.2 Legislative initiative

Several bodies have the authority to initiate legislation: the government, the Congress, the Senate and the assemblies of the autonomous communities. If the government takes the initiative, or if a regional assembly proposes that the former should adopt a particular bill, the draft law is known as a proyecto de ley. If the initiative, however, comes from either of the Houses of Parliament, or if the regional assembly submits a draft law direct to the Congress, it is known as a proposición de ley. Proyectos de ley submitted to the Congress by the government must previously have been approved by the Council of Ministers (5.5.3.1), and must be accompanied by a rationale (exposición de motivos) and all background material relating to the subject in question. With respect to proposiciones de ley emanating from a regional assembly, the latter may designate a maximum of three of its members to defend the bill in Parliament. In the case of proyectos de ley, it is considered to have delegated this task to the government, which has 'adopted' the bill.

In addition to these sources of legislation, article 87 of the Constitution permits recourse to a direct popular initiative, provided that it is backed up by 500,000 signatures and an appropriate rationale. However, such draft laws, known as proposiciones de ley, cannot refer to tax affairs, international affairs, the prerogative of pardon, or indeed any matters that would normally be dealt with by an organic law (4.7.1.1).

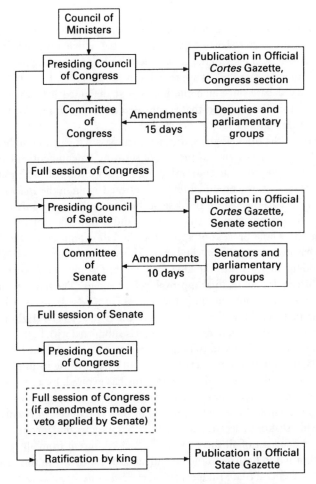

Figure 4.3 *Legislative process for draft laws, 1995*

4.7.3 Legislative process

4.7.3.1 Draft laws (proyectos de ley)

As can be seen in figure 4.3, the first political decisions to enact legislation of this kind is taken in the Council of Ministers. A preliminary draft law (*anteproyecto de ley*) is then prepared by the relevant minister or ministers concerned with technical help from the appropriate departments before being submitted for approval by the Council of Ministers. The bill is then submitted to the Presiding Council of the Congress (4.4.2), and is simultaneously published in the *Boletín Oficial de las Cortes, Sección del Congreso*. Deputies are allowed fifteen days from publication to present amendments either to the whole bill or to particular clauses. The committee concerned elects a working party (*ponencia*) which, on the basis of any amendments, draws up a report (*dictamen*) containing recommendations for improving the text. This modified text is then debated in the committee, article by article. If rejected, the bill is normally sent back to the government for reconsideration, and the whole process must then be repeated. If approved, it is passed on to the full Congress for a parliamentary debate, in which the bill is first defended by a member of the government. At this stage, a text that is considered obscure or inconsistent may be sent back to the committee for further study.

If approved by the full Congress, the president passes the text on to his counter-part in the Senate where a similar process of scrutiny, amendment and approval is carried out by the appropriate committee and plenary sitting of the Upper House. At the time of receipt, the modified text is published again in the *Boletín Oficial de las Cortes, Sección del Senado*. In the case of the Senate, however, only ten days are allowed for the presentation of amendments and a limitation of two months is imposed for the whole process of approving the bill submitted by the Congress. Once a bill has been approved in the Upper House, it is returned to the Congress and its president submits it to the king for final ratification. This must be carried out within fifteen days of its final approval in Parliament. The bill is then promul-gated and prepared for publication in the *Boletín Oficial del Estado* (4.5.7).

According to article 90 of the Constitution, the Senate has the right to veto the whole law, provided that a statement of reasons is submitted with it, or it can simply table amendments to it. A veto must be approved by an overall majority of the Senate. The Congress is empowered to overturn the veto by approving its initial text by an overall majority or, after a period of two months has expired, by a simple majority. Amendments can be accepted or rejected straight away by a simple majority. The two-month period required for Senate approval of bills is reduced to twenty days for legislation which has been declared urgent by either the government or the Congress.

The most important of all the *proyectos de ley* – different from all the others in that it is submitted to Parliament on an annual basis (normally in the autumn) – is the Bill on the General State Budgets (*Proyecto de Ley de los Presupuestos Generales del Estado*), which takes precedence over all other legislative business. Amendments which involve an increase in spending under one head must include a correspond-ing reduction under another. Final debate on the budgets then allows the bill to be approved section by section. It is worth noting that each regional parliament accords the same status to the budget bill for the autonomous community concerned (7.6.1).

From the foregoing, it can be clearly seen that the Lower House of the Spanish Parliament takes precedence over the Senate. Using its veto, the latter can delay a bill for twenty days but, provided that there has been no change in the voting inten-tions of the deputies since their approval of the original text, there is little chance that the bill will not become law. Apart from its limited capacity to delay the approval of legislation, the most that the Senate can hope for is that the Congress will accept some of its amendments. In these circumstances, it is not surprising that between 1982 and 1986 a frustrated opposition preferred to obstruct government legislation by referring laws or clauses of laws to the Constitutional Court (2.5). In practice, the latter has often become an alternative and, in some ways, more effective Upper Chamber.

4.7.3.2 Draft laws (proposiciones de ley)

In the case of *proposiciones de ley*, the nearest equivalent to UK private members' bills, only the initial stages of this process are different. In the case of a bill proposed by the Congress, the initiative can be taken by one deputy with the signatures of fourteen other members of the House, or by a parliamentary group with the signature of their spokesman alone (*Reglamento*, Article 126). Following publication, the government has a right to decide (i) whether or not to 'take it into consideration' and/or (ii) whether its approval would imply an increase in borrowing or a reduction in budgetary income. If, within thirty days, the government presents no objections to the bill, it is submitted to the full Congress for a special debate to decide whether or not to accept it for parliamentary processing. If the outcome is positive, the bill is passed on to the appropriate committee and processed in the same way as a *proyecto de ley*. The procedure for initiating a bill in the Senate is similar to that of the Congress, except that the initiative must come from a parliamentary group or from twenty-five senators, and the detailed text must be accompanied by a rationale. *Proposiciones de ley* issuing from a regional assembly or a popular initiative must first be examined by the Presiding Council of the Congress to ensure that all legal requirements have been fulfilled, after which they are submitted for special debate as outlined above.

Although the vast majority of laws start life as *proyectos de ley*, in the first legislature of 1979–82 as many as 206 bills were tabled in the Congress. It should be remembered, however, that *proyectos de ley* have priority over *proposiciones de ley*, which can never be declared priority or emergency bills.

4.8 Parliamentary control

This is examined in section V of the Constitution and refers basically to the accountability of the government to Parliament. Article 108 of the Constitution makes it clear that the government is accountable to the Congress for its actions. The government is obliged to give account of itself or subject itself to parliamentary control in a number of ways including: (i) measures of political control, such as the votes of confidence and censure motions (4.6.3.4); and (ii) budgetary and fiscal control, which is ensured by parliamentary scrutiny and approval of the annual state budgets (4.7.3.1) as well as the activities of the Audit Tribunal (9.9.3).

Legislative control is also exercised through Congress' right to approve or reject decree-laws, including those referring to states of alarm, exception and siege (4.6.3.2). To a large extent, these can be regarded as means of extraordinary control, since they are only used on rare occasions. Day-to-day control over the government is exercised through a series of parliamentary rights and conventions, which are itemised in articles 109–111 of the Constitution.

4.8.1 Right to information

Both Houses of Parliament and their committees have the right to demand, through their presidents, that the government, its departments or any authorities of the state or autonomous communities provide them with any help or information that they may require for the exercise of their duties (article 109).

4.8.2 Right to governmental presence

Both Houses and their committees can demand that members of the government should appear before them. In theory, the prime minister is absolved from this obligation, and in practice recent premiers seem to have taken too much advantage of this provision; on the other hand, ministers have a generally good record of making appearances (*comparecencias*) both in plenary sittings of Parliament and in the committees. As a counterweight to this right, the government has the right to attend all sessions of the Houses and their committees, including the right to be heard in them; they may also request that officials from their departments report to them (article 110).

4.8.3 Right to question

Article 111 of the Constitution grants the Houses of Parliament the right to submit two kinds of question to the government or to any of its individual members, and requires that the standing orders of both Houses shall devote a minimum amount of weekly parliamentary time to them. These are known as *preguntas* and *interpelaciones*. Question time is normally Wednesday afternoons; the prime minister, in a new initiative for the Spanish Parliament, appears each week at this time to answer questions, but not usually for more than fifteen or twenty minutes.

4.8.3.1 Questions (preguntas)

These must be presented to the presiding council of the House concerned in written form; members must specify if they wish to receive an oral reply, in default of which they will receive a written reply from the member of the government concerned. If an oral reply is specified, and if the question is accepted as valid by the appropriate Presiding Council, it will be included on the agenda of the corresponding plenary session. A maximum period of five minutes is allowed for the defence of and reply to the question. A similar formula applies to questions requiring an oral answer in committee. At the end of any legislative session, outstanding questions are dealt with by written answer. In any case, these must always be answered within a period of twenty days, unless agreed otherwise by the government or the Presiding Council.

4.8.3.2 Questions (interpelaciones)

These are similar to *preguntas* but may be formulated by parliamentary groups, as well as individual members of Parliament. These too must be presented in written form to the appropriate Presiding Council, and in this case they must refer to the reasons for or intentions underlying the conduct of either the Council of Ministers or any ministerial departments in matters of general policy. *Interpelaciones* are often presented in the form of a motion which is then debated in the full House concerned. At the end of any legislative period, any outstanding questions are dealt with as if they were questions requiring a written answer. These are a device commonly used by parliamentarians to attract publicity either to themselves or to a particular cause.

4.9 Comment

After a lapse of four decades, parliamentary life in Spain has, over the last eighteen years or so, been steadily revitalised. Indeed, Spain has now enjoyed the longest unbroken period of authentic parliamentary government in its history. Following the first democratic elections for forty years in 1977, the reformed *Cortes* slowly began to acquire the long-lost habits of parliamentary democracy. By the end of 1978, parliamentarians had completed the mammoth task of drawing up Spain's first democratic Constitution for nearly half a century. Subsequently, they undertook the even more daunting task of fleshing out the skeletal provisions of the Constitution, enacting hundreds of organic, ordinary and other laws, with the object of imbuing all the political, economic and other institutions of public life with the spirit and practices of democracy. Not the least arduous of these tasks was the challenge of transforming the very nature of this once strongly centralised state into one composed of self-governing regions, each endowed with its own legislature.

Sadly, however, there is a debit side to the story. Quite apart from a number of allegations of corruption and scandals involving government ministers (1.1.5 and 5.10) – most of whom are themselves parliamentarians – the nature of the relationship between government (especially the prime minister) and Parliament, the very processes by which parliamentary business is conducted and the weaknesses of the electoral system, have led to considerable alienation between Parliament and the citizens it is supposed to represent. There is little doubt that in both Houses individual parliamentarians are eclipsed in their influence by the all-dominant party machines which, through the system of *portavoces* (4.4.6), tightly control both procedure and outcomes. Such criticisms can probably also be levelled at other Western democracies in an age when parliaments have, to a large extent, become the legislative chambers of the government, and many prime ministers, if not 'elected dictators', display strong presidential tendencies. However, the Spanish malaise is compounded by two other inherent weaknesses. Firstly – and this is probably a legacy from the days of the tightly-controlled Franco *Cortes* (4.1) – spontaneous political debate is very rare (most interventions are uninspiring, read speeches) and parliamentarians are accorded few opportunities to question the premier. Secondly, the electoral system of closed and blocked lists (4.3.1) means that electors are voting not for individuals but for parties; parliamentarians do not represent their constituents in any active way (no local 'surgeries' are held, for example), and the voters do not identify with the deputies or senators whom they have sent to Madrid.

Considering all the flaws in the system, it is perhaps remarkable that overall turnout levels in Spanish elections compare very favourably with most other EU countries and in several cases are higher. In May 1995, for example, no less than 70 per cent of the electorate turned out for the regional and local elections. Evidently, citizens still have some confidence that their vote will make a difference and that from time to time they can force a change of government.

Chapter 5

Central government

Preliminary note

Since it is not easy to draw a line between 'government' and 'administration', log-ically these should be dealt with in one chapter. However, for reasons of presenta-tion and balance, it has been thought preferable to make a break, however artificial, between the two. Thus, chapter 5 will deal with the executive or decision-making tier, including the prime minister, the ministers and the Council of Ministers, as well as those bodies which advise the government and central civil service. Chapter 6 will examine the administrative levels, including the ministerial departments and the various autonomous administrative bodies dependent on them. It is accepted, however, that there are risks in any neat form of categorisation and that, particularly in Spain where the term 'central administration of the state' is commonly used to embrace all the above institutions, there will inevitably be some measure of overlap between the two. This is especially so in the case of the ministers who belong to the executive but head large departments of public administration. Thus, chapters 5 and 6 should be regarded as a continuum.

In the course of chapters 5–8, it will also become apparent that in present-day Spain government and administration operate at three theoretical levels, which in practice function as four. These are: (i) central; (ii) regional (relating to the autonomous communities); and (iii) local – the latter being divided into the pro-vincial and municipal tiers of administration (figure 5.1). It should be stressed that, while the central and regional authorities enjoy basic legislative and decision-making power, the provincial and municipal institutions, although exercising authority over minor matters, in general tend simply to administer policies agreed at higher levels.

5.1 Introduction

The separation of powers was acknowledged theoretically in the more progressive constitutions of nineteenth century Spain and clearly accepted in the republican Constitution of 1931. Franco, however, made no pretence of following this tradition, affirming that his preference was not for the separation of powers but their unity. In practice, of course, this meant that the legislature and the judiciary played sub-ordinate roles, becoming in effect simply instruments of an all-powerful executive, which was accountable to no body outside itself. In reality, the executive was a tool

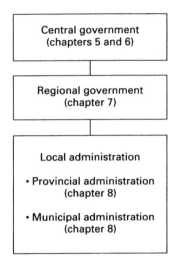

Figure 5.1 *Tiers of government and administration, 1995*

in the hands of one man, who ensured that both government and administration remained strongly centralised in Madrid.

Only with the promulgation of the Constitution of 1978 was the traditional division of powers between the three main branches of central authority restored, as Spain became, as we have seen, a 'social and democratic state based on the rule of law' (article 2).

5.2 Prime minister (*presidente del gobierno*)

5.2.1 Method of appointment

According to article 99 of the Constitution, after elections to the Congress, the king, following consultations with representatives of the main political groups in Parliament, will propose a candidate for the premiership, indicating his choice to Parliament through the president of the Congress. The candidate must then present his programme to the Congress and attempt to secure the support of the House by means of a vote of investiture (*voto de investidura*). (It is worth noting that it is *his* programme that is voted on and not that of the government which, of course, at that stage has not yet been appointed.) If this support is granted by the required overall majority, the king will then name the candidate prime minister; if this is not achieved, there will be a second ballot, forty-eight hours later, when a simple majority will suffice.

If this procedure fails to produce a premier, the king must propose other candidates until one eventually gains the confidence of the House. If no candidate has succeeded within two months of the first vote, the king is obliged to dissolve both Houses of Parliament and convene new elections with the backing of the president of the Congress. Naturally, all efforts would normally be made to avoid the necessity of having recourse to a second round of elections and, at least up to 1996, there had been no need for this procedure to be enacted.

5.2.2 Method of dismissal

A prime minister will normally leave office in one of the following three circumstances: (i) if the Congress denies him its support in a vote of confidence (article 114.1 and 4.6.3.4); (ii) if the Congress approves a motion of censure against him (article 114.2 and 4.6.3.4); or (iii) if his party or the coalition of parties that he leads is defeated in the general election. In these circumstances, he will stay in office until the new premier-designate has been sworn in as prime minister. Clearly, a head of government may resign of his own accord for reasons of his own choosing – such was the case of Adolfo Suárez in January 1981. This eventuality, and indeed the possible death of a premier while in office, is provided for in article 101. The latter states that in both cases the king, after consultations with the various political groups represented in Parliament, must propose another candidate who, as stated in article 99.2, is required to present his programme to the Congress and seek a vote of investiture. In the case of death, a deputy prime minister or senior minister will automatically assume the premiership until the above procedure has been followed. It should be stressed that resignation or death does not automatically need to involve new elections, although a new premier may feel that, as well as the confidence of Parliament, he requires a popular mandate.

It is interesting to note that it was during the investiture of Leopoldo Calvo Sotelo, following the resignation of Suárez, that the attempted *coup* of 23 February 1981 took place. At the time, it was doubtful whether the new premier-designate would secure an overall majority because of defections from the ruling UCD party; after the *coup* he was given quite a convincing overall majority, no doubt because Parliament was determined to stabilise the severely threatened democratic system.

It should also be stressed that if a prime minister leaves office for whatever reason, his government, i.e. his Council of Ministers, must also resign with him. However, to ensure continuity, the government stays on in a caretaker capacity until a new government has been installed. He is then known as the acting premier (*presidente del gobierno en funciones*). Politically a vacuum may exist, but constitutionally it may not.

5.2.3 Role

Just as the king is the symbol and highest representative of the state, so the prime minister, according to the 1957 Law on the Organisation of the Administration (*Ley de Régimen Jurídico de la Administración/LRJA*) is the symbol and highest representative of the government. Unlike the king, he is responsible for his actions, as well as those of the whole government. According to article 98 of the Constitution, 'the head of government directs the activities of the government and coordinates the functions of the other members of the government'. This means that he plays the major political role in the preparation, promotion and execution of the government's programme. He also performs the key administrative role, in the co-ordination of the work of the various ministries.

5.2.4 Powers

Expressed in more concrete terms, the most important powers and functions of the Spanish premier are as follows:

(i)   He can propose the appointment and dismissal of his ministers (article 100). He also has a similar right to recommend appointment to hundreds of junior ministerial and high-ranking civil service posts, as well as the civil governors in each province and the government delegates to the autonomous communities. Moreover, in practice, as the leader of the dominant party in Parliament, he has the right to select the persons to be elected presidents of the Congress and the Senate. In addition, he proposes the nomination of the heads of important state institutions like the Council of State (5.7) and the National Institute for Industry (9.4.2.2).

       It should be stressed that technically it is the king in all these cases who appoints and the prime minister who nominates candidates for appointment, following approval in the Council of Ministers (5.5). In reality, of course, the real decision-making power rests with the premier, not the king.

(ii)   He can propose the dissolution of the Congress, Senate or the Joint *Cortes* (article 115.1).

(iii)   He can endorse the acts of the king, for which he, the premier, is ultimately responsible (article 64.1).

(iv)   He can request that the king should preside over the Council of Ministers (article 62g). It should be noted that the king does not have the right to do so whenever he thinks fit.

(v)   He can propose the convening of a referendum on an issue of overriding national importance (article 92.2).

(vi)   He can request a vote of confidence from the Congress (article 112).

5.2.5 Prime Minister's Office (*Presidencia del Gobierno*)

In addition to all his other functions, the premier is in nominal charge of the prime minister's office, which over the years has grown from a small department with limited and specific responsibilities into a kind of ministry embracing a wide range of affairs. Its major purpose, however, is to provide a direct advisory service, on both political and technical matters, to both the prime minister and the vice-premier, particularly in relation to issues to be discussed at the Council of Ministers (5.5).

    Apart from a general secretariat (*secretaría general*), the major sub-division is the office of the presidency (*gabinete de la presidencia*). This is headed by a director

Table 5.1 *Prime Minister's Office, 1995*

Service	Name in Spanish
General Secretariat	*Secretaría general*
Office of the Presidency	*Gabinete de la Presidencia*
• Institutional Affairs	• *Asuntos institucionales*
• Economic Affairs	• *Economía*
• Social Labour Affairs	• *Asuntos sociolaborales*
• International Affairs	• *Asuntos internacionales*
• Education and Culture	• *Educación y cultura*
• Analysis	• *Análisis*
• Defence and Security	• *Defensa y seguridad*
• Research	• *Estudios*
• Directorate for Infrastructure and Monitoring of Crisis Situations	• *Dirección de Infraestructura y Seguimiento para Situaciones de Crisis (DISSC)*

Source: Presidencia del Gobierno (1995).

(*director*), who holds the rank of an under-secretary of state (6.2.4) and is responsible to the first deputy premier. Within this *gabinete*, there are eight departments (*departamentos*), each in the charge of a director, who holds a lower rank. These are shown in table 5.1.

Included here is the special Directorate for Infrastructure and Monitoring of Crisis Situations (*Dirección de Infraestructura y Seguimiento para Situaciones de Crisis/DISSC*). This was originally set up in December 1986 as a further delegated committee of the government (5.6). Its role is to ensure that the government is able to react immediately and effectively when crisis situations occur at either national or international level. It was very active at the time of the Gulf War, in which Spain played a minor role as part of the allied response to Iraq's invasion of Kuwait in 1990.

5.2.6 Limitations to powers

The powers of the prime minister are limited either by the need to consult with the Council of Ministers or the need to seek the authorisation of the Congress. Indeed, article 98 makes it clear that the prime minister directs the government's actions and co-ordinates the functions of his ministers 'without prejudice to the powers and direct responsibility of the latter in the running of their own department'.

5.2.7 Accountability

When we examine the accountability of the premier, it is hard to escape the conclusion that he becomes almost synonymous with the government. One example of this is that he himself, rather than the government, is the object of a motion of censure, and in this motion an alternative head of government must be named (4.6.3.4). Like his ministers, he is politically accountable to the Congress and criminally responsible to the courts. With regard to the latter, if the crime involves treason or any offence against the security of the state, he is answerable to Congress, four-fifths of which must propose an accusation, which must in turn be approved by an overall majority. This, of course, is another way in which the prime minister may leave office, i.e. as a result of being dismissed or being persuaded to resign. In this case, the Constitution does not actually state that the premier would be forced to leave office, but one can safely assume that this would be the case. It would also presumably be the consequence of any successful court case against the head of government involving criminal proceedings.

5.3 Deputy prime minister (*vicepresidente del gobierno*)

Article 98.2 envisages the possible existence of one or more deputy prime ministers, a post that was first created as long ago as 1823. Although neither the Constitution nor other legislation says so, one can assume that he is appointed and dismissed in the same way as other ministers (5.4.1). Again, there are no constitutional guidelines with respect to specific duties and powers, and it would seem that this depends very much on the premier of the day. In fact, in order to fill this constitutional and legal vaccuum, the government drafted the Law on the Organisation of the Administration of the State (*Ley de Organización de la Administración del Estado/LOAE*) which the *Cortes* approved in August 1983. This law spells out what are to be the ministries and their major divisions; of relevance here is article 3 which outlines the role of the deputy premier. This states that he will assume the functions of the head of government if the latter should die, be ill or absent abroad, and in practice this has already been applied in the case of presidential visits abroad, when the prime minister is never accompanied by his deputy.

Apart from such anticipated functions, the role of the vice-president is still very much a matter for the discretion of the incumbent premier. Under the governments of the UCD (1977–82) the prime minister appointed more than one vice-president, each in charge of a particularly important department, such as defence or economic affairs. Under the PSOE, however, the practice was to appoint only one deputy and he was never responsible for any of the traditional ministries. Rather he tended to play a co-ordinating role working closely with the prime minister and the ministers, in particular the Minister of the Presidency (6.2.1 and table 6.1). In contrast, José María Aznar, in forming his cabinet in May 1996, appointed a first and second vice-president, in charge respectively of the portfolios of the Presidency and Economy and Finance (table 6.1).

More recently, in 1993, a royal decree defined his position rather more clearly. As well as the general responsibilities outlined above, he was given the more precise task of chairing the weekly meetings of the General Committee of Secretaries of State and Under-secretaries (*Comisión General de Secretarios de Estado y Subsecretarios*) (6.2.4), as well as the delegated committees of the government (*comisiones delegadas del gobierno*) (5.6). Under Aznar, the *Comisión General* is chaired by the first vice-president (minister of the presidency) and the chairing of the *comis-*

iones delegadas is shared between him and the second vice-president (minister for economy and finance).

Following the resignation in June 1995 of the long-serving Narcís Serra, held politically responsible for the CESID phone-tap scandal that had recently shook the government (1.1.5), Felipe González left the post vacant (presumably temporarily) and reallocated his responsibilities. The minister of the presidency assumed the chair of the General Committee of Secretaries of State while, in the case of the delegated committees of the government, either the premier himself was to preside or in his place the senior minister of the committee concerned. The royal decree of 7 July 1995 (still in force) specifically attaches the delegation of the Committee for Economic Affairs (5.6.3) to the minister of economy and finance.

5.4 Ministers (*ministros*)

5.4.1 Method of appointment and dismissal

Ministers are appointed and dismissed by the king on the recommendation of the prime minister, who in reality exercises the power to 'hire and fire'. On appointment, like the premier, they must swear loyalty to the Constitution before the king. Government ministers must resign, as we have seen, following the departure of the premier but will continue in a caretaker capacity until a new government is formed (article 101.2).

5.4.2 Role

As heads of the large ministries (*ministerios*), the ministers carry immense responsibilities and, within certain limitations, enjoy a good deal of discretion and autonomy. They are ultimately responsible to the prime minister for the efficient running of their departments. They exercise initiatives of both a legislative and executive nature and they manage and inspect all the services within their departments. They are nominally in charge of the departmental inspectorate. They are also responsible for the autonomous bodies (6.3) linked to their ministries.

5.4.3 Powers

These can usefully be divided into three categories: those concerned with legislative, executive and judicial matters.

5.4.3.1 Legislative responsibilities

Each minister is ultimately responsible for presenting to the Council of Ministers the outline draft laws (*anteproyectos de ley*) or draft decree-laws (4.7.3.1) which have been prepared within his department. He is also responsible for exercising rule-making powers (*potestad reglamentaria*) where these are required to implement government policy as reflected in higher laws approved in Parliament. Specifically, he may issue ministerial orders (*órdenes ministeriales*) without the approval of the Council of Ministers.

5.4.3.2 Executive responsibilities

Where the responsibility has not been expressly granted to either the Council of Ministers (5.5) or the delegated committees of the government (5.6), the ministers have the right to appoint and dismiss other high-ranking civil servants within their departments; they are also responsible for the management of the civil servants and all disciplinary matters relating to staff within their departments. Moreover, they are empowered to sign state contracts related to matters concerning their ministries. In addition, they are required to draw up a draft budget for their departments as well as to allocate expenditure for departmental matters outside the competence of the Council of Ministers, making arrangements with the Ministry of Economy and Finance (*Ministerio de Economía y Hacienda*) (13.2) for payment of such amounts.

5.4.3.3 Judicial responsibilities

In the last resort, each minister can be called upon to resolve administrative disputes concerning the work of his department or its dependencies, provided that neither a lower nor higher authority is competent to deal with them. He is also empowered to resolve conflicts within his department related to the distribution of responsibilities between its different branches.

5.4.4 Limitations to powers

All ministers with departmental responsibilities can be called to account for or to explain their policies or actions before one or both of the Houses of Parliament or before one of the parliamentary committees linked to either House. In a general sense, of course, the ministers are always individually responsible for their actions to the Council of Ministers (5.5), even for those which require the signature of the king (article 98.2). At meetings of the Council of Ministers, of course, it usually soon becomes clear if an individual minister is failing to implement the policies agreed at cabinet level, in which case he may be subject, without appeal, to dismissal.

5.4.5 Accountability

Like the prime minister, the ministers may be held responsible for actions committed against the criminal code, in which case they will be brought before the criminal division of the Supreme Court (*Tribunal Supremo*) (14.5.1). If the crime concerns treasonable offences or any other offence against the security of the state, Parliament must take the initiative to prosecute. Such an initiative must have the backing of a quarter of the members of the Congress and the vote to prosecute must receive an overall majority in the House. Although the Constitution and other laws are silent on the subject, it can be safely assumed that in this way they would be dismissed from office. It is interesting to note that, according to article 102.3 of the Constitution, neither the premier nor his ministers can hope to benefit from a royal pardon (*prerrogativa real de gracia*) for such offences.

5.4.6 Incompatibility

Article 98.3 of the Constitution requires that government ministers shall not be able to hold representative posts other than those in Parliament, nor will they be permitted to occupy any public post that is not directly related to their governmental office. They are also debarred from indulging in any professional or commercial activity. The aim of such measures was clearly to prevent a re-occurrence of the kind of corruption that was common in the Franco era with senior government ministers occupying important positions in the financial and business world, as well as, on many occasions, more than one post within the system of public administration. The theory of this provision was originally fleshed out in the December 1983 Law on the Incompatibility of Offices among Senior Civil Servants (*Ley de Incompatibilidades de Altos Cargos*), the preamble of which stresses the need for the law to respect the principle of the separation of functions. A further law of 11 May 1995 went further in attempts to clarify and 'tighten up' the position of both government members and high ranking public officials. In practical terms, the legislation makes it impossible for a whole range of high-ranking personnel, from junior ministers down to the assistant directors of state enterprises, to hold either two paid posts within the civil service or one within the administration and one in certain areas of private enterprise (articles 2 and 7). Ministers are also required to make a public declaration of their assets and extra-governmental activities, which are to be recorded in the register of the activities of high-ranking public servants (*registro de actividades de altos cargos*); they must also state the social objectives of any companies in which they have an interest (article 6 of May 1995 Law).

5.5 Council of Ministers (*Consejo de Ministros*)

This is the highest political and executive body in the land, corresponding to the British cabinet. Normally, it consists of the prime minister, the deputy prime minister, where appointed, and the ministers, including minister of the presidency (5.3) who acts as the Cabinet secretary (*ministro secretario del Consejo de Ministros*). On rare occasions, a secretary of state (6.2.3) may be invited to attend but, although there has been some pressure in recent times to include them, these junior ministers do not form part of the cabinet. Meetings of the Council of Ministers are normally chaired by the prime minister, unless the king is present or unless the premier is ill or absent abroad, in which case, as we have seen, his place is taken by his deputy or the minister of the presidency (currently the same person).

5.5.1 Procedure

The Council of Ministers normally meets once a week in ordinary sessions on Fridays, even during the vacation periods, although extraordinary sessions can be held at any time should the political situation or some emergency require it. For many years decision-making meetings (*consejos decisorios*) alternated with discussion meetings (*consejos deliberantes*), the former being more technical and specific in character and the latter tending to have a more political flavour and covering a wider range of issues. These days, however, such distinctions have become more blurred and present meetings of the cabinet cover the whole range. Although no norms are laid down in this respect, it is assumed that votes are taken over matters requiring definite decisions where unanimity has not been achieved.

Preparation of the cabinet meetings is in the hands of the General Committee of Secretaries of State and Under-secretaries (5.3), chaired by the first deputy premier. This vitally important committee meets on Wednesdays and prepares the agenda for the weekly cabinet meetings. Nothing is allowed through to the Council of Ministers without passing first through this Committee. The latter, in fact, has the power to approve certain matters without reference to the cabinet, matters which are then 'nodded through' the Council of Ministers; such items appear under what is known as the 'green index' (*índice verde*). More important items, including draft laws and decree-laws are classified as 'red index' (*índice rojo*) and must be referred to the Council of Ministers for discussion. The Committee of Secretaries of State and Under-secretaries may also refer proposals back to their source, usually to the directorate general of some ministry (6.2.6), for further study before they are resubmitted for approval.

5.5.2 General responsibilities

The general responsibilities of the Council of Ministers are those outlined in article 97, which refers to the role of the government. This article states that 'the government directs internal and foreign policy, the civil and military administration and the defence of the state. It exercises the executive function and rule-making powers'. Like the prime minister, it has both a political, i.e. policy-making, and an administrative role. In the latter capacity, it controls the activity of the various branches of public administration and ensures that it is following agreed guidelines. It should also be stressed that, in addition to its control over the civil administration, it has ultimate control over military affairs and is responsible for national security and defence.

A further point worth making is that, since the government must endorse the acts of the king, it exercises the rights, or at least participates in the rights, granted to the king in the Constitution (articles 56, 64 and 65, for example). However, the government has no powers relative to the dismissal of the prime minister nor to the dissolution of the *Cortes*. Above all, it should be emphasised that it is ultimately accountable, in all its decisions and actions, to Parliament.

5.5.3 Specific responsibilities

These fall into the following four categories: (i) legislative; (ii) executive; (iii) judicial; and (iv) defence/security. Each will now be examined separately.

5.5.3.1 Legislative

It may seem a paradox that a basically executive body may exercise some legislative power under a constitutional system that recognises the separation of powers. However, in most liberal democracies, it is common for Parliament to grant the Executive the opportunity to share in the legislative process. The areas in which the cabinet participates in the legislative process, i.e. through draft laws, decree-laws and legislative decrees, have already been examined (4.7.2).

5.5.3.2 Executive

The Council's major function is to formulate and approve national policy over the whole area represented by the various ministries; it takes the initiative in preparing draft bills (*anteproyectos de ley*) which are normally drawn up in particular departments or joint departmental committees prior to being approved by the cabinet and then being submitted to the *Cortes*.

Under its rule-making power (*potestad reglamentaria*), the Council of Ministers proposes to the head of state a series of regulations or minor laws designed to implement laws already approved by Parliament. The cabinet, prior to submission to the king, considers the proposals of the head of government for the appointment and dismissal of high-ranking civil and other public servants; these include ambassadors, under-secretaries of state, director generals, civil governors, government delegates to the autonomous communities, captain-generals of the army (2.3.1) and so on.

The Council of Ministers is required to establish and disband the delegated committees of the government (5.6) which are permanently constituted, as well as certain other inter-ministerial committees set up on an ad hoc basis.

The Council must ensure the smooth running of all public services, intervening with emergency measures where necessary. It also has the right to call elections at regional and local, although not at national, level (this is, as we have seen, the prerogative of the king, on the advice of the prime minister) (3.4.2.2).

The cabinet enjoys certain executive rights related to the autonomous communities:

(i) It appoints and dismisses the government delegates who direct state administration within their respective regions (6.5.2).

(ii) It has the right to oblige the autonomous communities to carry out their responsibilities according to the Constitution.

(iii)   It also has the right to bring a regional authority before the constitutional court, if the latter adopts regulations which contravene the Constitution, and has the power to suspend such regulations.

5.5.3.3 Judicial

The Council of Ministers can nominate a candidate to be appointed attorney general (*fiscal general del estado*) (14.4.3), as well as two members of the Constitutional Court (2.5).

The Council is also expected to resolve certain appeals that are brought before it involving disputes between ministries where these cannot be solved by other competent authorities.

5.5.3.4 Defence and security

Article 97 of the Constitution makes it clear that the government, through the Council of Ministers, is responsible for the control of military affairs and for the defence of the state. This is clearly a role which it shares with the head of state who, as we have seen, is the commander-in-chief of the armed forces (3.4.1). Article 104 also assigns to the Council of Ministers responsibility for the security and police forces of the country, whose role is 'to protect the free exercise of rights and liberties and to guarantee public security'.

5.6 Delegated committees of the government (*comisiones delegadas del gobierno*)

These are inter-departmental committees composed of the ministers concerned and established with the approval of the Council of Ministers. They are the equivalent of UK cabinet committees. The royal decree of December 1981, which specified the membership of each one, reduced their number to five, which are as follows.

5.6.1 Foreign Policy Committee (*Comisión de Política Exterior*)

Members: the minister of foreign affairs plus members who may be co-opted by the premier depending on the area of policy under discussion. In recent years, a key figure on this committee has been the secretary of state for the European Union (15.4.2.1).

5.6.2 State Security Committee (*Comisíon para la Seguridad del Estado*)

Members: the ministers of foreign affairs; home affairs; presidency and the director general of state security.

5.6.3 Committee for Economic Affairs (*Comisión de Asuntos Económicos*)

Members: the ministers of economy and finance; promotion; labour and social affairs; industry and energy; agriculture, fisheries and food; presidency; health and consumer affairs; and the under-secretary of state for the economy. This Committee is currently chaired by the minister of economy and finance (5.3) who is the second deputy premier.

5.6.4 Autonomy Policy Committee (*Comisión de Política Autonómica*)

Members: the ministers of home affairs; economy and finance; public administration (and his deputy); and the secretary of state for the European Union (15.4.2.1).

5.6.5 Committee for Educational, Cultural and Scientific Policy (*Comisión para Política Educativa, Cultural y Científica*)

Members: the ministers of education and science; culture; presidency; the secretary of state for the universities and research; and any other ministers who may be co-opted, depending on the policy area under discussion, by the premier.

These committees meet when required, normally on Thursday mornings. They are chaired by one of the two deputy premiers. Naturally, the prime minister has the right to attend any of them whenever he wishes. The deputy premier concerned may invite other members of the government to meetings of the committees, as well as secretaries of state and other high-ranking civil servants. The deputy premier normally acts as secretary for all meetings of these committees, for which minutes must be kept.

The main function of these delegated committees is to provide a forum for specialists within the government to come together to discuss problems relating to areas of inter-departmental interest and enable co-ordination between ministries to take place. In fact, these specialised bodies may exercise decision-making powers in matters which do not need to be approved at the level of the Council of Ministers. Thus, although they often act in an advisory capacity, they are technically important components of the executive authority.

It should be noted that, in addition to these quite powerful committees, there are a large number of inter-ministerial committees (*comisiones interministeriales*), which again bring together experts from a variety of fields, but which can only make recommendations to the government. One of the most important of these is the Interministerial Committee for Economic Affairs related to the European Communities (*Comisión Interministerial para Asuntos Económicos relacionados con las Comunidades Europeas*), which was established by royal decree in September 1985. (This is not to be confused with the Interministerial Conference for Community Affairs referred to in 15.4.4.) Such committees may be permanent like this one or ad hoc; an example of the latter is the Organising Committee for the Spanish Presidency of the European Union (*Comité Organizador de la*

Presidencia Española de la Unión Europea), which was very active in 1994 and the first half of 1995.

5.7 Council of State (*Consejo de Estado*)

Since it is referred to in the Constitution (article 107), this advisory body has constitutional status and, in fact, constitutes one of the *órganos constitucionales* (1.2.3 and figure 1.1). Indeed, it constitutes the highest consultative organ of the government. It has no executive functions. Its president is appointed by the Council of Ministers, although he is not expected to be a political appointment; he is usually a jurist of recognised experience and prestige. Apart from the president and a general secretary, the Council of State includes various categories of counsellors (*consejeros*).

5.7.1 Permanent counsellors (*consejeros permanentes*)

These come from the following categories: minister; a high-ranking representative of the autonomous communities; a counsellor of state (from one of the other categories); the senior legal adviser (*letrado mayor*) of the Council of State; a high-ranking member of one of the royal academies; a senior academic from the legal, economic or social disciplines of a university faculty, with at least fifteen years' service; an officer from one of the legal corps of the armed forces; and a senior member of the civil service, with at least fifteen years' service and holding a university degree. Such members are appointed by a decree of the Council of Ministers for an indefinite period and each heads a department (*sección*) of the Council of State.

5.7.2 Ex-officio counsellors (*consejeros natos*)

This group includes such high-ranking national figures as: the director of the Spanish Royal Academy; the presidents of the royal academies of moral and political sciences, and of jurisprudence and legislation; the president of the Economic and Social Council (5.8); the attorney general (14.4.3); the president of the General Council for the Legal Profession (*Consejo General de la Abogacía*); the president of the General Council of Codification (*Consejo General de Codificación*); the director general of the State Legal Service (*Dirección General del Servicio Jurídico del Estado*) (5.9); and the director of the Centre for Constitutional Studies (table 6.2).

5.7.3 Elected counsellors (*consejeros electivos*)

The ten elected counsellors are appointed by decree for a period of four years among persons who have held various specific offices; these offices include: ministers or secretaries of state; parliamentary deputies or senators, magistrates (*magistrados*) of the Constitutional Court (2.5); the ombudsman (2.6); the president or members of the General Council of the Judiciary (*Consejo General del Poder Judicial*) (14.4.2); president of the Audit Tribunal (9.9.3); president of the Joint Chiefs of Staff (*Junta de Jefes de Estado Mayor/JUJEM*); ambassadors; the presidents or ministers of autonomous communities; mayors of provincial capitals; presidents of provincial or island councils; and university vice-chancellors (*rectores*).

In its day-to-day work, the Council is assisted by other technical officials, including the financial controller (*interventor delegado*), the director of the archives and library, and the head of computing (*informática*).

5.7.4 Structure

The Council functions either in plenary session (*pleno*) or through its standing committee (*comisión permanente*). The latter consists of the permanent counsellors plus the president and the general secretary of the council. The Council also functions through sections (*secciones*) headed by the permanent counsellors and specialising in specific areas of concern. These departments prepare material for deliberation by both the standing committee and the full Council.

5.7.5 Role

The basic function of the Council is to advise the government and the autonomous communities on a wide range of administrative and legal matters where doubts, queries or potential conflicts between organisations may exist in order to pre-empt litigation at a later stage. As well as attempting to resolve conflicts that may be referred to it, the Council also has the right to present proposals to the government. The full list of areas in which the Council has competence is given in the Law on the Council of State (*Ley del Consejo de Estado*) of 22 April 1980.

5.8 Economic and Social Council (*Consejo Económico y Social/CES*)

This body was envisaged in article 131.2 of the Constitution, which makes it clear that its main function would be to assist the government in economic planning, in collaboration with the unions and business and professional organisations. However, for political reasons, it was only formally set up by the law of 17 June 1991. For many years, an impasse had existed since the unions and others wished to see the Council have a planning and decision-making role, while the government was equally determined that it should be purely advisory and consultative in nature. In the end, an unsatisfactory compromise has been reached in which in certain circumstances (which are far from clear) the Council does have certain executive-type functions, although in general the government view of its role has tended to win the day.

5.8.1 Composition

The Council consists of sixty-one members, including the president, and twenty members in each of three clearly defined groups. The president is appointed by the government on the recommendation of the minister of economy and finance, and the minister of labour and social affairs, following consultation with the three groups in the Council. He must have the support of at least two-thirds of the Council members. The president holds office for four years. He is assisted by a general secretary, who is in charge of administrative affairs, and two vice-presidents who are elected by the *pleno*; one of these is nominated by the unions and the other by the business organisations. As well as the plenary group, the Council also has a standing committee (*comisión permanente*) and working committees (*comisiones de trabajo*), which may be permanent or ad hoc.

The three component groups of the Council are as follows:

5.8.1.1 Group 1: Union representatives (representantes de las organizaciones sindicales)

These members are nominated by the unions concerned in proportion to their official representation (11.3.2.5).

5.8.1.2 Group 2: Representatives of business organisations (representantes de las organizaciones empresariales)

These members likewise are nominated by the organisations concerned in proportion to the numbers of members in each (12.11).

5.8.1.3 Group 3

This is a mixed group consisting of the following sub-groups: agriculture (three members); sea-faring and fishing (three members); consumers and users (four members); social economy (four members); and six experts. The latter are appointed by the government on the recommendation of the ministers of economy and labour, following consultation with the other groups in the Council; these experts must be persons who have appropriate qualifications and recognised experience in the fields of socio–economic affairs and labour relations.

All Council members serve for four years and may be re-appointed for further four-year terms.

5.8.2 Functions

The Council's main function is to give expert advice to the government in economic, labour and social policy. The specific areas referred to in the 1991 law are: economy; taxation; labour relations; employment and social security; social affairs; agriculture and fishing, education and culture; health and consumer affairs; environmental affairs; transport and communications; industry and energy; housing; regional development; the EU internal market; co-operation for development. On the basis of rigorous research, the Council presents recommendations related to the above fields and prepares reports (*dictámenes*) on draft bills submitted to it by the relevant ministries. The ministries concerned are, in fact, obliged to submit such draft bills to the Council. In theory, the government is bound by *dictámenes* relating to certain areas of policy, but on the whole, as is the case with the Council of State, the Council of Ministers is not obliged to implement the recommendations of the CES. The latter meets approximately once per month in plenary session.

5.9 Directorate General of the State Legal Service (*Dirección General del Servicio Jurídico del Estado*)

This organisation, which, following the royal decree of 5 June 1985, replaces the former Directorate General for State Litigation (*Dirección General de lo Contencioso del Estado*), is the highest legal consultative body for central public administration. Unlike the Council of State, however, it does depend on a government department, in this case the Ministry of Justice (14.8). Like the Council of State and the Economic and Social Council, it has no executive functions. This body, through its various departments, advises when required all ministries, including autonomous administrative bodies (6.3) and at regional and provincial level, attached respectively to the offices of the government delegate (6.5.2) and the civil governor (6.5.3), provides a similar service for the *administración periférica del estado* (6.5.1), replacing the functions of the former state lawyers' offices (*abogacías del estado*).

5.10 Comment

At least in theory, Spain now has democratic government that is no longer, as in Franco's time, all-powerful and impervious to any pressure from the legislature or judiciary. In theory at least, there is a clear separation of powers between the executive, legislature and judiciary. Though formally appointed by the head of state, the prime minister owes his position, as in the United Kingdom, to his leadership of a parliamentary group that has won power via democratically held elections. Constitutionally, the executive is accountable to the legislature; the prime minister and his ministers must be prepared to explain and justify their policies in Parliament, and in the last resort the public is theoretically protected against arbitrary or illegal government behaviour by the courts.

In recent times, however, the government, and the premier in particular, have not always resisted the temptation (offered by an initially unassailable parliamentary majority) to act in ways that have been allegedly authoritarian, if not illegal. The premier's appearances in Parliament, for example, have, until relatively recently, been rare events, being reserved for 'big occasions'. Undoubtedly, too, appointments of members of the ruling party to many high institutions of state, while by no means illegal, have smacked a good deal of political patronage. Much more serious, however, have been the corruption and scandals that have reached into the highest echelons of government, culminating in the GAL affair (1.1.5) for which the then premier long refused to set up a committee of investigation (4.5.4). Whatever the extent of the government's level of responsibility in this affair, there is little doubt that the premier, as well as some of his ministers and senior civil servants, had been less than open both with Parliament and with the public.

Clearly such behaviour brings institutions and even democracy itself into disrepute. However, it should be borne in mind that, in spite of everything, combined pressure from sections of the press, the opposition parties in Parliament and the rigorous action of the courts, which refused to bow to intense pressure from the Executive, did in fact succeed in 'bringing the executive to heel'. In short, the institutions of democracy have been seen to work.

Chapter 6

Central administration

Preliminary note

The term 'public administration' (*administraciones públicas*) in Spain is used to cover a variety of institutions and services operating at central, regional and local level, as can be seen in figure 6.1. Since the departmental reorganisation of July 1986, the co-ordination and overall control of this vast bureaucracy has been the responsibility of the Ministry of Public Administration (*Ministerio de Administraciones Públicas*).

This particular chapter is organically linked, as we have seen, to chapter 5 on central government and is primarily concerned with examining central public administration. The regional and local authorities are dealt with respectively in chapters 7 and 8. This chapter examines the structure and functions of the ministerial departments, with a section that examines the 'anatomy' of one particular ministry, the social security system and the numerous autonomous administrative bodies (*organismos autónomos administrativos*) (6.3) which are dependent on the government departments. However, autonomous commercial, industrial and financial bodies, which are linked to most departments, are seen as forming part of 'public sector enterprises', and they are thus dealt with in chapter 9. Finally, although recent years have seen the transfer of many powers and functions from central administration to the autonomous communities, reference is made to the institutional structure through which central government is administered at a local level through the system of delegated administration (*administración periférica del estado*) (6.5.1).

6.1 Introduction

Spain has a long tradition of strong control from the centre dating back to the beginning of the nineteenth century when the foundations of the modern system of administration were laid. Even under the Second Republic, which granted autonomy to Catalonia and, belatedly, to the Basque Country, the basic structure was barely modified. Indeed, while Franco's system of government differed radically from that of the republicans, the system of administration had many features in common. One of these features was the delegation of central administration to provincial outposts which, as we shall see (6.5), has even now survived in some form.

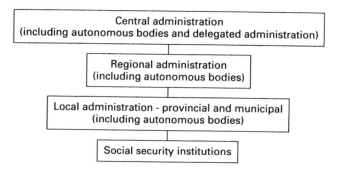

Figure 6.1 *Public administration in Spain, 1995*

However, two tensions emerged in the post-Franco era. On the one hand, there was clearly a need to rationalise the structure in order to improve control and co-ordination; on the other, the regions claimed a greater say in the running of their own affairs, a situation which led to the transfer of the functions of many of these bodies to the domain of the autonomous communities (chapter 7).

6.2 Ministries (*ministerios*)

The selection and denomination of the ministries, a responsibility which has recently reverted from the Council of Ministers to the premier himself, are clearly important in that they reflect the priorities and emphases attached by a particular government, and indeed by a given society, to areas of economic, social, political and cultural concern. Table 6.1 shows the ministerial departments first established by the government of José Mariá Aznar in May 1996. This list is, of course, alphabetical and not hierarchical; in terms of their political importance, which is in part related to size and the budget handled, the ministries regarded as most pre-stigious are: the Presidency; Economy and Finance; Foreign Affairs; and Home Affairs.

6.2.1 Overall structure

The overall structure of ministries, at least up to very recent years, and the system of public administration, were established at the beginning of the nineteenth century, when the Napoleonic model of the state was imported into Spain. Though certain modifications were made towards the end of the century, basically the system remained unchanged until the 1980s, when the governments of Adolfo Suárez and Felipe González (particularly the latter), set about reforming government administration. Apart from the re-arrangement of ministries, and indeed the reduc-tion of their number, the most important change introduced by the first government of Felipe González, at least as far as the top echelons of power were concerned, was to introduce secretaries of state (6.2.3) and general secretaries (6.2.5) in certain

Table 6.1 *Ministerial departments, May 1996*

Ministry of	Ministerio de
Public Administration	*Administraciones Públicas (MAP)*
Agriculture, Fisheries and Food	*Agricultura, Pesca y Alimentación (MAPA)*
Foreign Affairs	*Asuntos Exteriores*
Defence	*Defensa*
Economy and Finance*	*Economía y Hacienda*
Education and Culture	*Educación y Cultura*
Promotion+	*Fomento*
Industry and Energy	*Industria y Energía (MINER)*
Home Affairs	*Interior*
Justice	*Justicia*
Environment	*Medio Ambiente*
Presidency	*Presidencia*
Health and Consumer Affairs	*Sanidad y Consumo*
Labour and Social Affairs	*Trabajo y Asuntos Sociales*

Notes:
* Includes Commerce and Tourism
+ Includes Public Works
Source: El País (May 1996); BOE (6 May 1996)

departments. An important ministerial restructuring, following the election of June 1993, involved the creation of the super-Ministry of Public Works, Transport and the Environment, a new Ministry of Industry and Energy (Industry having formerly being linked to Commerce and Tourism), and a complex operation involving the suppression of the former Ministry of Relations with the *Cortes* and the restructuring of the Ministry of the Presidency (*Ministerio de la Presidencia*). (This ministry should not be confused with the *Presidencia del Gobierno* described in 5.2.5.) Under the control of the *ministro de la Presidencia*, this department consists of three major areas: the first is an under-secretariat which includes the technical general secretariat and the government secretariat; the second includes relations with Parliament and is in the charge of a *secretario de estado*; and the third is the Secretariat of State for Communication (*Secretaría de Estado de la Comunicación*), which replaces the former Government Spokesman's Department (*Oficina del Portavoz del Gobierno*).

The most recent changes to the pattern of ministries came in May 1996 following the election victory of José María Aznar two months earlier. On the one hand, two ministries, Culture and Social Affairs, were suppressed and merged respectively with Education and Labour, while the new prime minister carried out his election pledge to separate Home Affairs and Justice (14.8.1); on the other hand, he established a brand new Ministry of Promotion (*Fomento*), covering such areas as economic development and public works (figure 6.2). While the evident promotion given to the separate Ministry of Environment suggests forward thinking, the crea-

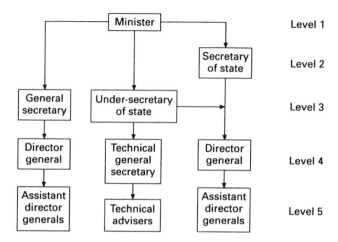

Figure 6.2 *Typical ministerial hierarchy, 1995*

tion of the *Ministerio de Fomento* has distinctly historical and conservative connotations.

It should be noted that, in addition to the conventional divisions of a ministry as shown in figure 6.2, all ministries include several (and, in some cases, a large number of) autonomous bodies, both of the administrative and commercial kind, plus a number of other entities (*entidades*) which fall outside the basic ministerial structure. As we have seen (5.6.5), each ministry also has attached to it a number of inter-departmental committees (*comisiones interministeriales*). Finally, all ministries now have at least one public information office (*oficina de información al público*) and, normally, a publications office (*centro de publicaciones*), also open to the public.

6.2.2 Hierarchy within ministries

Figure 6.2 illustrates the hierarchy that obtains at the apex of each ministry. As we saw in 5.4, the minister is the head of the department concerned and is responsible to the prime minister and the Council of Ministers, and ultimately to Parliament, for the efficient running of that department. In his task, he is aided by a team whose size varies according to the size of the ministry in question. Not all the ministries, for example, include a secretary of state, though more of these posts have been created in the last few years in the larger ministries such as Home Affairs, Foreign Affairs, Defence, Public Administration and even Education. On the other hand, in some small departments, the minister is aided only by an under-secretary of state and a variable number of director generals. Not all departments by any means are staffed by general secretaries. All, however, contain the all-important offices of under-secretary of state and the technical general secretary, both of whom can in many ways be regarded as the pivots of the activity of every ministry.

All the above offices are within the appointment of the Council of Ministers, though recommendations for appointment or promotion are usually made by officials at one level higher than the one concerned. Thus, the under-secretary will often recommend the appointment of staff at the level of director general. Strictly speaking, no official below the rank of minister is expected to resign when the prime minister leaves office, not even the secretary of state; in practice, however, government changes since 1977 have often led to wide-ranging reshuffles at all these levels – and there have even been changes, for political reasons, at the level of assistant director general. However, up to and including the technical general secretary, it is a requirement that the office holders should be career civil servants (*funcionarios de carrera*). Until recently the general trend was towards a greater professionalisation of all but the very top ministerial posts.

6.2.3 Secretary of state (*secretario de estado*)

This relatively new ministerial rank, equivalent to a British minister of state or junior minister, was created by the royal decree of July 1977. At the time of writing (1995), within nine of the fifteen ministries, there are now seventeen secretaries of state (compared with only nine in 1986), whose permanent nature, title and location were enshrined in the Organic Law on the Administration of the State (*Ley Orgánica de la Administración del Estado/LOAE*). Three of these secretariats, perhaps surprisingly, are situated within the Ministry of Education, in charge respectively of education (a general remit), universities and research, and the Higher Council for Sport (*Consejo Superior de Deportes*) (table 6.2). The secretary of state enjoys fewer powers than a minister but, being in charge of a large and clearly defined area of a ministry, including several directorates general, he does wield considerable power. However, unlike the minister, he has no power with regard to the legislative function, he cannot resolve demarcation disputes and he is not involved in the drawing up of the draft budget for the department. He is, however, permitted to stand in for the minister to make a statement to Parliament or to answer parliamentary questions and, as we have seen, some of these figures are members of the delegated committees of the government (5.6). He attends the weekly meetings of the General Committee of Secretaries of State and Under-secretaries (5.3 and 6.2.4). Indeed, the fact that this Committee (formerly only composed of the under-secretaries) has recently been remodelled to include the secretaries of state suggests that the latter's prestige is steadily being enhanced.

During 1995, at least one attempt was made by the minister for public administration to introduce the Government Law (*Ley del Gobierno*), one aim of which was formally to designate secretaries of state as members of the government, thus enabling them to attend meetings of the Council of Ministers (5.5). At the time, this was controversial since it was seen by the opposition as an attempt to provide ministerial immunity (*fuero*) for at least one former holder of such an office, then held in jail pending enquiries into the GAL affair (1.1.5).

6.2.4 Under-secretary of state (*subsecretario de estado*)

The under-secretary has played an important part in Spanish administration since the post was first established by the royal decree of 1834. In a ministry without a secretary of state (for example, Health and Consumer Affairs and Agriculture), and in practice in many cases where one exists, he is the most powerful figure after the minister. The under-secretary or *subse*, as he is often known, performs a dual function: on the one hand, he is directly responsible under the minister for the administration of the whole, or a large part, of the ministry; on the other, he exercises an important role of communication between the different divisions of the department, as well as with other departments and any other bodies that might be related to his ministry. He also has the responsibility for drawing up legislative drafts, as well as other legal documents, and implements budgetary allocations agreed within the department. Moreover, he is in charge of all the staff within the ministry and, where appropriate, it is his responsibility to resolve all matters related to staffing. In addition, he has the authority to inspect all the centres and dependencies connected to the ministries concerned, including autonomous bodies.

One of the most important functions of the under-secretary is to attend the weekly Wednesday meetings of the General Committee of Secretaries of State and Under-secretaries (5.3); one of the main purposes of this meeting is to draw up the agenda for the meetings of the Council of Ministers, in consultation with the cabinet secretary who chairs the meeting (5.3 and 5.5.1). (Currently the first deputy premier performs this function (5.3).)

6.2.5 General secretary (*secretario general*)

As we have seen, the figure of the general secretary was only created relatively recently, and has, consequently, had only a limited time in which to establish itself. In March 1995, there were twelve such posts (compared to nine in 1986), situated in seven ministries, no less than four of these being located in the Ministry of Agriculture, in charge respectively of: agricultural production and markets; food; agrarian structures; and marine fishing. Like the ranks already mentioned, this has been officially 'institutionalised' by the LOAE. In theory, the general secretaries have the same rank as the under-secretaries, but, partly because of their lack of tradition and partly due to the under-secretary's special responsibilities within the department, they do not, in practice, enjoy the same prestige. None the less, since they are in charge of a whole area of the ministry, including often several directorates general, they are important figures, especially in those departments where there are no secretaries of state.

6.2.6 Director general (*director general*)

In accordance with the need of modern administration to divide and delegate labour, departmental divisions or sections headed by director generals have been established. Thus the director general is responsible, under the minister and under-secretaries, secretaries of state and general secretaries, for a specific area of departmental work. All ministries contain several directorates general but, since their number and the internal organisation of any one department fall within the discretion of the minister in consultation with his subordinates, there is no reference to them in the LOAE. The specific responsibilities of the director general include: directing the services and resolving any problems within his section; monitoring the activities of all the bodies dependent on his section; and providing the minister with an annual report on the progress, expenditure and revenue of his section. In addition, like the under-secretaries, he may dictate circulars and instructions concerning the internal organisation of the bodies and services dependent on his section. The director general is normally assisted in his duties by one or more assistant director generals (*subdirectores generales*). In line with the general expansion in recent years of government administration, these particular appointments have tended to proliferate.

6.2.7 Technical general secretary (*secretario general técnico*)

The office of the technical general secretary was created in 1952. Unlike the above-mentioned officials, this figure was traditionally likely to be appointed more for his professional or administrative expertise than for his political leanings and was thus more likely than many of his colleagues to survive a change of government. In recent times, however, even this post has tended to be politicised. He is appointed, on the recommendation of the minister concerned, by the Council of Ministers. In spite of being technically on a lower level than the under-secretaries and the general secretaries, his particular function and the prestige attaching to his office have always enabled him to maintain a direct line to the minister in his capacity as head of an important team of technical experts, statisticians and researchers, whose task is to provide a continuous advisory service for the whole of the department concerned.

Surprisingly, perhaps, the office of the technical general secretary is not mentioned in the LOAE, but the fact is that not only is the office very well established, but every single ministry is endowed with one. The office is, however, institutionalised in the Law on the Organisation of Administration (*Ley de Régimen Jurídico de la Administración/LRJA*), which states that the responsibilities of the technical general secretary include the following: drawing up draft general plans and programmes required within the department; providing technical and administrative assistance (including the compilation of statistics) for the minister when the latter judges such assistance to be vital to the co-ordination of services; recommending reforms designed to improve the services provided by the different bodies within the ministry; and suggesting organisational reforms, paying strict attention to costs and productivity.

It is interesting to note, and a reflection of the influence wielded by the technical general secretary that, in order to carry out his responsibilities, he is able to insist that director generals and other officials within the ministry supply him with as many reports, data and documents as he may require.

6.2.8 Minister's private office (*gabinete del ministro*)

Each minister, in addition to the technical general secretariat, is assisted by a more personal team of advisers (*asesores*). The latter, unlike those in the secretariat, are appointed directly by the minister concerned and will normally be obliged to resign the moment the minister leaves office, as was the case following the July 1995 resignation of the minister of defence, and his replacement by the former minister. They are nearly always members of the same party as the minister and may well be long-standing confidants. The advisers in the private office may make proposals along certain political lines, which for technical or administrative reasons are rejected because the technical secretariat argues strongly against them. On the whole, in spite of the close relationship between the minister and his personal advisers, in such situations the views of the secretariat are likely to prevail because of the latter's greater experience of the ministry, as well as greater experience in general of administration.

6.2.9 Anatomy of a ministry: the Ministry of Public Administration

In order to show how the above officials relate to each other within particular ministry, the Ministry of Public Administration has in figure 6.3 been dissected into its major component parts. This ministry is of particular interest since, as well as heading the whole of the Spanish civil service, it is the department responsible for liaison with the autonomous communities and local authorities, and for the ongoing operation of making transfers of staff and resources to the regional authorities (7.7.5).

As can be seen, this ministry is divided into three major branches, headed respectively by the secretary of state for public administration, the secretary of state for territorial administration and the under-secretary for public administration. The first secretary of state is responsible under the minister for the whole area of the civil service at all levels of administration; as well as controlling two directorates general and the civil service inspection service, he is also responsible, more indirectly, for the two autonomous administrative bodies, the General Benefit Agency for State Civil Servants (*Mutualidad General de Funcionarios Civiles del Estado/MUFACE*), and the National Institute for Public Administration (*Instituto Nacional de Administración Pública/INAP*) (see table 6.2, p. 103). The second secretary of state is in charge of three directorates general, each dealing with one aspect of relations with the regional and local authorities. The Directorate General for Territorial Co-operation, for example, contains three subdirectorates general (*subdirecciones generales*), one of which, the Subdirectorate General for Bilateral Co-operation with the Autonomous Communities (*Subdirección General de Cooperación Bilateral con las Comunidades Autónomas*), is responsible for the day-to-day process of transferring

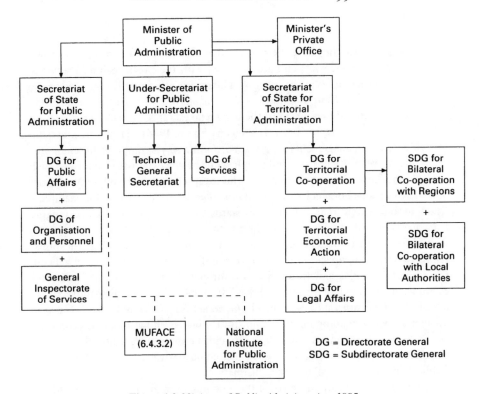

Figure 6.3 *Ministry of Public Administration, 1995*

staffing and resources to the regional authorities. The under-secretary, to whom the technical general secretary and the director general of services are accountable, has a pivotal role within the department, particularly in relation to the provision of technical services, budgetary and financial affairs, staffing and resources. Figure 6.3 also shows the autonomous nature of the minister's private office (*gabinete del ministro*), as well as the similar offices (*gabinetes*) which in recent years have sprung up in support of the secretaries of state.

It should be noted that, in addition to the numerous subdirectorates and bodies of equivalent rank within the ministry (a total of fifty-one), there are also the two autonomous bodies referred to above, nine bodies listed as 'other bodies and entities' (*otros organismos y entidades*) and a dozen or so inter-ministerial committees attached to this ministry, as well as three public information offices.

6.3 Autonomous administrative bodies (*organismos autónomos administrativos/OO.AA.AA*)

These are organisations which operate under the auspices of the various ministries in order to carry out specific administrative responsibilities. They are intended to give greater flexibility in the day-to-day operation of particular functions, while overall policy and budgetary control remain with the ministry responsible. They enjoy a separate legal status, they have their own budget allocation, they employ their own internal auditor (*interventor*) and are endowed with their own technical services, including a legal service (*servicio jurídico*). Their status was initially regulated by the Law of Autonomous State Bodies (*Ley de Entidades Estatales Autónomas*) of 1958 which, among other things, exempts them from taxes, rates, duties and registration fees, and was updated by the General Budgetary Law of 1988 (9.1). The membership of their boards of management (*consejos de administración*) is composed of senior officials from the relevant ministry and people with specific expertise or interests, such as union and employers' representatives who are appointed by the relevant minister. They have various nomenclatures – *instituto, consejo, servicio, centro*, for example – which to some extent reflect their varied status and are headed by a figure, ranging from *presidente* to *director* who, depending on the status given to the body concerned, may report to a director general, to a secretary of state or even directly to the minister. Most of these figures have a status theoretically equivalent to a director general, though in the case of some prestigious institutions they enjoy a higher status; for example, the president of the Higher Sports' Council is equal in rank to the secretary of state for universities and research. The General Budgetary Law (article 4) makes a distinction between autonomous administrative bodies and autonomous commercial, industrial and financial bodies (9.3) – though it is interesting to note that the official structure diagrams (*organigramas*), meticulously drafted by the Ministry of Public Administration, fail to make a distinction!

In 1995 there were around forty of these bodies, located in nearly all the fifteen ministries of state. In 1992, it was calculated that they accounted for 37.6 per cent of the total number of autonomous bodies, yet spent over 70 per cent of the 3.5 billion peseta budget allocated to the whole of the *administración institucional* (1.2.3). Interestingly, during the last government of Felipe González, in the Ministry of Culture, below the level of the *Subsecretaría de Cultura*, half of the ten divisions with the rank of directorate general or equivalent were autonomous bodies. The proliferation of these autonomous administrative bodies, perhaps not surprisingly, has in the past given cause for concern, though there seems to have been an attempt in recent years to reduce their number (albeit simply converting them into autonomous commercial bodies or into directorates or subdirectorates general). There is also considerable difference between the scale and importance of their operations. Some of them, for example, are entrusted with substancial financial resources, adding to the complexity of overall budgetary control and co-ordination. Thus, the National Employment Institute (*Instituto Nacional de Empleo/INEM*) (6.4.3.3), a very large entity which has been described as a 'miniature ministry' and which comes under the auspices of the Ministry of Labour and Social Affairs, has the important task of supervising the whole area of unemployment, assisting unemployed workers with retraining and providing unemployment benefits. The INEM even has dependent offices in all the provincial capitals of Spain. The fifty-one universities, including the Open University (*Universidad Nacional de Educación y*

Distancia / UNED) also figure as autonomous bodies, a status which is embodied in the University Reform Law (*Ley de Reforma Universitaria / LRU*) of 1982.

Some of these bodies have major functions delegated to them by the relevant ministry, but at times this appears to cause an overlap of responsibilities. The Ministry of Agriculture, Fisheries and Food, for example, has a number of bodies under its tutelage which carry out major aspects of the ministry's work. Thus the Institute for Agrarian Reform and Development (*Instituto Nacional de Reforma y Desarrollo Agrario / IRYDA*) is involved in a wide variety of activities, including infrastructural improvements, the modernisation of access roads and drainage schemes and, since 1992, the co-ordination of the EU rural development scheme, the Plan LEADER (French acronym 'Links between Actions for the Development of the Rural Economy'), for which it allocates funds to rural development centres (*centros de desarrollo rural / CEDERs*) in collaboration with the regional governments concerned. In this case, the situation is further complicated by the fact that more than one body may be functioning in a particular area of responsibility, as is the case in the training of agricultural workers with the involvement of IRYDA, the Agrarian Development Service (*Servicio de Extensión Agraria*), the Institute for Agrarian Relations (*Instituto de Relaciones Agrarias / IRA*) (which is now a commercial autonomous body) and INEM.

Sometimes, there may be other ministries which have responsibilities within an area covered by one of these bodies. Thus, while irrigation comes within the ambit of IRYDA, its plans in this respect are co-ordinated in conjunction with the *Dirección General de Obras Hidráulicas*, which was formerly under the Ministry of Public Works, Transport and Environment (*Ministerio de Obras Públicas, Transportes y Medio Ambiente / MOPTMA*), now the Ministry of Promotion (*Ministerio del Fomento*). There are also several important agricultural bodies which have commercial and marketing functions and which, therefore, come under different classifications, as will be seen in 9.3.

On the other hand, other autonomous administrative bodies are involved in more narrowly defined areas of activity. Some are concerned with research in subjects ranging from consumer affairs to constitutional studies like the *Instituto Nacional del Consumo*, and the *Centro de Estudios Constitucionales*, recently transferred back to the Ministry of the Presidency, having spent several years in the former Ministry for Relations with the *Cortes*. Others operate in the cultural area, such as the Prado Art Gallery and the Queen Sofía Arts Centre, or sport in the case of the Higher Sports Council (*Consejo Superior de Deportes*). The Institute for Women's Affairs (*Instituto de la Mujer*), attached to the Ministry of Labour and Social Affairs (*Ministerio de Trabajo y Asuntos Sociales*) (6.4.4.3), is a relatively new autonomous body created in the mid-1980s. Many ministries produce a considerable amount of documentation, research papers and books, and for this purpose they have their own publications departments (*servicios* or *centros de publicaciones*), which are likewise run as autonomous bodies.

The number of these bodies is not static and, as we have seen, in recent years some attempt has been made to reduce them wherever possible in order to avoid duplication and to secure economies. This sometimes means the incorporation of their function within a ministerial department. Thus, in 1985 the Arbitration and Conciliation Service, the *Instituto de Mediación, Arbitraje y Conciliación* (*IMAC*) and its personnel were transferred to a newly created subdirectorate general, the *Subdirección General de Mediación, Arbitraje y Conciliación*, within the Ministry of Labour and Social Affairs (6.4.3).

Some examples of these bodies, and the ministries to which they are responsible, are shown in table 6.2. The overall financial control and co-ordination of these bodies, and of other areas of public administration, is dealt with in 9.9. Autonomous administrative bodies at the regional and local levels are dealt with in chapters 7 and 8 respectively.

6.4 Health and social security

6.4.1 Background

When the foundations of Spain's nation-wide health service were laid during the Franco era, the term normally applied to the whole structure, perhaps rather misleadingly, was *seguridad social*. Until 1978, in fact, there was only one ministry dealing with health and social security affairs and this was the *Ministerio de Sanidad y Seguridad Social*. On the other hand, in parallel with state institutions, there were a large number of private bodies involved in both health care and social security provision. By the early 1990s, attempts over a long period to rationalise a complex system had come to fruition and a clear demarcation established between the National Health System (*Sistema Nacional de Salud/SNS*), comprising both national and regional provision, and the system of Social Security (*Seguridad Social*), which is now used in its more restricted, but more widely accepted sense as far as Spain's European neighbours are concerned.

The SNS, first established in its present form in 1986, is delivered by the Ministry of Health and Consumer Affairs (*Ministerio de Sanidad y Consumo*), while social security is the responsibility of the Ministry of Labour and Social Affairs (*Ministerio de Trabajo y Asuntos Sociales*), formerly called the Ministry of Labour and Social Security (*Ministerio de Trabajo y Seguridad Social*). In 1995 expenditure on social security alone accounted for 34 per cent of the Spanish national budget; this figure does not include health care which represents a further 11 per cent. It should also be borne in mind that the main vehicle for delivering social services, as opposed to social security, INSERSO, was transferred to the new Ministry of Social Affairs (*Ministerio de Asuntos Sociales*) in 1988 (6.4.4), though in May 1996 this was again merged with the *Ministerio de Trabajo*.

This section, therefore, will examine the major institutions under their functional headings: health service (6.4.2); social security (6.4.3); and social services (6.4.4). An overview of the relevant ministries and bodies is given in figure 6.4. It should be noted that the three major autonomous bodies in these areas, INSALUD (6.4.2.1), INSS (6.4.3.1) and INSERSO (6.4.4.1) all constitute management entities (*entidades gestoras*) referred to in 1.2.3 and table 1.3.

Table 6.2 *Examples of autonomous administrative bodies, 1995*

Ministry responsible	Name in English	Name in Spanish
Public Administration	National Institute for Public Administration	*Instituto Nacional de Administración Pública (INAP)*
Agriculture, Fisheries and Food	Institute for Agrarian Reform and Development	*Instituto de Reforma y Desarrollo Agrario (IRYDA)*
Foreign Affairs	Spanish Agency for International Co-operation	*Agencia Española de Cooperación Internacional (AECI)ᵃ*
Labour and Social Affairs	Institute for Women's Affairs	*Instituto de la Mujer*
Economy and Finance	Spanish Institute for External Trade	*Instituto Español de Comercio Exterior*
Education and Culture	Queen Sofia Arts Centre National Gallery	*Museo Nacional Centro de Arte 'Reina Sofía'*
Defence	Social Institute of the Armed Forces	*Instituto Social de las Fuerzas Armadas (ISFAS)*
Economy and Finance	National Statistics Institute	*Instituto Nacional de Estadística (INE)*
Education and Culture	Higher Sports' Council	*Consejo Superior de Deportes*
Industry and Energy	Spanish Office for Patents and Brand Names	*Oficina Española de Patentes y Marcas*
Justice	Centre for Legal Research into the Administration of Justice	*Centro de Estudios Jurídicos de la Administración de la Justicia*
Promotion	Centre for Research and Experimentation into Public Works	*Centro de Estudios y Experimentación de Obras Públicas*
Presidency	Centre for Constitutional Studies	*Centro de Estudios Constitucionales*
Health and Consumer Affairs	National Institute for Consumer Affairs	*Instituto Nacional del Consumo*
Labour and Social Affairs	National Employment Institute	*Instituto Nacional de Empleo (INEM)*

Note:
ᵃ Includes the Institute for Latin American Co-operation (*Instituto de Cooperación Iberoamericana (ICI)* and the Institute for Co-operation with the Arab World, the Mediterranean and Developing Countries (*Instituto de Cooperación con el Mundo Arabe, el Mediterráneo y Países en Desarrollo*).
Source: Centro de Información Administrativa, Ministerio de Administraciones (1996).

6.4.2 Health service institutions

Although amendments to structures have been made in subsequent legislation (such as the royal decree of 10 July 1992), the General Health Law (*Ley General de Sanidad*) remains the basic policy document guiding administrators in recent times. As already stated, health services are delivered by the Ministry of Health and Consumer Affairs and, increasingly, by the corresponding health departments of the regional authorities, to which responsibilities in this area have been transferred. In fact, the transfer of powers in this way has led to a significant slimming down of this central ministry, to the extent that it now has no secretariats of state or general secretariats. There are eight directorates general, all accountable to the under-secretary of state, who is also indirectly responsible for two of the three important autonomous bodies located within this ministry. These are the Carlos

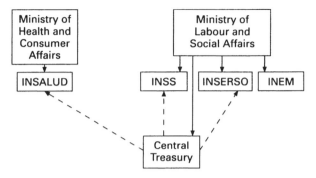

Figure 6.4 *Major health and social security institutions, 1996*

III Health Institute (*Instituto de Salud Carlos III*) (table 9.2, p. 166) and the National Institute for Consumer Affairs (*Instituto Nacional del Consumo*) (table 6.2). The third, and most important autonomous body, directly responsible to the minister, is the National Health Institute (*Instituto Nacional de la Salud/INSALUD*), the main institution providing health care to the nation. In recent years, the SNS has been making strenuous efforts, against a backdrop of difficult economic times, to bring the level of health care in Spain up to that of the more developed members of the European Union. An indication of the progress achieved in this regard can be found in the Ministry's published findings about the state of the nation's health when Spain recently participated in the European 'Health for All' programme.

6.4.2.1 National Health Institute

This body, set up in 1978, is responsible for executing government policy throughout the health service, including outpatient hospitals (*ambulatorios*), residential hospitals (*hospitales*), medical centres (*centros de salud*) and home care. Originally, it worked in collaboration with other public and private institutions (rather than replacing already existing facilities). In recent years, however, the social democratic governments of Felipe González have striven to extend the services of INSALUD and the national health system in general to increasing numbers of the population. In 1995 the Ministry claimed to be providing cover for no less than 99 per cent of Spain's population of over 38 million. As an autonomous body, INSALUD has its own legal identity, a separate budget and control over its own financial and legal affairs. The Institute comprises two major divisions, general coordination and general secretariat, and is in the charge of a director general, who is directly responsible to the minister. By a royal decree of 16 July 1992, a ministerial reorganisation included a tightening up of the structure of INSALUD which, it was felt, had hitherto acted with too much autonomy. Thus, it must now adhere more strictly to a department management plan (*plan de gestión*) which is drawn up in the General Secretariat for Planning (*Secretaría General de Planificación*). This move seems rather paradoxical, coming at precisely the time when new legislation was emerging which would transfer even more responsibilities in the health area to the regional authorities. In fact, in the case of certain regions, powers were transferred as long ago as 1982 (Catalonia) and 1983 (Andalusia); the latter has established its own regional health service, known as the *Sistema Andaluz de Salud* (*SAS*) (chapter 7).

6.4.2.2 Directorate General for Public Health (Dirección General de Salud Pública)

This is one of the most important divisions within the ministry, with certain responsibilities (for example, external health and veterinary affairs) which are not likely to be transferred to the regional authorities. It is responsible for the broad area of public health, covering the promotion of healthy living through education, food hygiene, food imports, vaccination programmes and epidemiology. It has taken over functions that were once performed by the now defunct *administración institucional de la sanidad nacional*, which had been set up as long ago as 1972.

6.4.2.3 Carlos III Health Institute

This increasingly prestigious research centre, working for the whole of the national health system, was established in Madrid in April 1986. It employs a total of 2,136 staff, of whom 484 have higher degrees in the medical field. The latter, using the latest equipment, carry out high level research in a wide area of fields, including epidemiology, microbiology, environmental risks to health, nutrition and genetics. The Institute has libraries that contain 16,000 volumes and 757 professional journals. The director of the centre, who is accountable to the under-secretary (the number 2 in this case) of the Ministry, is responsible for the three major divisions within the Institute: the General Secretariat, the Subdirectorate General for Research (*Subdirección General de Investigación*) and the Subdirectorate General for Training (*Subdirección General de Formación*). Within the latter is included the National Health School (*Escuela Nacional de Sanidad*), which provides high level training courses for professionals in this field, both from inside and outside the national health system. The Institute is classified as a commercial autonomous body (9.3).

6.4.2.4 Health Advisory Council (Consejo Asesor de Sanidad / CAS)

As long ago as 1986, the General Health Law (articles 40 and 110) envisaged the creation of some body in which the public would be represented at the highest level in matters of health; this was seen as part of the state's constitutional obligation in regard to health protection. In fact, however, establishment of such an entity was delayed until November 1992, when the Health Advisory Council was set up by ministerial order. The Council consists of a president, secretary (who must be a health consultant from the ministry itself) and a maximum of twenty-five members, all of whom are appointed by the minister from among professionals of 'recognised prestige' in the health, medicine, health sciences or social science disciplines. The full Council must meet at least twice a year and working committees as and when required. The Council's brief is to advise and inform the minister in respect of scientific, ethical, professional and social matters which may have a bearing on policy formulation.

6.4.2.5 Inter-regional Council of the National Health System (Consejo Interterritorial del Sistema Nacional de Salud)

This body was first envisaged in the General Health Law of 1986 and set up in 1987. Subsequently, its internal structure and brief have been modified in line with other legislation affecting the health service in particular (such as the Medication Law of 1990) and, more generally, the wider question of harmonisation between the various tiers of Spanish administration (such as the Law on Public Administration and Common Administrative Procedure (*Ley de Administraciones Públicas y Procedimiento Administrativo Común*) of November 1992). Thus, the present structure dates from December 1993. The Council consists of one representative from the health ministries of each of the autonomous communities with responsibilities in health, plus an equal number of top officials (*altos cargos*) from the Ministry in Madrid. The minister presides over plenary sessions of the Council, which by law must take place at least four times a year. Attached to the Council is a consultative committee (*comité consultivo*), composed of experts drawn from the Ministry itself. The Council's principal objective has been, and continues to be, to ensure the harmonisation of and co-ordination of policy between the central government and the government of the autonomous communities with responsibilities in health plus an equal number of top officials from the Ministry in Madrid. This is without prejudice to the complete autonomy enjoyed by certain regions in matters of health care provision; these regions at the time of writing (1995) are: Andalusia, the Basque Country, Catalonia, the Canaries, Galicia, Navarre and Valencia (chapter 7). Among its numerous, more specific remits, the Council is expected to concern itself with the contents of international agreements which bind Spain to co-operate with other countries in health affairs and with international health organisations. The Council is also required to encourage the involvement of the autonomous communities in the formulation of a common approach to health policy in its relations with the European Union. Although designated an 'advisory' council, in fact its decisions, unlike those of the Health Advisory Council, are regarded as binding.

6.4.3 Social security institutions

The early 1990s witnessed a whirl of legislative activity relating to social security, to the point where it was felt that a reformulated text of all the relevant legislation covering this area was urgently needed. The result was the General Law on Social Security (*Ley General de la Seguridad Social*) of 20 June 1994, which covers all aspects of the subject. Having regained certain responsibilities once lost to the Ministry of Social Services, the Ministry of Labour and Social Affairs has become one of the largest and most important government departments, handling the largest of all ministerial budgets. Unlike the Ministry of Health, there has only been a limited amount of devolution of powers to the regional authorities. Moreover, it is this ministry, through the administrative unit (*unidad administradora*) of the Directorate General for Employment (*Dirección General de Empleo*) that receipts from the European Social Fund are distributed (15.4.2.3). It has three major structural divisions: (i) the Under-secretariat for Labour and Social Security (*Subsecretaría de Trabajo y Seguridad Social*); (ii) the General Secretariat for Employment and Labour Relations (*Secretaría General de Empleo y Relaciones Laborales*); and (iii) the General Secretariat for Social Security (*Secretaría General de Seguridad Social*). With the exception of the National Employment Institute, which is a free-standing autonomous body, whose director is directly responsible to the minister, the other institutions which will be studied here fall under the jurisdiction of the General Secretariat for Social Security.

6.4.3.1 National Social Security Institute (Instituto Nacional de la Seguridad Social/INSS)

The INSS, established by the royal decree of 30 July 1979, is the second (after INSALUD) of the major autonomous bodies working in the area of health and social security/social services. It is a very large institution and, in terms of the budget it handles and the number of staff employed, is larger than some ministries. Since social security has a special role within Spanish public administration, its institutions have a rather different status from the norm, and thus the INSS, like the other bodies within the group, is classified as a management entity (*entidad gestora*), since its major role is the management of funds. The head of the Institute is accountable to the secretary general for social security. This organisation is responsible for administering social security benefits (*prestaciones*) which include old age pensions, sickness benefit, widows' and orphans' benefits, invalidity pensions and family allowances. It replaced many of the separate private entities which existed previously, such as the mutual benefit agencies (*mutualidades laborales*) (see 13.19) and friendly societies (*mutuas*), which had been responsible for particular groups of employees, such as artists, writers and bullfighters. The participation of interested parties in the running of the social security system is specifically mentioned in article 129.1 of the Constitution; this takes place through the equal representation of unions, employers' organisations and the government on both the general council and on the executive committee of the INSS. The former is responsible for establishing general guidelines and for approving the estimates, while the latter supervises the implementation of policy decisions.

6.4.3.2 Institute for the Welfare of Seamen (Instituto Social de la Marina/ISM)

In view of the significant number of people employed both among the sailing community and in the fishing industry, a special body, founded as long ago as 1919, was created to provide social security for them. Like the INSS, it is classified as an *entidad gestora* and its manager answers directly to the secretary general for social security. Because of the peculiar nature of the working conditions of those it covers, the ISM acts as an administrative agency not only for social security but also for health and social services.

Similar entities providing for specialist groups are: the *Mutualidad General de Funcionarios Civiles del Estado (MUFACE)* (for civil servants) (6.2.9) and the *Instituto Social de las Fuerzas Armadas (ISFAS)* (for military personnel).

6.4.3.3 National Employment Institute

An area of social security which has continued to be very important, given Spain's unenviable position as the EU country with the highest level of unemployment, has been that relating to unemployment, training and retraining. INEM was founded as part of the overall health and social security reform in 1978 and, like the above institutions, operates as an autonomous body (6.3); its director, who handles a large budget, is accountable only to the minister himself. In recent years, some progress has been made in the process of devolving its activities to the directorates general of labour (*direcciones generales de trabajo*) of the regional governments, particularly in the area of training (*formación*). However, problems of co-ordination have arisen because of the competing claims of the INEM outposts within the ministry's delegated administration (*administración periférica*) (6.5) at the provincial level (other areas of this ministry being only rarely subject to transfer).

6.4.3.4 Central Treasury for Social Security (Tesorería General de la Seguridad Social)

In view of the economic importance of social security in general within the economy, this special organisation was originally set up under the Budget Law of 1977 but updated in section 7 of the General Budgetary Law of 1988. It has its own legal identity and in many ways it resembles other autonomous bodies already described. However, it is classified – rather uniquely – as a common service (*servicio común*) (table 1.3) and its function is to provide a unified treasury (*caja única*) for all the income and expenditure of the social security system. It provides overall financial co-ordination and control for the three major management entities, INSALUD, INSS and INSERSO (6.4.4), managing their finances, administering the collection of social security contributions (*cotizaciones*) and benefit payments (*prestaciones*), as well as implementing borrowing and investment programmes. The Central Treasury, which now functions on the basis of a highly sophisticated computer system, is an integral part of the Ministry of Labour and Social Affairs, and administrative responsibility is vested in the director, who is directly appointed by the minister. There are a number of assistant directors who are in charge of specific areas, such as resources payments, budgets and planning. At provincial level, the Ministry has a delegated office called the directorate general of labour, social security and social affairs (*dirección general de trabajo, seguridad social y asuntos sociales*); within each of these is a branch of the Central Treasury to which citizens can go to collect their benefits. Each province usually has one or two additional local offices called *unidades de recaudación ejecutiva*, situated in the larger towns, where such transactions can take place.

6.4.3.5 Social Security Audit Corps (Intervención General de la Seguridad Social)

Since social security constitutes such an important element within the Spanish economy, the 1977 Budget Law (updated by the Law of 1988) set up a special body to regulate and control its expenditure. It operates within each of the three major social security management entities described above in order to secure proper financial management and control. Its officers prepare plans and reports on prospective expenditure, carry out analyses of budget estimates and expenditure, and co-ordinate accounting and auditing procedures throughout the system. In turn, this body is responsible to the State Audit Corps (*Intervención General del Estado / IGAE*) which, as part of the Ministry of Economy and Finance (13.2), exercises overall control over state spending through delegates and inspectors working over the whole range of public administration (9.9.2). The social security budget is subject to parliamentary control and the accounts are scrutinised by the Audit Tribunal (9.9.3).

6.4.4 Social services institutions

As already stated, responsibilities in this area were transferred in July 1988 from the Ministry of Labour and Social Security to the newly created Ministry of Social Services (*Ministerio de Asuntos Sociales / MAS*). This move, made in the opinion of many for political rather than administrative reasons, marked a reversal in the previous trend of the 1980s towards a more unified approach to all these public services. On the other hand, an opportunity was provided to strengthen an area, which may have lacked influence and which certainly needed some rationalisation, particularly in terms of its relations with the disparate private and voluntary groups also working in this field. However, in the reorganisation of ministries carried out by José María Aznar in May 1996, this Ministry was dissolved and its functions once more transferred to the Ministry of Labour.

As well as a general technical secretariat, this Ministry is composed of four directorates general (social services, social action, legal protection for minors, and migrant workers) and three institutes organised as autonomous bodies (women's affairs, youth affairs, and social services). One directorate and all three institutes are briefly examined below, most attention being paid to the social services institute, by far the largest institution within the Ministry.

6.4.4.1 National Institute for Social Services (Instituto Nacional de Servicios Sociales or INSERSO)

Like INSALUD and INSS, INSERSO is an autonomous body, or more exactly an *entidad gestora* originally established in November 1978, with its own legal identity, budget and other privileges of such bodies (6.3). It has a general council (*consejo general*) and an executive committee (*comisión ejecutiva*), the structures of which were laid down in the royal decree of 30 July 1979 and updated by the royal decree of 1 August 1985. Its director general reports directly to the minister. It was founded to complement the state's social security provision (6.4.3) with a range of social services, including: residential homes and day centres for the elderly; assistance for the disabled; assistance to refugees and those seeking asylum; non-contributory pensions and invalidity payments; creches for the 0–3 age group; and holidays for special groups, particularly the elderly. In recent years, the Institute has been especially active in support of the disabled (*minusválidos*); by the end of 1994, it had established 32 basic centres for the disabled (*centros base para los minusválidos*) (offering a wide range of assistance), four recovery centres for the physically disabled (*centros de recuperación de minusválidos físicos/CRMP*), five centres for the care of the physically disabled (*centros de atención a los minusválidos físicos/CAMF*) and fifty centres for the care of the mentally disabled (*centros de atención a los minusválidos psíquicos/CAMP*), including fourteen directly run by INSERSO and thirty-six run in collaboration with other (mainly regional) institutions. The Institute has also been co-operating in this field with a wide range of international agencies, including the OECD, and is currently participating in the EU scheme for the occupational professional training (*formación profesional ocupacional*) of the disabled, for which community funds are available to member countries via the European Social Fund (15.4.2.7).

Even when the MAS was a separate ministry under Felipe González, the budget for INSERSO still derived from the then Ministry of Labour and Social Security, reflecting the fact that the contributions (*cotizaciones*) of tax-payers still paid for the major part of these services. Under this ministry, services in this area have become more rationalised: agencies and autonomous bodies, like the former National Institute for Social Assistance (*Instituto Nacional de la Asistencia Social/INAS*) and the National Social Assistance Fund (*Fondo Nacional de Asistencia Social/FONAS*) have been disbanded and their activities incorporated within the work of either INSERSO or the Directorate General for Social Welfare (6.4.4.2). On the other hand, over recent years, a large percentage of the above services have been transferred to the new regional authorities; in terms of non-contributory pensions, for example, seven regions already manage these independently, while nine others do so in collaboration with the national office.

6.4.4.2 Directorate General for Social Welfare (Dirección General de Acción Social)

Like INSERSO, this body is now located within the Ministry of Labour and Social Affairs. Much of its work involves liaison and collaboration with other ministries, regional authorities and EU institutions in the provision of a wide range of programmes targeted towards specific groups. One unit deals exclusively with nongovernmental organisations (*organizaciones no gubernamentales/ONG*) and much of the Directorate's work involves assessing, for the purposes of granting special status, charities (*beneficencias*), such as the Spanish anti-Aids Foundation (*Fundación anti-SIDA Española/FASE*) or the Madrid-based employment generation foundation, *Creación de Empleo mediante la Promoción de Nuevas Empresas* (*CEPNE*). It is through this Directorate too that Spain participates in international special days, such as the international day of the family (*día internacional de la familia*) organised in 1993.

6.4.4.3 Institute for Women's Affairs (Instituto de la Mujer)

This institute was first set up by the PSOE government in the 1983 as one tangible expression of its commitment to promoting equal rights for women. Apart from organising a wide range of courses for women in Madrid and elsewhere, the Institute provides grants for research into women's affairs, assistance for publications in this field and attendance at training courses. Existing academic courses with a non-sexist orientation qualify for support from the Institute. A particular group that is targeted for assistance is single mothers. As might be expected, much of the Institute's work involves liaison and co-operation with non-governmental organisations. Moreover, it collaborates closely with a number of regional ministries (7.6.4) which seek its support for locally-based initiatives of the type described above.

6.4.4.4 Institute for Young People's Affairs (Instituto de la Juventud/INJUVE)

This institute, founded in the early 1990s, is another autonomous body (in this case of a commercial nature) (9.3) within this ministry, with a similar status and structure to others of its kind. Like the Institute for Women's Affairs, it is concerned with promoting equal rights for a particular social group. On the whole, it seems that most of its activities are of an academic and cultural kind; for example, it has recently been sponsoring an annual competition for young researchers (*certamen de jóvenes investigadores*) and an exhibition of young people's art (*muestra de arte joven*), as well as courses for the young on the environment (1994). One example of a more socially-oriented programme is that drawn up between the Ministry of Social Affairs, the *Generalitat* of Catalonia (7.1) the town hall of Cerdanyola del Vallés and the Autonomous University of Barcelona; this programme was designed to provide additional accommodation for students.

It should be noted that the treatment centres for drug addicts, many of them young people, is no longer carried out under the jurisdiction of this Ministry or that of Social Affairs but within a department of the Ministry of Home Affairs, called the Directorate General for the National Drugs Plan (*Dirección General del Plan Nacional sobre Drogas*).

6.5 Delegated state administration (*administración periférica del estado*)

6.5.1 Background and recent developments

The present pattern for the administration of the state has its origins in the reforms carried out at the beginning of the nineteenth century, when provinces were first established. These provinces (see figure 4.1, p. 47) were clearly envisaged as institutions for the administration of central government policy and not authentic organs of local government. For many generations, indeed right up to the end of the Franco era, central government delegated administrative but not political autonomy to bodies established at provincial level as part of what came to be called the *administración periférica del estado*. This whole operation was co-ordinated from the Ministry of Home Affairs, which had ultimate responsibility for what were the major institutions of delegated local government, the civil governors' offices (*gobiernos civiles*) and the town halls (*ayuntamientos*), the activities of which were tightly controlled from Madrid. In addition to these major institutions, each ministry in Madrid had its provincial offices (*delegaciones provinciales*), each endowed with its own bureaucracy.

As the process of devolving political power to the regions has developed in the post-Franco era, increasingly powerful arguments have developed for radically slimming down, if not for eliminating altogether, large parts of the *administración periférica*, particular in the case of those areas for which the regional governments have now assumed 'full' legislative, as well as executive and administrative responsibility. In recent years, it is true, administrators of the state have been transferred, along with corresponding financial resources, to the bureaucracies of the new autonomous communities (chapter 7). Moreover, following the law of 4 May 1983, in the case of the rapid-route autonomous communities (7.3.1) what remained of the provincial delegations of various ministries were incorporated into the civil governor's office of each province. Subsequently, in 1985, the *delegaciones provinciales* were incorporated into the newly created *Ministerio de Administraciones Públicas* (6.2.9) and renamed *direcciones provinciales*, each the responsibility of a *director general* answerable to the minister in Madrid.

None the less, the anticipated reduction in this delegated central administration has materialised only to a limited extent, in spite of the fact that over the last decade the process of decentralisation to the regions has gathered considerable momentum. Thus, to quote only two examples, as recently as 1994, there was a provincial transport director (*director provincial de transporte*) in all fifty provinces, as well as in Ceuta and Melilla – and this in spite of the fact that, within this ministerial area (Promotion), a considerable number of powers have already been transferred to the regional authorities, which themselves have *delegaciones* located in the provincial capitals (7.6.5).

During 1995, the Council of Ministers submitted to the *Cortes* the Law on the Organisation and Functioning of the General Administration of the State and its

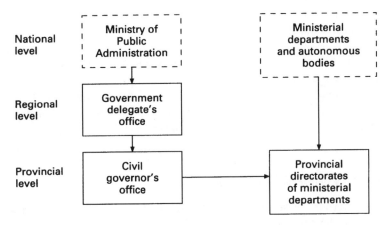

Figure 6.5 *Delegated central administration, 1995*

Public Bodies (*Ley de Organización y Funcionamiento de la Administración del Estado y de sus Organismos Públicos/LOFAGE*) which many had hoped would represent a radical restructuring of the *administración periférica*. In the event, this law has involved only tinkering with the roles of the government delegate (6.5.2) and the civil governor (6.5.3) and does not tackle the underlying issues of duplication and overlapping of functions, especially at provincial level.

An overview of the *administración periférica* is given in figure 6.5.

6.5.2 Government delegate (*delegado del gobierno*)

The figure of the government delegate is envisaged in article 154 of the Constitution, which states that 'he shall direct the administration of the state in the territory of the autonomous community and shall co-ordinate this with the administration of the community itself'. Under the LOFAGE (6.5.1), which slightly modifies his role as indicated in the Law of November 1983, the delegate is to be appointed by a decree of the Council of Ministers on the recommendation of the prime minister. The 1983 Law states that the government delegate, who is obliged to have his office in the same city as the regional seat of government, is the highest representative of the government in the autonomous community. In all official ceremonies, he takes precedence over other legal dignitaries, except if the president of the regional government is present (7.6.2). In his role as head of the state administration at regional level, he now exercises a three-fold role: firstly, he is in supreme charge of all the services of the central administration in his region; secondly, he has authority over the civil governors within the autonomous community (where these exist); and, thirdly, he is charged with co-ordinating the work of the state with that of the autonomous community concerned. A further minor modification introduced by the LOFAGE means that the corresponding *delegaciones del gobierno* are henceforth dependent, not on the Ministry of Home Affairs as hitherto, but on the Ministry of Public Administration. An important body which enables the delegate to carry out his function in this respect is the Co-ordinating Committee (*Comisión de Coordinación*) which he chairs and which is made up of all the civil governors in the region plus, when appropriate, the heads of all delegated services, i.e. the *directores provinciales*.

A small example of rationalisation has taken place in some of the larger autonomous communities; in Andalusia, for example, the government delegate, who is based in Seville, doubles up as the civil governor (6.5.3) for the province of Seville.

6.5.3 Civil governor (*gobernador civil*)

The civil governor, whose role was first defined as long ago as 1812, is the provincial equivalent of the government delegate and, therefore, the highest representative and executive of the state administration at provincial level. He is appointed by a decree of the Council of Ministers (5.5) on the recommendation of the ministers of home affairs and public administration 'on the initiative of the government delegate of each autonomous community'. An innovation of the LOFAGE, which updates the decree of October 1977 when his role was redefined, is that civil governors are henceforth to depend, not on the Ministry of Home Affairs as before, but on the government delegate. Thus, under the new legislation, the governor, who no longer depends directly on the central government, as was always traditionally the case, is seen as the provincial representative of the government delegate, as well as the chief administrative authority in the province. None the less, as in the Franco era, he continues, like the government delegate, to be a political appointee and there is normally a wholesale replacement of all civil governors when a government of a different party comes to power.

Basically, under the overall authority of the central government and the government delegate of the region, the civil governor is charged with the implementation of policies at provincial level for which the state is still responsible either fully or on a shared basis. His role is much more specific than that of the government delegate since for generations a whole provincial bureaucracy, the most important tier of the *administración periférica*, has been functioning under the control of the civil governor. Although this bureaucracy has been much reduced in recent years, as decentralisation has been implemented, the governor still retains a tight control over the elements that remain, working with his staff in the Office of the Civil Governor (*Gobierno Civil*). Since the decree of 1977 the *delegaciones provinciales* of central government, which used to depend on the ministries concerned, have been in theory brought within the ambit of the civil governor. In addition to overseeing the activities of the new *direcciones provinciales*, he has a number of specific functions, which traditionally were always part of his remit. These include what used to be called 'public order' and what under the 1978 Constitution is referred to as 'public safety' and the 'defence of citizens' rights and liberties'. Specifically, he is in charge of the state police and security forces that operate at provincial level. Related to this function, he plays a major role in cases of serious emergencies, such as large-scale fires, flooding, droughts and so on, which may affect the province. Another of his most important tasks is to make recommendations to central government about what he considers to be the investment requirements of the province in the public sector.

Like the government delegate, one of his major responsibilities is to ensure co-ordination at provincial level between the administration of the state and that of the local authorities, in particular the provincial council (8.4.1.1). In this respect, he is required to provide information and statistics that will help the local authorities function more efficiently, just as they are required to provide him with information about the functioning of local institutions.

Finally, it should be pointed out that, after 1977, in the single-province autonomous communities, all the powers of the civil governor were taken over by the government delegate. In these regions, therefore, the delegate assumed responsibility for more specific powers than his counterparts in the larger communities, since he must oversee the administration of the former delegations now absorbed into the *gobierno civil* (6.5.1), as well as taking on the commitments which were formerly the preserve of the civil governor of the province.

Following the agreements between the PP and CiU prior to the formation of Aznar's government in May 1996, it has been agreed that in the near future, following an act of Parliament, the post of civil governor will disappear. This office will become the assistant provincial delegate of the government (*subdelegado provincial del gobierno*) directly responsible to and appointed by the government delegate in the regional capital.

6.6 Comment

During the late 1970s and early 1980s the government and administration of the Spanish state underwent a profound transformation and, even at the time of writing (1995), the process is still not complete. As we saw in chapter 2, the impetus for such changes came from the new Constitution, which reflected a widespread desire for a new legal framework and a completely new set of principles for guiding public life. Democratisation, as well as embracing such notions as efficiency, communication and accountability, where without doubt some progress has been made, also enshrined the key concept of decentralisation, reflected in the creation of the autonomous communities. In this objective, too, a good deal has been achieved but, as will become clearer in chapter 7, certain difficulties remain. This is at least partly due to the fact that, in the constitutional and devolution processes, the final shape of the Spanish state was left an open question; if anything the constitution-makers opted for a model mid-way between a federal state, in which the communities would have sovereign institutions, and the centralised state which Franco bequeathed them. In practical terms, this has meant a certain duplication of responsibilities between central and regional authorities; at the regional level, the authorities are still hampered, to some extent, by the fact that they share certain powers with central government and, to a certain degree, are also subject to such watchdogs of Madrid as the government delegate and the civil governor.

A more rational restructuring of administration would seem to have demanded the disappearance of the civil governor and his dependencies which owe allegiance to the central government (at long last, this is soon to be implemented – ironically by the right-wing government of the PP). Moreover, the devolution process, while envisaging the elimination of many departments of the central administration as powers were progressively transferred to the regions, has in fact led not simply to the retention but even an expansion of departments in Madrid. This has been justified on the grounds of the need for co-ordination, but in reality reflects the desire to retain overall political control. Thus, it would seem that in Spain we have a classic case of Parkinson's Law which, if it spirals out of control could saddle the country with an impossibly expensive and oppressive bureaucracy; this could jeopardise the healthy evolution towards the freer, more democratic model of administration envisaged by the constitution-makers of 1978. This is the challenge now faced by the government of José María Aznar which has given a firm commitment to pruning the bureaucracy at all levels.

Chapter 7

Regional government and administration

7.1 Introduction

The political and administrative map of Spain is now radically different from what it was less than twenty years ago. Instead of a unitary state divided into some fifty provinces (figure 4.1, p. 47), the role of which was merely to administer the services of the central government, the country now has a semi-federal structure in which the powers of the state are shared with seventeen newly created autonomous communities (figure 7.1 and table 7.1), each endowed with its own president, parliament, executive and high court of justice. In the modern history of Spain, there is no precedent for such a major change in the structure of the state, nor for such a fundamental shift of power from the centre to the periphery.

The long and complex history of the tensions between the centre and the periphery in Spain falls outside the scope of this work and is well documented elsewhere. Suffice it to say here that, partly as a reaction to centuries of stifling centralism, culminating in the dictatorship of General Franco, and partly in response to deep-seated cultural differences – particularly manifest in the case of the Basques and the Catalans – the early post-Franco era witnessed considerable popular and official support for some form of decentralisation. This was conceived as an essential ingredient of the return to democracy. In the summer of 1977, following the UCD victory in the June elections of that year, Adolfo Suárez appointed a minister for the regions whose specific brief was to take some steam out of the clamour for regional autonomy and to negotiate provisional autonomy agreements with representatives of the regions.

Subsequently, between September 1977 when Catalonia's historic regional government, the *Generalitat*, was restored and the end of 1978, most of Spain's regions were endowed with institutions which, while enjoying only limited powers, represented an important symbolic first step on the road to self-government. The conversion of these provisional bodies into fully-fledged autonomous organs of government had to await the promulgation of the Constitution in December 1978.

7.2 Autonomy in the 1978 Constitution

During the sixteen-month constitutional debate, the autonomy issue was by far the most controversial. In some way a balance had to be struck between the fears of the parties of the Right that any reference to the nationalities of Spain represented a

1 País Vasco (Euskadi)
2 Cataluña (Catalunya)
3 Galicia
4 Andalucía
5 Principado de Asturias
6 Cantabria
7 La Rioja
8 Murcia
9 Comunidad Valenciana
10 Aragón

11 Castilla–La Mancha
12 Canarias
13 Navarra
14 Extremadura
15 Islas Baleares
16 Comunidad de Madrid
17 Castilla y León

Figure 7.1 *Autonomous communities of Spain: details of executive bodies, capitals and dates of Statute approval will be found in table 7.1, p. 119*

threat to national unity and the obvious preference of the Left for a federal-type solution. Certain parliamentarians were equally concerned that autonomy might be a disguise for mere administrative decentralisation, without any effective decision-making power being devolved to the regions. Many regionalists were unhappy about the distinction, drawn in article 2, between the 'nationalities' and the 'regions' of Spain, especially when transitional provision 2 of the Constitution suggested, although it did not actually state, that the former corresponded to the Basque Country, Catalonia and Galacia, which would be able to accede to full autonomy through an accelerated procedure.

Not surprisingly, the formula eventually agreed on was very much a compromise between the various political groups represented in Parliament, a compromise that

Table 7.1 *Autonomous communities of Spain*

Autonomous community	Executive body	Capital	Date Statute approved
País Vasco (Euskadi)	Gobierno Vasco (Eusko Jaularitza)	Vitoria	18.12.79
Cataluña (Catalunya)	Generalitat de Catalunya	Barcelona	18.12.79
Galicia	Junta de Galicia (Xunta de Galicia)	Santiago de Compostela	6.4.81
Andalucía	Junta de Andalucía	Sevilla	30.12.81
Principado de Asturias	Consejo de Gobierno de Asturias	Oviedo	30.12.81
Cantabria	Diputación Regional de Cantabria	Santander	30.12.81
País La Rioja	Consejo de Gobierno de la Rioja	Logroño	9.6.82
Murcia	Consejo de Gobierno de Murcia	Murcia	9.6.82
Comunidad Valenciana	Generalitat de Valencia	Valencia	1.7.82
Aragón	Diputación General de Aragón	Zaragoza	10.8.82
Castilla–La Mancha	Junta de Comunidades de Castilla–La Mancha	Toledo	10.8.82
Canarias	Gobierno de Canarias	Las Palmas	10.8.82
Navarra	Diputación Foral de Navarra	Pamplona	10.8.82
Extremadura	Junta de Extremadura	Mérida	25.2.83
Islas Baleares	Gobierno de la Comunidad de las Islas Baleares	Palma de Mallorca	25.2.83
Comunidad de Madrid	Consejo de Gobierno de Madrid	Madrid	25.2.83
Castilla y León	Junta de Castilla y León	Valladolid	25.2.83

Source: Own elaboration, based on *Anuario El País* (1982–84).

applied to both the procedure for attaining autonomy and the powers to be exercised by the new regional institutions. However, with the possible exception of the Basque Nationalists, who urged their electorate to abstain in the constitutional referendum, arguing that the pre-existence of Basque rights or *fueros* had not been expressly recognised, all major parties could accept the basic proposition of article 2. This states as follows:

> The Constitution is based on the indissoluble unity of the Spanish Nation, the common and indivisible motherland of all Spaniards, and recognises and guarantees the right to autonomy of the nationalities and regions of which it is composed and the common links that bind them together.

This basic principle is developed in considerable, if not always clear, detail in section VIII of the Constitution entitled, 'The Territorial Organisation of the State'. Article 143.1 spells out the territorial basis for the establishment of self-governing regions:

> Exercising the right to autonomy recognised in article 2 of the Constitution, adjoining provinces with common historical, cultural and economic characteristics, the islands and the provinces with a historical regional identity will be able to accede to self-government and form autonomous communities in accordance with the provisions of this section of the Constitution and of their respective statutes.

7.3 Three routes to autonomy

A consideration of the three routes to autonomy is relevant in that the method by which autonomy was obtained by any given region had an important bearing on the nature and extent of the self-government secured, and indeed continues to be a relevant factor in the ongoing devolution process. The eventual decision to provide three possible routes in fact represents part of the compromise reached in the course of the constitutional debate. At the heart of this issue were the claims of Basques and Catalans, and to some extent the Galicians and Andalusians, that, for historical and cultural reasons, they merited preferential status.

7.3.1 Rapid route (*transitional provision 2 of the Constitution*)

According to this provision, those regions which had in the past voted in a referendum in favour of autonomy would be permitted to proceed by a relatively simple process towards full autonomy. The already constituted pre-autonomous bodies would draw up a draft statute of autonomy which, following scrutiny by the Constitutional Committee of the Congress (2.1), would be submitted to a referendum in the regions concerned. The regions qualified to apply for autonomy via this route were: the Basque Country (*País Vasco* or *Euskadi*), Catalonia (*Cataluña* or *Catalunya*) and Galicia.

7.3.2 Slow route (*article 143*)

Initially, it was envisaged that, apart from the above three regions (the so-called 'historic nationalities'), this would be the normal route for all the regions in their progress towards autonomous status. This would involve a positive initiative on the part of all the provincial councils (8.4.1.1) and two-thirds at least of the municipal councils (8.3.2.1) in each region to set in motion the autonomy process. Subsequently, a statute of autonomy (*estatuto de autonomía*) would be drawn up by an assembly comprising members of the provincial councils, as well as deputies and senators elected in the provinces of the region concerned. This statute would be passed to the *Cortes* for approval as an organic law (4.7.1.1). When approved, the region would be able to assume responsibility for the limited areas of decision-making listed in article 148 of the Constitution. Only five years after the approval of its statute could a region proceed towards the full autonomy enjoyed from the outset by the historic nationalities. Since all the regions proceeding towards autonomy by this route did so between January 1982 and February 1983, no application to accede to full autonomy could be anticipated before January 1987.

7.3.3 Exceptional route (*article 151.1*)

During the constitutional debate, some regional representatives, particularly those from Andalusia, argued that the above two-tier arrangements made no provision for a region like Andalusia which, while not qualifying as a historic nationality, could still claim widespread popular support for full autonomy, as evidenced by mass demonstrations in its favour. A compromise solution was suggested involving an alternative route which, provided certain conditions were fulfilled, would allow such a region to follow an accelerated procedure towards full autonomy.

These conditions included the need for the initiative to be supported not only by all the provincial councils concerned but also by three-quarters of the municipal councils. To back this initiative, a popular referendum would have to be held and this would require the affirmative vote of an overall majority of the electoral roll in each province. Only when these steps had been taken could the region follow the procedure outlined in 7.3.2, and even then a second referendum was required to approve the actual text of the statute. Clearly there were political interests at work here determined to ensure that, at least in the short term, full autonomy was to be granted to no more than a privileged few. As we have seen, however, in the long term, all the regions would theoretically have the right to attain the same level of autonomy.

7.3.4 Navarre (*Navarra*)

This region merits special attention because of the unusual path which it has followed to autonomy. Navarre, an independent kingdom until the early sixteenth century when it was annexed by the joint Kingdom of Castile and Aragón, has subsequently enjoyed more autonomy than any other part of Spain, even surviving the centralising tendencies that occurred in the nineteenth century. Because it supported Franco in the Civil War, the region was able to retain its ancient rights (*fueros*), including the privilege, unique in Spain at that time, of being able to raise its own taxes. Culturally, the Navarrese of the north, many of whom speak Basque, feel a kinship with the three Basque Provinces to the west, while those of the south feel more affinity with Castile or simply prefer to retain their separate identity. For this reason, when other regions were deciding their future status within the new Spanish state, the people of Navarre found themselves deeply divided over whether to form their own autonomous community or join the community of the Basque Country. This dilemma is reflected in transitional provision 4 of the Constitution which offers the region the option of merging with the Basque Country at a later date should it so decide. This remains a long-term possibility. In the meantime, however, the political leaders of Navarre have negotiated with the state a pact which grants them autonomy, more or less along the lines of article 143, but includes their historic right to levy their own taxes. This pact culminated in the Organic Law on the Restoration and Development of the Autonomous Government of Navarre (*Ley Orgánica de Reintegración y Amejoramiento del Régimen Foral de Navarra*).

7.3.5 Ceuta and Melilla

Transitional provision 5 of the Constitution states that the cities of Ceuta and Melilla, former Spanish colonies on the coast of North Africa, may constitute themselves into autonomous communities if their local councils, by majority vote, should so decide. The *Cortes Generales* would then draw up and approve organic laws according to article 144, which allows Parliament to authorise the establishment of a community in territories which are not integrated into the normal local government structure. This procedure was in fact initiated as long ago as 1986, when draft statutes of autonomy in the form of organic laws were presented to the *Cortes*, but were not actually approved and promulgated until March 1995.

Up to this date, the two enclaves had simply enjoyed the status of municipal authorities. Now the status of both areas, which is virtually identical, is a hybrid between a municipal authority and an autonomous community of the slow-route variety (7.3.2). On the one hand, the institutions, albeit with different names, are similar to those of any *ayuntamiento* (8.3); the elections to the two assemblies take place at the same time and according to the same procedures as local elections elsewhere in Spain and, unlike the seventeen autonomous communities, there is no high court of justice (7.6.6 and 14.6.1). On the other hand, the very fact of having a statute of autonomy confers special status on them and this grants powers similar to those listed for other communities in article 148 of the Constitution (7.3.2). Moreover, in both cases, article 34 grant the cities financial autonomy and article 36.10, states that their revenue will include 'any other resources which may be attributed to the autonomous communities and local entities by state legislation and, through the general budgets of the state, [resources due] as a consequence of Spain's membership of the European Union'. Attached to each city too is the same rank of government watchdog – the government delegate (6.5.2) – as is the case with all seventeen autonomous communities.

7.4 Establishment of the autonomous communities

The first regions to attain autonomy under the 1978 Constitution were the Basque Country and Catalonia, where successful referendums were held in October 1979 and the statutes of autonomy of which were ratified in the *Cortes* by an organic law of December of that year. In March of the following year, elections were held to the Basque and Catalan Parliaments, as a result of which the first regional governments of the post-Franco era were sworn in. On the same day, a referendum was held in Galicia to approve that region's statute of autonomy. Elections, however, were not held until October 1981 when, simultaneously, the referendum to approve the Andalusian statute was held. The delay in holding these polls was partly due to the attempted *coup* of February 1981, which came close to destroying Spain's hard-won democracy (1.1.4).

A more significant effect of the *coup*, however, was that it strengthened the case of those who had been urging caution with regard to the autonomy process. The controversial Law on the Harmonisation of the Autonomy Process (*Ley Orgánica de Armonización del Proceso Autonómico/LOAPA*), one of four Agreements on Autonomy (*Acuerdos Autonómicos*) related to devolution approved in July 1981, was in essence a post-*coup* pact between the ruling UCD party and the opposition PSOE to ensure that the whole process was brought under tighter control. One of the major provisions of this law was that Andalusia was to be the first and the last region to accede to autonomy by the exceptional route; all the remaining regions would have to settle for the slow route laid down in article 143. As it happened, this did not present serious problems, since regional awareness and demands were undoubtedly less intense in the other regions, with the possible exception of Valencia and the Canary Islands. Thus, following the approval of their statutes of autonomy between late 1982 and early 1983, elections to the parliaments of the remaining thirteen regions took place in April 1983, simultaneously with the local elections scheduled for that period. By the summer of 1983, Spain's newly created autonomous communities, which would still have to wait a long time before the powers they had inherited were officially devolved to them, could at least see their new institutions in place and beginning to function. A whole new tier of government and administration was slowly being created.

It should be pointed out that, in the case of the six single-province communities that emerged in the course of this process, the provincial tier of government merged with the institutions of the new autonomous communities. Thus, for example, the *Diputación Foral de Navarra*, formerly a provincial level body, was upgraded to a regional level institution. The six regions concerned are: Asturias, Cantabria, La Rioja, Madrid, Murcia and Navarre.

7.5 Nature and implications of autonomy

'Autonomy' is not the easiest term to define and has a variety of different senses. In the Spanish case, however, whatever the limitations of the new decentralised structure and whatever state control over regional institutions still exists, autonomy is undoubtedly of a political nature. A serious attempt has been made to create alternative region-based centres of political power which, while in the last resort subservient to the central power, enjoy a generous degree of freedom to run their own affairs. It is generally accepted that political autonomy consists of a capacity to take decisions and to implement them on the basis of adequate resources. For it to be effective, political autonomy must include statutory, legislative and, above all, at least some financial autonomy. These three aspects will now be examined separately.

7.5.1 Statutory autonomy

All seventeen autonomous communities are now subject not only to the Constitution but also to their own statutes of autonomy which govern all aspects of political life at regional level. In effect, they constitute regional constitutions. Having been approved in the *Cortes* as organic laws (4.7.1.1), they can only be amended by an overall majority in both Houses of Parliament and only after a complicated procedure can they be overruled by Madrid. At the simplest level, a statute enables a region to organise its own institutions of self-government and establish the parameters of its own particular relationship with the central authorities.

It is interesting to note that, although the statutes have many features in common, because each is the result of a long process of political negotiation, they all have individual features which reflect their own special relationship with Madrid. The Basque Statute, as we shall see (7.5.3.7), enshrines the restoration of the economic agreements (*conciertos económicos*), involving certain tax-raising privileges, while the Catalan Statute grants the region considerable freedom in matters related to education, culture and language. As we have already seen (7.3.4), the Navarrese Statute (or *Fuero*) is also in many ways unique.

7.5.2 Legislative autonomy

In common with federal systems, with which the new structure of the state has much in common, the autonomous communities, endowed with their own legislatures, have the right to draw up and approve laws, as well as the right to execute and administer them either directly or through the provincial delegations (7.6.5). As we shall see, the areas of competence in which a community can legislate depend on the level of autonomy achieved, at least in the short term, and on the content of a given statute. Whatever their limitations, however, the regional parliaments had all begun to function by the summer of 1983, and subsequently, in each case, a large corpus of legislation has been approved and published in the regional equivalents of the *Official State Gazette*, such as the *Official Gazette of the Junta de Andalucía* (*Boletín Oficial de la Junta de Andalucía / BOJA*).

7.5.3 Financial autonomy

7.5.3.1 Sources of revenue

Authentic autonomy clearly implies control over financial resources. Article 156 of the Constitution, in fact, recognises the right of the autonomous communities to financial autonomy and this is guaranteed in the statutes of autonomy. From the outset, regional governments have been granted considerable freedom in the spending of revenue and in drawing up their own budgets but have been subjected to strict limitations with regard to the levying of their own taxes or to the sharing in taxes levied by the state. The state retains overall responsibility for taxation which, in line with the principles of solidarity and equality, must ensure an equal tax burden right across the country. None the less, over the last decade, the regional governments have become responsible for increasingly large budgets (that for Andalusia alone in 1995 was 1,905,488.2 million pesetas), and they manage substantial human, material and financial resources. The sources of these fall basically into three categories: regional resources; payments and grants from central government; and grants from the four funds of the European Union (table 7.2). Following an examination of the major law and institution governing the funding of autonomous communities, these sources will be looked at separately below.

Table 7.2 *Sources of revenue for autonomous communities, 1995*

Central government funds
1 For services transferred
2 For autonomous bodies
3 From the Inter-regional Compensation Fund (FCI)
4 Retention of certain taxes:
  • Personal income tax (*impuesto sobre la renta de las personas físicas/IRPF*) per cent
  • Inheritance tax (*impuesto sobre sucesiones*)
  • Wealth tax (*impuesto sobre el patrimonio*)
  • Capital transfer tax (*impuesto de transmisones patrimoniales*)
  • Luxury tax (*impuesto sobre el lujo*)
  • Gaming duties (*derechos de juego*)

Own sources
1 Taxes (*impuesto, tributos*) on property, products and activities
2 Charges (*tasas*) for services ranging from publications to health services
3 Surcharges (*recargos*) over and above state taxes
4 Borrowing: short-term, from banks; long-term, through issue of bonds
5 Investments and industrial, commercial and agricultural services
6 Others, such as fines (*multas*), donations (*donativos*) and legacies (*legados*)

Source: Data supplied by Subdirección General de Cooperación Bilateral, Ministerio de Administraciones Públicas (1996).

7.5.3.2 Organic Law on the Funding of Autonomous Communities (Ley Orgánica de Financiación de las Comunidades Autónomas/LOFCA)

This Law, foreshadowed in article 157.3 of the Constitution and approved in September 1980, details the financial arrangements and mechanisms to be applied to the funding of the autonomous communities (only two of which, of course, had been established at that time). The LOFCA set up the special Council for the Fiscal and Financial Policy (*Consejo de Política Fiscal y Financiera*), composed of the state minister for economy and finance, his counterpart in each region and the minister for territorial administration (now the minister of public administration). This is a consultative body which, as well as providing an intergovernmental forum for debate, concerns itself with the co-ordination of policy with particular regard to the distribution of state resources to the regions, as well as to public investment, the costs of services and public debt.

From the outset, it was recognised that, while the long and complicated process of devolving powers to the regions was being carried out, transitional arrangements would have to be put in place. Thus, for the period 1980–86, in the case of all the communities except the Basque Country and Navarre (7.5.3.7), the state guaranteed to cover the cost of services to be transferred, a fixed quota being paid out of the annual state budgets (*presupuestos generales del estado*). The annual share of the budget due to each region was worked out in proportion to the services transferred, as well as to the tax income (always a relatively small amount) which the regions were allowed to retain. At a later stage, in relation to share in state revenue (*participación en los ingresos del estado*), a more refined formula would be used taking into account

Table 7.3 *Decentralisation of public spending by tier of administration, percentage of total expenditure, 1980–94*

	1980	1982	1984	1986	1988	1990	1992	1994
Central administration	89.95	84.57	75.65	72.62	67.29	65.78	64.27	65.40
Regional administration	—	6.08	12.20	14.60	19.34	20.21	22.35	22.69
Local administration	10.05	9.35	12.15	12.78	13.37	14.01	13.38	11.91

Source: Informe Económico–Financiero de las Administraciones Territoriales en 1993, Ministerio para las Administraciones Públicas (1994).

such variables as population (by far the most important factor), land area, administrative units, dispersal of the population, relative poverty, fiscal pressure and insularity. For calculation purposes, state income, known as 'structurally adjusted state tax revenue (*ingresos tributarios del estado ajustados estructuralmente/ITAE*), includes direct and indirect taxation, as well as social security and unemployment contributions.

Already by 1985 more than 50 per cent of the state's education budget had been transferred to the autonomous communities and by the same date nine regions had been given the right to retain the taxes referred to in table 7.2. In addition, financial resources were transferred in relation to the specific services of the numerous autonomous bodies referred to in chapters 6–9, which included the budgets of the health and social security organisations, INSALUD (6.4.2.1) and INSERSO (6.4.4.1).

By the time the Council for Fiscal and Financial Policy produced the Agreement (*Acuerdo*) of November 1986 to cover the five-year period 1986–91, there had been a considerable advance towards the goal of achieving a ratio of public sector spending as between the state, the regions and the local authorities of 50:25:25. As can be seen in table 7.3, at the time of writing (1995), the ratio for the regions has come close to its target (approx. 23 per cent), though falls well short as far as the local authorities are concerned.

On 7 October 1993, the Council (consisting of central administration officials and the economy ministers of all the autonomous communities) produced another set of *Acuerdos* to cover the period 1992–96. The first and most far-reaching of these refers to the procedure for the application of joint tax responsibility (*corresponsabilidad fiscal*), already alluded to in the autonomy agreements of 1992 (7.7.5.2). Under this agreement, the group of fifteen autonomous communities were granted access, for the first time, to a fixed percentage (in most cases to be 15 per cent) of personal income tax (*impuesto sobre la renta de las personas físicas/IRPF*) generated at regional level. Pressure for this concession had come, not surprisingly, from the richer areas like Catalonia which stood to benefit most, while the strongest opposition came from the poorer areas like Extremadura and Galicia, which both voted against the proposal in the Council. For two years (1993–95), the Socialist government was dependent on the parliamentary support of the Catalan Nationalist Party, the CiU (10.4.5), and thus tended to concur with the views of forceful Catalan leaders like the regional president, Jordi Pujol. At all events, in spite of great reluctance in some regions, including Andalusia, from 1994 steps were taken to implement the new arrangements. A further development came in this area when, following the election victory in March 1996 of José María Aznar and his need to look to nationalists and regionalists for support (1.1.5), the PP government agreed, under pressure from the Catalan president to increase the percentage of income tax retained by the regions from 15 to 30, again with greater benefits for richer regions like Catalonia.

A further *Acuerdo* reached by the Council in 1993 – very much in line with the stress on harmonisation and solidarity in the 1992 autonomy agreements (7.7.5.2) – refers to the state's duty to ensure a minimum level of public services across the country. Hitherto, the experts involved have not reported, but it is clearly a matter which will exercise both national and regional politicians in the coming months.

7.5.3.3 Regional resources

Article 157 1 of the Constitution states that the regions can call on their own regional resources as part of their overall revenue. The range of possibilities is given in table 7.2 – though, in the case of some 'slow-route' regions, the right to levy certain taxes was not granted for several years. It should also be noted that so far no region has undertaken to impose a surcharge (*recargo*) on top of any state taxes – no doubt for fear of courting unpopularity at the polls. Borrowing, allowed from the outset, is certainly a facility which many regions have used in recent years; indeed, some, like central government itself, have incurred an alarming level of indebtedness (*endeudamiento*), notably Andalusia, Catalonia and Valencia – a development that does not augur well for a Madrid that is so anxious to be a front-runner in the quest for European convergence under the Treaty of Maastricht (15.1).

It should also be stressed that regional resources constitute a small percentage of total revenue for any of the fifteen autonomous communities (in the case of Andalusia in 1995 it was only 8.2 per cent). The fact is that, whatever autonomy regions have in terms of budget preparation and spending, their own local resources are still very limited. The bulk of revenue comes from central government, either via the shares in state taxes already mentioned or via certain special funds which will now be examined.

7.5.3.4 Inter-regional Compensation Fund (Fondo de Compensación Interterritorial/FCI)

This special fund was first envisaged in article 157.1c of the Constitution. Its aim was to correct imbalances between the regions by means of positive discrimination in favour of the less developed areas. The fund only came into being, however, with the Law of March 1984, the year after all seventeen autonomous communities had begun to function fully. According to this Law, a minimum of 30 per cent of the amount designated by the state for new public investment was to be channelled to the regions in accordance with a needs formula based on population density and other social and economic criteria. Initially, the FCI seemed to work, as intended, in favour of the poorer regions; for example, in 1985, Andalusia and Galicia received by far the highest proportion of the fund, 27 and 10 per cent respectively. Subsequently, however, the fund tended to operate to the benefit of the more developed areas; this was largely because not only was it being used for corrective purposes but also as a vehicle for covering the funding of services that were being progressively transferred as part of the autonomy process (more, of course, in the case of the rapid-route autonomies).

A further development of the mid-1980s was, of course, Spain's entry into the European Community. By 1990, a need was felt to develop a coherent investment policy in line with that of the European Community and to view the FCI and the European Regional Development Fund (ERDF) as complementary initiatives for promoting the development of backward areas. Specifically, formulae for the allocation of resources under the FCI were to be largely harmonised with those of the ERDF (15.4.2.2).

Thus, responding to the need for reform on both the above counts, the 1984 legislation was replaced by the Law of December 1990, whose avowed aim was to end the dualism referred to above and refocus the fund on its original redistributive purpose. In this process, help would be targeted to specific, poorer regions; in 1990 and 1991, for instance, the Law stipulated that the regions benefiting would be: Andalusia, Asturias, the Canaries, the two Castiles, Extremadura, Murcia and Valencia. (Special provision, it was recognised, would have to be made for Aragón, which includes the disadvantaged province of Teruel.) Subsequently, the regions to benefit would be listed in the annual state budget law (4.7.3.1). In 1993, in addition to the above-mentoned regions, Cantabria was also able to benefit from the fund. By this stage, it is also worth noting that the percentage set for the period of operation 1992–96 was 35 per cent, giving a further boost to the redistributive effect for the FCI.

Thus, in line with the criteria applied by the ERDF, the new Law amended the original formulae, giving a much higher priority to 'relative population' (density as compared to the average for all the autonomous communities) (87.5 per cent, in fact), while also including other factors such as relative income, level of unemployment, level of migration, population dispersal and insularity. The 1984 Law was also reformed in another sense, i.e. allowing the fund to finance not only real investment but transfers of capital, thus enabling co-ordination to take place with allocations received via the ERDF. The Law also streamlined and rationalised budgetary and auditing arrangements as between the central government and the autonomous communities relative to the fund.

7.5.3.5 Other forms of state aid

In addition to the FCI, since 1987, the state has been channelling aid to the regions relating to specific projects. One of these is the Regional Incentives Programme

(*Programa de Incentivos Regionales*) which is administered by the Ministry of Economy and Finance. In 1993, this scheme funded 424 projects all over Spain, with a total input of 29,193 million pesetas, representing an average subvention per project of 16 per cent, and creating over 8,600 new jobs. The regions to have benefited most from the scheme were Castile–León (116 projects), Andalusia (34), Valencia (32) and Castile–La Mancha (31).

In addition, central government provides matching funding for specific projects under the headings 'agreements' (*convenios*) and 'contract-programmes' (*contrato-programas*), the latter directed exclusively to projects relating to public transport. In 1993, the number of *convenios* signed was 231, amounting to 148,138 million pesetas; the regions to benefit most under this heading were (in order) Catalonia, the region of Madrid and Andalusia. The contract-programmes were worth 43,275 million pesetas and the main regional beneficiaries were Madrid, Catalonia, Valencia and the Canaries. Moreover, the state provided additional grants worth 187,782 million pesetas via specific ministries, of which by far the largest contributor was the Ministry of Labour and Social Affairs (6.4.3) with welfare allowances (*pensiones asistenciales*); the regions to gain most under this head were Andalusia (32 per cent), Catalonia, Galicia and Valencia.

7.5.3.6 European Union (EU) aid

A major change that has occurred in regional funding since 1986 has been the availability of EU money, notably from the ERDF, which in Spain is known as the *Fondo Europeo de Desarrollo Regional* (*FEDER*) (15.4.2.2), which has played a vital part in helping to update and modernise regional infrastructures. Help for employment and training has come via the European Social Fund (*Fondo Social Europeo/FSE*) (15.4.2.3) and assistance for agriculture and fishing has come from the guidance (*orientación*) section of the European Agricultural Guidance and Guarantee Fund (*Fondo Europeo de Orientación y Garantía Agrícolas/FEOGA*) (15.4.2.4). In addition to the above three structural funds (*fondos estructurales*), from 1993 the regions were also able to receive support for projects relating to the environment and transport infrastructure from the Cohesion Fund (*Fondo de Cohesión*) (15.5.3). Originally, all such monies from the three main funds were channelled to the regional authorities via the appropriate ministries and agencies of central government, and rather than in block grants aid came in the form of subventions tied to specific programmes. From 1994–95, however, regions were able to sign Community Support Framework agreements, known in Spanish as *Marcos Comunitarios de Apoyo* (*MCA*), with the European Union for periods of five years, thus allowing opportunities for greater long-term planning. Table 7.4 shows the agreement signed for the period 1994–99 with the *Junta de Andalucía*, which in total will receive 180,000 million pesetas per year over this period, representing 27.2 per cent of all EU money coming into Spain via these three funds.

Table 7.4 *Community support framework for Andalusia, EU grants and regional contribution, 1994*

	Grant from EU fund	Regional contribution
European Regional Development Fund (ERDF)	4,719,267	7,570,963
European Agricultural Guidance and Guarantee Fund (EAGGF)	606,521	836,581
European Social Fund (ESF)	1,315,271	1,814,168
Fund for Restructuring of Fishing	229,000	305,334
Totals	*6,870,059*	*10,527,046*

Source: Cinco Días – Special Report on Andalusia (23 December 1994).

7.5.3.7 Basque Country and Navarre

While fifteen of the autonomous communities rely largely on the state to transfer funds in their direction, the Basque Country and Navarre (7.3.4) enjoy the benefits of their historic rights (*fueros*). Two special economic agreements, the *concierto económico* for the Basque Country and the *convenio económico* for Navarre, grant the three Basque provinces of Alava, Guipúzcoa and Vizcaya, and the single province of Navarre, the right to levy and collect all taxes, except customs duties and the taxes on petroleum products and tobacco. These rights have to be exercised in conformity with the general state system of taxation, using the same terminology, criteria and classification of activities. The same rate of taxation has to be used as that imposed by the state in the case of personal income tax, company tax and VAT (known in Spain as *IVA*). While there is some flexibility allowed with the remaining taxes, the overall tax level cannot be lower than the state level.

From the income which is derived from taxation, the authorities in the Basque Country and Navarre have to deduct an annual quota (*cupo*) to be paid to the state in respect of those services and powers which the latter retains. This quota is agreed for a five-year period, but is subject to annual adjustment to take account of inflation.

Full details of all tax revenues have to be submitted to the Ministry of Economy and Finance in Madrid in order to enable the overall co-ordination of the fiscal system to take place. Furthermore, the accounts of these two communities, together with those of the other fifteen, are subject to scrutiny by the Audit Tribunal (9.9.3).

7.6 Institutions of autonomy

Article 152 of the Constitution lays down that in statutes of autonomy approved under the rapid-route system (that is, the four regions which first gained full autonomy), the institutions of the autonomous community will be: a legislative assembly or parliament, an executive or governing council, a president and a high court of justice (figure 7.2). Interestingly, in the case of the slow-route autonomous regions, no institutions are specified, and article 147 merely states that their statutes should

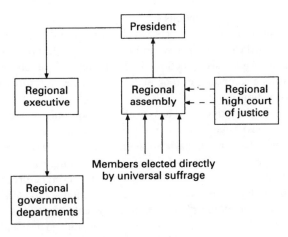

Figure 7.2 *Regional institutions*

contain 'the titles, structure and location of the autonomous institutions'. However, the texts of the four Agreements on Autonomy signed in 1981, including the LOAPA (7.4), assumed that all autonomous regions would have the same institutional structure, and in practice this has been the case. To a very great extent, these institutions are a regional reflection of national institutions and, like the latter, they must be organised along democratic lines. The institutions of an autonomous community are shown in figure 7.2.

7.6.1 Regional assembly (*asamblea regional*)

Except for the fact that it is composed of a single chamber, each regional assembly or parliament is more or less a mirror-image of the Madrid Congress. As with the latter, its members, known as deputies (*diputados*), are elected by universal, free, direct, equal and secret suffrage in accordance with the same system of proportional representation and seat allocation as operates for the general elections (4.3.1). Thus, the number of seats contested may vary between 135 for densely populated Catalonia to thirty-three for thinly populated La Rioja. The constituency in multi-provincial regions is the province, while the single-province regions operate as one constituency, unless the major parties (i.e. those represented in the Madrid Parliament) agree unanimously to adopt a different system, for example, one based on districts (*comarcas*) (8.5.2).

The normal life-span of the assembly is four years, after which elections must be held. The dates for these elections are fixed well in advance by the central government which since 1983 has opted for holding regional elections for article 143 autonomies at the same time as local elections.

Since the first elections in Andalusia, the Basque Country, Catalonia and Galicia took place on different dates, indeed in different years, these are likely to remain spaced out in the future, although there is nothing to stop the government deciding to make general elections or European elections coincide with one of these dates; for example, the general election of 1986 coincided with the Andalusian regional elections in 1986 and the European elections were held on the same day as the Andalusian elections in 1994. Since the first elections for the remaining thirteen communities took place on one date, in future these will all be held at the same time.

The internal organisation of each Assembly is also similar to that of the Madrid Congress and is enshrined in a *reglamento* similar to that drawn up for the Lower House in Madrid. Each has its own president, who controls the everyday running of the assembly; in this task he is helped by the presiding council (*mesa*) consisting of himself, often one or two vice-presidents and several secretaries, as well as a team of *letrados*. Each has established a standing council (*diputación permanente*) which looks after the affairs of the regional assembly when it is not in session. Moreover, each assembly has created its own bureaucracy to deal with a wide range of issues from relations with the regional executive to publications and public relations.

As in Madrid, the regional assembly works through plenary sittings (*plenos*) and committees (*comisiones*) and its ordinary working sessions are from September to December and from February to June. Extraordinary sessions can be called by the president at the request of the standing council, a fifth of the deputies or a specific number of parliamentary groups, or by the regional executive itself.

The powers and functions of the regional assembly are clearly laid down in the appropriate statute of autonomy. It has the right not only to draw up regional laws but to submit them to a vote and approve them without reference to Madrid. The procedure for initiating and approving legislation is very similar to that operating at the national level; the majority of draft laws (*proyectos de ley*) emanate from the executive. As well as these legislative powers, the assembly exercises a function of control, both economic and political, over the executive, which is thus made accountable to it. In addition, as we shall see, one of the important functions of the assembly is the right to nominate the president of the autonomous community concerned. The assembly also enjoys two further powers: first, the right to present bills (*proposiciones de ley*) to the national Congress (4.7.2) and, second, the right to present appeals (*recursos de anticonstitucionalidad*) to the Constitutional Court where it considers that there has been an infringement of the Constitution affecting the rights of the autonomous institutions (2.5.2.1).

7.6.2 President (*presidente*)

The president of the autonomous community, who is also the president of the regional executive, is designated by the regional assembly from among its members and appointed by the king. In practice, of course, what happens is that the leader of the majority party or coalition is elected following the presentation of his programme to parliament and a vote of investiture, as in Madrid. Essentially, the president has three functions:

(i)   He is the symbolic head of the region and as such he represents the community in its relations with the monarch, the government in Madrid and foreign dignitaries.

(ii) He is head of the regional executive (7.6.3); in this prime ministerial capacity, in collaboration with his ministers (*consejeros*), he has the responsibility for taking the important political decisions affecting the community as well as the obligation to ensure that official policy is translated into effective action. In this capacity, like his counterpart at national level, he is the titular head of both the regional executive and administration.

(iii) The president nominates and dismisses the members of the regional executive. He may appoint as his vice-president one of his ministers in charge of a particular department or a political colleague with no ministerial responsibility. The vice-president can assume powers delegated to him temporarily or permanently by the president and stands in for him when the latter is ill or absent.

Leaving aside the judicial aspects, the president can normally only be dismissed if he loses the confidence of the regional assembly. This can only be demonstrated by a constructive motion of censure presented to the assembly by the opposition, which must include the name of an alternative president. If the motion is approved, by an overall majority, this candidate is automatically sworn in as the new president of the autonomous community.

7.6.3 Regional executive (*consejo de gobierno*)

The regional executive consists of the president, the vice-president(s), where relevant, and the ministers, who collectively perform all the executive and administrative functions of the autonomous community. It is always accountable to the assembly, of which the president and his ministers are invariably members. The Constitution does not lay down how these ministers are to be appointed; while the normal procedure is for the president to name his ministers, usually from elected regional deputies, it is theoretically possible for the regional assembly itself to assume this responsibility. Like their counterparts at national level, these ministers are individually accountable to the president for the performance of their own ministries and collectively responsible to the regional assembly for the overall policies of the regional executive. Unlike the regional deputies, they receive a fixed salary plus expenses. Although the rank of regional deputy is obviously compatible with that of *consejero*, the latter is not allowed to hold office in any other branch of public administration. Like its counterpart at national level, the regional executive normally meets once a week under the chairmanship of the president. As well as approving draft laws to be sent to the assembly, one of its major functions is to issue decrees (*decretos*) and resolutions (*resoluciones*) which do not require the approval of the assembly. Likewise, the ministers themselves are authorised to issue orders (*órdenes*) over relatively minor matters relating specifically to their own

Table 7.5 *Composition of the Junta de Andalucía, 1996*

Regional Ministry of	Consejería de
Agricultural and Fishing	*Agricultura y Pesca*
Culture	*Cultura*
Economy and Finance	*Economía y Hacienda*
Education and Science	*Educación y Ciencia*
Home Affairs	*Gobernación*
Environment	*Medio Ambiente*
Public Works and Transport	*Obras Públicas y Transportes*
Presidency	*Presidencia*
Relations with Parliament	*Relaciones con el Parlamento*
Health	*Salud*
Labour and Industry	*Trabajo e Industria*
Tourism and Sport	*Turismo y Deportes*

Source: Agenda de la Comunicación, Junta de Andalucía, 1996

departments. Table 7.5 shows the composition of the government of the *Junta de Andalucía*.

7.6.4 Regional ministries (*consejerías*)

For economic reasons, the 1981 Agreements on Autonomy laid down that, at least in the case of the slow-route autonomous regions, no more than ten ministries would be allowed in each autonomous community. Neither the Constitution nor the statutes of autonomy specify which ministries are to be created in each region, and in fact in each case it has been left to the regional executive to decide on the structure of public administration. Thus, as can be seen from the example of the *Junta de Andalucía* (table 7.5), functions that at the national level are separate, have been combined.

In Aragón, the Basque Country and Navarre, the *consejerías* are known as *departamentos* (*departaments* in Catalonia) and in Valencia they are called *consellerias*. Within the various regional ministries, however, the internal structure is very similar and, to a large extent, reproduces the national pattern, with undersecretaries, director generals, and so on. It is interesting to note that article 4.2.5 of the first of the Agreements on Autonomy states emphatically that 'in the autonomous communities there will be no more staff appointed other than those strictly necessary for the immediate support of the political bodies concerned'. Article 4.2.5 goes on to stress that posts below and including the level of director general will be filled from among the ranks of professional civil servants. In spite of this stricture, however, political appointments have undoubtedly been made at these levels and, moreover, regional bureaucracies have tended to expand as regional governments, savouring political power for the first time, have seemed to vie with each other in creating a whole series of official and autonomous bodies dependent, to a greater or lesser extent, on the department of regional administration. The

Table 7.6 *Autonomous administrative bodies of the Junta de Andalucía, 1995*

Regional Ministry responsible	Name in English	Name in Spanish
Agriculture and Fishing	Andalusian Institute for Agrarian Reform	*Instituto Andaluz de Reforma Agraria (IARA)*
Culture	Andalusian Flamenco Centre	*Centro Andaluz de Flamenco*
Economy and Finance	Andalusian Institute of Statistics	*Instituto Andaluz de Estadística*
Education and Science	Andalusian Institute of Criminology	*Instituto Andaluz de Criminología*
Home Affairs	Andalusian Institute of Public Administration	*Instituto Andaluz de Administración Pública*
Labour and Industry	Andalusian Council for Consumer Affairs	*Consejo Andaluz de Consumo*
Environment	Andalusian Forestry Council	*Consejo Forestal Andaluz*
Public Works and Transport	Andalusian Cartography Institute	*Instituto Andaluz de Cartografía*
Presidency	Andalusian Institute for Women's Affairs	*Instituto Andaluz de la Mujer*
Health	Andalusian Health Service	*Servicio Andaluz de Salud (SAS)*
Labour and Industry	Andalusian Labour Relations Council	*Consejo Andaluz de Relaciones Laborales (CARL)*

Source: Agenda de la Comunicación, Junta de Andalucía (1995).

Junta de Andalucía, in fact, provides an illustrative example of the profusion of *organismos autónomos* operating in one region. The eleven listed in table 7.6 represent only a small proportion of the total number attached to the *Junta*; in addition, as we shall see in 9.6, this government, like other regional governments, has not been slow to emulate Madrid in the creation of a whole range of other autonomous bodies and public sector enterprises.

7.6.5 Delegated regional administration

In the eleven multi-province autonomous communities, each *consejería* is represented at provincial level in an office located in the provincial capital. These *delegaciones* are in some instances scattered in different buildings throughout the city concerned or, in some cases (for example, Málaga) have nearly all been brought together in purpose-built premises.

Each *delegación* is a mirror-image of the *consejería* at regional level, normally consisting of the same number of directorates general. In an ideal world, these *delegaciones* should have taken the place of their counterparts serving the *administración periférica* (6.5), but in practice most of these continue to function alongside the new regional bodies.

As their name implies, these *delegaciones*, which have no legislative or executive powers, are purely administrative agencies which serve to carry out regional policy at provincial level on the basis of budgets delegated to them. None the less, the *delegados* are important figures within the structure of regional government. They are likely to represent the regional government on co-ordinating bodies, such as tourist boards (*patronatos de turismo*) set up at provincial level. The most important of these *delegados* is the one in charge of home affairs (*delegado de gobernación*), since he acts as the representative for the whole group of *delegados* in any one provincial capital – for example, when there needs to be consultation between representatives of regional and local (provincial) government.

7.6.6 High Court of Justice (*Tribunal Superior de Justicia*)

While these courts have been established in all seventeen autonomous communities and are expressly referred to in each of the statutes of autonomy, they are more properly viewed as part of the indivisible, nation-wide structure of justice, which is an area of government that cannot be devolved to the regions. Hence, this institution is dealt with in more detail in 14.6.1.

7.7 Powers of autonomous communities

It is in the key area of powers (*competencias*) devolved to the autonomous communities that we see most clearly where contemporary Spain, at least for the moment, seems to differ from the classical federal state. In the latter, the regions tend from the outset to assume control over a clearly defined area and inherit clearly structured institutions. In Spain, however, not only was each region free to decide whether or not to request autonomous status, but it was able to some extent to decide on the level of autonomy required and, where applicable, the time-scale of progression to full autonomy.

According to the Constitution, the extent of powers initially granted to the communities depended on the route by which autonomy was achieved. Basically the slow-route autonomous communities assumed control over a minimum number of areas listed in article 148 of the Constitution. In reality, these included little more than one might expect of a local authority in a fairly centralised state like the United Kingdom. As we have seen (7.3.2), these thirteen areas were expected to wait at least until 1987 before they could advance to full autonomy. However, the Constitution failed to make clear what extra powers would be granted at that time and what the limits to autonomy (*techos autonómicos*) would be. In the case of the four rapid-route autonomous regions, experience in fact showed that the nature and extent of these powers could vary quite significantly from one region to another. This is partly because the particular demands and requirements of one region differed (and indeed still differ) considerably. It is also related to the imprecise wording of article 148.2 of the Constitution which stated that 'after five years and following reform of their statutes, these autonomous communities will be able progressively to extend their powers within the framework of article 149', but gave no indication what these new powers would be.

Yet article 149 lists what are called the 'exclusive powers of the state', which include such areas of competence as foreign affairs, defence, customs and international affairs, areas which even under a federal system would never be devolved to a regional authority. Clearly, regional authorities could only assume responsibility for some of the powers listed in article 149, although which fell within this category and which did not was far from clear.

7.7.1 Exclusive powers of the autonomous communities

Article 148 of the Constitution lists a series of powers to which slow-route regions could initially accede. These included: the organisation of their own institutions of self-government; town planning; housing; public works; forestry; environmental protection; museums; libraries; cultural affairs; the regional language (where applicable); tourism; sport and leisure; social welfare; health and hygiene; and non-commercial ports and airports.

7.7.2 Shared powers

By implication rather than prescription, articles 148 and 149 also indicate a number of areas in which power is shared between the national and regional institutions. These include: agriculture and cattle-rearing, which must be organised 'according to the overall structuring of the economy', the encouragement of economic development, which must be carried out 'within the objectives laid down by national economic policy', and the maintenance of historic buildings. In fact, such shared powers refer to areas over which, in the last analysis, the state claims ultimate sovereignty. Authority to share these powers is granted by way of basic legislation (4.7.1.5).

7.7.3 'Devolvable' powers

As we have seen, the so-called 'exclusive powers of the state' are indicated in article 149 of the Constitution. However, it is precisely by way of this list that a slow-route region is authorised, should it so wish, to extend its powers in the future: it would then enjoy these powers in common with the rapid-route communities. Again it is case-law, related to the individual statutes of autonomy, rather than the Constitution, which gives us some clue as to which of these powers may be acquired in this way. By implication these can be divided into two groups:

7.7.3.1 Delegated powers

Such powers, which in no way imply a ceding of sovereignty on the part of the central powers, include such areas as: the overall system of communications, ports and airports that are 'of general interest'; post and telecommunications; control of air-space and air transport; and academic and professional qualifications. Such powers can only be delegated by act of Parliament, in practice through framework laws (4.7.1.4).

7.7.3.2 Normally exclusive powers of the state

This section includes four areas of competence which are normally associated with national institutions only: justice, fiscal affairs, public security and international affairs. These areas are listed in article 149 and therefore fall, theoretically, under the 'exclusive powers of the state'. However, in certain respects they have been assumed by the rapid-route regions.

With regard to fiscal matters, article 156.2 of the Constitution lays down that 'the autonomous communities shall be able to act as delegates or collaborators of the state in the levying, management and allocation of the latter's tax resources'. Article 157, which includes a list of a region's financial resources, refers to the possibility of a community raising its own taxes. In practice, as we have seen, only the Basque Country and Navarre have so far achieved genuine autonomy in this respect (7.5.3.3) – although there has been considerable pressure from the Catalans to achieve similar status.

With respect to public security, article 149 allows the fully autonomous regions to create their own regional police forces. The first region to take advantage of this provision was the Basque Country which in 1980 created its own force, the *Ertzaintza*, followed by the *Diputación Foral de Navarra* and the *Generalitat*, which created the Catalán autonomous police force known as the *Mossos d'Esquadra*. These forces are administratively and financially dependent on the regional governments concerned but in the last resort are accountable to their political masters in the Ministry of Home Affairs in Madrid. In more recent times, three other regions – Andalusia, Galicia and Valencia – have assumed responsibility for units of the national police (*policía nacional*). It should be noted, however, that in all six cases the police forces concerned carry out similar functions and these are related to the powers of the autonomous communities themselves. Co-ordination between the state security forces, which still exist in all regions, and those of the autonomous communities is achieved through the Security Council (*Junta de Seguridad*).

As far as international affairs are concerned, the involvement of the autonomous communities is limited to such matters as the right to request information on treaties that might directly affect them, the right to make proposals relating to international matters and the right to participate in decisions of this nature through their regional representatives in the Senate.

7.7.4 Exclusive powers of the state

In view of the flexible nature of the Constitution, particularly in so far as it refers to the communities and their potential rights, it is difficult to be categorical about which powers belong exclusively to the latter and which to the state. However, again by implication rather than by prescription, it can probably be safely assumed that the state will always retain responsibility for such obviously national affairs as: nationality; immigration; political asylum; defence and the armed forces; customs and tariff barriers; foreign trade; the monetary system; general economic planning;

the authorisation of elections and referendums; the overall administration of justice; and the signing of international agreements and treaties.

It should be noted, however that, particularly since the Senate autonomy debate of September 1994 (4.3.2), there is every likelihood that in the future the regions will be invited to play some part in shaping policy relating to the European Union.

7.7.5 Transfer of powers (*traspaso de competencias*)

7.7.5.1 Early developments

Obviously the approval of the statutes of autonomy and the establishment of the institutions of self-government were only the first steps taken in the long and complicated process of transferring real powers to the seventeen autonomous communities. Subsequently, in each ministry mixed committees (*comisiones mixtas*) of officials, one half representing the state and the other half the communities, were established and charged with the onerous task of transferring not only the powers themselves but the human, material and financial resources required to convert such powers into reality. General guidelines for the transfer of powers were laid down in section IV of the Harmonisation Law, the LOAPA (referred to in 2.5.2.5 and 7.4). The Law clearly states that the royal decrees (*reales decretos*) by which these transfers are effected shall contain precise references to the transfer of the appropriate funds. It also protects the rights of civil servants transferred in this process: state functionaries who are transferred to the bureaucracies of the autonomous communities continue to belong to the same professional corps, remain on the same grade and retain all their financial, career and professional rights (article 32).

The process of transfers began soon after the elections to the Basque and Catalan parliaments in March 1980. Partly because of lack of clarity in the Constitution and the statutes of autonomy and partly due to underlying political problems, this process was not always smooth. In the case of the slow-route regions, more progress was made for the simple reason that, initially at least, fewer powers were being transferred. By 1984, however, most powers and resources due to be devolved, in the initial phase of the process, to both groups of regions had been transferred. In the case of the 'big four', this included such major areas as health, education, regional TV stations, police forces (Basque Country, Catalonia and Navarre) and tax-raising (Basque Country and Navarre). In subsequent years, three other regions, the Canaries, Navarre and Valencia, moved closer to full autonomy by acquiring full responsibility for education and health; transfers were effected by organic laws on transfers (*leyes orgánicas de transferencias*).

7.7.5.2 Autonomy Agreements of 28 February 1992

These agreements, signalled as a necessity by the Socialist government as early as a debate in the Senate in December 1987, represented a significant development, indeed a whole new phase, in the autonomy process. They were signed by the government, the PSOE and the PP, and constitute a commitment both to finalise the long, open-ended process of devolution and to provide as much harmonisation as possible across the whole system. Specifically, the Agreements envisaged the granting of additional powers to the ten remaining slow-route regions (whose five-year 'waiting period', stipulated in Article 148.2 of the Constitution, had now elapsed) so as to reduce the gap between them and the by now seven other regions which had advanced at a more rapid rate. The instrument for achieving this was the organic law of 23 December 1992, which spelled out the areas to be transferred and the mechanisms of transfer. In most cases, the statutes of autonomy had to be reformed.

The transfers covered three categories of powers: (i) exclusive to the regions, i.e. both legislative and executive; (ii) legislative development and implementation (*ejecución*); and (iii) implementation. The first category included such areas as water resources, planning and exploitation; charitable, cultural and other foundations; energy generation; and casinos, gambling and betting. The second, given separate treatment within the organic law, refers to education, involving the devolution of considerable budgets, while the third covers management of social security payments and social services under INSERSO (6.4.4.1).

It is clear that, once these transfers have been effected (and the process should be complete by the end of 1996) the 23 per cent share of public spending (table 7.3) will rise rapidly. Indeed, it has been calculated that they are likely to add a 6 per cent shift in resources and staffing from central to regional budgets. Even before the whole operation is complete, between 1980 and March 1995, it has involved the transfer from central to regional governments of nearly half a million staff. By the end of the process, it is estimated that the ratio of staff as between central, regional and local bureaucracies will be 2:6:2.

However, the 1992 Agreements were not only concerned with the completion of the transfer process, but with ensuring that there would be essential, on-going intergovernmental co-operation between the central and regional authorities, covering both political/administrative matters and financial and budgetary affairs. Hence, the Agreements proposed the creation of fifteen sectoral conferences (*conferencias sectoriales*), composed of specialists and practitioners from both central and regional governments. They would be basically of a consultative nature but would also provide a forum in which the autonomous communities could participate in decision-making in specific areas, looked at from both a state and regional perspective. These conferences, which have now begun to function, are listed in table 7.7. In addition, there is another conference attached to the Ministry for Public Administration (6.2.9), which is concerned with EU affairs; its aim is to ensure that the autonomous communities are able to participate in matters of general as well as of particular interest in this field.

Table 7.7 *Sectoral conferences, 1992*

Name in English	Name in Spanish
Agriculture	*Agricultura*
Social Affairs	*Asuntos Sociales*
Consumer Affairs	*Consumo*
Culture	*Cultura*
Industry	*Industria*
Infrastructure	*Infraestructuras*
Home Affairs; Civilian Protection	*Interior; Protección Civil*
Research	*Investigación*
Environment	*Medio Ambiente*
Fishing	*Pesca*
Public Health	*Salud Pública*
Health	*Sanidad*
Labour	*Trabajo*
Tourism	*Turismo*
Housing	*Vivienda*

Source: Acuerdos Autonómicos del 28 de febrero de 1992, Ministerio para las Administraciones Públicas (1992).

7.8 Controls over autonomy

7.8.1 Normal control

According to article 153a, the Constitutional Court (2.5.2.3) has the final word in adjudicating the constitutionality of any regional legislation. Article 161.2, for example, grants the government the right to challenge any measures adopted by the autonomous community; the challenge automatically leads to the suspension of these measures until the Court, within a period of five months, has either confirmed or lifted the suspension. Through the Council of State (5.7), the government exercises ultimate control over the powers which it is allowed to delegate to the autonomous communities (article 153b). The administrative divisions of the regional high courts of justice (14.6.1) have ultimate jurisdiction over the regional administration (article 153c). The Audit Tribunal (9.9.3) exercises ultimate control over economic and budgetary matters (article 153d).

7.8.2 Extraordinary control

According to article 155 of the Constitution, if an autonomous community fails to carry out its obligations under the Constitution or if it acts in a way likely to harm the general interests of the state, the government (with the agreement of the president of that community or, where this is not forthcoming, following an overall majority in the Senate), can adopt the measures necessary to oblige it to carry out its obligations or to desist from allegedly harmful activities. As yet, this extraordinary means of control has not been invoked and no ruling has appeared which indicates what precisely these 'necessary measures' might involve.

7.8.3 Financial control

It should already have become apparent that this is a major, if not the major, way in which the state exercises control over the activities of the regions. With the exceptions of the Basque Country and Navarre, the other regions enjoy only a limited capacity for the self-generation of funds and the greater part of funds spent at regional level derive from central coffers. The Inter-regional Compensation Fund (7.5.3.4) is also administered centrally via the annual state budgets.

7.8.4 Other controls

Although they do not appear in the Constitution under the heading of control, there are two other *de facto* controls over the activities of the communities:

7.8.4.1 Agreements of co-operation (acuerdos de cooperación)

The joint *Cortes* have the right to authorise co-operation agreements between autonomous communities (4.6.2.2). This ruling appears in the same article and conveys the same tone as the clause forbidding the federation of such communities (article 145).

7.8.4.2 Harmonisation (armonización)

According to article 150.3 the state can approve laws which establish the necessary principles to harmonise the legislation of autonomous communities even in areas of devolved competence, should the national interest so require it. The necessity for such legislation has to be approved by an overall majority of the two Houses of Parliament. It was through this article that the controversial LOAPA was introduced in 1981 (7.4). Article 4 of this law made it perfectly plain that, in the case of powers devolved under article 149 of the Constitution, state law would always prevail over the legislation and regulations approved by the autonomous communities. Article 6 of the same law permits the government and the joint *Cortes* (4.3) to request the provision of information on activities even within the exclusive competence of the communities. The most stringent requirement, however, appears in article 8 which states that, when the communities exercise state powers delegated or transferred to them through an organic law, 'the authorities of the autonomous communities must always regulate their activities to conform to the instructions given by the relevant state authorities'. Failure to comply with this would lead to a possible suspension of the transfer or delegation and to a re-assumption of state control in that area.

7.8.4.3 Conflicts between government and regional authorities

Constitutionally, regional governments have the right to appeal against central government legislation and vice versa, and appeals are made before the

Constitutional Court (2.5). Interestingly, over the period 1981–91, the autonomous communities contested central government legislation three times more than the central government appealed against regional laws. At the beginning of the period, however, when the UCD was in power, the centre had been much more critical. In recent years, and particularly after the pact on the Autonomy Agreements of 1992, appeals on both sides have virtually come to an end, thus giving a strong indication that the new regional state in Spain has reached a point of equilibrium and stability.

7.9 New role of the Senate

In June 1994, an inter-party working party was established to consider drafting an amendment to the Constititution by which the Senate (4.3.2) would be transformed into a more genuine parliament of the regions. Once this amendment has been agreed, it is likely that the composition and functions of this Upper House will be quite substantially altered. In terms of composition, for example, it is possible that in the future a majority of the senators will be elected directly by the regional assemblies (probably at the time of the regional elections and not, as now, following a general election) and, with regard to functions, the Senate is likely to assume the leading role in initiating legislation relating to the autonomous communities, and may well become the natural forum for such intergovernmental activities as the *conferencias sectoriales*. On the whole, there has been wide consensus over the need for this reform but, because of its constitutional importance, the parties involved are in no hurry to rush through any legislation.

7.10 Comment

Over the last fifteen years, it is clear that substantial progress has been made in the process of restructuring the Spanish state and establishing regional political authorities which share power with the central government in Madrid. With hindsight, what seemed once to be a potentially inherent weakness in the system – its failure to define from the outset the ultimate shape of the Spanish state – may well turn out to have been a positive advantage in that this very open-endedness and flexibility have probably encouraged a greater degree of co-operation between central government and the regions than would have otherwise been possible. On the whole, the new regional institutions are functioning well and seem to have attained a reasonable degree of public acceptance and approval. Moreover, there are statistics to show that, stimulated by their new-found freedom of action, a number of regions (some traditionally wealthy and others traditionally poor) have launched self-propelled initiatives for development, often grasping the new opportunities provided by EU funding. The Inter-regional Compensation Fund has also undoubtedly made a significant contribution during this period to the levelling out of some of the economic imbalances between the regions.

On the debit side, however, as regional governments have striven to consolidate their position, there is some evidence that, at least viewed from the perspective of the local authorities, regional centralism, especially in the larger communities, has tended to replace Madrid centralism. The central government, however, is not unaware of this and has recently announced that a future priority will be the strengthening of local autonomy.

A much more deep-seated problem concerns the Basque Country and Catalonia, regions which, paradoxically, have gained the most from devolution. These regions, where large sections of the population think of themselves as nations quite separate from the Spanish nation, may not for long accept the current political consensus that all the autonomous communities should soon reach the same level of autonomy. Jordi Pujol, for example, has already signalled that he expects the distinctiveness of Catalonia to be expressly recognised in the composition of the new-style Senate. The opportunities for political blackmail are even stronger in the Basque Country where serious and continuing clashes between moderate nationalists and the radicals who support ETA and Herri Batasuna (10.4.3) could lead the former, led by the PNV (10.4.1), to increase the level of its autonomy demands in order to pacify its more militant citizens. However smoothly the autonomy process may have been conducted over the last decade and a half – and undoubtedly in many respects there have been great successes – these two regions continue to pose the most serious threat to its long-term consolidation.

Chapter 8

Local administration

Preliminary note

The institutions making up what is most accutately referred to, at least in Spain, as 'local administration' but is often called 'local government' in the UK context, include the municipal and provincial authorities. In legal documents, these institutions are known collectively as local corporations (*corporaciones locales*). Although, since the devolution of powers to the regions (chapter 7), these local institutions are subject to the legal framework of the autonomous communities, they remain financially, to a large extent, dependent on central government. On the other hand, in recent years the trend has been towards increasing co-operation between these bodies and the regional authorities in whose ambit they are located.

8.1 Introduction

The Franco regime, in combining political repression with excessive bureaucratic centralism, presided over the effective demise of local democracy. During the Franco era, local institutions were basically instruments for administering the policies of central government and enjoyed no real autonomy. Such was the degree of central control that mayors, for example, were directly appointed by Franco's minister for home affairs or the civil governor of the province concerned, both of whom were directly appointed by Franco. Moreover, local elections were rigidly controlled by the dictator's single party, the National Movement (1.1.2) which ensured that, to those few seats open to direct election, only officially sponsored candidates were elected.

Furthermore, additional problems were created by the fact that over the quarter of a century between 1960 and 1985, as we have seen (1.1.3), Spain experienced unprecedented demographic, social and economic changes that were not accompanied by necessary corresponding changes in the territorial structure and administration of the country.

Thus, the governments elected after 1977 were confronted not only with the need to democratise government at all levels but also with the necessity of overhauling an anachronistic system of local administration. In order to underpin them, both sets of reform required a much higher level of economic support than had been available in the past.

8.2 Reform of local government

As at the national level, political reforms took precedence over administrative and economic change. Even here, however, change was slow to be enacted. Apparently for reasons of political self-interest, Adolfo Suárez was reluctant to hold local elections before April 1979, a month after the second round of general elections. Thus between 1977 and April 1979 a situation of often dangerous tension existed between the democratically elected central government and the non-reformed local institutions, still manned by Franco appointees. However, fully democratic local elections, based on the Election Law of March 1977, were eventually held, first in 1979 and subsequently in 1983, 1987, 1991 and 1995, the last three elections being held under the General Electoral Law of 1985 (LOREG) (4.3.1 and see below). As a result, the political map of local government was redrawn.

Administrative reform, however, lagged well behind political change. Although Calvo Sotelo's UCD government introduced limited changes in October 1981, basically local government was being run according to outmoded norms and practices. For a fundamental reappraisal of local administration, Spaniards had to wait until April 1985 when the Socialist government approved the Basic Law on Local Government (*Ley Reguladora de las Bases de Régimen Local/LRBRL*). This law laid down the ground rules for the organisation of local government within the framework of Spain's new democracy.

In some ways, and especially to those expecting substantial reform, the document was a disappointment in that the traditional pattern of administration was largely maintained. For example, the provincial tier of government, so maligned by the Left because of its associations with state centralism, was preserved and in some ways strengthened. However, it should, in fairness, be pointed out that this battle had already been lost during the constitutional debate, when the Left made substantial concessions to its political opponents in the interests of the consolidation of democracy. Even prior to the approval of the Constitution, it was clear that consensus politics was winning the day: it ensured the survival of the provinces as the electoral constituency in the Electoral Law of March 1977 and also in the Local Election Law of August 1978, both of which were incorporated into the updated LOREG of June 1985. Thus it came as no surprise when article 137 guaranteed that local administration would be based on provinces as well as municipalities.

In one important way the Law broke new ground in local government legislation: it outlined the services it expected local authorities to carry out, either on their own or in collaboration with other authorities, according to their size of population. Never before in the history of Spanish local government had such specific guidelines been laid down, nor had such flexible arrangements been agreed in terms of sharing responsibilities between the different tiers of administration.

8.3 Municipal administration

The 8,022 municipalities, centred in the town and city halls (*ayuntamientos*), have a much longer history and a higher level of popular acceptance than the provinces. These reasons, plus the fact that, except in times of dictatorship, such bodies have been popularly elected, possibly explain why there is more stress on municipal than provincial autonomy in the Constitution. It is interesting to note, however, that the LRBRL goes some way towards rectifying this, perhaps hoping to secure more popular support for the provinces. A feature of these municipalities, still not rectified by subsequent legislation, is that approximately 45 per cent of them have a population of less than 500 inhabitants and over 85 per cent a population of less than 5,000 inhabitants. This fragmentation into many tiny units, while encouraging local democracy, has created predictable administrative problems and is one major reason behind the decision to retain the provinces (8.4.3).

Article 140 of the Constitution states: 'The Constitution guarantees the autonomy of the municipalities. They shall enjoy full legal status. Their government and administration are the responsibility of their respective town halls, made up of the mayors and councillors.'

8.3.1 Municipal institutions

The basic institutions at municipal level are: the full municipal council (8.3.2.1) and the municipal commission (8.3.2.3), each headed by the mayor (8.3.2.2). These are statutory bodies, the existence of which is legally required. However, each town hall has the freedom to create any additional permanent or ad hoc entities that it considers necessary for the efficient running of municipal affairs. Clearly, the overall pattern will vary considerably from the large urban authorities to the small rural ones with responsibility for only a few hundred citizens. In fact, the freedom of action of these authorities in this respect is partly determined by the Organic Law of June 1985, which establishes the number of councillors to be elected in each municipality according to the latter's population (article 179).

Figure 8.1 shows the organisation of the institutions of the city hall of Málaga, a large urban municipality serving a population of over half a million.

8.3.2 Major municipal bodies

8.3.2.1 Municipal council (pleno del ayuntamiento)

The seat of municipal government is the town hall (*ayuntamiento*), a term which is also used, both officially and popularly, to refer to the whole body of municipal institutions and, sometimes, the municipal council. The LRBRL uses the term '*ayuntamiento*' in the broader sense and the full council is referred to as *el pleno del ayuntamiento* or, for short, *el pleno*. This is the rule-making, elected body of municipal government and roughly corresponds to an English city, or town, council. The

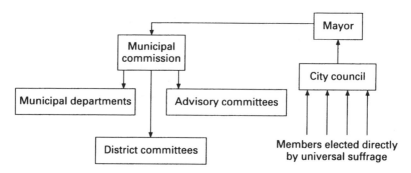

Figure 8.1 *Municipal administration in Málaga, 1995*

pleno is made up of councillors (*concejales*) who are elected, like politicians at the national and regional levels, by universal suffrage. A system of proportional representation operates similar to that used for the Congress and the D'Hondt system is employed for the allocation of seats. Electors vote in constituencies called *términos municipales*, the area served by each town hall, not for individual councillors representing wards or districts (as in the United Kingdom), but for municipality-wide lists on which there is a ranking order headed by each party's nominee for the post of mayor. The number of councillors per municipality is fixed in proportion to its population although, to safeguard the existence of small rural authorities, a minimum of five per municipality has been laid down in the LOREG. If councillors die, resign or are dismissed, their places are taken by the subsequent names on the list of the political party concerned, thus obviating the need for by-elections. Councillors serve for a period of four years and there is no limit to the number of terms of office they may serve. The council cannot be dissolved and elections, controlled by the central government, are called on a regular four-year basis. In 1995, for the first time, the resident nationals of voting age from four European countries (Denmark, Holland, Norway and Sweden) were able to vote in local elections in Spain, which had signed reciprocal agreements with these countries.

In normal circumstances, ordinary sessions of the full council must be held at least every three months; in fact, following the local elections of May 1995, the new PP-led administration in Málaga decided to convene seventeen *plenos* per year. Extraordinary sessions, in the case of emergencies, can be called either by the mayor or by at least a quarter of the council members. Councillors must be given a minimum of two days' notice of ordinary sessions, and the agenda for the meeting, with accompanying documentation, must be in their hands that same day. The quorum for meetings is a third of the full membership, and this must be maintained throughout the meeting. Agreements may be reached on the basis of a simple majority; if voting produces a tie, the mayor, acting as chairman, may use his casting vote (*voto de calidad*).

The municipal council does not have the authority to draft major laws but does have the right to draft and approve regulations (*ordenanzas*) which must conform to legislation emanating from either the *Cortes* or the regional parliament. One of its major functions is to control and oversee the work of the municipal commission (8.3.2.3). Moreover, the *pleno* is empowered to approve and, where appropriate, modify the budgets presented to it by the commission, to prioritise expenditure and to approve the accounts. Naturally the council has the right to establish its own internal organisation, including the appointment, payment and dismissal of full and part-time staff. As with its provincial counterpart, it may have recourse to the appropriate courts to ensure that the commission is operating legally. It may also approve a motion of censure against the mayor (8.3.2.2).

In two important ways, however, the municipal council is different from, and indeed more powerful than, its provincial counterpart. Firstly, it has the power to determine its revenue by raising its own taxes to supplement the grants from national and regional governments. Secondly, it has the right to participate in supra-municipal bodies, to create submunicipal bodies, to alter the municipal boundary, and to create or eliminate municipalities in consultation with higher authorities.

8.3.2.2 Mayor (alcalde)

Unlike most of his British counterparts, whose role has become honorary and dec-orative, a Spanish mayor always plays an active political as well as representational role. Indeed, there is so much prestige and tradition attached to his role that in pro-vincial capitals like Málaga he tends to be regarded as a more important figure than the president of the provincial council (8.4.1.2).

The mayor is elected by members of the full council meeting at its first session following local elections. He is normally head of the majority party or coalition in the council and must have headed the electoral list of the party concerned. It is pos-sible, of course, for the leader of a minority to become mayor if a candidate is accept-able to a coalition of parties and the latter is able to win a majority in the council. This occurred in Seville, for example, in 1991, when the leader of the *Partido Andalucista* (10.4.7), Alejandro Rojas-Marcos, became mayor. The Constitution allows for the direct popular election of mayors but, following several years of speculation, the 1985 Law opted solely for the method outlined above.

The mayor combines several functions in one person: he is the chief repre-sentative and president of the municipality, chairman of the full council, head of the municipal commission (8.3.2.3) and head of the municipal administration. He is, moreover, the highest representative of the state at municipal level. The mayor's main function is to direct municipal government, and it is his responsibility to convene and chair sessions of the *pleno*, the municipal commission and other municipal bodies. He must also direct, inspect and promote municipal works and services. He also has the right to issue edicts (*bandos*) on minor matters without con-sulting the council. It is the duty of the mayor to impose fines and other sanctions on those who flout these edicts or other orders of the council.

One of his major roles is that of head of the municipal police force (*policía local*), which is run from the town hall, usually through a department of security. The mayor must adopt urgent measures in the case of local emergencies or catastrophes (flooding, large-scale fires, explosions, etc.) when there is a grave risk to public safety, and he must immediately inform the *pleno* of his actions (see also 6.5.3).

The mayor also enjoys wide powers of appointment: he has the right to appoint not only the members of the municipal commission from among the members of the council, but also his deputy mayor(s) (*teniente(s) de alcalde*), who must be a member(s) of the commission. Moreover, the mayor can appoint members of other municipal organisations and must appoint all staff who are empowered to use fire-arms. In fact, in his name at least, all the employees of the town hall are appointed – although in practice posts are often filled by the heads of the departments concerned from civil servants qualified in particular fields.

One of the more pleasurable functions of the mayor, in his representational role, is to receive and often entertain visiting dignitaries to the town or city concerned. Visitors may range from the king and queen to foreign statesmen and members of national and international trade or cultural delegations. As one would expect, he is also much in demand to act as chair for many local organisations, and to open and close a whole range of events, from large fairs to Holy Week processions in the big towns and cities to school functions and talent contests. An additional function which mayors assumed in 1993 was the carrying out of civil marriage ceremonies, which was previously only possible in a local court (14.7). It is not surprising, then, that the local population tend to identify with him far more than with either the civil governor or the president of the provincial council, as he is in much more daily contact with the people. Since public relations are such an important aspect of his role, most mayors are assisted by a usually non-political head of protocol (*jefe de protocolo*).

8.3.2.3 Municipal commission (comisión municipal de gobierno)

This body normally exists only in municipalities with over 5,000 inhabitants. It consists of the mayor, the deputy mayor and a number of councillors, not exceeding a third of the total of the latter, appointed by the mayor and subject to dismissal by him. Normally all the members of the commission belong to the majority party.

The principal task of this commission is to assist the mayor in the exercise of his duties. In practice, especially in the large authorities, each member is given responsibility for a particular area of administration (8.3.3.1) or for a particular district of the municipality (8.3.3.3).

8.3.3 Other municipal bodies

It should again be stressed that, while the above institutions are statutory, the following have only optional status and their existence or otherwise depends on the size of the municipality.

Table 8.1 *Major departments of the Ayuntamiento de Málaga, 1995*

Department	Area
Mayor's Office	*Alcaldía*
Social Welfare	*Bienestar social*
Traffic and Transport	*Circulación y Transportes*
Culture and Tourism	*Cultura y Turismo*
Economy and Finance	*Económico–Financiera*
Education	*Educación*
Control and Supervision	*Fiscalización*
Legal and Administrative Affairs	*Jurídico–Administrativa*
Environment, Public Health and Commercial Activities	*Medio Ambiente, Salud Pública y Actividades Comerciales*
Human Resources	*Recursos Humanos*
Civil Protection and Fire-extinguishing Services	*Servicios de Protección Civil y Extinción de Incendios*
Security Services	*Servicios de Seguridad*

Source: Guía de Málaga, Ayuntamiento de Málaga (1993).

8.3.3.1 Municipal departments (delegaciones or áreas)

In all but the smallest authorities, municipal administration has been divided up into units specialising in particular spheres of interest and usually headed by an elected councillor. The internal departmental structure of the city hall of Málaga, shown in table 8.1, is not dissimilar to that found in other large municipalities.

The heads of these departments are responsible, under the mayor, for appointing and dismissing their administrative, technical and secretarial staff within the guidelines established by the Basic Law. However, appointments at this level must be made according to administrative and professional and not political criteria. Thus, below the level of head of department, the local government officers may belong to any or no political party, and normally remain in post when there is a change in the council.

8.3.3.2 Municipal autonomous bodies (organismos autónomos municipales)

Attached to the larger *ayuntamientos* there are often a number of autonomous bodies operating like the *áreas* but with more budgetary freedom. They are the municipal equivalents of the bodies already referred to in 6.3 and 7.6.4. Each is headed by a *director* who is not normally a councillor but may be a *persona de confianza* i.e. a person known and trusted by the mayor; his appointment must be approved by the *pleno*. Examples of such bodies in the case of Málaga are given in table 8.2. It should be noted that there are in fact two types of autonomous body: those of a non-profit-making nature, such as the *Fundación Municipal Deportiva* and the *Fundación Casa Natal Pablo Picasso*, and those run as commercial entities, such as the *Empresa Malagueña de Transportes SA* (*EMT*) and the *Empresa Malagueña de Aguas SA* (*EMASA*). The latter are municipal equivalents of the public enterprises at state level described in 9.3 and will thus be examined in more detail in chapter 9.

Table 8.2 *Autonomous administrative bodies of the Ayuntamiento de Málaga, 1995*

Autonomous body	Organismo autónomo
Municipal Computing Centre	*Centro Municipal de Informática*
Municipal Sports Foundation	*Fundación Municipal Deportiva*
Pablo Picasso Birthplace Foundation	*Fundación Casa Natal Pablo Picasso*
Municipal Botanical Trust	*Patronato Botánico Municipal*
Municipal Housing Institute	*Instituto Municipal de Vivienda*
Municipal Agency for Town Planning, Public Works and Infrastructure	*Gerencia Municipal de Urbanismo, Obras e Infraestructuras*

Source: Guía de Málaga, Ayuntamiento de Málaga (1993).

8.3.3.3 Municipal district committees (juntas municipales de distrito)

While clearly, even in small municipalities, local administration needs to be sub-divided into functional units, the existence of territorial divisions and their number depends exclusively on the size of the municipal authority. A small municipality will have no such divisions, while Málaga, with a rapidly expanding population, has recently increased the number from six to ten. In the latter case, each of these areas is the responsibility of a nominated councillor or delegate (*delegado*) who may or may not be a member of the commission, but who will almost always be a member of the ruling party. Local residents with complaints, who are reticent about approaching the town hall directly, may seek help from their *delegado* or from the local committee over which he presides. These committees are usually composed of respected citizens who reside in the district and who are appointed by the *delegado* with the approval of the *pleno*. The responsibility of the members is to represent the interests of local residents (*vecinos*) and channel their complaints, problems, and so on, to the council.

8.3.3.4 Advisory committees (comisiones informativas)

These non-elected bodies are found in only some of the larger municipalities. In Málaga, for instance, there are now six such committees headed either by members of the commission or councillors from the ruling party. Each committee consists of a chairman and eight members representing the major political groups on the council and the independents, in proportion to their share of seats on the council. Currently, in Málaga, each advisory committee consists of four members of the PP, including the chair, three members of IU (10.3.2), and two members of the PSOE. To some extent, these committees mirror the departmental organisation of the city hall. For example, some of the major committees in Málaga are: finance; works and public services; town planning; security; and health and social services. The main function of these advisory committees is to enable councillors of all political persuasions to participate in an advisory role in specific areas of policy in which they may have a special interest or expertise. They also serve as channels of communication between the commission and the minority political groups.

8.3.4 Open assembly (*concejo abierto*)

In municipalities of less than 100 inhabitants, a system of open assembly operates. Article 29 of the Basic Law recognises these cases and also allows such an arrangement to exist where geographical location or other factors make their establishment advisable. In order to establish such a system, the majority of the inhabitants concerned must send a petition to the town hall concerned which must approve the request by a two-thirds majority before final approval is granted by the regional government.

Under such a system the government and administration of the municipality is the responsibility of a mayor who is elected by a neighbourhood assembly (*asamblea vecinal*) composed of all the voters. The latter have the right to take decisions and vote on all matters affecting the municipality.

8.3.5 Responsibilities of municipal authorities

Each municipality is required to carry out certain minimum functions in accordance with legislation emanating from the central or regional government. Article 26 of the Basic Law lays down what these responsibilities are, depending on the size of the *término municipal*.

- *All municipalities* are responsible for public lighting, cemeteries, refuse collection, street cleaning, sewers, road access, pavements and food and drink inspection.
- *Municipalities with a population of over 5,000* are in addition responsible for public parks, public libraries, markets, water supply and sewage treatment.
- *Municipalities with a population of over 20,000* are in addition responsible for social services, police and fire services, sports facilities and abattoirs.
- *Municipalities with a population of over 50,000* are in addition responsible for urban transport and environmental protection.

One must distinguish between the above responsibilities, which are the compulsory minimum in each case, and additional services, outlined in article 25, for which the municipal authority can claim either exclusive or shared rights. Exclusive rights include: public security and traffic control, the promotion and management of housing, cultural activities and the care of historic buildings; rights shared with the regional government include: collaboration in the provision and maintenance of educational facilities, in the management of local education and in the provision of primary health care.

Municipalities which find themselves unable to provide the basic services required by law may be granted official dispensation by the regional government, in which case the latter is likely to charge the provincial council (8.4.1.1) with the task of providing them (Basic Law, article 26.2, 26.3). On the other hand, the central or regional authorities may decide to delegate additional powers to municipalities deemed capable of exercising them. In such circumstances, they must be persuaded that either efficiency or public participation is thereby enhanced. Some of the areas in which the municipalities are encouraged to assume additional powers are: education; culture; housing; health; the promotion of opportunities for women; and the protection of the environment. Obviously, funds would be made available by the state or the regional authority to enable the municipality to exercise such powers (8.6).

The interests of all local authorities, especially in relation to their financial dealings with the state, are represented by the Federation of Municipalities and Provinces (*Federación de Municipios y Provincias/FEMP*) which has become an important pressure group defending local government in both financial and legal respects. At the regional level, in the case of Andalusia, for example, the *Junta de Andalucía* has recently set up two bodies, the *Consejo de Municipios* and the *Consejo de Provincias* in order to provide a forum where the *Corporaciones Locales* can air their grievances and share experiences.

8.4 Provincial administration

The provinces (figure 4.1) were established as the main units of the *administración periférica del estado* (6.5) through which the central government hoped more easily to impose its policies. There are now effectively only forty-four of them since six have been transformed into single-province autonomous communities (chapter 7). According to article 141.1 of the Constitution, the province is defined as follows: 'The province is a local entity with its own legal status, consisting of a group of municipalities and representing a territorial division designed to carry out the activities of the state.'

Thus we can discern a certain duality in the role of the province. On the one hand, as an entity which brings together several municipal authorities, it clearly has a local function and in fact one of its major roles is to provide a range of services not available to the smaller municipal authorities within its ambit. This function is carried out by the *diputaciones provinciales* (8.4.1.1). On the other hand, it is also evident that the provinces retain their traditional role as outposts of central government; this function, as we have seen (6.5), is carried out by the *gobierno civil* operating as part of the *administración periférica del estado*. The funding for both spheres of responsibility, as with municipal government, comes very largely from central government. This section is concerned only with the role and functions of the *diputaciones provinciales*.

8.4.1 Provincial institutions

The basic institutions of the *diputación provincial* are: the full provincial council (8.4.1.1) and the provincial commission (8.4.1.3), each headed by the president (8.4.1.2). These are statutory bodies which must exist in all provincial capitals, although the council, like the municipal council, is free to create other bodies should it so decide. Figure 8.2 shows the major institutions of the Provincial Council of Málaga, although the pattern varies little from one province to another.

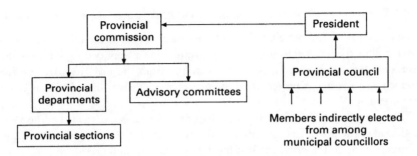

Figure 8.2 *Provincial administration in Málaga, 1995*

8.4.1.1 *Provincial council (pleno de la diputación provincial)*

The seat of provincial administration is the 'county hall' (*diputación provincial*), a term which is also used to refer to the whole body of provincial institutions as well as the full provincial council. The Basic Law on Local Government uses the term *diputación* in the broader sense and the full council is referred to as *el pleno de la diputación*. This is the rule-making body of provincial government.

The provincial council is made up of provincial deputies (*diputados provinciales*) who, except in the case of the three Basque Provinces (8.4.2), are elected indirectly by the municipal councillors elected in the preceding municipal elections. As with the latter, seats are allocated according to a system of proportional representation. Initially, a fixed number of seats is established for each province, the electoral board (*junta electoral*) of which allocates seats to each *partido judicial*. The latter, which is a territorial division for the administration of justice (14.7) and contains several municipalities, is the constituency for these elections. The allocation is not rigidly proportional since, however small its population, every *partido* has one deputy while no single constituency can have more than three-fifths of the total for the province. Provincial deputies hold office for four years and, provided that they are re-elected as municipal councillors, they may be re-elected as deputies. The procedure for meetings of the council is exactly the same as that outlined for municipal councils (8.3.2.1).

The provincial council does not have the authority, any more than the town halls, to draft major laws. In certain areas, it enjoys the right to draft orders or regulations (*ordenanzas*) which flesh out and must conform to laws emanating from the *Cortes* or the regional parliament. One of its principal functions is to control and oversee the work of the provincial commission (8.4.1.3), which is accountable to it. The council may have recourse to the courts to ensure that the commission is operating within the limits laid down by national and regional law. Another major function is to approve annually a provincial co-operation plan (*plan de obras y servicios*) concerning municipal works and services; the municipalities are obliged to participate in this plan.

8.4.1.2 President of the provincial council (presidente de la diputación provincial)

The president of the council is elected by all the members of the full council from among those members at its first meeting. Any provincial deputy is eligible to be the president. He tends to be a person of standing from the majority party on the council and is often a mayor of an important municipality, though this is not a requirement.

The president is the chief representative of the *diputación*, chairman of the *pleno* and head of the provincial commission with responsibility for the government and administration of the province. It is his duty to convene and preside over sessions of the full council, the commission and any other provincial institutions that may be established by the *diputación*. One of his major duties is to direct, inspect and promote the services and works of the provincial government, including those delegated to it by the regional government. The president must also see that the decisions of the council are enacted and published in the *Official Provincial Gazette* (*Boletín Oficial de la Provincia*). One of his major functions is to appoint vice-presidents of the council as well as the members of the provincial commission from among the provincial deputies. All the staff of the *diputación* are officially appointed in his name.

8.4.1.3 Provincial commission (comisión provincial de gobierno)

The commission consists of the president of the council, his vice-president(s) and a number of provincial deputies whose number may not exceed one-third of the legal total for the province. As we have seen in 8.4.1.2, the members are appointed by the president and are subject to dismissal by him. The principal task of the commission is to assist the president in his duties and to carry out the tasks which may be delegated to it either by the president or by act of the national or regional parliament. The president may, and frequently does, delegate responsibility for specific tasks to individual members of the commission; indeed, he may also delegate in this way to deputies who do not belong to the commission.

8.4.1.4 Provincial departments (áreas)

As with the municipal tier of government, the administration of the *diputación* is divided up into several departments (*áreas*), each headed by a delegate (*delegado*) who is certainly a provincial deputy and may well be a member of the commission.

In the case of the province of Málaga, the *diputación* consists of six major departments, each of which is sub-divided into a number of divisions or sections, as shown in table 8.3. In total, the department of culture and education consists of twelve divisions, while that of social welfare also has twelve. In addition, the *diputación*, like the *ayuntamiento* (and indeed all tiers of government and administration), has established a number of autonomous bodies, which are listed in table 8.4.

Table 8.3 *Major departments of the Diputación Provincial de Málaga, 1995*

Department	Area
Social Welfare	*Bienestar Social*
Municipal Liaison	*Co-operación Municipal*
Culture and Education	*Educación y Cultura*
Finance and Special Accounts	*Hacienda y Especial de Cuentas*
Internal Organisation and Personnel	*Régimen Interior y Personal*
Supramunicipal Affairs and Environment	*Supramunicipal y Medio Ambiente*

Source: Memoria de Actividades, Diputación Provincial de Málaga (1993).

Table 8.4 *Autonomous administrative bodies of the Diputación Provincial de Málaga, 1993*

Autonomous body	Organismo autónomo	Department
Centre for Women's Affairs	*Centro de la Mujer*	Social Welfare
Provincial Centre for Drug Dependency	*Centro Provincial de Drogadependencias*	Social Welfare
Civic Centre[a]	*Centro Cívico*	Culture and Education
University Nursing School	*Escuela Universitaria de Enfermería*	Culture and Education
Data Processing Centre	*Centro de Proceso de Datos*	Internal Organisation and Personnel
Rural Employment Plan	*Plan de Empleo Rural (PER)*	Supramunicipal Affairs and Environment

Note:
[a] This is not the equivalent of a UK town hall, but simply a social centre.
Source: Memoria de Actividades, Diputación Provincial de Málaga (1993).

8.4.2 Special arrangements

Within the above arrangements there are four exceptions to the rule which are outlined in the Basic Law: the single-province autonomous communities, including Navarre; the Basque Country; the Balearic Islands; and the Canary Islands.

8.4.2.1 Single-province communities (comunidades uniprovinciales)

As we have seen in 7.4, the single-province autonomous communities assumed all the powers, responsibilities and resources of the former provincial authorities once they had been established in 1983. Subsequently, therefore, provincial institutions as such in those areas ceased to exist; there areas are now run by regional bodies which, unlike the *diputaciones*, have their own statutes of autonomy (7.5.1) like any other region and enjoy political as well as administrative autonomy.

8.4.2.2 Basque Country (Euskadi)

As we have already seen in 7.5.3.7, the three Basque Provinces, Alava, Guipúzcoa and Vizcaya, which were recognised as 'historic territories' in the *concierto económico* negotiated with the central government in 1981, were able to recover their long-lost privileges, which relate particularly to the levying of taxes. Such privileges are not available to any other provinces, with the exception of Navarre. The *diputaciones forales*, as they are called, whose members are directly elected at the same time as municipal councillors (8.3.2.1), exercise these rights (including tax collection) in addition to those described above, thus making them much more powerful than most provincial councils. Indeed, in addition to the long-standing friction between Madrid and Vitoria (the seat of the Basque government), tensions have arisen from time to time between those advocating virtually autonomous provinces (reflecting, in fact, a past historical reality), and the supporters of a strengthened Basque government.

8.4.2.3 Balearic Islands (Islas Baleares)

The organisation of the Islands (*Islas*) is laid down in article 41.4 of the Constitution and, in much more detail, in the statutes of autonomy of the Balearic Islands (*Islas Baleares*) and the Canary Islands (*Islas Canarias*), each of which forms a separate autonomous community. The problem here is the geographical separation of certain units belonging to the same community. In the case of the Balearics, this has been solved by devolving substantial powers to the three island councils, known as *consejos insulares*, of Majorca, Menorca and Ibiza–Formentera. Each of these councils is composed of the national deputies elected in these islands who are empowered to head the government and administration thereof. Article 39 of the statute spells out in some detail the powers which they may exercise in addition to those normally exercised by a *diputación provincial*.

8.4.2.4 Canary Islands (Islas Canarias)

In a similar way, the government and administration of the Canaries is entrusted to seven island councils (*cabildos insulares*) which also enjoy greater powers than their equivalent provincial councils on the mainland. Unlike their counterparts in the Balearics, the members (*consejeros*) of the *cabildos insulares* are elected by universal suffrage at the same time as the municipal elections. It should be noted that the Canary Islands are part of the European Union but as yet do not belong to the customs union.

8.4.3 Responsibilities of the provincial authority

According to article 36 of the Basic Law on Local Government, the major powers of the *diputación* are as follows: (i) to co-ordinate municipal services and to ensure an adequate and complete provision of services across the whole province; (ii) to give legal, economic and technical assistance to the municipalities, particularly to those of limited economic and administrative capacity (8.3); (iii) to provide public services of a supra-municipal nature; and (iv) to develop support for and administer interests that are peculiar to that province. Article 31(b) of the Basic Law makes it clear that one major role of the province is to share in the co-ordination of local administration, collaborating with regional and central authorities. In recent years, an important aspect of this has centred on financial collaboration in joint public works projects, sometimes involving European as well as national and regional money (8.6).

8.5 Other local administration entities

As well as the provincial and municipal tiers of administration, the Basic Law envisages the creation, where appropriate, of both sub-municipal and supra-municipal bodies. The aim of the former is to provide an outpost of local administration in small communities separated from the seat of local administration within the *término municipal*.

8.5.1 Minor local entity (*entidad local menor*)

The major example of the former type of unit is the *entidad local menor* which may be established at village, hamlet or parish level. In 1992 the *diputación* in Málaga, for example, designated a district in Antequera, Villanueva de la Concepción, as such an *entidad*. The institutions of these bodies are the 'suffragan' mayor (*alcalde pedáneo*) and the neighbourhood council (*junta vecinal*) which is composed of all the electors of the area concerned who, through a majority system, elect one of their number as mayor. The size of the council varies according to the size of the population. In reality, these bodies are subject to the local *ayuntamiento*, though the latter may devolve certain concrete responsibilities to them.

The purpose of the supra-municipal bodies is to represent and promote the common interests of several municipalities; two examples of these are the district and the metropolitan area.

8.5.2 District (*comarca*)

Some areas of Spain, for example Catalonia, would have preferred this traditional administrative and political division of the region which, in different political circumstances, might have replaced the provinces both as electoral constituencies and as administrative units. It is significant that in certain regions the political parties and trade unions, notably the Socialist party and UGT, have adopted the *comarca* rather than the province as the base for their immediate sub-regional institutions. Article 42 of the Basic Law permits the creation of *comarcas*, provided that two-fifths of the municipalities concerned are not expressly opposed to the idea.

Interestingly, it is possible for a *comarca* to be formed from municipalities within more than one province provided that both provincial councils approve. Such arrangements, including the territorial limits, the organs and their composition, are subject to approval by laws emanating from the regional parliament.

In recent years, many of the *comarcas* have assumed greater importance in relation to the receipt and distribution of EU monies. For example, many of the fifty-two development centres (*centros de desarrollo rural/CEDERs*), established since 1992 for the purposes of bidding for grants under the EU's 'Plan Leader', (6.3 and 15.4.2.4) have been based on the *comarcas*. There are nine of these, for example, in Andalusia, including the *Comarca de la Alpujarra*, which includes municipalities in both Almería and Granada provinces.

8.5.3 Association of municipalities (*mancomunidad de municipios*)

This is similar in many ways to the *comarca*, but is usually a larger association of municipalities created for a wide variety of purposes, ranging from sewage/waste disposal and water supply to tourism and sport. In the autonomous community of Andalusia, for example, there are currently no less than ninety of these entities, located in all eight provinces of the region. Two of the largest are the coastal associations along the *Costa del Sol*, one for the western and one for the eastern side of Málaga. A number of these associations are actually named *consorcios* – consortia – though their composition (two or more adjacent municipalities) and their co-ordination and co-operation functions are exactly the same.

8.5.4 Metropolitan area (*área metropolitana*)

The *área metropolitana*, as its name suggests, may be established in large urban areas where the joint co-operation of adjacent municipalities is essential to providing a fair, rational and well co-ordinated service across an area that is likely to have many common economic and social problems. Regional law determines the organs of government and administration to be established, and ensures the equal representation of all the municipalities involved. The establishment of such an area is particularly useful for large conurbations, such as Barcelona, Córdoba, Málaga, Valencia and Zaragoza which have recently established a long-term strategic plan (*plan estratégico*) based largely on US models.

8.6 Financing

Naturally, the key factor in the revitalisation of local government and administration in Spain has been finance and resources. Article 142 of the Constitution states that local authorities will be financed by their own taxes and from a share in those levied by the state and the autonomous communities. According to national and regional legislation, local authorities have a right to supplement the grants or shares in taxes due to them from higher levels of government by raising their own revenue

Table 8.5 *Sources of revenue of the Ayuntamiento de Málaga, 1994*

English	Spanish
Transfers from central government[a]	*Transferencias del gobierno central[a]*
• Current	*•Corrientes*
• Capital	*• Capital*
Transfers from EU[b]	*Transferencias de la UE[b]*
Direct taxes	*Impuestos directos*
• Property Tax	*• Impuesto sobre bienes inmuebles (IBI)*
• Business Tax	*• Impuesto sobre la actividad económica (IAE)*
• Vehicle Tax	*• Impuesto sobre Vehículos*
Indirect taxes	*Impuestos indirectos*
• Capital gains tax	*• Impuesto sobre Plusvalía*
Charges and other income	*Tasas y otros ingresos*
Income from own assets	*Ingresos patrimoniales*

Notes:
[a] These are paid from the National Fund for Municipal Co-operation (*Fondo Nacional de Cooperación Municipal*).
[b] These are channelled via various ministries of central administration.
Source: Presupuesto 1995, Ayuntamiento de Málaga (1994).

from local sources. The major part of this local revenue comes from taxes and charges of various kinds, such as the Spanish equivalent of rates, licences for property, businesses and vehicles, income from public transport, fines for driving, parking and other offences, as well as revenue from local cultural and historic attractions. In fact the December 1988 Law Regulating Local Finance (*Ley Reguladora de las Haciendas Locales*), in addition to extending the freedom of municipalities to set tax rates, made a long-overdue attempt to simplify and rationalise local taxes. Thus, now there are only three compulsory taxes; these are: (i) the tax on real estate (*impuesto sobre bienes inmuebles/IBI*); (ii) the tax on economic activities (*impuesto sobre la actividad económica/IAE*); and (iii) the tax on vehicles (*impuesto sobre vehículos*). Two optional taxes which they may levy are a tax on the increase of urban land value and a tax on construction, installations and works.

The various sources of income available to the Málaga *ayuntamiento* are shown in table 8.5. Obviously, the local sources constitute only a small fraction of the global financial needs of any municipal authority. In addition to annual block grants to both the *diputaciones* and *ayuntamientos* paid for out of the annual state budgets, both provincial and the larger municipal authorities can bid for additional support for specific projects under the government-run Local Economic Co-operation Programme (*Programa de Cooperación Económica Local/CEL*), which works on the basis of a five-year cycle and is administered via the Ministry of Public Administration (6.2.9). In recent years, the same authorities have also been able to bid for EU grants, sometimes with the aim of supplementing funds for a CEL project; the greater part of this kind of funding has tended to come from the ERDF and be linked to so-called local operative plans (*planes operativos locales/POL*).

Every year each local authority is obliged by law to approve and publish a single budget (*presupuesto*) covering all revenue and expected expenditure during the coming financial year. During a fixed period of time, this budget is on view to members of the public who have the right to make complaints; subsequently the budget is published in the *Official Gazette* (*Boletín Oficial*) of that authority. Final approval of the budget must be given by the full council of the appropriate authority before 31 December prior to the financial year concerned; if approval is not granted, the budget for the previous year stands.

In line with the policy of greater accountability of both public and private organisations in Spain, the accounts of local authorities must be scrutinised each year by a special audit committee, the *comisión especial de cuentas*, of each local authority. This body is made up of members from the various political groups represented in the full council. Like the annual budget, the accounts must be available to the public before being approved by the council. In addition the accounts must be submitted to the state Audit Tribunal (9.9.3).

8.7 Comment

From the foregoing, it can be seen how, in many ways, local administration in Spain has been transformed in comparison with the rigid and ossified structure and practices of the past. Some of the most important moves in this direction relate to the more flexible arrangements between different tiers of administration and to the tightening up of accounting practices, as well as legislation to ensure that devolved responsibilities will be accompanied by devolved resources. In one other important way, too, that is in the field of communication and public involvement, the system is slowly being modernised.

At least as far as the man in the street is concerned, this is perhaps the most obvious way in which, both in theory and in practice, local government is being modernised. Article 69 of the Basic Law in fact states: 'The local corporations shall provide the fullest information about their activities and facilitate the involvement of all citizens in local life.' Article 70 lays down that sessions of the *plenos* must be open to the public and, of course, to the media, with the exception of meetings of the commissions.

Decisions taken by the local authorities must be made public, including the annual budget. All citizens have the right to obtain copies of the decisions taken by local councils and any background to such agreements, as well as a right to consult archives and registers. Another form of popular involvement is the referendum, which mayors and presidents of provincial councils may call, on matters of 'a local nature which are of special interest to local residents', with the exception of financial matters.

Article 72 is worth quoting in full because it shows how those originally concerned with the reform of local government were determined to encourage more open government and more popular involvement in local affairs:

> The local authorities favour the development of associations for the defence of the

general or sectoral interests of residents, they provide them with the fullest information about their activities and, as far as possible, they make public resources available to them, give them access to the economic aid required to meet their objectives, and they encourage their participation in the running of the authority.

There is little doubt that the sort of reforms outlined above, plus the fact that local elections are now carried out in a fully democratic manner, have begun to reawaken a genuine interest in local affairs in recent years. In the main, local authorities, particularly at the municipal level, have responded to this and have been much more prepared than in the past to provide information on the activities and plans of the councils, as well as to stimulate more involvement in local activities – be they economic, political or cultural.

On the negative side, however, in addition to the continuing problems related to the multiplicity of small municipalities (8.3), three developments should be highlighted. Firstly, as already observed (7.5.3.1), while the regional share of public spending has increased substantially in recent years (and obviously local authorities will have benefited from this to some extent), the local share of spending has actually declined, currently representing no more than 12 per cent of the total when parity with the regions at approximately 25 per cent was the stated original goal. Secondly, the *diputaciones* have seen some of their powers (particularly in the area of health provision) assumed by regional governments, which in some cases seem to be applying a new form of centralism. Thirdly – and this reflects the overall economic situation of the country in the mid-1990s – local authorities, in their haste to provide a much greater range of services than have ever been available in the past, have in many cases over-reached themselves and are in a serious state of indebtedness, only matched by many regional governments, as well as central government itself, which until the recovery becomes long and sustained will not be in any position to bail them out.

Chapter 9

Public sector enterprises

9.1 Introduction

This chapter aims to cover those sectors of the state public sector (1.2.3) which, unlike the autonomous administrative entities dealt with earlier (6.3), can be defined as entities (*entidades*) or enterprises (*empresas*) rather than bodies (*organismos*) because of their more active involvement in the market economy. Some attention will also be paid to their counterparts at regional and local level which, according to some definitions, do not form part of the state public sector, although they are clearly part of the 'public sector' in its widest sense.

The Spanish Constitution of 1978, while recognising and protecting in article 38 the right to free enterprise, also acknowledges, in article 128, the right of the state to intervene in the economy in the public interest. Article 129, as well as providing the framework for the state's substantial involvement in social security and other welfare programmes (6.4, for example), also states that 'the authorities will effectively promote the diverse forms of participation in public ownership'. Thus, the Constitution appeared to be recognising the mixed economy inherited by post-Franco policy-makers – an economy in which, for historical, political and economic reasons, the state sector had acquired a large share of the economic cake (1.1.2).

Under Franco, the pragmatic approach to economic policy had led to the creation of a complex web of entities which seemed to possess a momentum of their own, often removed from their original objectives and the prevailing needs of the time. Diverse in character and purpose, and located in a variety of ministries, these entities enjoyed considerable administrative and financial autonomy. Little attempt was made at that time either to regulate and audit them or to provide a co-ordinated legal or economic framework for their activities. Under the prevailing system of political patronage and the general trend towards bureaucratisation, many posts were filled as rewards for past military or political service by people with little interest in or knowledge of economic affairs.

In the post-Franco era, while the ministerial location of these enterprises has been left largely unchanged, more entrepreneurial attitudes and practices have been adopted, and regulation and controls are now much tighter. An updated, reformulated text (*texto refundido*) of the General Budgetary Law (*Ley General Presupuestaria/LGP*), approved by a royal legislative decree of 23 September 1988, not only brought together all previous legislation dealing with budgetary, treasury, debt and accounting matters, but provided an overall financial framework for the whole of the state public sector.

9.2 Classification of public sector bodies

Although, as suggested in 1.2.3, classification of this sector is notoriously complex and may take various forms according to whether it be for legal, administrative or financial purposes, the LGP in fact divided the sector into five groups. The first two of these, state administration (ministries) and social security, have already been dealt with in chapter 6. The third covers so-called *administración institucional* and covers autonomous bodies, with two subgroups; the first of these, administrative bodies (*organismos autónomos de carácter administrativo*), has already been covered in chapters 6, 7 and 8; the second is entitled autonomous bodies of a commercial, industrial, financial or similar nature (*organismos autónomos de carácter comercial, industrial, financiero o análogo*). The commercial and industrial bodies will be dealt with in this chapter (9.3), while those of a financial nature will be covered in chapter 13.

The fourth group comprises so-called state 'enterprises' (*sociedades estatales*), known also as 'public enterprises' (*empresas públicas*), which will also be dealt with in this chapter (9.4). The fifth group, known as 'entities with special legal statute' (*entes con estatuto jurídico especial*), will also be dealt with here (9.5). Public sector enterprises dependent on regional and local administrations will be dealt with in 9.6 and 9.7, respectively. An overview of the whole range of public sector enterprises is given in table 9.1

9.3 Autonomous commercial, industrial, financial and similar bodies (*Organismos autónomos de carácter comercial, industrial, financiero o análogo*)

These entities are, on the whole, organised like the administrative bodies described in 6.3. They too are attached to particular ministries and, because of the nature of their activities, are given a considerable degree of latitude in their day-to-day running. They are distinguished from these other bodies in that they pursue commercial, industrial or financial objectives, which justifies a more independent structure and mode of functioning (see table 9.2). Although not all have the status of public limited SA companies (12.3), they can, to all intents and purposes, be regarded as public sector enterprises and, indeed, as we shall see, do have the right to create such entities. These bodies constitute 62.4 per cent of the sector known as 'institutional administration', while the remaining 37.6 per cent is accounted for by the administrative bodies referred to in 6.3.

In 1995, there were sixty-three of these bodies, seventeen fewer than in 1985, reflecting a general, albeit slow, trend over recent years to rationalise some bodies working in the same field and to privatise others. They are located within a wide range of ministries, including the ministries of defence, home affairs, agriculture,

Table 9.1 *Public sector enterprises, 1995*

Title in English	Title in Spanish
1 Autonomous commercial, industrial, financial or similar bodies (state)	*Organismos autónomos de carácter comercial, industrial, financiero o anólogo (estatales)*
2 State enterprises	*Sociedades estatales*
• Public law entities	• *Entidades de derecho público*
• Trading enterprises with state majority share	• *Sociedades mercantiles con participación estatal mayoritaria*
3 Public entities with special legal statute	*Entes públicos con estatuto jurídico especial*
4 Regional public sector enterprises	*Empresas públicas autonómicas*
• Public law entities	• *Entidades de derecho público*
• Trading enerprises	• *Sociedades mercantiles*
5 Local public sector enterprises	*Empresas públicas locales*
• Public law entities (provincial and municipal)	• *Entidades de derecho público (provinciales y municipales)*
• Trading enterprises (municipal)	• *Sociedades mercantiles (municipales)*

Sources: Various.

Table 9.2 *Examples of commercial, industrial, financial and similar bodies, 1992*

Ministry responsible	Name in English	Name in Spanish
Agriculture, Fisheries and Food	National Service for Agricultural Products	*Servicio Nacional de Producios Agrarios (SENPA)*
Labour and Social Affairs	Institute for Young People's Affairs (6.4.4.4)	*Instituto de la Juventud (INJUVE)*
Economy and Finance	Spanish Tourism Institute	*Instituto de Turismo de España (TURESPAÑA)*
Education and Culture	National Institute for Scenic Arts and Music	*Instituto Nacional de las Artes Escénicas y de la Música (INAEM)*
Defence	Military Construction Service	*Servicio Militar de Construcciones*
Economy and Finance	Official Credit Institute	*Instituto Crédito Oficial (ICO)*
Education and Culture	Higher Council for Scientific Research	*Consejo Superior de Investigaciones Científicas (CSIS)*
Industry and Energy	School of Industrial Organisation	*Escuela de Organización Industrial*
Home Affairs	Civil Guard Housing Trust	*Patronato de Viviendas de la Guardia Civil*
Promotion	Water Authority for the South of Spain	*Confederación Hidrográfica del Sur de España*
Presidency	*Official State Gazette*	*Boletín Oficial del Estado (BOE)*
Health and Consumer Affairs	Carlos III Health Institute	*Instituto de Salud Carlos III*

Source: El Sector Público Estatal, Secretaría del Estado de Hacienda, Ministerio de Economía y Hacienda (1992).

economy and finance, promotion, health and consumer affairs, labour and social affairs, education and culture, and the presidency. The largest number is located in Promotion, which among other entities is responsible for the management of Spain's numerous port authorities (*juntas de puerto*), as well as nine regional river and water authorities (*confederaciones hidrográficas*). Otherwise, the largest number are to be found in the Ministry of Agriculture, including, for example, the National Service for Agrarian Products (*Servicio Nacional de Productos Agrarios/SENPA*), the Fund for the Organisation and Regulation of Agrarian Production and Pricing (*Fondo de Ordenación y Regulación de Producciones y Precios Agrarios/FORPPA*, which is involved in price support and intervention schemes), and the Institute for Nature Conservation (*Instituto para la Conservación de la Naturaleza/ICONA*). These bodies handle large budgets and employ significant numbers of staff. As is the case with the autonomous administrative bodies, they must by law be attached to a government department.

9.4 State enterprises (*sociedades estatales*)·

The General Budgetary Law of 1988 distinguishes between two types of state enterprise: (i) entities governed by public law (*entidades de derecho público*) and (ii) trading enterprises (*sociedades mercantiles*) in which the state has a majority share but which must conform to private law (*derecho privado*). In 1993, there were almost 500 of these enterprises; only seventeen of them belonged to the first group and the rest were trading enterprises.

9.4.1 Public law entities

This group, which in fact in 1993 comprised only 3.4 per cent of the whole of this group, consists of a variety of wholly owned public companies, including the Spanish National Railway Network (*Red Nacional de Ferrocarriles Españoles/RENFE*, in fact known as an *ente público*), the ports of Barcelona, Bilbao, Valencia and Huelva, the Institute for the Diversification and Saving of Energy (*Instituto para la Diversificación y Ahorro de la Energía/IDAE*), the Centre for Industrial Technological Development (*Instituto para el Desarrollo Tecnológico Industrial*), and Narrow Gauge Railways (*Ferrocarriles de Vía Estrecha/FEVE*). This group also includes one entity under the auspices of the Directorate General for State Assets (9.4.2), the Official Tourism School (*Escuela Oficial de Turismo/EOT*) and the Official Credit Institute (*Instituto Crédito/ICO*) (13.4). The other 96.6 per cent of this group is constituted by the *sociedades mercantiles de participación estatal mayoritaria* which, as their name implies, involve enterprises where the state has a majority share holding. This wide range of different enterprises encompasses the thirty-five official categories of the economy, but are particularly prevalent in industry, energy, mining, construction and transport.

9.4.2 Trading enterprises with state majority share

Within the sector known as trading enterprises (*sociedades mercantiles*), there are three major economic groupings, which at least until recently (9.4.2.4) have all acted as holding companies for a very wide range of trading companies. These are the Directorate General for State Assets (DGPE, 9.4.2.1), within the Ministry of Economy and Finance, the National Institute for Industry (9.4.2.2), and the National Institute for Hydrocarbons (9.4.2.3); the latter two holdings are both attached to the Ministry of Industry and Energy (*Ministerio de Industria y Energía/MINER*). As major players in the economic field, these will now be examined separately.

9.4.2.1 Enterprises attached to the Directorate General for State Assets (Dirección General del Patrimonio del Estado/DGPE)

The legal framework for this body consists of two major laws. The first is the Law on State Assets (*Ley de Patrimonio del Estado/LPE*) approved by royal decree as long ago as 15 April 1964; the second is the *Ley General Presupuestaria* (*LGP*) approved by royal legislative decree on 23 September 1988 (see above), which brought together in one updated document all the relevant legislation on the subject. The group of bodies and enterprises controlled by the Directorate General, which acts as a holding company, came to be known as the *Grupo Patrimonio*. Structurally, all these enterprises are very similar to any other private or public limited company: each has a board (*consejo de administración*) headed by a chairman (*presidente*) and composed of a variable number of board members (*vocales*), as well as a management committee (*comisión directiva*) headed by a managing director (*director gerente*), and composed of a number of directors, plus in some cases the government delegate (*delegado del gobierno*) to protect the interests of the state.

Of the three major holding groups, *Grupo Patrimonio* encompasses the widest range of social and economic activities, including financial, industrial, agrarian, commercial and service enterprises. Group reports tend to place them in three sub-groups: financial enterprises; industrial, commercial and service enterprises; and 'enabling' enterprises (*empresas instrumentales*). In 1994, the *Grupo Patrimonio* consisted of thirty-three of these enterprises, employing a total of 141,000 staff and representing a state share holding that varied from 20 to 100 per cent. All these enterprises are constituted as *sociedades anónimas* (*SA*) (12.3) and are, therefore, unlike the holding companies and autonomous bodies, subject to private law (*derecho privado*). The same applies to the many subsidiary companies which are dependent on a number of these major enterprises. A list of the major enterprises of the *Grupo Patrimonio*, some of which will now be examined, is given in table 9.3.

The major enterprise within the financial sub-group is the Spanish Banking Corporation (*Corporación Bancaria Española/CBE – Argentaria*) which is a good example of a major enterprise incorporating a number of subsidiary companies, in this case seven. This will be examined in detail in 13.5.

Table 9.3 *Major companies in the Grupo Patrimonio, 1995*

Sector	Company	% state holding	Date founded
Financial	Compañía Española de Seguros de Crédito a la Exportación (CESCE)	50.25	1971
	Corporación Bancaria Española (Argentaria)	51.66	1991
	Sociedad Anónima Estatal de Caución Agraria (SAECA)	80.00	1988
Mining and construction	Minas de Almadén y Arrayanes SA (MAYASA)	100.00	1982
Agriculture	Empresa de Transformación Agraria SA (TRAGSA)	20.00	1977
Industry	Compañía española de Tabaco en Rama SA (CETARSA)	79.18	1987
	Tabacalera SA	52.36	1945
Commerce and services	Agencia EFE	99.38	1939
	ALDEASA SA	80.00	
	Empresa Nacional de Autopistas SA (ENAUSA)	100.00	1984
	Mercados Centrales de Abastecimiento SA (MERCASA)	42.66	1966
	Paradores de Turismo de España SA	100.00	1991
	Sociedad Estatal de Gestión Inmobilaria de Patrimonio SA (SEGIPSA)	100.00	1977
	Telefónica de España SA	31.86	1924
	Compañía Transmediterránea SA	95.24	1916
Enabling	Sociedad Estatal de Gestión de Activos SA (AGESA)[a]	100.00	1993
	Cartuja 93 SA	51.00	1991
	Barcelona Holding Olímpico SA (HOLSA)	51.00	1989
	Inmobilaria de Promociones y Arriendos SA (IMPROASA)	100.00	1984
	Sociedad Española de Estudios para La Comunicación Fija a través del Estrecho de Gibraltar SA (SECEGSA)	100.00	1981
	Madrid 1994, Organizadora de Conferencias Internacionales SA	100.00	1992

Notes:
[a] Originally founded in 1982 as the *Sociedad Estatal de Ejecución de Programas Conmemorativos del Centenario del Descubrimiento de América SA* and changed in 1985 to the *Sociedad Estatal para la Exposición Universal de Sevilla 92.*
Source: Grupo Patrimonio, *Memoria 1993 (Annual Report)* (1994).

Of the companies listed in the sub-group, the oldest is undoubtedly the *Compañía Transmediterránea SA*, which was founded in 1916. It is a large shipping company which is concerned with all aspects of the trade, including sea transportation, ship construction and repair, shipping insurance, package tours, etc. It plies the busy sea routes between Algeçiras and North Africa, and between other ports and the Balearics and the Canaries. The state has a 95.24 per cent holding in the company, which includes twenty-three subsidiary enterprises, including thirteen loading companies (*sociedades de estiba*) based in the major ports of Spain.

Another well-established and typically Francoist company, dating back to 5 March 1945, is *Tabacalera* which, as its name implies, is concerned with the import, manufacture and sale at home and abroad of tobacco products. The state's share in this enterprise is 52.36 per cent. Within the *Tabacalera* group, there are thirteen smaller companies, including several from abroad, and thirteen associated companies. Since Spain's entry into the EC in 1986, the company has had to concede its former monopoly status under laws passed in 1985. None the less, thanks mainly to a dynamic export drive, particularly in Eastern Europe, Japan and Germany, exports have been very buoyant.

On 18 January 1991, the former autonomous administrative body, *Administración Turística Española*, attached to the then Ministry of Industry, Commerce and Tourism, became the state enterprise known as *Paradores de Turismo de España SA*. This enterprise is responsible for the chain of eighty-five high quality state-run hotels or paradors, the first of which was founded as long ago as 1928. Located in every province of the mainland and islands, many of these have been created from tasteful conversions of historic buildings, such as palaces, monasteries and castles, often located in areas of outstanding natural beauty. In theory, its statutes state that the organisation is responsible for the management and development of all state-owned tourism establishments and facilities, but in reality the bulk of its work relates to the paradors. Currently, the state retains a 100 per cent stake in the enterprise, but a future public flotation of shares is a strong possibility, as is the privatisation of some individual paradors. The main aim behind the conversion from autonomous body to state enterprise was to inject more entrepreneurial approaches to management and the training of staff.

Unlike the enterprises already mentioned, those known as *sociedades instrumentales* have been set up for a specific and limited purpose, and are usually closed down once that purpose has been achieved – though Parkinson's Law seems in fact to have operated in a number of cases where life has gone on beyond the expected time of extinction! Thus, while the company set up to co-ordinate the commemorations for the 500th anniversary of the Colombus expedition, *Sociedad Estatal de Ejecución de Programas Conmemorativos del Centenario del Descubrimiento de América SA*, has now been wound up, the enterprise established in 1989, via a joint agreement with the city hall of Barcelona, to finance the infrastructure and facilities for the Olympic Games, *Barcelona Holding Olímpico SA (HOLSA)*, is still very much in existence, reflecting the long process required, following such a massive world event, to settle all payments and debts. The state has a 51 per cent share in this company, the rest being in the hands of the city hall of Barcelona. *Cartuja 93 SA*, on the other hand, constituted in October 1991 in relation to the World Fair, Expo 92, held in Seville the following year, was a conscious attempt to find ways of making profitable social and economic use of some of the pavilions and facilities left over after this major event. This enterprise is jointly financed by the state (51 per cent), the *Junta de Andalucía* (44 per cent) (table 7.6) and the city hall of Seville (5 per cent).

Worthy of special mention, as one of the most important companies in the group, is *Telefónica de España SA*, founded as a monopoly in 1924, and a major player in the Spanish telecommunications industry. *Telefónica* has been subject to restructuring in recent years; in fact, since the summer of 1995, the state's stake in the enterprise has been reduced to approximately 20 per cent, with the prospect of full privatisation in the not-too-distant future. This expanding enterprise wholly or partly owns 24 subsidiary companies, including telephone companies abroad, is associated with nine other companies and has shares in another eleven. It is easily the largest of the *Grupo Patrimonio* companies, with equity of 1,437,055 million pesetas and an average staff of over 84,000 (1993).

While a number of firms in the *Grupo Patrimonio* have recorded financial successes in recent years, in spite of the recession of the early 1990s, one company in particular has been in great difficulty. This is the textile giant *Intelhorce SA*, the largest textile company in Andalusia, which was founded in Málaga in 1960. Its sale to an Italian entrepreneur in 1989 led to the exposure of public and private corruption on a massive scale. After subsequently re-acquiring the ailing company on behalf of the state and attempting to relaunch it as *General Textil Española* (*GTE*), in June 1995, the Ministry of Economy and Finance announced its closure with the threatened loss of 1,700 jobs. Needless to say, this has aroused enormous opposition from the unions who are still hoping to persuade the government to keep the company afloat in some form and, at the very least, to ensure adequate compensation for the workers involved.

9.4.2.2 Enterprises attached to the National Institute for Industry (Instituto Nacional de Industria / INI)

INI was founded in the early years of the Franco regime, on 25 September 1941 (1.1.2). Following the devastation of the Civil War and in the face of Spain's subsequent international isolation, the government set about the task of rebuilding the Spanish economy, laying particular stress on the development of a home-grown industrial sector, historically a sector that hitherto had been very limited in scope. In fact, to a very large extent, INI was the major instrument of economic policy during the formative years of the Franco regime. Under the auspices of INI, the state set up a number of large, mainly public limited companies, particularly, though not exclusively, industrial. Examples of those established mainly during the 1940s are: *Empresa Nacional Siderúrgica SA* (ENSIDESA) (iron and steel), *Empresa Nacional de Electricidad SA* (ENDESA) (electricity), *Empresa Nacional Bazán de Construcciones Navales Militares* (BAZAN) (naval defence), *Empresa Nacional Santa Bárbara de Industrias Militares* (SANTA BARBARA) (military hardware), *Sociedad Española de Automóviles de Turismo* (SEAT) (car manufacture, originally in collaboration with Fiat) and *Iberia, Líneas Aéreas de España SA* (IBERIA) (the Spanish National Airline).

During the 1960s, INI became involved, as a minority shareholder in companies like *Empresa Nacional Hulleras del Norte SA* (HUNOSA) (coal mining), HISPANOIL (petroleum products) and *Astilleros Españoles SA* (AESA) (shipbuilding). During the economic crisis of the 1970s, INI developed a reputation as a 'hospital for private firms making losses' (*hospital de empresas privadas en pérdidas*), bailing out such firms as *Hijos de J. Barreras SA* (BARRERAS) (shipbuilding), *Astilleros y Talleres del Noroeste SA* (ASTANO) (shipbuilding and repairs), and *Minas de Figaredo SA* (FIGAREDO) (mining). During the 1980s, under the Socialist government of Felipe González, many INI companies were subjected to severe pro-grammes of industrial reconstruction (*reconversión industrial*) in an attempt to make Spanish companies more competitive prior to entry into the EC in 1986. While firms like *Altos Hornos del Mediterráneo SA* were forced to close down their factory at Sagunto, and the HUNOSA coal mining company in Asturias suffered drastic pruning and job losses, a number of firms were sold to the private sector, including SEAT (to Volkswagen), Viajes Marsans SA (travel agencies), *Empresa Nacional de Turismo SA* (ENTURSA) (tourism) and *Empresa Nacional de Autocamiones SA* (ENASA) (lorries). In fact, between 1985 and 1995, INI privatised no less than 21 companies, across a wide range of economic sectors.

In recent times, the most significant change – which has had far-reaching conse-quences – has been the creation of TENEO. In the State Budget Law (*Ley de Presupuestos Generales del Estado*) of 1991 (article 107), with effect from 1992, the government authorised INI to establish under its umbrella a large public limited company to which the shares of certain INI companies would be progressively transferred. The Council of Ministers had to authorise the creation of TENEO and subsequently, in consultation with the Ministry of Economy and Finance, to authorise any sale or purchase of companies. In a phased operation during 1992, no less than forty-seven companies were transferred to TENEO. At the same time, the material assets of INI headquarters in Madrid were made over to this new entity. The aim of this bold move was to group together those enterprises which INI con-sidered to be, at least in the future, potentially profitable (*potencialmente rentables*). One of the features of this new enterprise is that its member companies do not receive any funds from the state budgets (unlike INI itself), but it will be completely self-financing; in time, public share offers are likely to be on the agenda. In 1994, the TENEO group of companies employed 70,000 staff, had an income of 1.7 billion pesetas and exported goods worth half a billion pesetas.

Some of the major companies transferred to TENEO include IBERIA, ENDESA (electricity), *Construcciones Aeronáuticas SA* (CASA) (defence and aerospace), INESPAL (aluminium), *Indra-Sistemas SA* (INDRA) (electronics) and *Empresa Nacional Elcano de la Marina Mercante* (ELCANO) (maritime transport). Its share interest in these enterprises varies from 5.7 per cent in the case of the *Banco Exterior de España* (13.5.5) to 66.6 per cent in the case of ENDESA. As can be seen in table 9.4, the TENEO companies include the industrial development companies (*sociedades de desarrollo industrial/SODI*) which from 1972 onwards were established in the poorer regions to promote industrial growth. These can be recognised from the prefix SODI attached to the first letters of the region concerned: thus, SODIAN operates in Andalusia, SODIEX in Extremadura, SODIAR in Aragón, SODICAL in Castilla-León, SODICAMAN in Castilla–La Mancha, and SODICAN in the Canary Islands. (SODIGA in Galicia was recently privatised.) TENEO holds a 51 per cent share in these companies, the rest being provided by savings banks, com-mercial banks, the *Banco Exterior de España* (13.5.5) and the regional authorities themselves.

In its first few years of existence, TENEO seems to have fulfilled expectations in

Table 9.4 *Companies attached to TENEO, 1994*

Sector	Company	% state share-holding	Date founded
Energy	Empresa Nacional de Electricidad SA (ENDESA)[a]	75.62	1944
	Empresa Nacional del Uranio SA (ENUSA)	60.80	1972
	Red Eléctrica de España SA	53.07	1985
Air Transport	Aviación y Comercio SA (AVIACO)	99.94	1948
	Iberia, Líneas Aéreas de España SA[a]	99.93	1927
Aerospace/	Construcciones Aeronáuticas SA (CASA)	99.28	1923
Electronics	Indra–Sistemas (INDRA)[a]	60.00	1979
Engineering/	Babcock Wilcox Española SA (BWE)	100.00	1919
Construction	Empresa Nacional Adaro SA (ADARO)	100.00	1942
	Empresa Nacional de Ingeniería y Tecnología SA (INITEC)	100.00	1964
	Equipos Nucleares SA	100.00	1973
Aluminium/	Empresa Nacional de Celulosas SA (ENCE)	70.81	1968
Chemicals	Industria Española del Aluminio SA (INESPAL)[a]	98.32	1986
	Potasas de Llobregat SA	99.99	1990
Sea	Compañía Transatlántica Española SA (CTE)[a]	99.98	1881
Transport	Empresa Nacional Elcano de la Marina Mercante SA (ELCANO)	100.00	1943
Corporate	Empresa Nacional de Artesanía SA (ARTESPAÑA)	100.00	1969
Services	INFOINVEST[a]	100.00	1989
	Sociedad para el Desarrollo Industrial de Andalucía SA (SODIAN)	60.29	1977
	Sociedad para el Desarrollo Industrial de Castilla y León SA (SODICAL)	51.00	1982

[a] These are groups of enterprises, of which the named one is the parent company.
Source: Grupo TENEO 1993 (Annual Report) (1994).

spite of having been established at the height of the recession of the early 1990s. The company report for 1994 announced that all the member companies, with the notable exception of IBERIA (see below) were in profit. One encouraging feature is the extent to which it has become increasingly involved, as was indeed the aim, in the international market, 49 per cent of its sales going to countries of the European Union. TENEO, moreover, is constantly evolving; for example, as well as the privatisation of SODIGA, four other companies have been sold off and others, like the INDRA electronics group, have been restructured. TENEO has also acquired a large holding in the major electricity company *Sevillana de Electricidad SA*, as well as minority holdings in a number of power generating companies, such as the large thermal power station of Puertollano. TENEO companies, particularly in the field of energy, are making great progress on the international front; for example, in 1993 ENDESA signed an agreement with electricity companies in Peru and Santo Domingo. An area in which the TENEO companies have been very active recently has been that of research and development (R&D) (29,000 million pesetas in 1994); an increasingly important part of this budget is being earmarked for environmental

Table 9.5 *Companies still attached to INI, 1994*

Sector	Company	% state share-holding	Date founded
Naval	*Astilleros Españoles SA (AESA)*[a]	100.00	1969
Construction	*Astilleros y Talleres del Noroeste SA (ASTANO)*	100.00	1944
	Hijos de J. Barreras SA (BARRERAS)	99.99	1928
Mining	*Minas de Figaredo, SA (FIGAREDO)*	100.00	1932
	Empresa Nacional Hulleras del Norte SA (HUNOSA)	100.00	1967
	Prerreducidos Integrados del Suroeste SA (PRESUR)	99.64	1981
Iron and Steel	*Corporación Siderurgía Integral, SA (CSI)*[a]	50.00	1991
	Productos Tubulares SA	100.00	1992
	SIDENOR SA[a]	50.00	1991
Defence	*Empresa Nacional Bazán de*	100.00	1947
	Construcciones Navales Militares SA (BAZAN)		
	Empresa Nacional Santa Bárbara de Industrias Militares	100.00	1960
	SA (SANTA BARBARA)		
Insurance	*Musini, Sociedad Mutua de Seguros y Reaseguros a*	63.87	1966
	Prima Fija (MUSINI)		

Note:
[a] These are groups of enterprises, of which the named one is the parent company.
Source: Grupo INI 1993 (Annual Report) (1994).

aspects of company operations, TENEO claiming to be the Spanish market leader in co-generation and renewable energy.

It is interesting to note that most of the eleven major companies which INI has not transferred to TENEO are located in the heavy industrial sectors which both in Spain and world-wide have been in decline for at least the last two decades. The list, which can be seen in table 9.5, significantly includes some of the 'lame ducks' like BARRERAS and FIGAREDO, that were taken over by the INI 'hospital' in the 1970s, as well as others, like BAZAN and SANTA BARBARA, which came into being in the 1940s and early 1950s when state protectionism was at its height. What the future holds for such enterprises is uncertain, though, doubtless, opportunities will be sought to privatise any parts which in themselves might seem capable of generating profits, at least in the longer term.

During 1995 and early 1996, IBERIA has been frequently in the news as Spain pressed the EU Transport Commissioner, Neil Kinnock, to grant the ailing company permission to sell off some of its assets (specifically a large part of its 85 per cent share in *Aerolíneas Argentinas*) and to provide a second controversial injection of state subsidies (the first was in 1992). In spite of strong objections from both other national airlines in the Community and from private competitors in Europe, the Commission was persuaded to come to the aid of IBERIA in January 1996.

Like other public sector organisations, INI itself is subject to the General Budgetary Law of 1988, while the companies which it has spawned are governed by the Reformulated Text on Company Law (*Texto Refundido de la Ley de Sociedades Anónimas*) of 1989 (12.1). Structurally, INI is organised like most other autonomous bodies, with a board headed by a president and vice-president, who are assisted by the board members, plus a secretariat which deals with legal affairs; there is also an executive committee (*comisión ejecutiva*) which for day-to-day-affairs is run by the director general (*director general*), assisted by a financial director (*director financiero*) and a director for planning and control (*director de planificación y control*). TENEO in fact has a similar structure and co-ordination between INI and TENEO is ensured by the fact that the office holders for both are virtually the same, except that the posts of director general (one in INI and two in TENEO) are filled by different people.

9.4.2.3 National Institute for Hydrocarbons (Instituto Nacional de Hidrocarburos / INH)

The INH was founded in 1981 as a public entity (*ente público*) (in practice, one more state holding company) in order to combine that part of the energy sector which had previously been under the control of INI with two companies CAMPSA and *Petrolíber*, which had previously been under the auspices of the *Dirección General del Patrimonio del Estado* (9.4.2.1). It was structured and run in a similar way to INI before the latter ws restructured in 1992 with the creation of TENEO (9.4.2.2). The INH was established to co-ordinate and control all the public sector enterprises operating in crude oil, petroleum products, natural gas and petrochemicals. In general, the move proved to be successful since, as early as 1985, the ten companies then controlled by the INH accounted for as much as 1 per cent of Spain's gross domestic product. Entry into the European Community in 1986 presented an opportunity for further restructuring and rationalisation in an increasingly competitive market and EC law required, in any case, that the CAMPSA monopoly of the sales in Spain of petroleum products be terminated.

Thus, in October 1987, in a move similar in many ways to the creation of TENEO, the INH established a nucleus of public limited companies under the umbrella title of REPSOL, which includes *Repsol SA*, the parent company, plus the ten main affiliated companies listed in table 9.6. The aim was to create a company that, as an oil group, could compete internationally, drawing upon the experience and resources of oil sector companies of long-standing tradition. Today, in terms of sales and profits, *Repsol* can boast of being one of the most important oil companies in Europe and on a world scale is the sixth most important company in the sector. *Repsol* and its numerous subsidiaries and associated companies have a large number of shareholders from small retail holders to large institutional investors; its shares are listed on the Spanish Stock Markets and on the New York Stock Exchange (NYSE). In 1989, *Repsol* went public and floated 60 per cent of its shares on the stock exchange. In March/April 1995, another 20 per cent and in January/February 1996 a further 10 per cent, leaving only 10 per cent in state hands; most commentators regarded these ventures as highly successful. Until the announcement of fundamental changes to INI/TENEO and INH (9.4.2.4), one could certainly foresee the day when *Repsol* would retain no state share whatsoever and would soon become a totally privatised concern.

Table 9.6 *Major Repsol companies, 1995*

Company	Activity	% Repsol SA holding
Repsol Exploración SA	Oil and gas exploration and production	100.00
Repsol Petróleo SA	Runs four oil refineries	99.96
Petronor SA	Runs one oil refinery (Bilbao); one brand name for marketing petroleum products	87.82
Repsol Química SA	Production of high grade petrochemicals	100.00
Repsol Comercial de Productos Petrolíferos SA	Marketing and sale of petroleum derivative products	96.34
Grupo Gas Natural SDG	Marketing and sale of natural gas	45.26[a]
Repsol Butano SA	Purchase, sale and distribution of liquid petroleum gas (LPG)	100.00
Compañía Logística de Hidrocarburos (CLH)	Responsible for logistical services, including pipelines, and for service stations	59.87
Repsol Naviera Vizcaina	Sea transport of petroleum products and service stations	99.55

Note:
[a] *Grupo Gas Natural* owns 91 per cent of the shares in the old gas company ENAGAS; the remaining 9 per cent comes directly from INH.
Source: Oferta Pública de Venta de Acciones de Repsol, SA, Instituto Nacional de Hidrocarburos (INH) (1995).

The major companies listed in table 9.6, as well as their numerous subsidiaries, are predominantly public limited companies with boards and management structures similar to those of private companies and, like the companies of *Grupo Patrimonio* and *TENEO*, are subject to private law (*derecho privado*).

- *Repsol Exploración SA*, as its name implies, is concerned with oil exploration but also with production. i.e. with the so-called 'upstream' side of the whole oil/gas operation. Following in the footsteps of HISPANOIL, the company which began exploring for crude oil and gas over 30 years ago, *Repsol Exploración* has interests in eleven countries. Over recent years, in fact, the company has tended to concentrate its exploration production and reserves acquisition activities in areas of high potential, particularly in Latin America (Mexico, Venezuela, Colombia and Argentina), Africa, Indonesia, the Middle East (Libya and Egypt), the far East and the North Sea. The Mexican State Petroleum Company, *Petróleos Mexicanos* (*PEMEX*), which is a share holder in *Repsol* (5 per cent), has signed an agreement with *Repsol* to supply no less than 50 per cent of the company's oil needs. In Indonesia, *Repsol* has become one of the world's main producers of crude oil. In Spain, some limited exploration has been carried out near Burgos and off the Mediterranean coast near Tarragona.

- *Repsol Petróleo SA* is the company responsible for the country's well-established refineries in Bilbao, Cartagena, La Coruña, Puertollano and Tarragona, strategically placed near the main centres of consumption in Spain, Portugal and southern France. It is also concerned with the marketing of refined petro-leum. In the field of refining, *Repsol* has gained a high reputation and its conver-sion:distillation ratio is above the average for the European Union. This company belongs to the European Council for the Chemical Industry (*Consejo Europeo de la Industria Química*) and has signed the Mutual Assistance Pacts (*Pactos de Ayuda Mutua*) with other European oil producers, all concerned to improve safety and limit the environmental impact of oil conversion.

- *Petronor SA* is the company based in the north which both runs the refinery in Bilbao and whose name is used as one of the three brand names for marketing *Repsol* petroleum products at the numerous service stations throughout the country.

- *Repsol Química SA* is concerned with the production of high grade petrochem-ical products, especially at the refineries of Puertollano and Tarragona. Production of ethylene in these centres represents 60 per cent of national output and production of propylene at the refineries of La Coruña and Bilbao (*Petronor*) accounts for 61 per cent of total Spanish production. In addition, this company produces many chemicals which constitute basic materials for the plastics and fibres industries.

- *Repsol Comercial de Productos Petrolíferos SA* is concerned with the marketing and sale of numerous derivative petroleum-based products, including plastify-ing oils for the rubber industry, composites used to fill telecommunications cables and coke consumed by the steel industry. It is among the top companies in the world for waxes and paraffins, with application in the food and rubber industries, among others.

- *Grupo Gas Natural (SDG)* was recently formed as a result of a complicated merger of the old ENAGAS firm, run under the auspices of INH, and *Gas Natural*, forming thus the fourth largest natural gas group in Europe in terms of the number of clients. It sells 40 per cent of the natural gas currently con-sumed in Spain and has a 75 per cent share in the residential–commercial sector. *Repsol SA* is currently the major shareholder of this company, holding 75 per cent of the shares, while 25 per cent have been floated on the stock market.

- *Repsol Butano SA* is concerned with the purchase, sale and distribution of liquid petroleum gas (LPG). A more viable company was formed out of a dis-parate group of competitors when *Repsol* acquired, among other companies operating in the field, *Gas Madrid* and *Gas Barcelona*. The LPG network, now the largest in Europe, comprises more than 30 storage, bottling and despatch-ing centres, serving almost 14 million customers.

- *Compañía Logística de Hidrocarburos (CLH)* was formed partly as the result of the process of breaking up the CAMPSA monopoly. It is responsible both for the logistical services of *Repsol*, including the hundreds of kilometres of oil pipelines traversing the country, and the 1,300 or so service stations located everywhere in Spain. In fact, CLH is a conglomerate involving *Repsol* itself, the French ELF petroleum company, BP, Shell and the *Compañía Española de*

Petróleos (*CEPSA*), a private Spanish company trading in lubricants and carburants. Service stations trade under three brand names: *Repsol*, *CAMPSA* and *Petronor*. A number of *Repsol* service stations have been recently established in the United Kingdom and, in fact, the company has signed agreements with Trusthouse Forte (now Granada) for the establishment of motorway service stations trading under well-known brand names like Little Chef.

Repsol Naviera Vizcaina is a sister company based in Bilbao, which concentrates on sea transport and also controls a chain of service stations located mainly in the Basque Country.

In recent years, *Repsol*, like INI, has become involved in R&D geared to improving its record on emissions into the atmosphere; in this field *Repsol* put many measures into force in anticipation of the EU Directive of December 1994 referring to emissions of volatile organic compounds. Unlike INI, *Repsol* has also become heavily involved in sponsorship of cultural and sporting events, including, for example, the Festival of Spanish Arts held in London in the spring of 1994, and support of the Spanish effort for the Olympic Games in Atlanta in 1996.

This sector in general and *Repsol* in particular provide a very good illustration of the need to adapt structures and activities to the requirements of the Single Market. Between 1986 and 1992, the importation of petroleum products from the European Union was subject to a transitional programme of controlled expansion in parallel with a similar timetable for exports to the Community. At the beginning of the period, most EU exports to Spain were sold by importers to the state which fixed prices and then sold them on to the customer. Once liberalised, products could be sold via a new network of outlets, the so-called Parallel Network (*Red Paralela*), at a price determined by the market, subject to price maxima compatible with EU regulations. Petrol, diesel oil and other products from Spanish refineries for internal consumption had to be sold via service stations which formed the Concessional Network (*Red Concesional*). By the end of the transition period in 1992, all aspects of the industry were liberalised: ownership of all the transportation and network and sales outlets had been transferred from the state to Spanish petroleum companies, in particular *Repsol*.

9.4.2.4 Recent developments

In June 1995, the government announced a fundamental change to the structure of the INI and INH holding companies. By the royal decree of 16 July 1995, INI effectively disappears and the loss-making companies in the naval construction, mining, iron and steel sectors will be transferred to the new State Industrial Agency (*Agencia Industrial del Estado/AIE*). At the same time, the profit-making enterprises of TENEO and *Repsol*, plus remaining INI companies, will be transferred to the new State Company for Industrial Participation (*Sociedad Estatal de Participaciones Industriales/SEPI*). SEPI and AEI were created by an act of Parliament of 30 December 1995. One of the major aims of this shake-up is to ensure that, within six

Table 9.7 *Entities with special legal statute, 1992*

Name in English	Name in Spanish
National Airports and Air Traffic Authority	*Aeropuertos Nacionales y Navegación Aérea*
Bank of Spain (13.3)	*Banco de España*
National Stock Market Committee	*Comisión Nacional del Mercado de Valores (CNMV)*
Economic and Social Council (5.8)	*Consejo Económico y Social (CES)*
Council for Young People's Affairs	*Consejo de la Juventud*
Council for Nuclear Safety	*Consejo de Seguridad Nuclear (CSN)*
Spanish Radio and Television Company	*Ente Público Radiotelevisión Española (RTVE)*
Cervantes Institute	*Instituto Cervantes*
National Mutual Assurance Company for Local Government Workers	*Mutualidad Nacional de Previsión de la Administración Local (MUNPAL)*
Iron and Steel Restructuring Agency	*Gerencia de Reconversión Siderúrgica*

Source: *El Sector Público Estatal*, Ministerio de Economía y Hacienda (1992).

years, the debts of the INI companies within SEPI, currently 700,000 million pesetas, will be paid out of the overall profits of this new group, thus relieving the Treasury and the taxpayer of a massive debt. AEI will be a vehicle for a fundamental restructuring which is bound to involve severe cutbacks and closures, as well as the occasional privatisation where feasible. There is no doubt that such developments will be watched very closely by the unions and in July 1995 there were mass protests in shipyards owned by *Astilleros Españoles SA*. The scheme was also criticised by a former PSOE minister of economy, Carlos Solchaga, who lamented the lack of any parliamentary debate on the subject.

9.5 Entities with special legal statute (*entes con estatuto jurídico especial*)

These bodies, recognised as distinct for the first time in the 1988 State Budgetary Law, are difficult to categorise in that they seem to be a hybrid between the constitutional bodies referred to in 1.2.3 and autonomous bodies, both administrative and commercial (see table 9.7). The *Consejo Económico y Social* (*CES*), already dealt with as a consultative body in 5.8, could easily be regarded as a constitutional body since its creation was envisaged in the Constitution of 1978. The *Consejo de Seguridad Nuclear* (*CSN*), answerable direct to Parliament and concerned with citizen protection in matters of nuclear safety could, however, also be regarded as a constitutional body, although it is not referred to in the 'Law of laws'. The *Instituto Cervantes*, on the other hand, attached to the Ministry of Education and Culture, and established to promote and protect the Spanish language and culture at home and abroad, could easily be seen as just one more autonomous administrative body, an extension of a normal government service. The *Instituto Español de Comercio Exterior* is clearly of a commercial nature, while the *Agencia Estatal de la Administración Tributaria* is concerned with tax affairs. It is perhaps not surprising to find that the Spanish Radio and Television Network, *Radiotelevisión Española* (*RTVE*), defined as an *ente público*, has a special legal statute.

What all these entities have in common is that, while like many other state-controlled bodies their budgets are included in the annual state budgets (*presupuestos generales del estado*), and they are all subject to the normal budget control of such bodies, they have each been given a separate statute which clearly defines their particular role in terms of aims, operation, financing and control.

9.6 Regional public sector enterprises

It is not surprising to find that, since a whole structure of government and administration has been established at regional level following the creation of the seventeen autonomous communities (chapter 7), these public authorities should have themselves sought, like central government, to make a positive contribution to their own development, particularly in the economic sphere. Thus, we find that each regional administration has, over the last fifteen years or so, built up a body of public sector enterprises which in some cases collaborate with counterparts at national level. The regional authority chosen to exemplify this kind of development is the *Junta de Andalucía* which, in defining its public sector enterprises, uses the term *sector público empresarial*, (see table 9.8). In the 1983 General Law on Public Finance, the *Junta's* public enterprises are defined as 'those business enterprises in which the majority shareholder is the *Junta de Andalucía* or one of its autonomous bodies and entities governed by public law with legal personality which by law must adapt their activities to the requirements of private law'. Subsequent legislation of the Andalusian Parliament has brought Andalusian law, namely the *Ley de Patrimonio de la Comunidad Autónoma de Andalucía* relating to public sector enterprises, in line with the General Budgetary Law of 1988 (9.1).

9.6.1 Public law entities (*entidades de derecho público*)

Like their counterparts at national level, these are autonomous bodies (within the industrial, commercial and financial group) set up by the Andalusian government to promote economic activity or services in specific areas where it is felt that a more independent and entrepreneurial approach best suits the initiative concerned. They were created by an Act of the Parliament of Andalusia. By law, such enterprises must come under the auspices of a specific regional government department (*consejería*).

Of the above, although RTVA is the largest in terms of the number of people employed (808 in 1992), the most influential in economic terms is the IFA which has established seventeen companies of very varied size and spanning a multitude of activities, from the large Development and Economic Restructuring Agency of Andalusia (*Sociedad para la Promoción y Reconversión Económica de Andalucía SA/SOPREA*) – which itself has majority and minority holdings in a wide range of smaller companies – to small family concerns like the carpet-making company based

Table 9.8 *Public enterprises of the Junta de Andalucía, 1992*

Enterprise	Function
Entidades de derecho público	**Public law entities**
Empresa Pública de Puertos de Andalucía	Regional ports authority
Empresa Pública de la Radio y Televisión de Andalucía (RTVA)	Regional radio and TV authority
Empresa Pública de Suelo de Andalucía (EPSA)	Regional housing promotion agency
Instituto de Fomento de Andalucía (IFA)	Regional economic development agency
Sociedades mercantiles	**Trading enterprises**
Empresa Andaluza de Salud Pública SA	Public health promotion agency (especially in higher education)
Empresa de Gestión de Instalaciones y Turismo Juvenil SA (INTURJOVEN)	Management of tourism facilities for the young (including youth hostels)
Empresa de Gestión Medioambiental SA	Environmental management agency (including waste disposal)
Empresa de Gestión de Tierras SA	Land management agency (including agriculture, forestry and hunting)
Orquesta de Sevilla SA	Seville regional orchestra
Sociedad de Gestión y Financiación de Infraestructuras Sierra Nevada 95 SA	Management and finance agency for World Skiing Championships in Granada
Verificaciones Industriales de Andalucía SA	Vehicle inspection service

Source: El Sector Público Empresarial de la Comunidad Autónoma de Andalucía 1992 (1993).

in the Alpujarras, *Alfombras Alpujarreñas SA*. For a number of years, the IFA has also been helping to support a number of tourism projects, particularly those concerned with rural tourism, in the region, often providing matching funding from the *Junta de Andalucía* for funds emanating from EU sources, such as those provided under the 'Plan Leader' for rural development (8.5.2, 15.4.2.4).

9.6.2 Trading companies (*sociedades mercantiles*)

Currently, there are thirty such entities in the region. Nine of these have been set up directly by the government (*consejo de gobierno*) or one of its autonomous bodies and constitute what is called the *Grupo Patrimonio*. The remaining twenty-one have been established indirectly via one of the public law entities referred to in 9.5. As in the case of the latter, they have by law been ascribed to a *consejería*. Table 9.8 gives a complete list of both categories of companies, indicating what their function is in each case.

9.7 Local public sector enterprises

Even before the establishment of the autonomous communities, local authorities, as suggested in 8.3.3.2, had been setting up autonomous enterprises, sometimes in the form of public limited SA companies, to carry out certain services deemed to require more freedom of action in both the organisational and financial spheres. In

Table 9.9 *Public enterprises of the Ayuntamiento de Málaga, 1993*

Enterprise	Function
Companies wholly owned by Ayuntamiento	
Empresa Malagueña de Transportes SA (EMT)	Local bus service
Empresa Malagueña de Aguas de Málaga, SA (EMASA)	Water supply
Sociedad Municipal de Aparcamientos y Servicios SA	Car parks
Empresa Municipal de Iniciativas y Actividades Empresariales de Málaga SA (PROMALAGA)	Promotion of municipal entrepreneurial activities
Empresa Municipal de Recaudación de Málaga SA	Tax collection service
Joint Companies	
Parque Cementerio de Málaga SA (PARCEMASA)	Cemetery
Empresa Mixta de Limpieza de Málaga SA (LIMASA)	Cleaning/waste disposal
Mercados Centrales de Abastecimiento de Málaga SA	Central market suppliers
Parque Tecnológico de Andalucía SA	Regional science and business park

Source: *Guía de Málaga*, Ayuntamiento de Málaga (1993).

the city hall of Málaga, for example there are several such entities, which are listed in table 9.9. These are run as commercial organisations, fully or partly owned by the *Ayuntamiento de Málaga*, such as the *Empresa Malagueña de Transportes SA* (EMT) (municipal bus service) and the *Empresa Malagueña de Aguas de Málaga SA* (EMASA) (water company). These enterprises are the municipal counterparts of all state level SA companies (such as *Repsol SA*) and of the trading enterprises described in 9.6.2.

At the provincial level, in the *Diputación Provincial de Málaga*, for example, there are, as we have seen a number of autonomous enterprises, though the bulk of them fall into the category of administrative entities (table 8.4). There are no trading enterprises at this level of administration, though public law entities are quite common; the *Diputación de Málaga* has set up the Planning and Development Enterprise (*Sociedad de Planificación y Desarrollo/SOPDE*) to promote and stimulate economic development in the province. In this aim, it collaborates with similar agencies within the region, such as the IFA (9.6.1).

9.8 Co-ordination and political control

The fact that there are so many different entities (indeed, so many different categories of entity), makes co-ordination difficult to achieve. This is further compounded by the fragmentation of decision-making, leading to diffusion in authority. At times there is no clear demarcation between the holding companies themselves (the INI, for example, still has some shareholding interests in some of the DGPE companies), although the creation of the INH and, in more recent times, *Repsol* was a clear step in the direction of a clearer demarcation between their operations. A further obstacle is the fact that many of the enterprises are a mixture of private and public capital; this can sometimes lead to a conflict of interests. Thus, although the state may be a majority shareholder, decisions may be strongly influenced by the private sector, which increasingly includes foreign investors. At least in recent years, an attempt has been made to achieve some degree of co-ordination of the sector through one of the government's delegated committees, the *Comisión de Asuntos Económicos* (5.6.3), which meets regularly. Some political control is ensured through this committee and through the obligation resting on the heads of the holding companies to attend the relevant parliamentary committees when requested to do so.

9.9 Financial control

During the Franco era, when the *Cortes* exerted little or no influence over organs of government and administration, both political and financial control were often lax. The democratic Parliament, however, takes much more interest in the allocation of resources than was previously the case. The need, spelled out clearly in the Budgetary Law of 1988, for the budgets for all state-related bodies to be included in the annual statement, was a big step forward in this respect. Thus, budgets within the public sector are subject to substantial parliamentary scrutiny before being approved. Thereafter, control is exercised in a number of ways, depending to some extent on the nature of the enterprise concerned, e.g. whether it is subject to private or public law. In most cases, however, the enterprises dealt with in this chapter are subject to:

(i) internal audit by the financial controller (*interventor*) of the government department or enterprise concerned; (ii) treasury control from the Ministry of Economy and Finance; and (iii) the Audit Tribunal (9.9.3).

9.9.1 Internal audit

In recent years, the three state holding companies have strengthened their control over the companies in which they participate. Thus INI and TENEO, for example, each have a strong audit section with their own team of auditors who standardise reporting procedures and check the financial records and statements of the respective companies.

9.9.2 Treasury control

The Ministry of Economy and Finance has a large department, the State Audit Corps (*Intervención General de la Administración del Estado/IGAE*) with over 200 inspectors who are in regular, if not permanent, contact with the various entities of the public sector. There are also separate corps for the supervision of the regional and local authorities. Reports are submitted from the Ministry of Economy and Finance to the ministry responsible for co-ordinating the particular entity concerned and copies are sent to the Council of Ministers (5.5). The IGAE's main responsibility, outlined in article 126 of the Budgetary Law, is to draw up the general accounts of the state (*cuenta general del estado*), which must include the accounts, in separate categories, of general state administration, autonomous administrative bodies and commercial, industrial and financial autonomous bodies. If it is suspected that criminal irregularities have taken place, a report is submitted from the IGAE to the Directorate General of the State Legal Service (5.9). This Directorate will then decide whether or not to recommend that the case be forwarded to the attorney general (*fiscal general del estado*) (14.4.3).

9.9.3 Audit Tribunal (*Tribunal de Cuentas*)

This is one of the constitutional bodies listed in 1.2.3 and thus has constitutional status. Formerly, Parliament, in line with article 136 of the Constitution, delegated to it examination and control over all public sector accounts. This includes the three areas for which the IGAE is responsible (9.9.2), plus the accounts for the social security system (6.4) and those for state enterprises (*sociedades estatales*) and other entities making up the state public sector (article 132.3 of the LGP). Article 153 also gave it responsibility for the accounts of the regional governments; some of these have since created their own audit tribunals without prejudice to the power of the state Audit Tribunal. Thus, in Catalonia, for example, there is the *Sindicatura de Cuentas* and in Galicia the *Consejo de Cuentas*. Navarre, because of its traditional privileges (7.5.3.2), has its own independent system, the *Cámara de Cómputos*, which handles the accounts of local authorities without recourse to the *Tribunal de Cuentas* in Madrid. Indeed, the Navarrese rejected a demand to submit accounts to the state Audit Tribunal in 1985 on the grounds that this would merely duplicate the existing provisions.

The Audit Tribunal seeks to confirm whether the various bodies and entities of state have legally and efficiently discharged their responsibilities in accordance with the Constitution and the law. It presents an annual report (*memoria anual*) to the *Cortes* or to the legislative assemblies of the regional governments concerned, on the basis of its examination of the *Cuenta General del Estado*; by law it is required to do this within six months of receiving it.

The *Tribunal de Cuentas* is an independent body whose members (*consejeros de cuentas*) have the same status as senior members of the judiciary (chapter 14). They have to be suitably qualified as auditors, lawyers or economists with a minimum of fifteen years' professional experience. There are twelve members, each of whom is allocated a specific area of responsibility, according to expertise and experience. Six are designated by the Congress and six by the Senate by a three-fifths majority vote. They serve for a period of nine years. The chairman (*presidente*) is elected, from among the members, for a period of three years, at a plenary session of the Tribunal.

9.9.4 Independent audit

In recent years, it has become common, partly because of the influence of practices prevailing in other EU countries, for many of the major public sector enterprises to have (non-compulsory) audits carried out by independent auditors, usually drawn from the large international accounting firms. To some extent, this development also reflects an increased reliance on external foreign sources of finance and the need to indicate credit-worthiness, as well as being a measure of the increasing involvement of state enterprises in foreign trade and investment.

9.10 Comment

Although some steps have been taken towards the rationalisation of the vast array of public sector entities with the creation of INH–*Repsol* and of TENEO, a good deal of overlap still exists between the various bodies responsible for the co-ordination of the sector as a whole. It is still too early to tell whether the latest restructuring outlined in 9.4.2.4 will have any impact on this situation. The State Budgetary Law represented a bold attempt to bring together in one legal document all legislation relating to the legal, budgetary, financial and auditing situation and obligations of all public sector enterprises, but in certain areas, by introducing terms not previously used, it only succeeded in blunting rather than in sharpening definitions of categories within this highly complex sector. It remains the case, too, that, in spite of its being envisaged in the Moncloa Pacts of 1977, the proposed special Statute for Public Sector Enterprises (*Estatuto de la Empresa Pública*) has still not seen the light of day.

Nevertheless, considerable progress has been made in two areas. Firstly, the public sector in general has become subject to closer scrutiny. Aside from the recent allegations about slush funds (*fondos reservados*) being used to fund anti-ETA state terrorism (which naturally tend to dent confidence in the system), there apears to be a general acceptance that greater accountability is required at all levels of society and that auditing in both the public and private sector must be taken seriously. Secondly, there is little doubt that developments such as the creation of TENEO and *Repsol*, which seem to be thriving in very competitive markets, prove that the move towards less dependence on state financing and the adoption of more rigorous entrepreneurial approaches are beginning to bear fruit. In spite of all that has been written above about the public sector in Spain (a country, indeed, where the largest companies remain those linked to government or multinationals), it is worth bearing in mind that, after the United Kingdom and the Benelux countries, Spain's public sector is the smallest in the European Union – and, what is more, it is growing smaller day by day.

Chapter 10

Political parties

10.1 Introduction

Like many democratic organisations in Spain, political parties in the past often experienced a precarious existence. For long periods, they were either outlawed or saw their activities severely curtailed. For much of the nineteenth and twentieth centuries, the political scene was dominated by the military, which conferred upon itself the right to intervene in political life whenever it judged that stability was threatened. From the beginning of the nineteenth century to the 1970s, neither democracy itself nor political parties in particular had the most favourable opportunities to take root; prior to the post-Franco era, the party system was subject to severe economic, social and political pressures that prevented it from establishing and consolidating itself as it had done in other countries of western Europe.

After the Civil War, Franco abolished all political parties, except his own subservient National Movement which was an amalgam of loyal right-wing groups (1.1.2). With the exception of the PSOE, the PCE, the PNV and the ERC (tables 10.1 and 10.2, pp. 188 and 208), all the parties that had occupied the political stage in the 1930s sank without trace. However, in the wake of the Political Reform Law of 1976 (1.1.4), there occurred a veritable explosion of political parties, at national and regional level, all eager to participate in the first democratic elections for over forty years, scheduled for 15 June 1977. In total, it is estimated that there were some 200 parties in existence at the time, ranging from the extreme left to the extreme right. (Now in fact there are no less than 1,274 legally constituted parties, the great majority of which are of a regional or even local nature.)

Some of these, on the Left, had emerged clandestinely in the late 1960s and early 1970s to enjoy a precarious existence under Francoist repression; some in the Centre and on the Right had begun to form as political associations under the pseudo-democratic legislation of Carlos Arias Navarro, who in 1974 legalised political groupings under the limited umbrella of the National Movement. The majority, however, were formed as a consequence of the Suárez reform between late 1976 and the spring of 1977 (1.1.4).

While democracy now seems reasonably well-established in Spain, the party system over the last decade has been subject to considerable fluctuation. Of the three major groupings dealt with below (10.3), only the PSOE has remained largely unchanged – though not unaffected by serious internal divisions. On the other hand, a number of other parties formed in the 1980s, like the Democratic and Social

Centre Party (*Centro Democrático y Social/CDS*), the christian democratic *Partido Demócrata Popular* (*PDP*), the Liberal Party, (*Partido Liberal/PL*) and the Democratic Reformist Party (*Partido Reformista Democrática/PRD*), as well as many others, have been dissolved.

10.2 Constitutional, legal and financial position

Bearing in mind the vicissitudes of political parties in the past, the Constitution-drafters of 1978 inserted specific guarantees about their existence and their rights within the country's new Constitution. Article 6 states as follows: 'Political parties express political pluralism, they contribute to the formation and expression of the popular will and they are the major instrument of political participation.'

There is little doubt that reference to political parties, like that to the trade unions (chapter 11), was deliberately incorporated in order to pre-empt attempts to restore any kind of pseudo-democracy that limited or prohibited the participation of parties in the political process. Hence, in order to preserve and legitimise their vital role, they were, as it were, institutionalised. Moreover, the Law on Political Parties (*Ley de Partidos Políticos*) of 8 December 1978 spells out in detail the rights and obligations of parties, their mode of functioning, which must be democratic, and their legal status. According to article 2.1 of the Law, political parties become fully legal twenty-one days after their leaders have presented documentation containing personal details and the party statutes at the Ministry of Home Affairs, on the official register of which they must appear. In fact, this register and all official forms relating to political parties are kept in the Subdirectorate General of Electoral Processes (*Subdirección General de Procesos Electorales*) of this Ministry.

The financing of political parties was regarded as such an important issue that, albeit rather belatedly, it was dealt with in an organic law, approved on 2 July 1987. To some extent, this law merely reiterates the provisions contained in the Election Law of 1985 (LOREG) (4.3.1), which states that parties will be awarded annual subventions to cover the expenses of everyday administration, of election campaigns and of the parliamentary groups at both national and regional level. These subventions are calculated according to (a) the number of parliamentary seats gained at the last general election (one-third) and (b) the total number of votes obtained at the same election (two-thirds). The law also regulates party income from non-government sources; for example, anonymous donations cannot surpass 5 per cent of the amount received by a party in one financial year and no single donation, from an individual or corporate source, must exceed 10 million pesetas. In addition, the law insists that parties keep proper accounts, which must be submitted both to an internal audit and to the external audit of the Audit Tribunal (9.9.3).

Because of the severe degree of indebtedness in which all major national and regional parties find themselves currently (calculated to be in the region of 30,000 million pesetas or approx. £150 million in April 1995), it is likely that before long a new law regulating party finances will be drawn up. In the meantime, the Spanish Association of Private Banks (*Asociación Española de Banca Privada/AEB*) (13.6.1)

Table 10.1 *Major national parties in Spain, 1995*

Name of party in Spanish	Ideology	Founder(s)	Year founded	Leader(s) 1995
Partido Socialista Obrero Español (PSOE)	Socialist	Pablo Inglesias	1879	Felipe González
Partido Popular (PP)[a]	Conservative	Manuel Fraga	1989	José-María Aznar
Izquierda Unida (IU)[b]	Radical Left	Julio Anguita	1986	Julio Anguita
Partido Comunista de España (PCE)	Communist	Antonio García Daniel Anguiano Mesto García	1920	Julio Anguita

Notes:

[a] The origin of this party lies in the *Alianza Popular* founded by Manuel Fraga in 1976.

[b] This 'political federation' includes the PCE, as well as other small parties (10.3.2.1).

has presented a proposal to the Congress committee on the funding of political parties (4.5.4) under which, over a period between ten and fifteen years, the parties would be invited to pay back their debts at modest rates of interest, likely to be between 3 and 5 per cent. Currently, the parties with the greatest debt are the PSOE (with over 50 per cent of the total), the PP and the PNV (10.4.1).

10.3 Major national parties

The major national parties are now examined in detail, particular attention being paid to the Socialist Party, the United Left and the Popular Party; reference will also be made to the Communist Party, now part of IU (10.3.2) (see table 10.1). The Union of the Democratic Centre (*Unión de Centro Democrático/UCD*) is not examined here since, although it played a vital part in the rebirth of party politics during the restoration of democracy (1.1.4), it was disbanded in the spring of 1983. Inevitably, however, reference will be made to it when considering other parties and when assessing the electoral performance of all the parties concerned (10.6). The same applies to Suárez's second attempt to create a viable centre party, the CDS (10.1), which was effectively disbanded in 1993 (although it has still not been removed from the official register).

10.3.1 Spanish Socialist Workers' Party (*Partido Socialista Obrero Español/PSOE*)

10.3.1.1 Origins

The PSOE was founded in May 1879 by a group of print-workers in Madrid under the leadership of Pablo Iglesias. It is the oldest party in Spain and one of the oldest in Europe. From an early stage (1888), it had established its own trade union, the UGT (11.4.1), which helped it to grow into a mass party by the 1930s. Its major bases of support were the industrial areas of the north (the Basque Country and Asturias) and Madrid but, by the time of the Second Republic – which it helped to establish – it was widely supported all over the country. Like all political parties, it was outlawed during the Franco era; most of its leaders went into exile in France or Latin America and a number suffered persecution at the hands of the regime. The party was legalised again in February 1977. The PSOE has been a long-time member of the Socialist International and in the European Parliament is one of the largest members of the European Socialist Party (table 15.2, p. 311).

10.3.1.2 Ideology

The PSOE was traditionally a working-class party committed to the emancipation of the working classes and the destruction of the capitalist system. To a large extent, it drew its inspiration from Marx but in practice it has never been exclusively marxist. It has, however, been subject to tensions between the exponents of marxism and the advocates of social democracy. This was most recently illustrated in May 1979 when at its XXVIII Congress, against the wishes of its general secretary, Felipe González, a resolution was passed affirming the marxist nature of the party. Following González's resignation, the party adopted a collective leadership until an extraordinary congress was summoned the following September. On this occasion, a moderate resolution, supported by González, was approved; this resolution described marxism as 'a theoretical instrument for the analysis of social reality', an analysis which 'comprehends the various contributions, marxist and non-marxist, which have helped to make Socialism the great alternative for emancipation of our time'. Consequently, González was re-elected general secretary in a decision that was to prove historic in terms of improving the party's electoral credibility. Subsequently, the PSOE moved a considerable way towards the centre of the political spectrum, particularly in terms of economic and monetary policies, in a deliberate attempt to widen its electoral appeal. In thirteen years in power, the party if anything, moved even further towards the centre of the political spectrum, especially in terms of economic policy. In its manifesto for the 1993 general election, the party referred vaguely to 'a reformist and progressive project' for Spain, directed 'towards Europe, towards modernity and towards national cohesion and solidarity'.

10.3.1.3 Policies

Reflecting the above changes, the party's manifestos from 1977 to 1996 showed a steady progression from a 'traditional' socialist programme, a strong element of state intervention, for example, to a much more pragmatic platform. While the 1977 manifesto appealed for radical changes in economic direction, including the nationalisation of a wide range of private organisations and firms, and that of 1982 referred only to the nationalisation of the national grid, the programmes from 1986 to 1993 made no reference to nationalisation and stressed the need to strengthen both the private and public sectors of the economy. In common with the socialist parties of the European Union, it accepts that the mixed economy is here to stay. To a large extent, the accent has been on the modernisation and streamlining of existing institutions, an efficient and honest bureaucracy, a properly managed economy, an extended health service, and a more equitable and modern education system, rather than on sweeping changes. Education is an area to which the socialists attach great importance, but here the hand of pragmatism can very obviously be seen: whereas the resolutions of the XXVII Congress in 1976 were foreseeing the day when grants to private schools would be stopped and private education allowed to wither away, party policy since 1980 has been to preserve the private sector, including financial aid, while bringing it more closely under the scrutiny and control of the state, as evidenced by the Law on the Right to Education (*Ley de Derecho a la Educación/LODE*) of 1983. However, in certain social areas, the party at times presented a more definite left-wing image: for example, it argued consistently in favour of a more liberal divorce law than the one approved by the *Cortes* in 1981, and in 1985 it pushed through a limited abortion law while in government. Moreover, it has to be recognised that, in the area of social policies, the party has consistently laid stress on the need to bring health, social security and social services (6.4) up to the standard of its European partners. Over the last decade and a half, it has also designed a whole series of measures to improve the legal status of women – though its own record on the promotion of women to posts of responsibility at both party and government level still leaves a lot to be desired.

Historically, the PSOE, even in its early manifestos, was committed to the establishment of a federal republic. In two senses, this ideal was modified during the years of the transition to democracy. In the first place, convinced of the democratic commitment of King Juan Carlos, the party came to accept that the winning of the 'democracy versus dictatorship' battle was more important than winning the 'republic versus monarchy' contest. Secondly, although still theoretically committed to federalism, the party accepted the compromise formula, enshrined in the Constitution, of the state of the autonomous communities (*Estado de las Autonomías*) and indeed played a major part in consolidating and developing the process of decentralisation initiated under the governments of the UCD (1.1.4).

In terms of foreign policy, the party consistently argued, on political as well as economic grounds, for Spain's full membership of the then European Community and saw its ambition realised in January 1986 when Spain, with Portugal, was finally admitted. While in government, the PSOE proved to be consistently (some would say even uncritically) pro-Europe (15.2.1), putting itself clearly among the vanguard of countries pushing for faster economic and monetary as well as political integration.

Clearly more long-term in nature, but no less consistent, has been the party's determination to restore Gibraltar to Spanish sovereignty; the party took the first step towards normalising relations and preparing the way for serious negotiations with the United Kingdom when in February 1985 it re-opened the frontier with Gibraltar, closed since 1969. In one key area, however, pragmatism once again won the day and that was over the question of NATO, which Spain (then governed by the UCD) joined in May 1982. At the time, this decision was vigorously opposed by the party and, in the campaign for the 1982 elections, the party committed itself to holding a referendum to allow the people to decide on Spain's future status within the Atlantic Alliance. However, not long after assuming power at the end of 1982, the PSOE government became convinced that to remain in NATO was in Spain's best long-term interests. Thus, in the referendum campaign of 1985–6, the government found itself in the embarrassing position of recommending to the electorate that the country should remain a member of the organisation. However, the outcome of the referendum, held on 12 March 1986, was a comfortable majority in favour of the government's policy. Subsequently, Spain demonstrated its pro-Atlanticist commitment in such joint military ventures as the Gulf War of 1990.

With regard to Latin America, an area in which many expectations have been aroused over a number of years, policy has been couched in the general terms of the need to provide aid both unilaterally and through the European Union. Little is heard these days, however, of the PSOE's erstwhile ideological sympathy for such 'non-conformist' countries as Cuba and Nicaragua as foreign policy becomes increasingly indistinguishable from that of the United States and the European Union (see also 15.2.1 and 15.6).

10.3.1.4 Structure

The most obvious feature of the internal structure of the PSOE, shown in figure 10.1, is its federal nature. The party consists of autonomous federations or regional parties based on the autonomous communities. These federations are in turn made up of provincial and local branches known as *agrupaciones*. Another characteristic of party organisation, which endeavours to give a good example of democracy, is that at each level there is a decision-making body or congress which elects an executive committee to carry out its policies, as well as a management and control committee to monitor the activities of the latter. In each case, the executive organ is responsible in both a political and financial sense to the congress.

The basic unit of the party is the local branch (*agrupación local*). This consists of the local assembly (*asamblea local*), which performs both a decision-making and monitoring role, and the local committee (*comité local*), which acts as the executive. At the provincial level, the provincial congress (*congreso provincial*), elected directly from local assemblies, elects the provincial executive committee (*comisión ejecutiva provincial*), which is overseen by the provincial committee (*comité provincial*). A very similar pattern exists at the level of the autonomous community, where the party institutions are the regional congress (*congreso regional*), the regional executive committee (*comisión ejecutiva regional*) and the regional committee (*comité regional*). In the case of the historic nationalities, these bodies are known as *de nacionalidad*. The autonomous nature of the regional parties, which have their own general secretaries, is often reflected in the adoption of a distinct name, usually an addition to

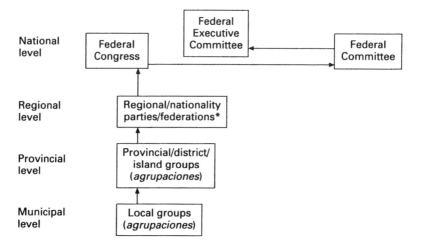

* At each of these levels, there is a structure similar to that at national level. Each regional party is headed by a president.

Figure 10.1 *Simplified structure of PSOE, 1995*

the PSOE acronym. Thus the Andalusian Party is known as the PSOE–A, the Catalan as the PSC–PSOE and the Galician as the PSG–PSOE. In practice, the autonomy supposedly enjoyed by these regional parties is often limited by the not infrequent intervention in the appointments of regional party leaders by the national party.

As can be seen in figure 10.1, the major organs of the PSOE at national or federal level are: the congress; the executive committee; and the federal committee. These will now be examined separately.

- Federal Congress (*Congreso Federal*): This is the sovereign body of the party, the major task of which is to formulate the official policy which it is expected that the parliamentary party will support in the *Cortes* and which a Socialist government will implement. It meets in ordinary session every two years and in extraordinary session when, as in 1979, circumstances dictate it. The congress is composed of delegates directly elected by the provincial congresses on the basis of proportional representation. The other organs of the party listed below are elected by secret ballot within this congress. Motions to the congress are presented by the provincial branches (*agrupaciones* or *federaciones provinciales*).

- Federal Executive Committee (*Comisión Ejecutiva Federal*): It is the function of the executive committee to carry out the policies or resolutions agreed either by the federal congress or by the federal committee (see below), taking whichever decisions are considered necessary to implement such policies. Its thirty-one members are elected by the federal congress for periods between three and four years. They include the president and the general secretary (i.e. the leader) of the party, a deputy general secretary, twenty-six executive secretaries (*secretarios ejecutivos*), including the presidents of the autonomous communities and eight departmental secretaries (*secretarios de áreas*), each responsible for specific areas, such as internal organisation, international relations, financial affairs and female participation. A similar structure is found in the executive committees of the regional parties. The executive committee is convened either by the general secretary, by the secretary for organisation or at the request of a simple majority of its members. In theory, at least, the president and the general secretary have no over-riding authority, but in practice their views carry enormous weight.

- Federal Committee (*Comité Federal*): Between congresses this is the highest authority in the party. It is composed of the federal executive committee, the general secretaries of the regional parties, representatives of these parties elected in their regional congresses and representatives directly elected by the federal congress. The total number of members is currently thirty-nine. The major functions of the federal committee are: to organise the party's electoral campaign, to oversee the activities of the executive committee, to check the statutes of the regional parties or federations and to appoint and dismiss the director of the party's journal, *El Socialista*. It is to this body, too, that the Socialist Youth Organisation, the *Juventudes Socialistas*, is accountable.

Other national organs of the party, all accountable to the federal congress, are:

- The Federal Guarantees Committee (*Comisión Federal de Garantías*), which is concerned with the protection of the rights and duties of party members.
- The Federal Auditing Committee (*Comisión Federal Revisora de Cuentas*), which is responsible for the internal auditing of national party accounts. (A parallel body exists in each of the regional parties.)
- The Committee for the Regulation of the Assets and Activities of Party Office Holders (*Comisión de Regulación de Bienes y Actividades de los Cargos Públicos del Partido*), whose cumbersome title clearly explains its purpose.

10.3.2 United Left (*Izquierda Unida/IU*)

10.3.2.1 Origins

The United Left was formally established in 1986 and currently includes the Spanish Communist Party (*Partido Comunista de España/PCE*), which is by far the oldest and largest of the member parties, the Party of Socialist Action (*Partido de Acción Socialista/PASOC*) and the Republican Left (*Izquierda Republicana*). Though initially a coalition, it is now formally registered as a federation of parties. The United Left grew out of a loose grouping of radical parties and pressure groups of the Left which was formed in 1985 to fight against the PSOE government's official policy of maintaining Spain within NATO (10.3.1.3). To some extent, its creation represented an attempt to re-align the radical Left both in the aftermath of the resignation of Santiago Carrillo as leader of the Communist Party (10.3.4) and as a response to the shift towards the centre of the PSOE. A number of the original members of the then coalition, such as the Carlist Party and the Progressive Federation (led by the well-known economist, Ramán Tamames), have now withdrawn and, indeed, particularly since the IV Federal Assembly of December 1994 (the statutes of which make no reference to the PCE), the United Left now gives every impression of having become a new, largely homogeneous party of the radical Left. In the European Parliament, IU is part of the group known as the Unitary European Left (table 15.2, p. 311).

10.3.2.2 Ideology

Clearly, IU owes a certain ideological debt to the PCE, out of which, to a large extent, it was born. However, long before the creation of the new formation, even the PCE had thrown off a large amount of its historical marxist baggage and moved some way towards the 'progressive' and away from the 'revolutionary' Left. In its current statutes, IU defines itself as follows 'Izquierda Unida is a political and social movement which comes together in an organisation that is politically sovereign, which has a single overall political line, a federal structure and is ideologically in tune with the pluralistic nature of the Spanish Left and its peoples.' Prefacing the statutes referred to above are seven fundamental principles which, while basically designed to apply to the internal organisation and workings of the party, in fact throw a good deal of light on its basic philosophies. These principles are: a decentralised, federal structure backing up a united programme; a democratic mode of functioning and consensus; openness to various currents of opinion (pluralism); limitations on terms of office for party officials; collective policy-making; priority for young people; and equality of the sexes. In line with its proclaimed support for all things federal, IU is still ideologically committed, as is the PCE, to a federal republic – although it has never made a big issue of the matter and seems, in general, happy to live with the democratic monarchy.

Since it was created, IU has sought to update its ideas and project an ideology that reflected its broader social base in terms of both party and voter support. Ecologists, 'greens', pacifists and other minority groups have been encouraged to join their ranks and, indeed, in some regions are organically linked to the party; in Andalusia, for example, the party's full name is Izquierda Unida – Los Verdes – Convocatoria por Andalucía (IU–LV–CA). At the same time, under Julio Anguita, currently leader (co-ordinator) of both the PCE and the IU, it has sought to preserve as many elements as possible of communist radicalism. While, electorally, the suppression of the PCE and its formal merger with IU might seem a pragmatic step, Anguita has thus far set his face firmly against such a move. Arguments over this issue are at the heart of ongoing internal struggles between the ortodoxos, who tend to look to the past, and the renovadores, who favour change.

10.3.2.3 Policies

In terms of economic policy, recent IU manifestos do not read very differently from those of the PSOE. However, in certain ways, the federation's approach is more radical: for example, more stress is laid on the need to reverse the current unemployment figures by means of a massive plan of public investment; the party would also go further than the PSOE in terms of nationalisation, taking into public ownership the so-called 'large monopolistic companies' – the banks, finance houses and insurance companies. A greater effort would be made to create a free health service paid for out of the national budget; and more attention would be paid to the needs of agricultural workers.

One interesting feature of IU's policies is that, while wishing to strengthen the state system of education, IU recognises the right to existence of the private schools – no doubt a concession to the new middle classes, which it is trying to woo. The party supported the introduction of a very liberal divorce law, civil marriage, family planning centres, a radical abortion law and measures designed to end discrimination against women.

In recent years, it has turned its attention to a wide range of 'progressive' or 'alternative' issues, such as the problems of the environment, refugees from North Africa, migrant workers, and the specific problems of women, young people and the elderly. At the heart of its domestic policies, however, is the commitment to use all the resources of the state to create full employment, to redistribute wealth and to develop the best possible public services for all citizens.

With regard to foreign policy, IU supports Spain's continued membership of the European Union but, like the two main trade unions (chapter 11), would like to see much more emphasis given to social, as opposed to economic, integration and would like to see a development of the full potential of the Social Charter. Moreover, it favours giving more democratic powers to the European Parliament to control the Council of Ministers and the Commission (15.5). It also supports a common European foreign and security, but is opposed to the creation of a European army. Since the federation was born out of the anti-NATO campaign of the mid-1980s, it is not surprising to learn that IU favours the disappearance of this military alliance, as well as that of the Western European Union, and advocates the denuclearisation of Europe. The party has consistently opposed the PSOE's pro-Atlanticist orientation; it is at odds with many policies of the US administration favouring, for example, the immediate lifting of the trade embargo against Cuba, Iraq and Libya. The party is firmly committed to international solidarity and was in the vanguard of the recent campaign, supported by many young people in Spain, to persuade the government to devote 0.7 per cent of gross domestic product (GDP) to development aid.

10.3.2.4 Structure

The present shape of IU, illustrated in figure 10.2, was approved at its IV Congress in December 1994. The essential feature of the party is that it is a federation of

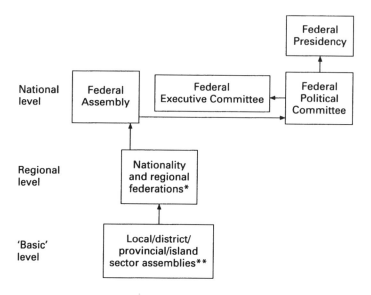

* Each of these has a structure similar to that of IU at national level,
  including a president.
** Each of these elects a political council (*consejo político*) to run
  the branch between meetings of the assembly.

Figure 10.2 *Simplified structure of IU, 1995*

parties constituted at the level of the autonomous community, plus one each for
Ceuta and Melilla. These are known as *Federaciones de Nacionalidad* or *Federaciones
de Región*. In article 2.2 of the statutes, the names of nine of these regional federations are spelt out individually; the Navarrese federation, for example, is to be
known as *Izquierda Unida–Ezker Batua de Navarra* and the Valencian as *Esquerra
Unida del País Valenciá*. The same article also spells out the different names to be
given to the Balearic federation in Majorca, Menorca and Ibiza–Formentera. Each
of these federations is sovereign (for example, it can elect its own candidates for
regional and local elections) and endowed with the same institutions as the federal
party. There is no federation of IU in Catalonia but its nearest equivalent,
Initiative for Catalonia (*Iniciativa per Catalunya/IC*), maintains close relations
with IU and is part of the same national and EU parliamentary groups. In addition to the eighteen regional federations, IU has established itself in five European
countries (France, Belgium, Germany, Luxemburg and Switzerland); these groupings are organised in the same way, and enjoy the same rights, as all the other
federations.

IU lays great stress on the grass-roots' nature of the party. The basic units of each
federation – which may vary from one area to another – are assemblies (*asambleas*),
which may be constituted at ward, local, sector, district, island or provincial level.
At the lowest level, except in the larger cities, the normal basic units are the local

assembly (*asamblea local*) and the sector assembly (*asamblea de sector*), a recent innovation which is unique to IU. Obviously, a number of the latter come together in any one area to form district assemblies and groups of them constitute provincial or island assemblies. These grass-roots' assemblies (*asambleas de base*) are sovereign within their own ambit and 30 per cent of the members can insist that an extraordinary meeting be called at any time. This demand is made of the political council (*consejo político*), which in the case of *asambleas* at all levels is the executive organ of each local branch. All the assemblies function in two modes, in open assembly and in closed session. In the former, the meetings are open to all IU sympathisers and interested parties from local groups, whether members or not; such sessions, which it is recommended be held at least twice a year, serve to encourage an open dialogue in which officials explain the party line and the rank and file express their opinions on the party's performance; such meetings are authorised to organise public demonstrations (*movilizaciones*) on particular issues, such as the 0.7 per cent GDP campaign mentioned above. In closed session, the assembly appoints party officials, basically to the *consejo político*, deals with all membership and financial matters, debates party policy and sends proposals, amendments, etc. for consideration by the federal party organs. In addition, the closed assembly, at local level, elects candidates for municipal elections and can make proposals regarding candidates for regional, general and European elections.

As can be seen in figure 10.2, at the national or federal level, the principal organs of the party are: the federal assembly; the federal political council; the federal presidency; the federal executive committee; and the office of the general co-ordinator. Each of these will now be considered in turn.

• Federal Assembly (*Asamblea Federal*): This is the highest body of IU at national level, equivalent to the party congress, and the one entrusted with drawing up the basic outlines of official policy. It is composed of the federal political council (see below) (which cannot constitute more than 20 per cent of the assembly) and representatives of nationality, regional and overseas organisations affiliated to IU. Delegates are elected from these federations on the basis of proportionality, bearing in mind the number of IU candidates elected in various levels of election, as well as the number of paid-up members. It is a requirement, however, that a minimum of 50 per cent of each delegation is composed of representatives from local, sectoral, district or provincial assemblies. The functions of the federal assembly, among others, are: to approve the party's programme for government at both national and European level; to analyse and debate the management report (*informe de gestión*) to be presented to it by the Presidency (see below); to decide on the overall political and organisational strategy of the party; and to elect members of the Federal Political Council (see below).

• Federal Political Council (*Consejo Político Federal*): This is the main governing body of the party between assemblies. The statutes describe it as 'the organ of government, representation, administration and decision-making of IU' and it enjoys very broad powers to act on behalf of the party, for example, before the courts or entities of public administration. In ordinary session, it meets at least once every three months. It is composed of: those elected at the Federal Assembly (see above); the departmental co-ordinators at national level (see below); from between one and twelve representatives elected by each federation; and representatives from federations located abroad. Among its wide range of functions, the Council is empowered: to organise and convene the Federal Assembly; to ratify the appointment of the general co-ordinator (*coordinador general*) or leader of the party, as proposed by the members of the Council elected by the Assembly, to elect the Executive Committee (*Comisión Ejecutiva*) proposed by the general co-ordinator; to ensure that the federations are acting in accordance with IU statutes at national level; to monitor, on a three-monthly basis, the work of the national and European parliamentary groups; to debate, approve or reject the report presented by the general co-ordinator on behalf of the Presidency; to approve the annual budgets; to debate and propose to the Federal Assembly the programme for European elections; to debate, approve and propose to the Assembly a candidate for the premiership and generally to direct policy and evaluate the political progress of the party.

• Federal Presidency (*Presidencia Federal*): The function of the Presidency is to ensure the continuity of political management between meetings of the Political Council. Normally it meets once a month. It is composed of: the General Co-ordinator (elected by the Political Council); the general co-ordinators or presidents of each of the territorial federations of IU; and the Executive Committee, including the federal co-ordinator for departments (see below). The Federal Presidency functions at two levels: (i) the full session (*pleno*) and (ii) the Executive Committee. The Executive consists of the general co-ordinator and members elected by the Federal Political Council. The main functions of the Federal Presidency are: to take political and organisational decisions in accordance with the resolutions of the Political Council; to convene meetings of the latter; to propose to the Council a candidate for the premiership, as well as candidates for the European elections; to propose to the same body the draft programmes for government and for European elections; to agree general strategies for national and European parliamentary groups; and to direct IU's national and international policy. It is worth noting, too, that article 47 of the statutes grants the Presidency the power to suspend or nullify any decisions taken by the nationality or regional federations which are deemed contrary to the party statutes.

The functions that are specific to the Executive Committee are to implement the decisions agreed in the Presidency and in the Political Council and to prepare proposals for study and discussion by higher level organs of the party. Although the party statutes appear to lay much less stress on the Executive Committee (or equivalent) and its organisational structure than the other two major parties (only six departments are mentioned by name), in fact there are currently as many as twenty-nine departments or *áreas*, including organisation and finance, human rights, elections, migrants and social marginalisation, women's affairs, European Parliament affairs, matters relating to the autonomous communities and international relations. A key figure on the Executive is the federal co-ordinator for departments (*coordinador general de áreas*) (see above), a liaison person who acts as a kind of deputy to the general co-ordinator in the general organisation of the Committee's affairs.

- General Co-ordination (*Coordinación General*): Although this is presented as yet another institution of the party in its statutes, in practice it is synonymous with the person of the General Co-ordinator (currently Julio Anguita) whose main briefs are: to represent the Federal Presidency as well as the whole of the party; to preside over meetings of the Presidency, Executive Committee and Federal Political Council; to propose to the Presidency the team which will make up the Executive Committee; to convene meetings of the latter to ensure co-ordination with the tasks of the Presidency and to implement agreements of the latter and the Political Council.

- Federal Guarantees Committee (*Comisión Federal de Garantías*): This body is elected either by the Federal Assembly or the Federal Political Council and its members, who must act 'with impartiality and independence', are not allowed to occupy a public or organisational post within the party. Its role is to protect the rights and duties of individual members of the party. Each regional federation is expected to have a similar body, which can refer cases of doubt or dispute to the Federal Guarantees Committee.

- Collective working groups (*áreas de elaboración colectiva*): Apparently counterbalancing the rather top-heavy and bureaucratic structure of party organs outlined above is this novel IU creation, which has no counterpart in the other major parties. Article 24 of the statutes describes these as 'the instrument of participation and social involvement which guarantees consistency with programatic and social alternatives . . . these groups must be the central element in dialogue and links with society and with social movements'. Through such groups, the party hopes both to influence and be influenced by formers of opinion acting in social groups and movements outside the structure of political parties. At national level, there are currently thirteen of these *áreas*, some of which correspond to the other kind of *áreas*, the departments of the Executive Committee; it is worth noting that among the thirteen are some 'progressive' groups, including: ecology and environment; peace and solidarity; migration; and young people. All federations of IU are also expected to establish a similar range of working groups. At national and regional level, liaison is ensured via the *coordinador de áreas*. The importance of these groups – to which no less than eleven pages of the party statutes are devoted – should not be underestimated: not only is each one of them endowed with its own technical and administrative 'back-up', but the regional federation working groups, having 'fed in' the views of the rank and file, are empowered to draft proposals for national and European party policy.

10.3.3 Popular Party (*Partido Popular/PP*)

10.3.3.1 Origins

This centre-right party is the successor to the Popular Alliance (*Alianza Popular/AP*) founded by the veteran conservative leader Manuel Fraga in 1976. AP was originally a loose coalition of seven right-wing groups, most of which were led by an ex-Franco minister like Fraga himself. After poor performances in the elections of 1977 and 1979, the Alliance tried to broaden its base by entering an electoral coalition with other like-minded national and regional parties. This was known as the Popular Coalition (*Coalición Popular/CP*), which improved the position of the Right in the elections of 1982 and 1986, but still failed to come within striking distance of the by then dominant PSOE.

Following a period of uncertainty and instability, sparked off partly by the resignation of Fraga in 1986 and partly by the desertion of most of the coalition partners, AP entered a new phase in January 1989 when its IX party conference was held. This historic conference, known as the Conference of the Refoundation (*Congreso de la Refundación*), took the decision to adopt the name *Partido Popular* and resolved to create a tightly structured single party, eschewing all attempts to retain the coalition formula. Members of other conservative, liberal and christian democrat parties, as well as independents, were invited to join the new party. Subsequently, in April 1990, the party held its X national conference in Seville, at which the president of Castilla–León, the youthful José María Aznar, was elected party president. A new, purely honorary role, that of founder-president, was given to Manuel Fraga. In 1983 the then *Alianza Popular* joined the International Democratic Union (IDU) of which PP has continued to be a member, and since 1991 has been a full member of the European Popular Party in the European Parliament (table 15.2).

10.3.3.2 Ideology

In the early years of its incarnation as the *Alianza Popular*, the party's ideology suffered from considerable ambiguity, as ex-Francoists and reformists jostled for its soul and opponents on the Left cast doubt on its democratic credentials. Certainly, Fraga seemed to project an authoritarian image, which in the early years of democracy tended to frighten an electorate that vividly remembered Franco. These days, however, such charges would be unthinkable. Since the 're-launch' of 1989, the party has established itself clearly as a party of the centre-right, incorporating the three main political strands of Spanish conservatism, liberalism and christian democracy.

10.3.3.3 Policies

When one compares the party's programmes of the late 1970s and 1980s with those of the 1990s, one is struck by the differences. *Alianza Popular*, the undoubted heir of Francoism in its early days, while accepting the need for a democratic state based on the rule of law and the wisdom of making certain concessions to the regions, tended to stress the over-riding necessity for a strong state, the unity of which would be guaranteed by the monarchy, an institution to which the party has been consistently committed. Moreover, the party laid great stress on public order and assigned an important role to the armed forces in the protection of the state and its institutions. AP was also the only major party to insist during the constitutional debate that there be an explicit reference to the role of the Catholic Church. Today, however, references of this kind are difficult to find in party documents and manifestos, and the accent is on such things as the strengthening of the *Estado de las Autonomías*, the defence of the rights and liberties, as well as the duties, of citizens, the creation of a more balanced, just and mutually supportive society and the need to ensure the correct balance of power between the major institutions of the state in order to ensure the better functioning of democracy.

The most recent insight into party policy was given in an interview with José María Aznar published in the daily *El Mundo* on March 27 1995. Clearly, one of the major domestic priorities of a PP government would be the completion, over a four-year period, of the autonomy process. At the end of this, it would no longer be possible for regions to negotiate futher extensions to their powers and the government would draw up a list of powers that were not transferable to the autonomous communities. During the same period, the system of a single administration (*administración única*) first proposed by Manuel Fraga would be implemented: this would involve ensuring that any one given area of responsibility would be wholly administered by only one tier of administration and would provide much greater administrative homogeneity than exists at the moment. As part of its programme to rationalise regional and local administration, the PP favours more devolution of powers from the regional to the local tiers of government. The party also supports the concept of reforming the Senate, whose members, it believes, should all be elected by the parliaments of the autonomous communities (chapter 7).

Economically, the party favours a social market economy. In this respect it does not differ so much from policies followed in practice by governments of the PSOE; however, the PP places much more stress on the market and the values of enlightened capitalism, the freedom to establish firms, private initiative and risk-taking entrepreneurship. It is very hostile to excessive state involvement in the economy, particularly nationalisation and high rates of taxation; currently, the party advocates reduced rates of direct taxation, as well as simplification of the system. To compensate for lost tax revenue, the party claims that public expenditure can be drastically reduced by cutting down the number of ministries and pruning the number of top governmental posts (*altos cargos*) by 5,000. As a party which admires the British Conservative Party, it is perhaps not surprising to find that it has recently outlined quite a wide-ranging policy of privatisation (by no means unknown during the years of PSOE rule, of course): as well as further developing the policy of privatising public sector firms capable of surviving in the public sector, the PP proposes the privatisation of public financial institutions such as *Argentaria* (13.5), all the nonbi-lingual television channels as well as one of the two state-run channels and large parts of the delivery end of the National Health System (6.4). On the other hand, the PP declares its intention to improve the value of state pensions, eventually raising the minimum level to that of the minimum wage (11.3.1.1) and encouraging the development of pension funds. Social security contributions would also be reduced by 5 per cent over three years.

The party, as might be expected, defends traditional values and social policies, though not as dogmatically as it did as AP. It stresses the need to maintain the private sector of education; not only are individuals and entities to enjoy the right to found and run such centres but parents must have the right to send children to the school of their choice. Its hostility to greater state control over education was demonstrated in its obstructive opposition to the PSOE's new education law, the LODE, during 1983 (2.4.3.4). The party was once very conservative in its attitude to policies concerning the family, but now, having long ago accepted the 1981 divorce law and the need for contraception, is even prepared to countenance abortion in certain circumstances (indeed, it has no proposals to reform the present law).

With regard to foreign policy, the party is firmly committed to the European Union, though it favours the 'Europe of nations' concept rather than that of a 'federal Europe'. On the other hand, in the interview quoted above Aznar states that a PP government would in all probability hope to take Spain into the European Economic and Monetary Union (EMU) by 1999. The party is equally committed to the Atlantic Alliance and as AP in 1982 supported the UCD in its decision to take Spain into NATO. Aznar is very pro-American and indeed favours strengthening links with the United States. On the other hand, party policy is to attach a higher priority to support for Latin American countries via the European Union and criticises the PSOE for insufficient attention to this area. The socialists are also criticised for not having put enough pressure on the British authorities with regard to Spain's historic claim to Gibraltar, consistently supported by the PP.

10.3.3.4 Structure

Alianza Popular could generally be described as a strongly centralised party, tightly controlled from the top, which made few concessions to the regional nature of the country; it was very much a voters' rather than a members' party, with no pretensions to build up a mass membership. Since the creation of the PP, however, significant steps have been taken to rectify what the new leadership came to acknowledge were inherent weaknesses. Now, not only has the party developed a much more federal structure, but it has recently made more serious efforts to build up and involve grass-roots' support – although it is still some way behind the PSOE and IU in this respect.

Thus, a substantial degree of autonomy has now been granted to the regional parties, each of which bears the name of the autonomous community concerned. Parties at the regional, provincial, district and island level are all endowed with similar institutions to the party at national level, i.e. congress (*congreso*), steering

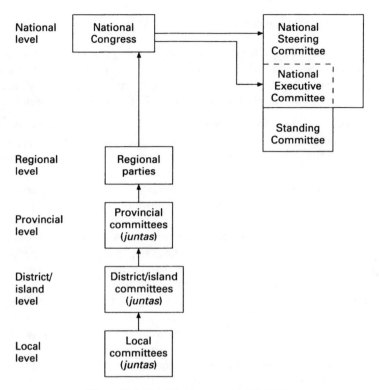

Figure 10.3 *Simplified structure of PP, 1995*

committee (*junta directiva*) and executive committee (*comité ejecutivo*). A novelty of the new PP structure, a simplified version of which is given in figure 10.3, is that an attempt has been made at all levels to integrate, on the one hand, party office holders and representatives and, on the other, parliamentarians from appropriate local institutions. Thus, for example, the provincial steering committee, as well as containing members of the Provincial Executive Committee and members elected at the Provincial Congress, also includes the president of the local committees (*juntas locales*), national and regional parliamentarians for the province concerned and the provincial deputies. Likewise, at the national level, the National Executive (see below) includes the spokespersons of the Congress, Senate and European Parliament, as well as the presidents of the autonomous communities.

If the structure retains a weakness – and this is reflected in the 1993 party statutes – below the district or island level, there are no clear guidelines regarding the number and nature of the institutions which should operate. Unlike the PSOE and IU, the local party groups do not seem to constitute the basic units of party organisation. On the other hand, the party claims to have established some kind of machinery in over 90 per cent of the country's municipalities, and boasts success in having even set up sub-municipal branches (*juntas de distrito*) in several of Spain's largest cities.

As can be seen in figure 10.3, at the national level, the principal organs of the party are: the National Congress; the National Steering Committee, together with its Standing Committee; the National Executive Committee; and the Presidency. Other bodies, operating only at national level, will also be briefly examined.

- National Congress (*Congreso Nacional*): This is the sovereign body of the party. It meets in ordinary session every three years and in extraordinary session whenever the National Steering Committee, by a two-thirds majority, decides to convene it. It is composed of delegates (*compromisarios*) elected by the territorial institutions of the party and the members of the National Steering Committee. The former members must constitute at least five times as many as the *ex officio* members and the number attending from territorial parties is related, on a proportional basis, to membership levels and to the number of votes obtained in preceding elections. The party's youth group, New Generations (*Nuevas Generaciones*), also has the right to send delegates. As well as electing the president, the members of the National Executive Committee and the twenty members of the National Steering Committee, the Congress's main functions are: to approve or censure the performance of the Executive and Steering Committees since the previous ordinary Congress; to shape the basic policies for the future direction of the party; to approve or reject the party accounts; and to debate all documents submitted to it relating to the electoral programme, party strategy or party management.

- National Steering Committee (*Junta Directiva Nacional*): This is the most important party body between congresses. It meets in ordinary session every four months and in extraordinary session when convened by the President of the party, either on his own initiative or by agreement of three fifths of the Executive Committee. It functions both in plenary session (*pleno*) and in standing committee (*comisión permanente*). The former is composed of the members of the National Executive Committee; the twenty members elected by the National Congress; national and European parliamentarians; regional, provincial and island party presidents; and the general secretary of New Generations plus the presidents and six elected members each from the regional branches of this organisation. The Standing Committee (*Comisión Permanente*) is made up of the party president, the members of the National Executive Committee, the regional party presidents and one representative each of the parliamentary groups of the Congress, Senate and European Parliament. The main functions of the National Steering Committee are to ensure that political agreements and directives of the Congress are implemented and to monitor the performance of the Executive Committee. In addition, it approves the establishment of party unions, federations or coalitions and designates the party's candidate for the premiership. The Standing

Committee, convened by the party president, lays down the party's policies for the autonomous communities and oversees all matters relating to election programmes and campaigns at regional level.

- National Executive Committee (*Comité Ejecutivo Nacional*): As its name implies, this is the principal executive and administrative body of the party. It is composed of: the national president and general secretary of the party; members elected at the national congress; the spokespersons (*portavoces*) of both Houses of Parliament plus that of the European Parliament; the presidents of the parties of the autonomous communities; the national president of New Generations; the vice-secretaries, co-ordinators and departmental secretaries (*secretarios de áreas*), if not already members elected by the party congress; and the presidents of the Electoral Committee and the Conflicts and Discipline Committee. The Executive Committee meets in ordinary session at least once a month and in extraordinary session when requested by three-fifths of the membership. Its main brief is to organise, co-ordinate and control all the activities of the party in line with party policy as laid down by the National Congress and Steering Committee, and it is empowered to draft all the necessary regulations and guidelines to ensure that this is put into effect. More specific tasks of the Executive include: appointing, among others, the general secretary, the general vice-secretary, the presidents of the National Electoral Committee and of the Conflicts and Discipline Committee and the party treasurer (*tesorero*); resolving conflicts between the various territorial divisions of the party; and drawing up and approving both the normal and the electoral budgets. Dependent on the Executive, which decides on their number, title and membership, are the so-called study committees (*comisiones de estudio*), whose task is to assist in the task of formulating sectoral policies.

- Presidency (*Presidencia*): Basically this comprises a triumvirate of the party hierarchy, namely the founder-president, the president and the general secretary. The first of these is purely honorary and temporary, currently invested in Manuel Fraga, who as the founder of the party carries enormous influence but little power. He is an automatic member of the Executive. The real leader of the party is the president, currently José María Aznar, who obviously has enormous powers – although the statutes ensure that in fact final decisions are made by the Executive, to which normally the president makes recommendations or proposals. The general secretary, for example, is appointed by the Executive Committee on the proposal of the president; his task is to implement, under the president, all agreements, directives and decisions adopted by the Executive and the Steering Committee. Accountable to him in turn are the general vice-secretaries, each responsible for an area of party activity, through whom he must co-ordinate the everyday work of the party.

  Other national organs of the party are:

- The Popular Party Interparliamentary Group (*Interparlamentaria Popular*), which is composed of the PP parliamentarians of the Congress, Senate, regional assemblies and the European Parliament; this body is accountable to the National Steering Committee and its main function is to provide a forum for intra-party political debate.

- The Popular Party Intermunicipal Group (*Intermunicipal Popular*), performs a similar role at the local level and comprises not only municipal, provincial and island councillors, but those occupying executive posts such as mayors and provincial presidents belonging to the party.
- The National Electoral Committee (*Comité Nacional Electoral*), whose members must not be election candidates, draws up and approves lists of candidates for the European, national and regional elections and also designates candidates for the presidencies of the governments of autonomous communities and provincial councils, as well as mayors in provincial capitals. With the approval of the party president, some of these powers may be delegated to the regional electoral committees.
- The National Conflict and Discipline Committee (*Comité Nacional de Conflictos y Disciplina*), as its name implies, is responsible for disciplinary affairs and disputes arising between members and the party organs; in particular, it is concerned with those members who belong to the national organs of the party as well as party parliamentarians. Regional counterparts of this body deal with such matters at the level of the autonomous community.

It should be noted that most of the national bodies listed above have their regional counterparts. Indeed, the party statutes, agreed at the XI Congress in December 1993, deliberately make reference to the party congresses, steering committees, etc. in the plural, thus stressing not only the decentralised nature of the party, but the similarity in structure of the regional parties.

10.3.4 Communist Party of Spain (*Partido Comunista de España/PCE*)

The Spanish Communist Party traces its origins to April 1920 when, influenced by the Bolshevik Revolution of October 1917, several members of the PSOE's youth organisation and other dissidents decided to adhere to the newly formed IV (Communist) International and found a new party. From its inception, the party announced itself to be marxist and revolutionary, and its policies were aimed at bringing down the capitalist system. For forty years, both inside Spain and in exile, its members bore the brunt of Francoist repression, since it was more often than not in the vanguard of resistance to the regime. The expected reward for all its efforts did not come following legalisation in April 1977 and the first democratic general election of the same year, even though the party had presented a moderate left-wing programme that was far from radical. Indeed, in all the general elections held between 1977 and 1982, the PCE, under its veteran leader, Santiago Carrillo, failed to win more than 10.7 per cent of the vote and, indeed, in 1982 sank to an all-time low gaining only 4.1 per cent of the vote and four seats in the Congress. Following the resignation of Carrillo after the debacle of 1982, the party's fortunes did not improve to any extent, even under the new leader Gerardo Iglesias, who was incapable of imposing party unity. The election as leader of the more dynamic Julio Anguita in 1987 gave a temporary boost to the party, but by then the process of creating the United Left (10.3.2) was well advanced. Anguita, though now well established as leader of the latter, has remained secretary general of the PCE and has refused to countenance the dissolution of the party, in spite of the fact that it no longer presents its own candidates independently in elections at any level. In the longer term, however, it would seem that its demise is inevitable.

10.4 Major regional parties

In a country where the regional issue has dominated politics on so many occasions, it is not surprising that political parties have emerged to defend the political interests of communities which are conscious of possessing a separate identity. In fact, it was only at the turn of the century, coinciding with increased local cultural activity and, in some areas, the beginnings of industrialisation, that parties were formed and nationalism assumed a more political character. With the development of the autonomous communities since 1980 and the increased sense of regional and local identity in many areas of the country, it is perhaps not surprising that literally hundreds of regional parties have sprung up in recent years (see table 10.2). As will be observed below, however, most of the best established and most successful parties are located in the historic communities.

10.4.1 Basque Nationalist Party (*Partido Nacionalista Vasco/PNV*)

This basically conservative, Catholic and at times radically nationalist, party was founded in 1895 by Sabino Arana with the aim of promoting the Basque language and culture and of providing a vehicle of political expression for the Basque people. The party headquarters is in Bilbao. It is by far the oldest of all the regional parties in Spain. Until the 1970s, it was the only nationalist party in the Basque Country (*Euskadi*) and, while rivals have sprung up, it continues to be the most important. The basis of its support has traditionally been the lower-middle class, the peasantry and the clergy. Its ideology, reflecting a variety of interests, has varied from outright independence from Spain to an accommodation with Madrid within a system of autonomous government.

In the post-Franco era, partly under pressure from extreme nationalists, it fought the Madrid government every inch of the way in its demands for a generous degree of autonomy within the Spanish state. Today, its political stance often seems somewhat ambiguous: on the one hand, it is a signatory with the PSOE and other moderate Basque parties to the 1988 Pacts of Ajuria Enea, which condemn ETA violence and advocate the peaceful resolution of the region's problems; on the other, in recent times, it has often called for self-determination (*autodeterminación*) a term which for

Table 10.2 *Major regional parties in Spain, 1995*

Name of party	Ideology	Founder	Year founded	Leader 1995
Partido Nacionalista Vasco (PNV)	Basque nationalist (Christian democrat)	Sabino Arana	1894	Xabier Arzallus
Eusko Ta Alkartasuna (EA)	Basque nationalist (Left)[a]	Carlos Garaicoechea	1986	Carlos Garaicoechea
Herri Batasuna (HB)	Radical Basque nationalist (pro-independence)	Telesforo Monzón	1978	Jon Idígoras et al
Euskadiko Ezkerra (EE)	Basque nationalist (Left)[a]	Francisco Letamendía	1976	Juan María Bandrés
Convergència i Unió (CiU)	Catalan nationalist	Jordi Pujol	1978	Miquel Roca
Esquerra Republicana de Catalunya (ERC)	Radical Catalan nationalist (pro-independence)	Francesc Macià	1931	Angel Colom i Colom
Partido Andalucista (PA)	Andalusian regionalist (centrist)	Alejandro Rojas-Marcos	1984	Antonio Ortega
Coalición Canaria (CC)	Regionalist and nationalist	Various	1993	Manuel Hermoso
Bloque Galego Nacionalista (BNG)	Galician nationalist	Various	1988	Xosé Manuel Beiras
Partido Aragonés (PAR)	Aragonese regionalist (centre-right)	Hipólito Gómez de las Roces	1977	José María Mur Bernard
Unió Valenciana (UV)	Valencian regionalist (liberal)	Vicente González Lizondo	1982	Vicente González Lizondo
Unión del Pueblo Navarro (UPN)	Navarrese regionalist (centre-right)	Jesús Aizpún Tuero	1979	Jesús Aizpún Tuero

Notes:
[a] This party now fights elections in collaboration with the PSE–PSOE (10.4.4).

many radical nationalists is synonymous with independence. In the general elections since 1977 the party has consistently been defeated by the PSOE, which is particularly strong in the industrial heartland around Bilbao, with its strong immigrant vote. In the 1986 general elections, the party's performance was particularly disappointing as it lost two of the eight seats which it had won in 1982 (table 10.3a, see p. 217). This was probably at least partly due to the serious schism which affected the party during 1985 and 1986 and led to the creation of a breakaway party, *Eusko Ta Alkartasuna (EA)* (10.4.2). In elections post-1986, it has managed to retain five seats in the Congress, but its share of the popular vote has tended to decline. After victories in the 1980 and 1984 regional elections, after which it formed one-party governments, the PNV has been unable to secure overall control and, for most of the last decade, has shared power in Vitoria (the seat of the Basque government) with the PSOE, though the presidency has been consistently held by the PNV politician, Antonio Ardanza, with a socialist as his deputy. Following the regional elections of 1994, the PNV shares power with both the PSOE and the EA (10.4.2) in a tripartite government (*el tripartito*). In recent years, the PNV has adopted a markedly pro-EU stance, no doubt seeing Europe as a forum in which pressure can be put on national governments for the benefit of the 'peoples of Europe'. Currently, the party has one Euro-MP, having fought the 1994 European elections as part of the Nationalist Coalition (*Coalición Nacionalista*), which includes EA, the ERC and the BNG (table 15.1). The present leader of the party is the veteran Xabier Arzallus who, following the narrow PP election victory in March 1996 (1.1.5), has, in exchange for certain concessions to the regions, been persuaded to give Aznar the support of the PNV in Parliament.

10.4.2 Basque Nationalists (*Eusko Ta Alkartasuna/EA*)

This party, based in Alava, was founded in October 1986 when the former Basque President, Carlos Garaicoechea, left the PNV to form a breakaway group, which favoured the strengthening of the new Basque institutions as opposed to the three provincial authorities. In general, it adopts a rather more radical line than the PNV in its dealings with Madrid. In 1993 it lost one of the two Congress seats that it won in 1989. Likewise, in 1994 it lost one of the eight seats in the regional parliament which it had won four years earlier and is only the fifth party in terms of seats and percentage of the popular vote. On the other hand, it has become one of the partners in the *tripartito* referred to in 10.4.1. In the 1995 local elections, it secured no less than 407 councillors. Like the PNV, it fought the 1994 European elections as part of the Nationalist Coalition, but won no seats. The EA is strongest in Navarre, the home province of Garaicoechea.

10.4.3 Basque Homeland and Freedom Party (*Herri Batasuna/HB*)

This party was founded in 1978 as a coalition of four left-wing nationalist parties whose declared aim was and is to establish the separate Basque and Socialist state of Euskadi. This is an aim shared with ETA (*Euskadi Ta Askatasuna*) the political arm of which HB clearly is. HB belongs to the wider radical nationalist movement known as the *Koordinadora Abertzale Socialista* (*KAS*), to which members of ETA also belong. The party headquarters is in Bilbao, though more of its supporters are to be found in San Sebastián, the capital of Guipúzcoa. Following the PNV's struggle to have Basque rights more explicitly recognised in the Constitution and to secure a more generaous autonomy for Euskadi, this coalition shot to prominence in the general elections of 1979, when it sent three deputies to the Congress in Madrid (subsequently they have consistently refused to occupy their parliamentary seats). This was followed by a spectacular performance in the regional elections of 1980 when the party came second to the PNV, gaining eleven out of the sixty seats in the Basque Parliament. This success was largely maintained in the general elections of 1982 and the regional elections of 1984. The party came close to parity with the PNV in the general elections of 1986, winning five seats in the Congress compared to the PNV's six. In recent years, the party appears to have embarked on a steady, albeit slow, decline as its share of the vote in all elections has fallen, probably reflecting a growing weariness on the part of many erstwhile supporters with the continued atrocities of ETA. In the 1993 general election, they lost two of their four seats and saw their share of the vote drop from 1.08 to 0.88 per cent as compared with 1989. A similar trend occurred in the 1994 regional elections in which the party lost two of its thirteen seats and in the same year lost its only seat in the European Parliament. Decline in support was further confirmed in the local elections of May 1995 when the party lost thirty of the 119 councils seats won in 1991 and in the general election of 1996 when, although it hung on to its two parliamentary seats in the Congress, saw a further erosion in its vote. However, as the third most important party in the regional parliament, it is clearly still a force to be reckoned with in the Basque Country – even discounting its present alarming capacity to mobilise considerable support against the anti-violence campaigners in the region.

10.4.4 Basque Left (*Euskadiko Ezkerra/EE*)

Euskadiko, also based in Bilbao, was founded by Francisco Letamendía in 1977 from a group of radical nationalist parties committed to a marxist view of society but preferring to use legal channels to gain power and opposed to ETA terrorism. Between 1977 and 1982, it managed to send one deputy to the Madrid Congress and in the general elections of 1986 and 1989 actually secured two. On the other hand, its performance in regional elections has been less encouraging, falling from nine seats in 1986 to six in 1990. In 1993 the party merged with the Basque Socialist Party (PSE–PSOE), but had to share the national disaffection with the ruling party whose share of the vote fell from 19.9 to 17.1 per cent between 1990 and 1994. As a part of the PSOE–EE merger, it now participates as one of the three ruling groups in the *tripartito* (10.4.1).

10.4.5 Convergence and Union (*Convergència i Unió/CiU*)

The main partner of this centre-right coalition is the Democratic Convergence Party of Catalonia (*Convergència Democrática de Catalunya/CDC*), founded in 1974 by the present president of Catalonia, Jordi Pujol, who in March 1995 celebrated fifteen years in power. The other partner is the christian democratic (and more conservative) Democratic Union of Catalonia (*Unío Democrática de Catalunya/UDC*). This coalition, whose headquarters is in Barcelona, was founded to fight the general elections of 1979 and has subsequently more or less coalesced as a single party. To some extent, it can be regarded as an updated manifestation of the first Catalan nationalist party, the Catalan Regionalist League (*Lliga Regionalista Catalana*), founded at the turn of the century by Catalan industrialists and businessmen. Although it has pressed hard for generous terms for the *Generalitat*, its relations with Madrid have generally been good; following the general election of 1993, when the PSOE failed to secure an overall majority, and up to September 1995, the party was involved in what amounted to a *de facto* coalition with the ruling party. The CiU has followed the pattern of the PNV in yielding to the national parties in general elections, taking second place, but in all the regional elections between 1980 and 1992 the party swept to overall victories, each one more convincing that the last, though a slight decline (possibly linked to the party's support for the unpopular PSOE central government) was recorded in the local elections of May 1995. It is worth noting that since democracy returned to Spain, Barcelona has always had a Socialist mayor, currently the dynamic Pasqual Maragall, re-elected in these same elections. Perhaps the most interesting feature of this party is that it appeals to a broad cross-section of Catalan voters, including many non-Catalan speakers from outside the region; its secret has been to present a modern, progressive image and to convey an impression of efficiency as a government. The party has been led for several years by Miquel Roca, the unsuccessful CiU candidate for mayor of Barcelona in May 1995. The early regional elections held in November 1995 saw Pujol claim a fifth successive triumph; any electoral risk he might have been taking in shoring up the national government in Madrid had obviously been only marginal. Following the inconclusive PP victory in the general election of March 1996 (1.1.5), the Catalan president again found himself wooed from Madrid and in a strong position to extract important concessions from the new Conservative government of José María Aznar, which is largely dependent on the votes of the CiU.

10.4.6 Republican Left of Catalonia (*Esquerra Republicana de Catalunya/ERC*)

This Catalan nationalist party, based in Barcelona, was founded in 1931 by Francesc Macià. During the Second Republic, it replaced the more conservative *Lliga Regionalista Catalana* (10.4.5) as the major force of Catalan nationalism. As its name implies, the party has traditionally had a strongly republican orientation. In the post-Franco period, it has been eclipsed by the coalition led by Jordi Pujol (10.4.5), both in general and regional elections, never winning more than one seat in the Congress or more than 9 per cent of the regional vote. However, under its forceful new leader, Angel Colom, the party has since 1992 adopted a stance in favour of complete independence for Catalonia, which appears to have helped it to improve its position in the regional elections of that year when it gained eleven seats, a significant improvement on the six of 1988. A further advance came in the local elections of 1995 when the party increased its number of councillors from thirty-one to sixty-nine. Reflecting a general trend among nationalist parties, the ERC, while improving its position in the regional elections of November 1995 (pushing its number of seats from 11 to 13), tended to fall back somewhat in the national poll of March 1996.

10.4.7 Andalusian Nationalist Party (*Partido Andalucista/PA*)

This party, whose headquarters are in Seville, was founded as the Andalusian Socialist Alliance (*Alianza Socialista de Andalucía/ASA*) in 1973, became the Socialist Party of Andalusia (*Partido Socialista de Andalucía/PSA*) in 1976 and finally changed its name to the *Partido Andalucista* in 1984. It was founded by Alejandro Rojas-Marcos as a radical socialist and regionalist (later nationalist) party; in general, however, it seems to have appealed more to the liberal-centrist voter disillusioned with the state parties of Right and Left. Its most striking success was in the general elections of 1979 when it sent five deputies to the Madrid Congress and in 1980 when two of its candidates were elected to the parliament of Catalonia. Subsequently, its fortunes declined rapidly, even in regional and local elections. It won no seats in the general elections of 1982 or 1986 and in the regional elections of 1986 lost one of the three seats in the regional assembly which it had won in 1982, Benefiting from general disillusion with the PSOE, the party saw its fortunes improve slightly in subsequent polls, gaining two seats in the general election of 1989 and ten in the regional elections of the following year. However, this boost was to prove short-lived, for in 1992 tensions within the party led to the withdrawal to form a separate grouping of the charismatic and influential mayor of Jerez, Pedro Pacheco, thus splitting an already small vote. Hence, in the general election of 1993, the party lost its two seats, while the splinter group, the Andalusian Progress Party (*Partido Andaluz de Progreso / PAP*) failed to win a single seat in the Congress. Even when the two parties came together in an electoral coalition, known as Andalusian Power (*Poder Andaluz*), for the regional and European elections of June 1994, they were roundly rejected by the voters: the PA lost seven of its ten seats in the regional Parliament and its single seat in Europe. The vote in the local elections of 1995 only served to confirm this trend; while the PAP leader was confirmed as mayor of Jerez, Rojas-Marcos, who had been mayor of Seville thanks to support from the PP, was forced to stand down in favour of his conservative partner. Thanks to recent efforts to unify the *andalucista* groups under one umbrella, the party improved its position in the regional elections of March 1996. Indeed, the party will have some influence in the new Andalusian government since the Socialist leader, Manuel Chaves, has been forced to form a coalition with the PA in order to form a stable administration. Currently, two members of the PA hold ministerial office in the *Junta de Andalucía*.

10.4.8 Canary Islands Coalition (*Coalición Canaria / CC*)

This coalition, formed in 1993, and centred in Santa Cruz de Tenerife, comprises several parties which all define themselves as nationalist, although they range from the Left to the Right of the political spectrum. The major partner in the coalition, founded in 1983 and which has been fighting general elections since 1986, is the Association of Canary Islands Independents (*Agrupación de Independientes de Canarias / AIC*); it has eighteen seats out of sixty in the regional parliament and thus constitutes the largest group. It also controls the island councils (*cabildos insulares*) (8.4.2.4) of Tenerife and Lanzarote. In the general election of 1993, the CC gained a very creditable four seats in the Congress, which it retained in the election of 1996. Previously it had already reinforced its position in the regional elections of May 1995, winning twenty-two out of the sixty seats in the parliament, where it is now the largest party and the major party in the coalition government. Thanks to José

María Aznar's failure to win an outright victory in the March 1996 election, the CC, under Manuel Hermoso, has negotiated its way into the parliamentary pact which the Conservative leader has been obliged to construct. Though currently riding the crest of a wave, the Coalition's lack of ideological coherence does not bode well for its long-term political future.

10.4.9 Galician Nationalist Block (*Bloque Nacionalista Galego/BNG*)

This left-wing nationalist coalition was founded in the late 1980s, but has only recently become the best supported of the various regional parties in Galicia, eclipsing the Galician Coalition (*Coalición Galega/CG*) and the Galician Left (*Esquerda Galega/EG*), both of which seemed more likely to prosper in the mid-1980s. However, from a base of one seat and only 4.2 per cent of the vote in the regional election of 1985, the party advanced considerably in subsequent years, to the point where in the regional election of 1993 it won thirteen seats (out of eighty-five) and 18.7 per cent of the vote. This success was followed up in the local elections of 1995 when the BNG added 23 to its tally of 67 council seats won in 1991. It forced itself dramatically onto the public scene in the general election of 1996 when it increased its popular vote to the point where it won representation (two seats) in the national Congress. It is now quite clearly the major nationalist party in Galicia and, after the PP and PSG–PSOE, has established itself as the third force in Galician politics under the leadership of one of the great political survivors of the region, Xosé Manuel Beiras.

10.4.10 Aragonese Party (*Partido Aragonés/PAR*)

This centre-right party, which used to be called the *Partido Aragonés Regionalista*, was founded in Zaragoza in December 1977 by Hipólito Gómez de las Roces. It is a regionalist party, which has fought for the widest possible autonomy for Aragón, but now defines its position as 'the nationalism of renewal' (*nacionalismo renovador*). At its VI Congress in 1989, it decided to suppress the adjective *regionalista* but retains the original acronym, PAR. In the general elections of 1986, 1989 and 1993, it sent one deputy to the Madrid Congress. In the regional election of 1987, it won nineteen seats (out of sixty-seven) with 28.5 per cent of the vote; though these figures fell to fourteen and 24.7 respectively in 1991 and fourteen and 20.5 in 1995. Currently, after being the second regional party for several years, the PAR now occupies third position in the regional parliament but still enjoys the privilege of deciding which of the two major national parties will govern in Aragón. During the period 1987–95, Gómez and his successor, Emilio Eiroa, were elected president of Aragón, being able to form a coalition with the PP, a party with which it has strong ideological ties but, following the regional elections of 1995, the PP provided the leadership with the PAR in the supporting role. Currently, the party has 11,000 members.

10.4.11 Valencian Union (*Unió Valenciana/UV*)

UV was founded in Valencia city in 1982 by Vicente González Lizondo. As a liberal, centrist party, it has fought for more autonomy for the *Comunidad Valenciana*. In general elections since 1986, it has never had less than one deputy in the Congress and obtained two in 1989. In the regional election to the Valencian *Generalitat* in 1987, it gained six seats (out of eighty-nine) with 15 per cent of the vote and in 1991 it slightly improved its position by winning one more seat with 16.2 per cent of the vote; in 1995, however, it declined to five seats and 7 per cent of the vote. In these last elections, it was overtaken by IU as the third force in Valencian politics but remains clearly the main regional party, and has 18,000 members.

10.4.12 Union of the Navarrese People (*Unión del Pueblo Navarro/UPN*)

The UPN was founded in the late 1970s in Pamplona by Jesús Aizpún Tuero. It sent one deputy to the Madrid Congress in 1979 in its own right, but in subsequent general elections has preferred to campaign alongside the PP, with which it maintains fraternal links. Thus, conversely, in regional elections the PP does not stand separately but supports UPN candidates who are more likely to appeal to voters in regional polls. In 1987, the UPN was narrowly defeated by the PSOE in elections to the *Diputación Foral de Navarra*, winning fourteen out of the fifty seats contested with nearly 25 per cent of the vote. In 1991, the roles were reversed and the UPN, with twenty seats and 35 per cent of the vote, came top of the poll. Subsequently, the UPN, with the help of independents, was able to form a regionalist party government, with Juan Cruz Alli as president. However, following an internal feud within the party, Cruz Alli, only a few months before the regional elections of 1995, set up a separate party, the Democratic Convergence of the Navarrese People (*Convergencia Democrática de los Navarros/CDN*), and came third in the polls with ten seats and 18.5 per cent of the vote; subsequently, the UPN–PP coalition needed the support of the CDN to form a viable government.

10.5 Membership and financing of major national parties

Compared to other countries of the European Union, membership figures in Spain are consistently low, with the exception of certain regional parties. It is interesting to note that the current membership of the PSOE is much lower than it was in the 1930s and that the ratio of member to party stands at only 1:26. Although all three major parties have seen an increase in recent years, they remain largely the parties of voters rather than members; party loyalty is not high and, prior to all general elections, there is always, up to the last moment, a high percentage (sometimes up to 30 per cent) of undecided voters.

10.5.1 Spanish Socialist Workers' Party

The PSOE experienced a dramatic increase in support between 1976, when membership was claimed to stand at only 8,000, and 1983, when it was estimated to have reached 140,000. Subsequently, the pace of increasing membership tended to slacken, but was claimed to be 167,000 in 1986. Over the last decade, in spite of declining popularity among voters, the PSOE has managed to increase its membership substantially to 350,173 (1994 figure). By far the largest group of members is to be found in Andalusia (91,910) followed by the *Comunidad Valenciana* (41,934) and Castile–La Mancha (25,255). Worthy of note is the fact that over the last decade there has been a healthy improvement in the number of women members, rising from 10 per cent in 1986 to 23.3 per cent in 1994. A worrying trend, perhaps, for the party is that the average age of members is as high as 46.

Apart from the state grants, which in the case of all parties account for up to 90 per cent of total revenue, the party's income derives from membership fees (*cuotas*). The party Congress lays down a minimum figure which all members must pay (with special rates for the unemployed and the retired), but expects members to pay more in relation to their income. The statutes of the XXXIII Congress of 1994 laid down that the minimum fee would be 100 pesetas per month, though this can be revised on a yearly basis by the Federal Committee. Members pay their fees to their local branch or *agrupación*. In addition, the party receives donations from individuals and organisations sympathetic to its aims. In recent years, a vital source of revenue has been loans from financial institutions. Indeed, of all the parties, the PSOE is currently in the worst plight, with debts amounting to no less than 11,000 million pesetas, more than a third of the total indebtedness of all the political parties. Sadly, in recent years too, in its attempts to secure additional sources of revenue, the party appears to have resorted to irregular financial dealings (the so-called *Filesa* affair) which have done nothing to improve its image.

10.5.2 United Left

Since its creation in 1986, IU has seen its membership rise steadily. It now claims to have 52,711 members, plus a further 20,000 or so who belong to its sister party in Catalonia, the IC (10.3.2.4). Interestingly, over two-thirds of IU members are claimed to be new recruits to the new party and not members of the PCE or other member parties. (Membership of one of these does not confer automatic membership of IU and vice versa.) Of the IU's 52,711 members, the largest group is to be found in Andalusia (19,097), followed by Madrid (7,295), Valencia (4,267) and Asturias (4,042).

IU derives about 10 per cent of its revenue from membership fees. A minimum rate is set by the Federal Assembly and members are expected to pay an additional amount related to their ability to pay. Members pay their dues monthly to their local branch or *asamblea de base*. This revenue is supplemented by fund-raising events. For a party which loudly proclaims its commitment to the federal cause, it is interesting to note that all revenues are forwarded to the centre in Madrid, which redistributes it on a percentage basis relating to membership. The PCE does not make a contribution to party funds nor does IU help to finance the PCE. Like other parties, *Izquierda Unida* is currently in debt, though party HQ claims that its problems are not serious in this regard.

10.5.3 Popular Party

Unlike IU, the PP did not have to start from scratch in establishing its membership, being able to build on the 100,000 or more bequeathed to it by AP in the late 1980s. At the end of 1994, the party claimed to have 429,293 members, which compared to the 284,323 of 1990, represents a dramatic increase of 33 per cent. Of these members, the largest number are in Andalusia (57,133), followed by Galicia (42,978), Madrid (36,167) and Valencia (35,282). Only 25.92 per cent of members are women, though this compares very well with figures for the PSOE (10.6.1). A trend that must worry the latter party, however, is that the largest increase in new members to the PP in the last few years was in the age range 18–23. The traditional association between age and conservative voting has apparently been broken down: students account for 12.88 per cent of the membership. Another trend has been the ability of the PP to eat into the traditional urban strongholds of the PSOE, particularly in the capital; it is very significant that the province of Madrid, with 11 per cent, has by far the largest concentration of party members.

The healthy increase in membership has undoubtedly had a beneficial effect on party finances, coupled with donations from the employers' side of the business and industrial community, which looks favourably on PP economic policies. None the less, the party is no more free from debt than the other parties, although the fact is that the 6,000 million pesetas which it owes to financial institutions is almost all due to debts incurred by AP. The new PP claims to have cleared all debts incurred since 1989.

10.6 Electoral achievements

The performance of the major national and regional parties in the general elections held between 1977 and 1996 are given in table 10.3. Fears expressed prior to the 1977 election that the large number of parties in the field might lead to a dangerous fragmentation of Parliament and to weak coalition governments were not borne out by events. In all the elections of the period, no more than four parties made any significant impact on the electorate and of these, since 1982, by far the most dominant have been the PSOE and the AP–PP, which together in 1993 and 1996 respectively polled 70.90 and 75.93 per cent of the popular vote. If anything, concerns today tend to focus not on the danger of fragmentation but on the way in which the electoral system appears to favour large parties and, to some extent, discriminates against the smaller groups.

Table 10.3a *Results of general elections in Spain, 1977–86*

Party	1977 Seats	Election % votes	1979 Seats	Election % votes	1982 Seats	Election % votes	1986 Seats	Election % votes
National								
UCD	166	34.62	168	35.02	12	7.14	–	–
PSOE	118	29.27	120	30.49	202	48.40	184	44.06
PCE–IU	20	9.38	24	10.74	4	4.13	7	4.61
AP–CD–CP[a]	16	8.33	9	5.96	106	26.18	105	26.00
CDS	–	–	–	–	2	2.89	19	9.23
Regional								
PCD–CiU	10	3.70	9	2.50	12	3.69	18	5.02
ERC	1	0.80	1	0.70	1	0.70	0	0.42
PNV	7	1.70	7	1.50	8	1.89	6	1.53
EE	1	0.50	1	0.50	1	0.48	2	0.53
HB	–	–	3	0.96	2	1.01	5	1.15
PSA–PA	0	0.30	5	1.81	0	0.40	0	2.80

Notes:

[a] AP fought the 1979 election within the CD (*Coalición Democrática*) coalition and the 1982 and 1986 elections as part of the CP (*Coalición Popular*) coalition, which included regional parties.

Source: El País (June 1977–June 1986).

Table 10.3b *Results of general elections in Spain, 1989–96*

Party	1989 Seats	Election % of votes	1993 Seats	Election % of votes	1996 Seats	Election % of votes
National						
PSOE	175	40.02	159	36.08	141	37.48
PP[a]	106	25.61	141	34.82	156	38.45
IU	18	8.99	18	9.57	21	10.58
CDS	14	7.71	0	1.75	–	–
Regional						
CiU	19	8.99	17	4.95	16	4.61
ERC	0	–	1	0.80	1	0.67
PNV	5	1.25	5	1.24	5	1.28
EA	2	0.68	1	0.55	1	0.46
HB	4	1.08	2	0.88	2	0.73
EE	2	0.52	0	–	–	–
PA	2	1.06	0	–	0	0.54
AIC[b]/CC	1	0.26	4	0.88	4	0.89
BNG	0	–	0	0.54	2	0.88
PAR[c]	0	0.36	1	0.61	–	–
UV	2	0.72	1	0.48	0	0.37

Notes:

[a] Includes votes for the UPN (10.4.12).

[b] Stands for *Agrupación de Independientes de Canarias*, a coaliation of independent parties which since 1993 has been part of *Coalición Canaria* (10.4.8).

[c] Fought 1996 election allied to PP.

Source: Anuario El País (1994) and *El País* (6 March 1996).

10.6.1 Performance of the Socialist Party

Following defeats by the UCD in 1977 and 1979, the PSOE has gone on to win four general elections: 1982, 1986, 1989 and 1993 (table 10.3). However, from the high point it reached in 1982, winning over 48 per cent of the vote and 202 out of the 350 seats in the Congress (a clear overall majority), the party went on to lose overall control in 1989, with only 175 seats, and in 1993, while remaining the largest single party (and paradoxically gaining more votes than in 1989), plummeted to 159 seats with only 38.79 per cent of the vote. To a large extent, this decline has also been reflected in regional and local elections. At the regional level, the party controlled thirteen out of the seventeen autonomous community governments in 1987; by 1991 this figure had dropped to ten and by 1995 to three (and in only one of these – Castile–La Mancha – did it have an overall majority). Symptomatic of the party's troubles was the result of the Andalusian elections of June 1994 when, for the first time in twelve years, it lost its overall majority and had great difficulties in getting its programme approved in the regional parliament. At the municipal level, a similar decline has been observed: in 1991 opposition parties gained local councils in traditionally Socialist urban areas and the PSOE lost control of several large cities, including Madrid, Seville and Valencia. A further embarrassment came in the European elections of 1994 when it was convincingly defeated by the PP, losing nine percentage points compared to the previous poll in 1989 (table 15.1, p. 308). However, its greatest humiliation occurred in the local and regional elections of 1995 when it lost control of several regional governments and the majority of the major cities in Spain, with the exception of Barcelona and La Coruña. As expected, the PSOE lost the general election of March 1996. However, the margin of defeat was so narrow (just over one percentage point) that Felipe González – buoyed up also by the victory in the simultaneous regional elections in Andalusia – could already claim to have begun to reverse the apparently inexorable PP advance.

10.6.2 Performance of the United Left

Since its foundation, IU's electoral fortunes have been mixed, although the most recent trend, from a low base, is steadily upwards. In general elections, the party has gone from seven seats with 4.6 per cent of the vote in 1986 to eighteen with 8.99 per cent in 1989 to eighteen with 9.57 per cent in 1993. While this improvement seems quite substantial, it should be recalled that, at least in percentage terms if not in terms of seats, it still falls short of the PCE's best performance in 1979 when it secured 10.74 per cent of the vote. However, to a large extent, the party's strength lies in its local bases. In regional governments, the party may not hold power (though the PSOE has depended on it recently to govern in the *Comunidad de Madrid*), but in recent years its share of the vote in several regions has risen quite dramatically. For example, in the Basque Country, from no seats and 1.4 per cent of the vote in 1990, the party went on to gain six seats with 9.2 per cent of the vote in 1994. In Andalusia, where its base has always been strong, in the 1994 regional elections IU, in coalition with the Greens, won 20 seats with 19.14 per cent of the vote, which compares very favourably with the eleven seats and 12.67 per cent of the vote four years earlier. At the local level, while retaining overall third position in the country, IU witnessed a slight fall in its position between 1987 and 1991, although it considerably improved its position in the elections of 1995, obliging the PSOE to depend on it to remain in power in several large cities, including Málaga. The party's most impressive performance of recent times came in the 1994 European elections when it more than doubled its number of seats (from four to nine) as well as its share of the vote (from 6.1 to 13.5 per cent) compared to the previous poll in 1989. In theory, particularly given the problems besetting the PSOE, the outlook for the party in recent times should have been good – and its performance in the regional and local elections of 1995 hinted at better things to come. However, probably owing to underlying divisions within the IU itself, the left-wing electorate in March 1996 seemed still more inclined to trust the PSOE than the 'new Left'; thus, while at these polls IU marginally improved its position, its performance fell far short of expectations.

10.6.3 Performance of the Popular Party

Following poor performances in the general elections of 1977 and 1979 the then AP, profiting from the UCD's rapid decline, established itself as the main party of the Right in 1986, winning 106 seats with 26.18 per cent of the vote. In the elections of 1986 and 1989, it seemed incapable of rising above this ceiling. However, by the time of the 1993 election not only had the party restructured itself and appointed a new leader (10.3.3), but the PSOE government was losing a substantial degree of popularity. Hence, the PP came within four percentage points of the PSOE (34.82 to 36.68) and won 141 seats in the Congress as well as 93 in the Senate. Over the last five years, a similar improvement has taken place at regional and local level. As a result of the elections of 1991, the party was able to form single party or coalition governments in five autonomous communities and made substantial inroads into traditional Socialist heartlands in the municipal elections, significantly winning or sharing power in Madrid, Seville and Valencia, as well as sixteen other provincial capitals. In the 1993 regional elections in Galicia, the party won a resounding victory under Manuel Fraga, gaining an overall majority for the first time, with no less than 52.21 per cent of the vote and 43 out of 75 seats contested. In some respects, its achievement in the less promising terrain of the Basque Country in the regional elections of the following year was even more remarkable: on that occasion, the party gained eleven seats (out of 75), which compared very favourably with the six seats and 8.23 per cent of the vote in 1990. An even more impressive result was undoubtedly that of the European elections of June 1994 when it convincingly defeated the PSOE, winning 40.2 per cent of the vote (compared to the socialists' 30.7 per cent) and sending 28 *eurodiputados* to Strasbourg. However, the most spectacular result of recent times occurred in the regional and local elections of May 1995 when the party won overall or relative control in nine out of the thirteen regions contested and overall control of most of the major cities in the country. In addition, the PP, thanks to changes in the composition of regional parliaments, seized overall control of the Senate, as well as control of the all-important Council for Fiscal and Financial Policy which determines policy for their autonomous communities (7.5.3.2). The general election of March 1996 was, in reality, a disappointment for the PP; while it emerged triumphant as the largest single party, its performance fell well short of expectations (and, indeed, of all poll predictions) and José María Aznar was obliged to do deals with three nationalist parties, notably the CiU (10.4.5), in order to put together a reasonably stable government. Some commentators, ironically, were already speaking of the beginning of the PP's decline.

10.7 Comment

In any democratic country, political parties play a crucial role in legitimising the system. This is no less the case in Spain today than in other democratic nations. It should be clear from the foregoing that all the major parties are system-supportive in that they accept the values of democratic politics and, indeed, offer relatively moderate programmes to what still appears to be a moderate electorate. The only exceptions to this are radical Basque parties like *Herri Batasuna* (10.4.3). It is significant that over the last decade both the major parties have moved towards the centre of the political spectrum, the PSOE now clearly established as a social-democratic party and the PP as a party of the centre-right. Popular support for the system has been reflected in the generally high turnout in most elections, especially general elections. At times of crisis, such as the attempted coup of 1981, the attempt on the life of José María Aznar in April 1995, and the ongoing struggle against ETA terrorism, reflected in the 1988 Pacts of Ajuria Enea, there has been abundant evidence of inter-party co-operation. Thus, in terms of their relationship with the state and with each other, the Spanish parties would seem to have passed the test of legitimisation.

On the negative side, however, few major parties (IU is the main exception) can claim a blameless record in terms of financial propriety, and several have succumbed to the temptation of exchanging political favours for contributions to party coffers. In terms of this kind of corruption, the PSOE has without doubt been the major culprit – as the party of government between 1982 and 1996 its example has been lamentable at national, regional and local level. Shortage of funds has, of course, been the main cause in most cases of such shady dealings although, as we have seen (10.2), extra dubious sources of funding have not prevented most of them falling into serious indebtedness. However, while there may be a strong case for reviewing the law on party funding, the principal causes lie partly in a system that has allowed a proliferation of elections (most years witness either a European, general or major regional election) and partly in simple mismanagement of funds.

Perhaps in part due to public scepticism regarding such financial matters, but also related to the wider European malaise of a growing alienation between parties and public, doubts persist concerning the extent to which the former carry with them their electorates and the degree to which citizens consistently identify their interests and goals with those of any one political party. It has to be recognised that none of the parties can claim to be a mass party with a stable electorate. Compared to their counterparts in western Europe, the Spanish parties, in terms of membership, remain small. Moreover, allegiances can change dramatically as the UCD found in 1982 and the PSOE found in the period 1993–95 – although it can be argued, and with good reason, that such changes are healthy and, indeed, good for democracy, particularly if one party has been in power for a long time.

Chapter 11

Trade unions

11.1 Introduction

As with political parties (chapter 10), the fate of trade unions in the past depended very much on the kind of political system prevailing at the time. For example, while they were allowed freedom to form and operate during the Second Republic (1931–36), during the Franco era all union organisations were proscribed by law and driven underground or into exile. The major unions affected in this way – indeed the major unions in existence since the nineteenth century – were the UGT (11.4.1) and the CNT (11.5.3); the latter, having been associated by Franco with the Anarchist movement, came in for particularly harsh persecution. In the place of these unions, the dictator established his so-called 'vertical syndicates' (*sindicatos verticales*), which in reality amounted to little less than submissive instruments of offical labour policy, strongly controlled by government. The 1960s, a period of rapid economic expansion (1.1.3), witnessed growing confidence and solidarity among workers and a tendency among certain employers to prefer to negotiate with the authentic representatives of labour in order to introduce new methods and to improve productivity. For a while, there was tacit toleration of unofficial bodies, such as the Workers' Commissions (11.4.2), until they were declared illegal in 1967. With the return of democracy after 1975, all unions were allowed to operate freely again and, reflecting the changed social and labour scene of the post-Franco era, a number of new unions were created at both national and regional level.

11.2 Trade unions in the Constitution

Article 7 of the Constitution acknowledges the rights of unions and employers' organisations to defend their own legitimate interests within the provisions of the Constitution and the law, provided that they are democratically constituted and run. The right to join a union is granted to all citizens other than members of the armed forces (article 28.1) and members of the judiciary, such as judges, magistrates and public prosecutors (article 127.1). There is an equal right not to join (article 28.1).

Article 28.2 expressly recognises the right of workers to strike in defence of their interests, but reference is also made to exceptions to this in the public interest, to be clarified by subsequent legislation. This point is reiterated in article 37, which guarantees the right to collective bargaining (2.4.3.2) and the right to adopt collective conflict measures (2.4.3.3).

Reference is made in article 40 to the need to ensure a limit to the length of the working day, as well as the proper provision of paid holidays. Indeed, these matters were adopted in the subsequent legislation of 29 June 1983 which established an effective 40-hour week and a minimum of 23 days' annual holiday.

Article 35 lays down the right and duty of every Spanish citizen to work and to earn a living wage without discrimination between the sexes. Section 2 of this article also recognises the special issue of workers' rights by referring to their enshrinement in a special Workers' Statute, a commitment that was embodied in the law of 10 March 1980, later modified by the law of 24 March 1995 (11.3.1).

It should be stressed that, following the approval of the Constitution, in signing key agreements of the International Labour Organisation (ILO) (numbers 87 and 98, which refer to the right to form trade unions, the right to join one and the right to collective bargaining), and with the approval of a subsequent body of detailed legislation, Spanish trade union law was effectively coming into line with that of other Western democracies. Spain is also a signatory to the European Social Charter which, among other things, emphasises the freedom of workers and employers to establish organisations.

11.3 Legal position of trade unions and trade unionists

While general principles concerning unions and labour relations were laid down in the 1978 Constitution, subsequent detailed legislation, on which union representatives were consulted, was needed in order for these to be implemented in practice. While most of this legislation was enacted in the early 1980s, to some extent, this has been an ongoing process, as one might expect in a democratic system that is still to some degree 'feeling its way'. Thus, an updated Workers' Statute was approved as recently as 24 March 1995.

11.3.1 Workers' Statute (*Estatuto de los Trabajadores*) (*1980/1995*)

This Statute, first approved in 1980 and updated by the reformulated text of 24 March 1995, elaborates on workers' rights under three broad headings: (i) the relationship of the individual to work; (ii) worker representation; and (iii) collective bargaining.

11.3.1.1 Relationship of the individual to work

This is the title of section 1 of the Statute which covers the rights and duties of workers at their place of work, as well as details of the various kinds of contracts to which they may subscribe. Article 4 deals with equal opportunities and forbids all kinds of discrimination. However, there is also reference to the concept of the minimum wage (*salario mínimo interprofesional/SMI*), to be fixed annually by the government in consultation with unions and employers, bearing in mind the anticipated consumer price index (*índice de precios al consumo/IPC*) and other economic indicators.

Articles 34, 35.3 and 37 of the reformed Statute cover a variety of basic rights and conditions for Spanish workers, bringing them into line with their fellow citizens of the European Union. For example, the maximum working week, worked out on an annual basis, is 40 hours – though a maximum of 9 hours per day prevents employer exploitation in this regard. Workers under the age of eighteen are given special protection: they cannot be expected to do more than 8 hours per day and this must include any time off given for training (*formación*). All workers must have a minimum break of 12 hours between shifts. Rest periods are guaranteed and limits are put on night work. A recent addition to the Statute refers to the right of women with a child of up to nine months old to be absent for the equivalent of one hour a day for breast-feeding. In addition to statutory annual holidays, time off is given for a wedding (15 days), the death or serious illness of a close relative (two days, or four if travel is involved) and moving house (one day).

In order to safeguard workers in cases of bankruptcy (*quiebra*) or closure (*cierre*), the Statute established the Guaranteed Wage Fund (*Fondo de Garantía Salarial*) (article 33) to provide wages for up to a maximum of 120 days, derived from specific employer contributions. The *Fondo* was constituted by royal decree in March 1985 as an autonomous administrative body (6.3) within the Ministry of Labour and Social Affairs; both unions and employers' organisations have a right to be represented on this body.

11.3.1.2 Worker representation

Section 2 of the Statute deals with rights of assembly and collective representation in the work place, as well as with election procedures. Article 66 stipulates that, in firms which have fewer than fifty and more than ten employees, workers are represented by staff delegates (*delegados de personal*), elected on the basis of one delegate for up to thirty employees and three for between thirty-one and forty-nine. In firms which have more than fifty employees, workers are represented by works' committees (*comités de empresa*), the size of which is in proportion to the number of employees, as shown in table 11.1. If elections are required, candidates are presented in lists containing at least as many names as there are places to fill, with a clear indication of the union or the group of workers who have proposed the candidates. Voting is then by secret ballot and the term of office for those elected is usually four years. The composition of the committees, therefore, usually reflects the relative strengths of the unions at the work place. Before it had consolidated itself as a major challenger to the UGT, *Comisiones Obreras* favoured this system; they were not so keen to see changes which would transfer negotiating rights from the broader-based works' committees to plant-based single union branches.

The works' committees receive regular statistical information, financial statements and end-of-year reports (*memorias*) from management. They issue reports to the work force on the implications of any pending restructuring, organisational changes or financial adjustments. They monitor the fulfilment of legislation concerning industrial relations, social security and health and safety (article 64). In

Table 11.1 *Representation on works' committees*

No. of employees in company	No. of employees on works' committees
50–100	5
101–250	9
251–500	13
501–750	17
751–1000	21
1000+	21+2 per thousand employees up to a maximum of 75 members

Source: Ley Orgánica de Libertad Sindical (1984).

general, therefore, their role is to negotiate on behalf of the employees concerning their day-to-day work and their job security. This may also include local wage agreements, although such negotiations may well take place at another level.

11.3.1.3 Collective bargaining

The procedure for negotiating collective agreements (*convenios colectivos*), their format and their status is established in section 3, article 88, of the Workers' Statute, with subsequent modification resulting from the Organic Law of Union Freedom (11.3.2). Collective agreements can be negotiated at a variety of levels, depending on the consent of the parties involved. When they occur at company level, the works' committee is the appropriate body to represent the workers, with a maximum of twelve representatives per side. If they are negotiated at local, provincial, regional or national level, a negotiating committee (*comisión negociadora*) has to be formed consisting of representatives from those unions which have the status of 'most representative union' (11.3.2.4). This committee can have a maximum of fifteen union representatives, as can the committee representing the employers. Negotiations have to start within one month of a properly constituted request being presented by either side and agreement must be reached by 60 per cent of each party before it can be finalised. Once agreed, it is binding on both parties for as long as stipulated. The agreements have to be lodged with the Subdirectorate General for Mediation, Arbitration and Conciliation (11.8) and they have to be published in the *Official State Gazette* or its regional equivalent.

11.3.2 Organic Law of Trade Union Freedom (*Ley Orgánica de Libertad Sindical/LOLS*) 1985

This law was first approved in July 1984 but, due to the fact that an appeal against it was lodged with the Constitutional Court (2.5), it did not come into effect until 2 August 1985. The law stems from article 28.1 of the Constitution which recognises, but does not spell out, the basic freedoms and rights of unions. Because of the fundamental and far-reaching significance of the details of these freedoms, they required a law with the status of organic law (4.7.1.1). Hence, this is the law which currently establishes the *modus operandi* of unions in Spain and it therefore merits some attention.

11.3.2.1 Right to join a union

Section 1, article 1, of the Law recognises the constitutional right of all workers freely to join a union and this includes those working in public administration. However, it stipulates two exceptions: members of the armed forces and members of the judiciary. Furthermore, the right to exercise trade union rights for certain groups, such as members of the police force, is governed by specific regulations.

11.3.2.2 Right to found a union

The right to found, suspend or to disolve a union, via democratic procedures and without prior notice to any authority, is granted in section 1, article 2, of the LOLS, which also reinforces the right of workers to join the union of their choice and freely to choose their own representatives within the union concerned. The law protects union activity both inside and outside the work place, and unions cannot be suspended or disbanded by the authorities other than by order of the courts following a serious infringement of the law.

11.3.2.3 Legal responsibility of unions

Unions are liable for their own acts but not those of individual members, unless they are acting in accordance with union instructions. According to article 5.3 of the Law, fees (*cuotas*) paid by union members cannot be sequestrated.

11.3.2.4 Representation

Although all legally constituted unions enjoy the same basic freedoms, this Law recognises the special position of the 'most representative union' (11.3.2.5). The criterion used to decide which unions qualify for this status is that of election results rather than membership. Originally, the Law stipulated that the election process must be completed within three months, but legislation was brought in during 1994 to allow for a more flexible timetable. The conciliation department (11.8), in which was set up the National Committee for Union Elections (*Comisión Nacional de Elecciones Sindicales/CNES*), is the body responsible for agreeing election periods and for recording union election results.

11.3.2.5 'Most representative unions'

This classification is given to those unions which have obtained 10 per cent or more of the total number of delegates or members of works' committees. Based on

Table 11.2 *Trade union election results, per cent of representatives elected, 1978–90*

	UGT	CC.OO	USO	CSI–CSIF	ELA–STV	CIG[a]	Workers' group	Other unions
1978	21.70	34.50	3.90	–	0.90	–	18.20	20.80
1980	29.30	30.90	8.70	–	2.40	1.00	14.60	14.60
1982	36.71	33.40	4.64	–	3.30	1.17	12.09	8.69
1986	40.90	34.80	3.20	–	3.30	1.30	6.70	9.50
1990	42.00	37.00	2.90	1.40	3.20	1.50	3.60	6.40

Note:
[a] Figures for 1982–86 refer to the INTG (11.6.2)
Source: Elecciones Sindicales – Resultados Nacionales, Ministerio de Trabajo y Seguridad Social (1991).

the 1990 results (table 11.2), the UGT (11.4.1) and CC.OO (11.4.2) attained this status at national level, as indeed they had done in previous elections. This means that all the unions and federations which belong to these bodies also enjoy that status within their own ambit, even if they have not directly obtained 10 per cent of the delegates. To acquire this status at regional level, it is necessary to obtain a minimum of 15 per cent of the delegates, who must correspond to at least 1,500 individuals. Therefore, in addition to the UGT and the CC.OO, the Basque union, ELA–STV (11.6.1), and the Galician union, CIG (11.6.2) (which lost this status in 1986), both qualified.

11.3.2.6 Rights of 'most representative unions'

These unions are automatically entitled to become part of a negotiating committee for collective agreements above the level of the single company and to nominate representatives to the boards of public bodies, such as the Economic and Social Council (5.8) and the National Institute for Social Security (6.4.3.1). Since 1986, this right has *de facto* been extended to membership of EU bodies like the Economic and Social Council (15.3.8.1). These and other rights are restricted to the specific region where the status was achieved in the case of those unions which qualified on a regional basis.

11.3.2.7 Union rights within companies

Formal recognition is given to the single union, plant-based branch or section (*sección sindical*), as a representative and negotiating force within individual firms. Within a given firm, unions are granted a range of facilities, such as, for example, time and location for holding meetings, a union office and the right to publicise information for union members.

11.3.2.8 Protection of union freedom

Ample protection is built into this Law to protect unions and individual members from any form of discrimination by employers. A formal procedure for recourse to the courts is laid down starting with the newly established social or labour courts (*juzgados de lo social*) (14.7.6) and extending as far as the Constitutional Court (2.5), with penalties in the form of fines for acts of discrimination. Legislation in this field, which needed to be brought into line with the 1985 Organic Law of the Judiciary (14.3.1), was updated in the Law of Labour Procedures (*Ley de Procedimento Laboral/LPL*) of April 1990.

11.3.2.9 Collection agreement levy

In order to help unions defray some of their costs, they can establish provision within a collective agreement for the employer to deduct a payroll levy (*canon de negociación*) from those workers who opt into the scheme. Likewise, unions can request that firms, with the agreement of the employee, deduct union fees from the payroll (*descuento de nómina*).

11.3.2.10 Election of workers' representatives

The procedure was laid down in the Workers' Statute of 1980, modified by subsequent legislation in 1983, and updated in the new version of the Statute in 1995. In 1985 the LOLS had established a four-year period for elections (instead of every two years as before), and this was applied between 1982 and 1990. However, following a long process of negotiations and parliamentary activity, it has subsequently been agreed with the unions that there could be a more flexible procedure under which elections are carried out over a much longer period, dates to be agreed by unions and employers. Thus, the most recent round of elections has been spread out during the autumn of 1994 and the whole of 1995. In these elections, for the first time since 1980, the CC.OO edged ahead of the UGT taking an average lead over the latter of nearly three percentage points.

The results of the 1990 elections for delegates and members of works' committees (table 11.2) – the last time when elections took place more or less simultaneously – indicate that the only 'most representative unions' on a national basis in terms of the 1984 Organic Law are the UGT and the CC.OO, as was the case in all previous elections dating back to 1982. The number of unaffiliated delegates, now known as the Workers' Group (*Grupo Trabajadores*), elected in 1982 was quite significant but, as can be seen, has steadily diminished with succeeding elections. The category 'others' consisted of a relatively large number of delegates representing unions which may be relatively strong only in particular localities or firms. As a result of the LOLS, open lists (*listas abiertas*) which gave workers the opportunity to choose from a wide range of candidates, some of whom would be selected because of their personal attributes, were replaced by closed and restricted lists (*listas cer-*

Table 11.3 *Major trade unions in Spain, 1995*

Name of union in Spanish	Orientation	Founder	Founded	Leader
National				
Unión General de Trabajadores (UGT)	Socialist	Pablo Iglesias	1888	Cándido Méndez
Confederación Sindical de Comisiones Obreras (CC.OO)	Radical Left	Marcelino Camacho	1964	Antonio Gutiérrez
Unión Sindical Obrera (USO)	Christian democrat	Collective	1959	Manuel Zaguirre
Confederación de Sindicatos Independientes y Sindical de Funcionarios (CSI–CSIF)	Independent	Various	1978	Antonio Corrales
Regional				
Euzko Langilleen Alkartasuna–Solidaridad de Trabajadores Vascos (ELA–STV)	Independent	Manuel Robles Aranguiz	1911	José Elorrieta
Converxencia Intersindical Galega (CIG)	Galician nationalist	Various	1990	Fernando Acuña
Sindicato de Obreros del Campo (SOC)	Radical Left	Juan Manuel Sánchez	1976	Juan Manuel Sánchez

Source: IMAC, Ministerio de Trabajo y Seguridad Social (1995).

radas y bloqueadas). The latter had the effect of limiting choice to candidates drawn from the unions in direct relation to the number of delegate posts to be filled. Thus, by 1995 unions controlled no less than 90 per cent of work place delegates.

11.4 Major national unions

Over the last decade, the trend – already discernible in the early 1980s – towards domination of the labour scene by two powerful unions has continued. Currently, the UGT and CC.OO account for up to 80 per cent of work place delegates. In specific regions, sectors or even firms, however, other unions, such as USO (11.5.1) and CSI–CSIF (11.5.2), can enjoy a good deal of influence. Another trend, common to most national unions, is that, aside from their organisation according to sector, they now have a decentralised structure, with regional federations which enjoy considerable autonomy. On the other hand, the larger unions at least have become increasingly involved with their labour affairs at the level of the European Union. Table 11.3 shows the major trade unions in Spain, both national and regional.

11.4.1 General Workers' Union (*Unión General de Trabajadores/UGT*)

The General Workers' Union was founded in Barcelona in 1888 by Pablo Iglesias (10.3.1.1). For the first hundred years of its existence, it was closely allied to the PSOE (10.3.1). It was strong prior to the Civil War but was savagely repressed during the Franco era. In the post-1975 period, especially following legislation in April 1977, the union emerged as the strongest numerically and was very prominent in negotiating national agreements on economic and social matters both with the government and the employers (11.8). However, the mid-1980s onwards witnessed a growing disillusion, on the part of leadership and members, with the economic policies of the PSOE, which the UGT saw as favouring employers and big business in particular; industrial restructuring (1.1.4) and radical changes in the labour market not only led to severe unemployment but also weakened the organisational base of the unions. Thus, in 1988 – a year which witnessed the first general strike of the new era – the UGT decided to sever its formal links with the PSOE, symbolised by the abandonment of his parliamentary PSOE seat by the union's veteran general secretary, Nicolás Redondo. At its XXXV Congress in April 1990, the UGT formally confirmed its total autonomy from the PSOE.

In the late 1980s, the UGT seemed to benefit from its new-found independence and growing co-operation with CC.OO. In the early 1990s, however, not only was the union rocked by the scandal surrounding its property development initiative, the *Promotora Social de la Vivienda* (*PSV*), but internal divisions were beginning to occur over the future model of the union; some, like Redondo and his successor Cándido Méndez (elected at the XXXVI Congress in April 1994), favoured a strong executive with the power to negotiate at the highest levels, while others argued for stronger regional unions and sectoral federations. Such divisions culminated in the spring of 1995 when three opponents of Méndez on the Executive forced the latter to resign pending the calling of an Extraordinary Congress; this was duly held on 29 April 1995, but Méndez's narrow 53 per cent victory could hardly be claimed as convincing, and is not likely to dampen discontent with his leadership, which in the view of many was too sympathetic towards the PSOE government.

11.4.1.1 Principles

In a statement of principles emanating from the XXXVI Congress in December 1994, the UGT declares itself to be

> an institution that is predominantly composed of producers, organised into related groups of occupations and liberal professions which . . . respects the widest freedom of thought and action among its members, provided that they fall within the revolutionary direction of the class struggle and support the creation of forces that will ensure the complete emancipation of the working class.

Bearing in mind the evolution of the PSOE between 1979 and 1988 (10.3.1.3), it is perhaps not surprising that the union severed its links with the party that had long previously abandoned such a radical doctrine. However, as recently as the XXXIV Congress in April 1986, the UGT, in its *Resoluciones*, states that the PSOE is 'the only political option capable of offering acceptable solutions to the problems of society'. Yet, four years later at the 1990 Congress, the wording had changed; on this occasion, in much vaguer language, we read: 'the UGT reaffirms the Socialist direc-

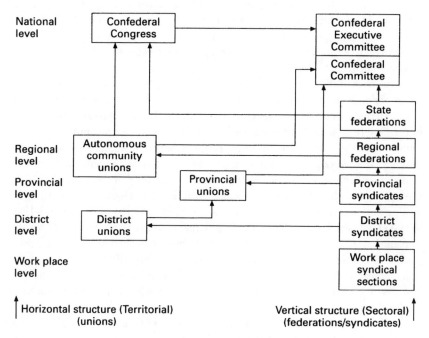

Figure 11.1 *Simplified structure of UGT, 1995*

tion of union activities and the need for combined political and union action ... [as well as] co-operation with those political and social forces which pursue the same objectives.'

11.4.1.2 Structure

As shown in figure 11.1, the UGT has both a horizontal and vertical structure, with institutions which reflect this. Vertically, the union is divided into twelve sectoral organisations known as *federaciones estatales* and horizontally it is structured into territorial groupings known as *uniones*. The *federaciones* represent branches of the whole range of employment from agricultural workers through various branches of light and heavy industry to various parts of the service sector. Many of these federations, such as the Federation of Land Workers (*Federación de Trabajadores de la Tierra/FTT*), were established as long ago as the 1930s; others, like the Union of Small Farmers (*Unión de Pequeños Agricultores/UPA*) – which is particularly active in Andalusia – are of relatively recent creation (1987). Currently, the largest federations are the Public Services Federation (*Federación de Servicios Públicos/FSP*), the Federation of Iron and Steel Workers (*Federación Siderometalúrgica*, known simply as METAL, and the Federation of Associated Industries (*Federación de Industrias Afines/FIA*), which represents, among others, workers in the chemical and textile industries. Altogether these federations account for nearly 60 per cent of the total membership of the UGT. Regional syndicates, corresponding to the seventeen autonomous communities plus Ceuta and Melilla, have considerable autonomy. Nationally and regionally, these federations each have their own national organs, including a federal congress which meets every four years and elects its own executive committee.

At the base of this vertical structure are the all-important syndical sections (*secciones sindicales de empresa*) which group together all UGT members in one work place. All these sections come together at district level in *sindicatos comarcales*, which in turn are represented at the higher levels of the province, the autonomous community and the state. The *secciones sindicales* have considerable autonomy; for example, they have a right to negotiate local collective agreements and can call a strike if a collective agreement has been signed at the level of the work place. (This was the case in the long-running dispute with Santana Motors of Linares during 1994, involving particularly *Comisiones Obreras*.) During the early and mid-1980s, the UGT favoured the idea of giving negotiating power to these *secciones* rather than to plant-based multi-union committees, a preference facilitated to some extent by provisions in the organic Law of Trade Union Freedom (1985) (11.3.2); in recent years, however, the union has tended to place less emphasis on this since the trend has been for section members to be precisely those who stand for election to the *comités de empresa* (11.3.1.2).

Horizontally, the UGT consists of 40 *unions territoriales* (more often known simply as *uniones*) of workers, taken from the whole range of *federaciones*. Currently, there are 20 *uniones regionales*: one for each of the seventeen autonomous communities (usually adopting the name of the latter, such as *UGT del País Valenciano*), one each for Ceuta and Melilla, and one for members working abroad (*UGT del Exterior*). In addition, in the provinces of four geographically large regions – Andalusia, Aragón, Castile–La Mancha and Castile–León – there are 20 *uniones provinciales*, which enjoy a good deal of organisational autonomy, though less than that accorded to regional unions. Both the regional and provincial unions in parallel with the *federaciones*, have the right to organise their own congresses and to elect their own executive committees. Moreover, regional unions, provided that they can muster 15 per cent of the delegates in their territory (with a minimum number of 1,500 members), have the right to be represented on certain state institutions, such as INSS (6.4.3.1) and the Economic and Social Council (5.8).

At the national level, the apex of the UGT pyramid is composed of the following national (confederal) institutions:

• Confederal Congress (*Congreso Confederal*)
  This is the highest decision-making body of the union and consists of 800 delegates. It meets every four years in ordinary session, to agree union policy and lay down guidelines for future action. Following the Congress, the union publishes its *Resoluciones* which, as well as updating if necessary the basic principles of the party and its internal statutes (*estatutos*), lays down general union policy on a wide range of issues from regional and national affairs to interna-

tional matters, covering not only labour and social but also political aspects. The Congress may also meet in extraordinary session as decided by the Confederal Committee (see below) or at the request of more than 50 per cent of the *federaciones estatales* and the *uniones*, which in turn represent more than 50 per cent of the total membership of the UGT. The most recent example of this, as indicated above, occurred on 29 April 1995, when there was an unsuccessful challenge to the leadership of the present general secretary, Cándido Méndez.

• Confederal Committee (*Comité Confederal*)
  This is the major representative group of the union between congresses. It meets in ordinary session twice a year and in extraordinary session when requested either by an overall majority of its members or by the Confederal Executive Committee (see below). The *Resoluciones* of the XXXVI Congress state that 'participation and democracy between congresses is guaranteed by means of the Confederal Committee since this is the Confederation's instrument of participation and control'. The membership of this Committee is made up according to criteria of proportionality and is thus composed of representatives of the *federaciones estatales* and of the *uniones de comunidad autónoma* and *uniones provinciales* according to rules laid down by each of the bodies concerned. Each Federation is represented by its general secretary and by a minimum of two more members, the rest being allocated proportionally according to the number of members up to a maximum of 100. The *uniones* are represented by their general secretaries plus those elected proportionally up to a maximum of sixty-eight. All members of the current Executive Committee (see below) are automatically members. The membership of the Confederal Committee is currently 205, of whom 181 are members with full voting rights.

• Confederal Executive Committee (*Comisión Ejecutiva Confederal*)
  The Executive Committee consists of eleven members, including the general secretary, and is elected every four years at the Confederal Congress, which reviews its performance during the previous term of office. Each member, except the general secretary, is a *secretario* responsible for one of the ten departments of the Executive. The function of this Committee, which meets on Tuesdays every week, is of course to implement the overall policies of the union in co-ordination with the federations and unions. To a large extent, this co-ordination process is carried out via the Executive's participation on the Confederal Committee. It should be noted that, as in the case of the other two major organs at national level, the regional and twenty provincial unions also have their own executive committee, elected at Congress every four years.

• Other national bodies
  In addition to these three major bodies, the UGT possesses two other national level organs. These are the Guarantees Committee (*Comisión de Garantías*), whose function is to control and protect the rights of members, as well as apply

sanctions where rules are broken, and the Control Committee (*Comisión de Control*), which deals with all the financial and budgetary affairs of the union. Both committees, which have a president and four ordinary members (*vocales*), are elected at the same time as the Executive at the Confederal Congress and, as we have seen, are represented on the Confederal Committee.

11.4.1.3 Individual membership (afiliación)

Workers can become members (*afiliados*) of the UGT by joining through their *sección sindical* at their place of work. Members pay a basic fee (*cuota*), plus an additional percentage related to their income, as recommended at Congress. They thus become members of one of the several *federaciones*. This automatically grants them membership of the appropriate regional union. Fees are normally paid monthly either via direct bank debit (*domiliación bancaria*) or by payroll deduction (*descuento de nómina*); 61 per cent of members pay by the former method. At the end of 1993, the total membership of the UGT stood at 747,636. In fact, between 1989 and 1993, the union claimed a dramatic increase of 250,000 members (an increase of over 50 per cent), which may be partly attributed to the decision by the union to distance itself from the increasingly unpopular PSOE government and its more militant stance in favour of workers, especially those in the hard-pressed and expanding public sector. As already stated, the FSP is the largest of the *federaciones* with over 150,000 members, followed by METAL with 116,000 and FIA with nearly 80,000. The largest regional *uniones* are Andalusia (111,828), País Valenciano (84,460), Madrid (86,670) and Catalonia (83,806).

11.4.1.4 Membership of international bodies

Over the last decade or so, the UGT has developed very strong international links, as reflected in the ninety delegates (including twenty-four from all over Europe and seventeen from Latin America) who attended the Congress of April 1994. Moreover, a large part of the *Resoluciones* document published after this Congress is devoted to international policy, with one important section devoted to the European Union and Spain's role within it. Thus, the UGT is a member of the European Trade Union Confederation (ETUC) and has its own office in Brussels. Currently, the union is also a member of the International Confederation of Free Trade Unions (ICFTU) and the International Professional Secretariats (IPS), an international organisation which brings together members of national sectoral syndicates or federations. Recently, the UGT has become a member of the European Syndical Committees whose aim is to provide a forum for sectoral interests at the European level. Altogether there are fifteen of these, of which one – to which METAL is affiliated – is the European Federation of Metalworkers (*Federación Europea de Metalúrgicos*).

11.4.2 Union Confederation of Workers' Commissions (*Confederación Sindical de Comisiones Obreras/ CS de CC.OO*)

As stated above (11.1), the Workers' Commissions first emerged in the changed economic climate of the mid-1960s, when a need was felt on both sides of industry for more genuine dialogue between more authentic workers' representatives (many of whom had in any case infiltrated the official vertical syndicates) and employers anxious to improve economic performance. While never an exclusively trade union arm of the Spanish Communist Party, the Commissions in their early days certainly had a majority of PCE members – probably because the latter were the most active political group at grass-roots' level (10.3.2). Although founded much later than the historic UGT, the Commissions were in a strong position to take advantage of the new situation provided by the return to democratic rule after the death of Franco and their legalisation in May 1977. In recent years, they have gained considerable ground on the UGT, partly because of the latter's internal and financial problems (11.4.1), and partly due to the dynamic leadership of their youthful general secretary, Antonio Gutiérrez.

11.4.2.1 Principles

The most recent statement of CC.OO principles is contained in the Statutes (*Estatutos*) published after the union's V Congress in 1991. The union declares itself to be democratic and independent (i.e. with no party affiliation) and, in defending the interests of male and female workers, directs its efforts towards 'the suppression of the capitalist society and the construction of a Socialist, democratic society'. In addition to improving the lot of its members – and that of the working class in general – the union clearly has a political agenda: it supports the concept of a federal state and recognises the 'right to self-determination of those peoples who desire to exercise it', echoing demands consistently made by more radical Basque and Catalan nationalists. The union also commits itself to joint struggle with other unions. The principles include a strong, indeed utopian, commitment to the eventual creation of an international syndicalist movement. In view of the way in which labour relations and Spanish society in general have evolved in recent years, the language of much of this section of the Statutes is surprisingly reminiscent of the class-based attitudes and images of the 1930s; indeed, they virtually echo those of the UGT (11.4.1.1).

11.4.2.2 Structure

As shown in figure 11.2, *Comisiones*, like the UGT, has both a vertical and a horizontal structure, with corresponding set of institutions. Vertically, the union is divided into some seventeen syndicates (*sindicatos*), each representing a branch (*rama*) of industry in the widest sense of the word, including agricultural workers, miners, construction workers, iron and steel workers and workers in many branches

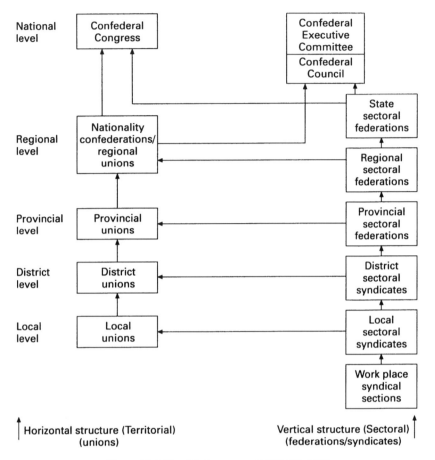

Figure 11.2 *Simplified structure of CC.OO, 1995*

of public administration. These syndicates operate at factory, local, district, provincial, regional and national level. Regional syndicates, corresponding to the seventeen autonomous communities plus Ceuta and Melilla, have considerable autonomy and often have their own names and/or acronyms; in Andalusia, for example, the union is known as *Comisiones Obreras de Andalucía* (*COAN*). Nationally, these trades syndicates are known as state federations (*federaciones estatales*) like those of the UGT. Horizontally, the union consists of *uniones* of workers, taken from a range of *sindicato* branches, and operates at the same levels, except that of the work place. Regional unions which, like their trades counterparts, enjoy a good deal of freedom of action, are known either as *uniones regionales* or, in the cases of the historic nationalities (chapter 7), as *confederaciones de nacionalidad*.

The basic unit of the syndical structure, to be found at the work place, is the syndical section (*sección sindical*). This consists of all the CC.OO members in any one centre. Its main function is to apply the union's policy in the factory or work place and draw up guidelines of policy which its representatives must take to the corresponding works' committee (*comité de empresa*) when, for example, collective bargains are being negotiated. In addition to a general secretary, the section must elect the legally agreed number of union delegates (*delegados sindicales*) to represent the union on the above committee. One of the other main tasks of the delegates is to collect membership fees (*cuotas*). As suggested in figure 11.2, composition of a local (normally municipal level) union branch (*unión local*) is made up of CC.OO members from a variety of local branch syndicates (*sindicatos locales de rama*) which in turn are composed of members drawn from a range of work place syndical sections (*secciones sindicales de empresa*).

As indicated in figure 11.2, all local syndicates are represented on district syndicates which in turn are represented on provincial syndicates; the latter elect delegates to the regional and the national *federaciones de rama*. The horizontal (territorial) unions function very much in the same way. There is co-ordination, via periodic meetings, at all levels between the syndicates and the unions.

The main national institutions are as follows:

* Confederal Congress (*Congreso Confederal*)
  This is the highest decision-making body of the union. It is composed of an equal number of delegates from the state federations, on the one hand and, on the other, from the nationality confederations (corresponding to the autonomous communities) and the regional unions. The Congress meets in ordinary session every four years; notice must be given at least six months in advance and all motions and relevant documents forwarded at least four months beforehand. Extraordinary meetings can be called either by an overall majority of the Confederal Council or by territorial and/or federative organisations that together make up two-thirds of the union membership. As well as determining the official policy of the union for the next four years, the Congress has to carry out certain specific tasks, including (i) approval of the Statutes, modified if necessary; (ii) approval of the composition of the Confederal Congress; (iii) election, by free and secret vote of the secretary general (leader) and president of the CC.OO (a more or less honorary post); and (iv) election of the Executive Committee (see below). The most recent Congress was held in January 1996, when, to the surprise of many, the veteran founder of the CC.OO, Marcelino Camacho, was ousted from the presidency and hence from the union's Confederal Executive Committee (see below). At the same time Antonio Gutiérrez was re-elected general secretary for another four-year term.
* Confederal Council (*Consejo Confederal*)
  This is the highest management and representative body between congresses. It is composed of: the Confederal Executive Committee, including the secretary general and president of the CC.OO; two members of the Free Syndicate of the Merchant Marine (*Sindicato Libre de la Marina Mercante*); the confederal secretaries (i.e. leaders of regional unions) who are not already members of

the Confederal Executive Committee, as well as the economic and legal co-ordinator (*coordinador económico y jurídico*) of the national Technical Office (*Gabinete Técnico*) (all elected by the Confederal Council); and an equal number elected by the state federations, nationality confederations and regional unions at their respective congresses. The total membership is currently 150. The Council is convened by the Executive Committee in ordinary session at least five times a year; it may meet in extraordinary session whenever this is requested by a third of its members. Its main general function is to debate and discuss union policy between congresses and to control its implementation by the Executive Committee. More specifically, it convenes the Confederal Congress; it approves the annual budget as proposed by the Executive Committee; it fixes membership fees; it receives annual reports from the Financial and Guarantees Committees (see below); it elects the editor of the union's official mouthpiece organ, the *Gaceta Sindical*; and, if agreed by an overall majority of members present, it can revoke the election of members of the Executive Committee or elect additional members provided that the initial number is not increased by 10 per cent.

- Confederal Executive Committee (*Comisión Ejecutiva Confederal*)
  This is the highest union body for implementing policy agreed at Congress and guidelines agreed in the Council. As we have seen, it is elected every four years at the Confederal Congress; members must have been members of the union for at least four years. It is convened by the General Secretary or by a third of the total membership. It tends to meet once a week. In order to organise the everyday work of the union at national level, the Executive is divided into sec-retariats (*secretariados*); the number of these can vary, but at present there are eighteen, covering a wide range of areas, including: employment; industrial policy; environmental matters; training; women's affairs; peace and disarma-ment; relations with the European Union; and international relations. In addi-tion to the general functions referred to above, the Committee has specific responsibility for the organisation of the union's central services, for the appointment of all technical and administrative staff, for publishing central official publications and for maintaining contact with all union federations, confederations and unions. It is accountable to Congress at the end of its term and to the Council between meetings of Congress.

Other national level institutions are the Guarantees Committee (*Comisión de Garantías*), whose task is to take care of internal disciplinary matters, and the Administrative Control and Finances Committee (*Comisión de Control Administrativo y Finanzas*), established to control administrative affairs and to check the accounts of all national level organs. Both committees are elected to serve for four years at the Confederal Congress; in neither case can members (five in each case) be members of the major union bodies described above.

A point worth noting is that since 1982 there has been no close connection between the Spanish Communist party and CC.OO. The union's claims not to have any particular bias in favour of one party is reinforced by the fact that not one of the current members of the Executive Committee belongs to the party.

11.4.2.3 Individual membership (afiliación)

Membership is organised either at the work place, where a worker signs on as a member of his *sección sindical*, or at the district or provincial office to which the syndical section is affiliated. Members (*afiliados*) pay a fee (*cuota*) every month which includes a fixed amount plus a certain percentage extra calculated according to income. The most normal way of paying is via deduction from one's monthly wage. Special arrangements are made for migrant workers through the *Secretaría de Emigraciones*. Members enjoy all the rights accorded to their counterparts in other European unions.

At the end of 1995, the total membership of CC.OO stood at 636,413. This represents a slow but steady increase since 1981 when the figure stood at 389,237. The sectors best represented by CC.OO members are mining and engineering (125,475) and iron and steel (113,871). In terms of the regional share of total membership, Catalonia (111,555), Andalusia (98,712) and the region of Madrid (86,249) are the best supported in global terms. (Interestingly, for work place delegates in the 1990 elections, the CC.OO triumphed over the UGT in both Madrid and Barcelona.) Between the late 1980s and early 1990s, however, certain regions, in particular Asturias, recorded drops in the number of members, reflecting the heavy unemployment registered in areas of traditional and heavy industry.

11.4.2.4 Membership of international bodies

The CC.OO, reflecting its total commitment to international co-operation in union and labour affairs, is a member of the European Trade Union Confederation (ETUC). Currently being debated (and likely to go ahead in the near future) is membership of the International Confederation of Free Trade Unions (ICFTU).

11.5 Other national unions

As indicated already (11.4), at national level only the UGT and the CC.OO have most representative union status. Since the latter moved away from indentification with specific political parties and adopted a more independent stance, other unions have seen their position eroded from their already low base of the early 1980s.

11.5.1 Workers' Syndical Union (*Unión Sindical Obrera/USO*)

Such has been the fate of this small national union which, as can be seen in table 11.2, saw its percentage of elected representatives fall from 4.64 in 1982 to 2.9 in 1990 and its overall ranking during the same period drop from third to fourth. Like the CC.OO, this union arose from a group of workers who were opposed to the official Franco unions. Many of its founder members came from a Catholic workers' background, being members of the Catholic Youth Workers (*Juventud Obrera Católica/JOC*) or the Catholic Action Workers' Brotherhood (*Hermandad Obrera de Acción Católica/HOAC*). Its strength was largely centred in large organisations such as Spanish Railways (*Red Nacional de Ferrocarriles Españoles/RENFE*) and the heavy industries of northern Spain, coal and iron/steel, which for many years now have been in serious decline. At its V Congress in 1991, the union declared itself to be a free, sovereign, class-based, democratic union, based on the autonomy of its member unions, with a willingness to collaborate with other unions and an international vocation. Territorially, the USO's basic unit is the district centre (*sede comarcal*); these centres are affiliated to *uniones* at the provincial, regional and national level. In sectoral terms, it is divided into sixteen professional federations (*federaciones profesionales*). Its national bodies are similar to those of the UGT and CC.OO, except that the Executive Committee has as many as thirty members, including the current general secretary, Manuel Zaguirre. In 1994 it had only 70,000 members but of these 6,860 (over 10 per cent, a higher percentage than that of the UGT or *Comisiones*) were union representatives. The USO is a member of the christian democratic-oriented World Labour Confederation. It has a monthly publication known as *Unión Sindical*.

11.5.2 Confederation of Independent Syndicates and Civil Service Union (*Confederación de Sindicatos Independientes y Sindical de Funcionarios/CSI–CSIF*)

The CSIF part of this twin union was formed in 1978, bringing together as many as 180 union groups that had grown up independently in the immediate post-Franco period. In July 1991, at a special unification conference, the CSIF and CSI, representing respectively the public and private sectors, joined forces. Like other unions, the CSI–CSIF is organised both territorially and sectorally; on the one hand, it is divided into regional and provincial *uniones* and, on the other, into twenty-four sectors or branches of economic activity. At the national level, the union consists of four major institutions: as well as the National Congress (*Congreso General*), the Union Council (*Consejo Sindical*) – the body which acts in place of the latter between congresses – and the National Executive Committee (*Comité Ejecutivo Nacional*), the union also has a Confederal Committee (*Comité Confederal*), which acts as a delegated committee of the Union Congress and must ensure that all agreements and resolutions of Congress are carried out. At the head of the CSI–CSIF is the general secretary, currently Antonio Corrales. Unlike the USO, which seems to be on the decline, the CSI–CSIF, in large measure because its members come from the expanding services sector, seems to be on the increase. In 1994 the union had a membership of 116,000 and in the 1990 union elections, secured 6,300 representatives; however, paradoxically, its percentage of work place representatives was lower than that of the USO (2.5 per cent). CSI–CSIF is not yet one of the most representative unions, but could well become so in the near future.

11.5.3 Other unions

In the first flush of freedom granted by the new right to register unions in 1977, more than 400 were said to exist at one time, both national and regional. Many have since disappeared. The national level unions that remain can be divided into two groups: (i) those calling themselves independent unions, whose members come from a variety of occupations; and (ii) those which represent specific occupations or professions. In the first group are the Confederation of Independent Workers (*Confederación de Trabajadores Independientes/CTI*) and the Confederation of Independent Unions (*Confederación de Sindicatos Independientes/CSI*). The second group includes unions catering for the needs of special interests, such as the Free Union of the Merchant Navy (*Sindicato Libre de la Marina Mercante/SLMM*) and the Spanish Union of Airlines (*Sindicato Español de Líneas Aéreas*). This group of unions is sometimes referred to as 'unitary unions' (*sindicatos unitarios*).

Three unions which achieved more than 1,000 representatives nationally in the 1990 union elections were the following:

- the General Confederation of Labour (*Confederación General del Trabajo/CGT*), with 1,670
- the State Convergence of Doctors and Technical Health Assistants (*Convergencia Estatal de Médicos y Ayudantes Técnicos Sanitarios*), with 1,247
- the Federation of Independent Unions of Spanish State Education (*Federación de Sindicatos Independientes de Enseñanza del Estado Español*), with 1,054.

A union which played a historic role in the working-class struggles of the early decades of this century is the National Confederation of Labour (*Confederación Nacional del Trabajo/CNT*), (11.1) founded in 1910 and based on anarcho–syndicalist thinking. Although still in existence, over the last decade this union has shrunk to almost insignificant proportions. Its very radical ideology prevents it from participating in any electoral processes.

11.6 Major regional unions

The only two regional unions which have gained sufficient support to qualify for negotiating status have been the Basque union, *Eusko Langilleen Alkartasuna – Solidaridad de Trabajadores Vascos* (ELA–STV), and the Federation of Unions in Galicia (*Converxencia Intersindical Galega/CIG*). In 1982, both unions gained more than the 15 per cent of representatives legally required at regional level to give them a formal place on negotiating bodies under the provisions of the Organic Law of Trade Union Freedom (11.3.2). Throughout the period 1982–90, the Basque union maintained its most representative status, gaining in 1990 no less than 37.8 per cent of the regional vote; the Galician union, however, has seen its fortunes fluctuate somewhat: having won representative status in 1982 and then lost it in 1986, its percentage share rose to an encouraging 23 per cent of the regional vote in 1990.

11.6.1 Basque Union (*ELA–STV*)

The Basque union, which has members in the three Basque provinces as well as Navarre, is a regional union with its headquarters in the industrial port of Bilbao, the capital of the Basque province of Vizcaya. Although its origins lie in the Basque nationalist movement centred on the PNV (10.4.1), it now proclaims a fierce independence – to the point where members of any political parties are debarred from standing for posts of office in the union. One of its primary objectives is to set up and develop a system of independent industrial relations in the autonomous region of Euskadi. Like most other unions, it has a territorial structure (composed of eighteen district-based unions) and a sectoral structure (with seven professional federations). Currently, it has 90,000 members and in the 1990 union elections it secured 6,836 work-place representatives, a percentage relative to membership of 13.2. In the region, it has always faced strong competition from the UGT, traditionally strong in the industrial heartland of Bilbao, but is currently the strongest union in the Basque Country.

11.6.2 Galician Union (*CIG*)

The Galician union, which has members in the four provinces of Galicia, is a regional union with its headquarters in the port and ship-building town of Vigo in the province of Pontevedra. It was established in April 1990 as the result of a merger between the Federation of Galician Workers (*Intersindical Nacional de Traballadores Galegos/INTG*) and the Regional Confederation of Galician Workers (*Confederación Xeral de Traballadores Galegos/CXTG*). Structurally, it is composed of eleven sectoral branches known as *coordinadoras de federación* and of six territorial unions, located in the six major cities of the region. Although still a relatively new union, it is the heir to a long tradition of unionist activity in the region and, as stated above, recovered most representative status in the elections of 1990. In 1990 it secured 3,527 work place representatives.

11.7 Other regional unions

Over the last decade the consolidation of the autonomous communities (chapter 7) has given a certain impetus to the formation of regional unions; indeed, it is at this level that more and more collective agreements are being signed. The Catalan leader, Jordi Pujol, is on record as stating his preference for a regional framework for labour relations in his region. This region, in fact, has one of the most active and best supported of the non-representative region-based unions, the Syndical Confederation of Catalonia (*Confederación Sindical de Catalunya/CSC*). In the Basque Country, a radical union with a heavy political bias is the so-called Patriotic Workers' Commissions (*Langile Abertzale Batzordea/LAB*), which has close links with Herri Batasuna (10.4.3) and which, like the latter, forms part of the KAS organisation (10.4.3). This union secured no less than 2,836 representatives in the union elections of 1990. An equally radical union in Andalusia – though not one that would defend violence – is the Union of Rural Workers (*Sindicato de Obreros del Campo/SOC*), founded in 1976 in Antequera, which over the last two decades has often resorted to direct action (such as land occupation) in defence of the interests of the unemployed and casually employed land-workers of the region. Its leader, Juan Manuel Sánchez, mayor of Marinaleda, achieved national notice in the spring of 1995 after being sent to prison (for 24 hours) by the High Court of Justice of Andalusia for his activities.

11.8 Subdirectorate General for Mediation, Arbitration and Conciliation (*Subdirección General de Mediación, Arbitraje y Conciliación*)

This body was first established in 1979 as an autonomous administrative body (6.3) within the Ministry of Labour and Social Security; it was initially called the Institute for Mediation, Arbitration and Conciliation (*Instituto de Mediación, Arbitraje y Conciliación/IMAC*) and is still often referred to by its former acronym. By a royal decree of December 1985, which involved a reorganisation of this ministry, its functions were transferred to the above-named Subdirectorate within the Directorate General for Labour (*Dirección General de Trabajo*). Originally, it operated with a good deal of autonomy, with its own director and a governing council, which included union and employers' representatives, as well as ministry appointees. Now it functions more or less as just one more government department.

The aim of establishing IMAC, as well as its subsidiaries at regional and provincial level, was to provide both sides of industry, groups as well as individuals, with mechanisms for resolving disputes as an alternative to going to law. Indeed, the law states that parties in dispute must have recourse to the conciliation service prior to going to court. Although it was intended to perform the role of arbitrator between unions and employers, for many years this was not put into effect and its role was confined to that of providing conciliation services. These are largely aimed at individual workers seeking information on their rights prior to having recourse to the labour courts. Subsequently, just at a time when IMAC was assuming more of its theoretical powers in this field, moves were made to transfer such responsibilities to a number of the autonomous communities (7.7.5). In any case, many of the cases were (and continue to be) handled by the provincial office (*dirección provincial*) of the Ministry of Labour within the *administración periférica del estado* (6.5).

If arbitration fails, parties in disagreement have at their disposal a range of newly established social courts which after 1985 gradually replaced the Francoist *magistraturas de trabajo*. These function, as will be seen in chapter 14, at various levels. At local level there are several social or labour courts (*juzgados de lo social*) (14.7.6) which handle most ordinary cases of dismissals, breaches of contract and social security problems. More serious matters and appeals are sent to the social divisions of the regional high courts (*tribunales superiores de justicia*) (14.6.1) and at the highest level to the social division of the Supreme Court (*Tribunal Supremo*) (14.5.1). In these cases, IMAC, or one of its provincial offices, acts as a filter by resolving approximately half the complaints it receives from individuals before they need to go to court.

To a large extent, this department has become a registry for the results of union elections, statutes, collective agreements and private agreements concerning termination of employment; in addition, it publishes a very detailed annual statistical report, the *Anuario de Estadísticas Laborales* on all aspects of labour affairs.

11.9 Pacts with government and employers

The consensus approach adopted in the post-Franco era by political and labour groups towards major economic and political problems was undoubtedly important in securing a relatively smooth transition from one system of government to another. As part of this process, lengthy negotiations took place in order to achieve major agreements on, for example, wage restraint, employment, industrial restructuring and social security. The discussions were not always carried out between the same parties because at the time no permanent consultative structure had been established. Article 131.2 of the Constitution envisaged the creation of the Economic and Social Council (*Consejo Económico y Social/CES*) (5.8) to assist the government in economic planning. In fact, because the unions argued for this body to have executive rather than just advisory and consultative status, its creation was delayed until as late as June 1991, the unions in the end losing the battle to give it 'teeth'.

Various attempts were made in the immediate post-Franco years to achieve a measure of unity and solidarity among labour organisations. A co-ordinating body for the UGT, the CC.OO and the USO, the *Coordinadora de Organizaciones Sindicales* (*COS*) was tentatively established in 1976, when it succeeded in organising a general strike. However, it only survived a short time and it has not been resurrected since – although the *unidad sindical* policy of the UGT and CC.OO (11.10) since 1988 has gone a long way towards restoring union co-operation. On the other hand, the employers' organisations have been very successful in settling their differences and in creating an Employers' Confederation, the *Confederación Española de Organizaciones Empresariales* (*CEOE*), which is described in 12.11. Nevertheless, despite the lack of cohesion on the union side, between 1978 and 1986 several major pacts (*pactos*) and agreements (*acuerdos*) were signed (table 11.4).

11.9.1 Moncloa Pacts (*Pactos de la Moncloa*) (1977)

Following the UCD general election victory in June 1977, an economic package was agreed by the major political parties (1.1.4). It included pay guidelines which related wage increases to the level of inflation (penalised firms paying above the norm) and allowed for the shedding of labour if pay increases were due to union pressure. It covered a whole gamut of other measures, including tax reform, social security,

Table11.4 *Social pacts, 1977–86*

Year	Pact	Organisations involved	% wage band agreed	% consumer price index (yearly average)
1977	Moncloa Pacts	UCD, PSOE, AP, PCE	–	–
1980 and	Inter-Confederation	UGT, USO,	13–16 (1980)	15.30 (1980)
1981[a]	Framework Agreement	CEOE (12.11)	11–15 (1981)	14.4 (1981)
1982	National Agreement on Employment	UGT, CC.OO, CEOE Government	9–11	13.9
1983	Inter-Confederation Agreement	UGT, CC.OO, CEOE CEPYME (12.11)	9.5–12.5	12.3
1984	No agreement		–	–
1985 and	Economic and Social	UGT, CEOE, CEPYME,	5.5–7.5 (1985)	8.2 (1985)
1986[a]	Agreement	Government	7.2–8.56 (1986)	8.3 (1986)

Note:
[a] Agreements lasted for two years.
Sources: Boletín de Estadísticas Laborales, Minsterio de Trabajo y Seguridad Social (various years); Instituto Nacional de Estadística (INE) (various years).

housing, employment, prices and monetary policy. Although, on this occasion, the employers and labour representatives were notable by their absence in the negotiations, the Pacts established a pattern which was to be followed by subsequent employer–union and tripartite negotiations involving the government.

11.9.2 Inter-Confederation Framework Agreement (*Acuerdo Marco Interconfederal/AMI*) (1980)

This Framework Agreement was signed in January 1980 by the UGT and Spanish Employers' Confederation, CEOE. As such, it was not legally binding but it provided pay guidelines which were revised in 1981 in the light of price rises. The parties agreed to co-operate in reducing working hours, banning overtime and increasing productivity. The success of this agreement prompted a more ambitious tripartite agreement.

11.9.3 National Agreement on Employment (*Acuerdo Nacional de Empleo/ANE*) (1982)

This agreement was signed in 1981 by the government, the CEOE and the two major unions, the UGT and CC.OO, to come into effect for 1992. It established pay norms with provision for their automatic modification in accordance with changes in the consumer price index. The unions also secured the promise of government measures to boost employment and reform social security. The government also acknowledged the need to compensate the unions for their assets (*patrimonio sindical*) which had been expropriated during the Franco era. Even at the time of writing

(1995), however, this issue had not been resolved to the satisfaction of the UGT and the CNT.

11.9.4 Inter-Confederation Agreement (*Acuerdo Interconfederal/AI*) (1983)

This was a further agreement, without the participation of the government, between the employers and the two largest unions, the UGT and the CC.OO. It set pay norms with an adjustment mechanism along the lines previously established in the tripartite national agreement of 1981. It also stressed the importance of co-operation on working conditions.

11.9.5 Economic and Social Agreement (*Acuerdo Económico y Social/AES*) (1985–86)

This Economic and Social Agreement was designed to apply to the two-year period 1985–86. It was a return to the tripartite system of 1981 involving government, management and workers and the first therefore to be entered into by the Socialist government of Felipe González. This was the most far-reaching of the agreements signed to date. It included a number of commitments which the government under-took to honour, including measures concerning unemployment, health and safety at work, and training. Agreement was reached to boost job creation through the ser-vices of the National Employment Institute, INEM, an autonomous administrative body (6.3) created by a royal decree in 1978. Over the years, this large institution, with offices in all provincial capitals, has become particularly significant in the light of Spain's high unemployment level, estimated in 1995 to be in the region of 22 per cent. In addition to being responsible for administering unemployment benefits, the INEM is empowered to negotiate public works schemes with regional governments and generally to act as a catalyst in job creation in both the public and the private sector.

The UGT and the employers' organisations, the CEOE and the CEPYME (12.11), entered into a legally binding contract regarding pay norms and productiv-ity. They undertook to introduce a voluntary disputes procedure, as they were dis-satisfied with the services of IMAC (11.8).

The growing divisions on the union side were highlighted by the refusal of the CC.OO to enter into the agreement, although they subsequently sought to be involved in aspects of its implementation. One of the major stumbling blocks was the agreement between the participants to pursue a more flexible approach towards the hiring and firing of labour in line with other EU countries. The CC.OO, however, saw this move as a sell-out of the safeguards against dismissal traditionally enjoyed by Spanish workers. Although half-hearted attempts were made in the early 1990s to resurrect such pacts, they came to nothing in the end; thus the AES can be regarded as the last of these global agreements. Subsequent collective agreements have been achieved either at the local or regional level or within a sector. The nearest thing to a global agreement in recent times was the 1993 agreement which the major unions and the employers of INI (9.4.2) signed; this linked workers' wages to the performance of individual INI companies. The attempt in the same year to reach a global agreement between the government and the unions ended in deadlock when the unions demanded a minimum wage rise of 8 per cent and the government and Confederation of Employers' Associations (12.11) were only prepared to offer 5 per cent.

11.10 Joint union action (*unidad sindical*)

More or less simultaneously with the divorce between the UGT and PSOE, i.e. from about 1988, came the beginning of a highly significant development in the Spanish union movement. This was partially facilitated by the election of the energetic young leader of CC.OO, Antonio Gutiérrez, at the Congress of 1987; the new general secretary was strongly committed, in the long term, to a unified union movement and the UGT leader, after his disillusioning experiences with the PSOE government, was more receptive than hitherto to such collaborative developments. The result, indeed, has been not only growing convergence in terms of ideology, policies and strategies but also in organisational terms, where in many respects the unions seem to be increasingly similar in structure.

Over recent years, the two major unions have collaborated increasingly, at local and national level, in the publication of joint documents, presenting a common front in terms of analysis of Spain's particular social and economic problems, policies to be adopted and strategies to be followed. One example of such a document, published in November 1991, was that entitled 'Union Initiative for Progress' (*Iniciativa Sindical de Progreso*), which sets the unions' ideas for reform clearly within the context of Spain's still relatively weak position within the European Union. This document – and indeed many others published independently by the two unions – conveys the view that, while economic integration has gone on apace, social integration has lagged far behind, to the detriment of workers' interests, especially in areas of social protection, professional training, unemployment benefits and working conditions. Consistently, the unions repeat their concerns about the existing imbalances between the countries of the European Union and between the regions of individual countries. Thus, the UGT and CC.OO have waged a long campaign both on the home front, urging the Spanish government to pursue policies that tend to distribute wealth more widely, and on the EU front, in collaboration with the ETUC, in support of policies that work for controlled development through cohesion rather than purely market-led, monetarist measures. In common with their counterparts in ETUC, the two Spanish unions support the establishment of a more democratic EU executive controlled by a more powerful European Parliament (15.3.2).

In recent times, the two most potent expressions of union convergence and solidarity among workers from a wide range of sectors have been the two, well-supported general strikes of December 1988 and January 1994. Though given less publicity, perhaps more significant in terms of tangible benefits for workers have been the increasing number of regional level collective agreements which the UGT and CC.OO have reached jointly with the employers.

11.11 Comment

To a large extent, the position of the trade unions in society over the last two decades has reflected the changing political and economic situation of the country as a whole. During the 1976–82 transition period, considerable euphoria was generated in the heady atmosphere of the new democracy; not only did membership of existing unions rise dramatically, but many new unions, at both national and regional level, first saw the light of day. At this time, political parties, employers' organisations and unions accepted that the national priority was to consolidate this fledgling democratic state. In the social pacts that characterised the period 1977–86 (11.9), the unions made considerable concessions in the national interest; indeed, due partly to the economic crisis of the late 1970s and early 1980s (compounded by the industrial restructuring policies of the government) and partly to the attempted *coup* of 1981, they allowed themselves to continue in this mode of social consensus long after the point when, at the grass-roots' level, much disillusion had set in, both with politicians and with the unions who had supported them. Thus, between 1980 and 1988, union membership underwent a steady decline. Since then, however, particularly in the case of the CGT and CC.OO, there has been an encouraging reversal of this trend, particularly explicable in terms of the unions' exchange of confrontation for collaboration and partly due to the creation of new and secure jobs in the expanding area of public administration, especially at regional and local level. However, union leaders are not under any illusion about the reality of a situation, in which under half the working population is unionised, well below the average for the European Union. There is little doubt that, to a large extent, the causes of this lie on the one hand, in fundamental recent changes in the labour market (including considerable deregulation) and, on the other, in structural changes affecting Spanish labour; the latter includes both permanent job losses in traditional heavy industries (historically areas of high union recruitment) and the high percentage of insecure jobs (some estimates give as much as 30 per cent) affecting women in particular (part-time, temporary, short-contract, etc.) which were created during the short employment 'boom' of the mid- and late 1980s. Alongside ensuring that 'modern' issues, such as work organisation, the impact of technological innovation and the working environment, are included in collective agreements (which historically has often not been the case), the unions' major challenge for the future remains that of persuading governments to tackle seriously the question of wealth redistribution and achieving more job opportunities and greater job security for their members. Increasingly, this battle will be fought both at the regional level and in the European context, where there is likely to be increasing collaboration with other EU union organisations like ETUC and the European Syndical Committees.

Chapter 12

Business and professional associations

12.1 Introduction

Article 39 of the Constitution recognises and guarantees the rights of private enterprise in Spain. It specifies that this right is to be exercised in accordance with the overall needs of the economy and within the general framework of economic planning. The scope for private enterprise in Spain is, thus, similar to that of business in other EU countries and, in fact, the private sector has flourished under the PSOE despite initial fears to the contrary. Harmonisation with EU legislation has led to significant changes in Spanish company law in recent years. The Commercial Code (*Código de Comercio*) is the basic source of mercantile law in Spain and this has been subject to revision from time to time since it was first enacted in 1885. It was necessary therefore to introduce a substantial number of modifications to the Code in 1989 in order to bring Spain's mercantile legislation into line with EU directives on companies. This was done initially through the 1989 Law on the Partial Reform and Adaptation of Mercantile law to the Directives of the European Economic Community in regard to Companies (*Ley de Reforma Parcial y Adaptación de la Legislación Mercantil a las Directivas de la Comunidad Económica Europea en materia de Sociedades*). This was followed by other measures designed to consolidate the changes in specific area of business organisation. Thus the 1989 Reformulated Text of the SA Company Law (*Texto Refundido de la Ley de Sociedades Anónimas*) was, in effect, a redrafting of the 1951 Law on SA Companies (*Ley de Régimen Jurídico de las Sociedades Anónimas*), illustrative of the practice of building upon existing law wherever possible through reformulation and insertion of new clauses. Changes to the legal framework of the smaller SL form of limited company (*sociedad de responsabilidad limitada*) envisaged in the harmonisation legislation of 1989 were likewise finally brought together in March 1995 in the Law on Limited Liability Companies (*Ley de Sociedades de Responsabilidad Limitada*).

Alterations to the regulations concerning the Mercantile Registry (*Registro Mercantil*) were also introduced in 1989 which, *inter alia*, added the obligation to file audited annual accounts with the Registry (12.3). All businesses, with the exception of the sole trader, have to register their existence with the Mercantile Registry in the capital of the province in which the registered head office of the company is located. Thereafter a record of the main details is kept in the Directorate General for Registration (*Dirección General de los Registros y del Notariado*) in Madrid. The basic data which must be entered includes name, address, nature of business, date of foundation, capital and the appointment and removal of directors and auditors. Subsequent changes in any of these particulars must be reported. The importance of the Registry lies in the fact that the filed data is assumed to be public knowledge. The corollary of this is that failure to register a particular aspect could lead to a charge of fraud. Members of the public may visit the Registry and request access to data held on any company, and this is generally provided in the form of a print-out at a small charge. The reference number relevant to a company's entry with the Registry is usually included on the company's official stationery.

12.2 Sole traders (*comerciantes*)

The one-man business is still the most common form of business organisation in Spain. This is regulated in the Commercial Code and, although registration with the Mercantile Register is not compulsory for sole traders, it does nevertheless have the advantage of giving legal status to their documentation. Examples of sole traders are found in many sectors, especially in retail sales, food and drink, crafts and many personal services. They are automatically members of their local chamber of commerce from which they can derive technical and legal support (12.12). In addition, Spanish law, following an EU directive of 1989, has recognised that in some instances sole proprietor businesses may expand to the point where limited liability is desirable although control is to remain vested in a single person (or company). Hence the 1995 Law on Limited Liability Companies (12.5) incorporated the concept of the single proprietor limited liability company (*sociedad de responsabilidad limitada unipersonal* or *sociedad anónima unipersonal*).

The significance of the contribution to the economy of the small and medium-sized business (*pequeña y mediana empresa / PYME*), which may or may not be in the hands of a sole proprietor, is recognised by a number of institutions which exist to support it. These range from the state-run Institute for Small and Medium-sized Businesses (*Instituto de la Pequeña y Mediana Empresa Industrial / IMPI*) under the auspices of the Ministry of Industry and Energy, to the private Institute for Family-owned Businesses (*Instituto de la Empresa Familiar*) which includes some of Spain's top industrialists in cosmetics and wines (12.11).

12.3 SA companies (*sociedades anónimas/ SA*)

The Reformulated Text on Company Law of 1989 (*Texto Refundido de la Ley de Sociedades Anónimas*) recognised that the category of public limited company (*sociedad anónima / SA*) was being applied to many business organisations which in practical and financial terms were too small to merit this designation. It therefore stipulated that as from 30 June 1992 any businesses wishing to preserve or acquire this status would need to have a minimum share capital of 10 million pesetas. The impact of this could be gauged by the large number of formal announcements in the financial pages of the press at the time as smaller companies were transformed into the alternative *sociedad de responsabilidad* (*SL* or *SRL*). Many were prepared to forfeit the undoubted prestige which went with the SA title in order to have to supply less detailed information. It is difficult to obtain accurate figures for the number of companies actively trading according to categories, but figures issued by the Mercantile Registry in 1995 (January) indicated that there were twice as many SRLs (525,542) as there were SAs (254,910).

The SA, however, is clearly the most significant form of business enterprise in terms of the major economic indicators. It is the type that is likely to be quoted on the stock exchange and to be adopted by foreign entities seeking to establish themselves in Spain. Their importance is further heightened by the fact that public sector companies (chapter 9) are also organised on this basis and hence generally carry the suffix SA.

Full details are included within the law of the classes of shares which these companies may issue, as well as details of the rights and obligations of shareholders (*accionistas*) on whom ultimate authority rests through their annual general meeting (*junta general ordinaria*) or extraordinary meeting (*junta general extraordinaria*). Although such meetings are normally formalities, there are signs of increased interest in some of the issues involved as the economic climate and any suspicion of financial scandal have made investors more anxious to see how management performs. Notification (*convocatoria*) of a meeting has to be given in a major newspaper in the appropriate province, as well as in the *Official Bulletin of the Mercantile Registry* (*Boletín Oficial del Registro Mercantil*). It is customary to provide notification (*segunda convocatoria*) of an alternative meeting should, as may often be the case, there be insufficient shareholders present to meet the initial quorum. In some instances where the share capital is in the hands of only two or three shareholders, their total attendance and unanimous consent is all that is required for a shareholders' meeting to be valid. This then carries the impressive title of *junta universal*. In practice, control of each company is in the hands of the board of directors (*consejo de administración*) formally elected by the shareholders.

A main area of concern in recent years has been the financial accountability of companies, as it was widely accepted that much of the data published by Spanish companies had previously been of a cosmetic nature for tax purposes. In a major attempt to convince foreign investors of the reliability of information and to ensure harmonisation with EU requirements, four further pieces of legislation have been put in place. Firstly, the 1988 Auditing Law (*Ley de Auditoría*) introduced the long overdue mandatory audit of accounts by independent external auditors. Secondly, new Regulations concerning the Mercantile Registry (*Reglamento del Registro Mercantil*) were approved in 1989 which, *inter alia*, obliged companies to file their annual accounts with the Registry and, hence, place them in the public domain (12.1). Thirdly, the General Accounting Plan (*Plan General de Contabilidad*) of 1973 was substantially revised both in the light of experience and in order to reflect EU directives more accurately, and this came into effect through the royal decree approving the General Accounting Plan of 1990 (*Real Decreto, por el que se aprueban el Plan General de Contabilidad*). The Plan is compulsory for all enterprises irrespective of their legal form of organisation which means that, in theory at least, there should be a certain uniformity in the financial statements issued by companies. Naturally, however, there will be differences which stem from the nature of individual businesses. Nevertheless, the most important contribution made by the Plan lies in its mandatory accounting principles, its valuation rules and its rules for drawing up the annual accounts. The legislation also made provision for the establishment of the Institute of Accounting and Auditing (*Instituto de Contabilidad y Auditoría de Cuentas/ICAC*) as the main regulatory body in the field of accounting and auditing in Spain. Fourthly, in 1991 formal recognition was given to the increased significance of groups of companies within the Spanish economy. A royal decree approving rules to draw up annual consolidated accounts (*Real Decreto 1815/1991, por el que se aprueban las normas para la formulación de las cuentas anuales consolidadas*) introduced detailed regulations to bring together the financial statements of parent companies and subsidiaries in the form of consolidated accounts. Further modifications, for example the broadening of the scope for submitting a more simplified or abbreviated form of accounts, were introduced under additional provisions (*disposiciones adicionales*) of the 1995 SL law (12.5).

12.4 Worker-controlled limited liability companies (*sociedades anónimas laborales/SAL*)

This is a variation of the SA company described above (12.3) which results when employees mount a bid to rescue an ailing firm, sometimes utilising their compensation funds in order to do so. This status, which attracts tax benefits, requires a minimum 51 per cent of the capital to be owned by permanent employees. A revision of the legal provision for this type of company is expected in the near future. According to the Mercantile Registry 1,206 such enterprises were constituted in 1994. Alternatively, in order to salvage divisions of companies which their owners have decided to sell off or close down, workers have elected to establish co-operatives (12.7).

12.5 SL companies (*sociedades de responsabilidad limitada/SRL/SL*)

The legislation concerning SL companies, which has been subject to various modifications as a result of the harmonisation process referred to above, was eventually rationalised and codified in the 1995 Law on Limited liability Companies (*Ley de Sociedades de Responsabilidad Limitada*). This type of company, which previously had no minimum size, is now required to have a minimum capital of 500,000 pesetas and its accounts have to be prepared, audited and filed along similar lines to those of the SA companies, albeit in more simplified terms. Existing SLs have been given three years (until 31 May 1998) in order to adapt their articles of association to the terms of the new legislation. The overall intention, however, is to provide a more flexible type of organisation, requiring less documentation and formality, for the smaller and family type of business. Here members (*socios*) enjoy the benefits of limited liability but there are restrictions on the transfer of their holdings (*participaciones*) in order to keep ownership within the hands of the founder members. Previously the number of members was limited to fifty; however, this limit was removed in the 1995 law. It was argued that it was cumbersome to monitor the details of ownership to this degree and that the restrictions on transfers would effectively preserve the closed nature of this form of business organisation. This type of organisation can be found particularly in the service, transport and retail sectors.

12.6 Partnerships (*sociedades colectivas*)

There are two basic kinds: the general partnership with unlimited liability (*sociedad colectiva/SC* or *sociedad regular colectiva/SRC*); and the limited partnership with at least one general, unlimited partner and one limited partner (*sociedad en comandita/S en C* or *sociedad comanditaria/S Com*). A variant of the limited partnership is the hybrid partnership limited by shares (*sociedad comanditaria por acciones/S Com por A*).

Although partnerships are recognised in the Commercial Code and they must be recorded in the Mercantile Registry in the same way as the forms of business organisation described above, they are not widely found in Spain. In 1994, for example, there were only seven new partnerships registered with the Registry. A few US investors have favoured this form of organisation for tax advantages in the United States and, in theory, the lack of need to file accounts with the Registry could be an attraction. In Spain professional people tend to act on their own account or, in view of the risks inherent in the more unpredictable economic climate of the time, they seek the benefits of limited liability through the SL form of organisation or, if of sufficient size, the SA form. A notable exception at the time of writing is Spain's largest firm of accountants and auditors, *Arthur Andersen y Cia, S Com*.

12.7 Co-operatives (*cooperativas*)

Much interest has been shown recently, both inside and outside Spain, in this form of organisation and the Spanish Constitution expressly refers in article 129.2, to the encouragement of the development of co-operatives. They are currently regulated by the *Ley General de Cooperativas* of 1987. There is a special Co-operative Register (*Registro de Cooperativas*) in which co-operatives must be recorded and their statutes must be approved by the Ministry of Labour and Social Affairs. There is separate legal provision in the autonomous communities of the Basque Country (Euskadi), Catalonia, Valencia and Andalusia, testimony to the significance of co-operatives in these regions.

In recent years, the use of co-operatives has grown considerably across a wide spectrum of economic sectors particularly in their traditional stronghold, the agricultural sector, where the Ministry of Agriculture, Fisheries and Food, which has a separate institute (*Instituto de Fomento Asociativo/IFA*) to encourage the work of co-operatives, has promoted legislation to facilitate financial assistance and training.

This is the form of organisation which has been favoured in the promotion of land development programmes to counter the problems of the large estates (*latifundios*) on the one hand, and excessively small holdings (*minifundios*) on the other. The newly autonomous regional governments have been active in this area and, despite bureaucratic and technical difficulties, an increasing number of co-operatives are now functioning, for example, in some of the traditionally neglected areas of Andalusia. On the other hand, the motivating force in many cases has been the realisation of the opportunities available for Spanish farmers to compete in EU markets and elsewhere, especially in regard to marketing and distribution.

However co-operatives are no longer the prerogative of the agricultural sector. A lot of attention in recent years has centred on Mondragón, a town in the Basque province of Guipúzcoa. In 1956 the seeds were sown for the growth of a significant movement through the creation of ULGOR, a co-operative taking its name from the initials of its five founder members. It initially employed twenty-three people making paraffin heaters but by 1994 it had grown to include some 100 enterprises employing over 25,000 people. In 1991 it adopted corporate status and became known as the *Mondragón Corporación Cooperativa* (*MCC*). This was in order to seek external funding and to extend its activities more easily into foreign markets. Among the individual co-operatives is the original ULGOR, a major producer of consumer durables, as well as others responsible for foundries and forges, capital goods, component industries and construction. One of the significant strengths of the movement has been its strong financial organisation based on its own bank, the *Caja Laboral Popular* (*CLP*) with some 700 staff distributed among ninety-three branches throughout the Basque region. In addition to carrying out normal banking business with the public, it lends money to the co-operatives and has become the commercial headquarters of the movement, responsible for technical research and planning. The Mondragón movement also includes its own social security organisation, a medical and hospital service, a laundry and meals service, a technical college, housing co-operatives and an agricultural co-operative.

The significance of the co-operative movement in the Basque country is further illustrated by the formation in 1995 of the Federation of Basque Co-operatives (*Federación de Cooperativas de Trabajo Asociado de Euskadi*), which brought together forty co-operatives representing more than 260 separate undertakings in order to act collectively to raise additional capital.

A further growth area in recent years for this type of organisation has been in housing through the collective funding of house-building and ownership. Unfortunately the much publicised scandal arising from the collapse of the co-operative *Promotora Social de la Vivienda* (*PSV*) and the implication of the trade union UGT has dented the image of this particular aspect of co-operatives (11.4.1). Other sectors where co-operatives are found include transport, education, health, credit institutions (13.5) and consumer organisations.

As co-operatives are open to the admission of new members, their capital is variable and they therefore require a different organisational framework to that of the SA company. Hence use is made of a general assembly (*junta general*) as the supreme body which meets when required and takes decisions by majority votes on issues such as the initial contributions of new members and the modification of internal regulations. This elects a board of control (*consejo de vigilancia*) which in turn appoints the board of management (*junta rectora*) to look after the day-to-day running of the co-operative. Within each enterprise there is a social council (*consejo social*) which, like the works' committee in SA companies, acts as a channel of communication between management and shop-floor workers with powers in matters such as health, safety and welfare.

12.8 Joint and collaborative ventures

A common feature of business organisation in recent years has been the formation of joint ventures. This has been particularly important in regard to carrying out major expansion programmes, promoting a particular service or product, acquiring and exploiting new technology and research, developing export markets and tendering for public works schemes. The government has provided a number of financial and fiscal incentives to encourage firms to act together and this is one way in which foreign technology and know-how has been acquired. There are various ways in which these joint ventures may be formed. Thus, for example, temporary consortia of companies (*uniones temporales de empresas/UTE*) have been provided for since the 1982 Law on the Tax Treatment of Temporary Associations and Unions of Companies (*Ley sobre Régimen Fiscal de Agrupaciones y Uniones Temporales de Empresas*). These are contracts of co-operation established between companies for a maximum period of ten years, often used in the construction industry and between Spanish and foreign companies in order to undertake public works schemes.

Where organisations wish to enter into formal agreements to share facilities such as central purchasing, R&D or information systems, then a separate joint legal association (*agrupación de interés económico/AIE*) can be set up for such a specific purpose. Thus, for example, in the high technology field a number of undertakings, including the National Scientific Research Council (*Consejo Superior de Investigaciones Científicas*), *Alcatel*, *Barcelona Tecnología* and *Mondragón Corporación Cooperativa/MCC*), linked up early in 1995 to form *Diseño y Tecnología Microelectrónica/AIE*. This type of agreement is also often found among the liberal professions. When such a joint collaborative association includes participants from other EU countries it is referred to as an *agrupación europea de interés económico/AEIE*. Both these forms of association have to be registered with the Mercantile Registry (12.1) and the basic legal stipulations are contained in the 1991 Law on Economic Interest Associations (*Ley sobre Agrupaciones de Interés Económico*). Small and medium-sized firms (*pequeñas y medianas empresas/PYMES*), which often find it difficult to obtain access to external finance, can now obtain the benefit of underwriting and guarantees through membership of a mutual guarantee companies (*sociedades de garantía recíproca/SGR*) (13.11). This type of organisation, regulated by the 1994 Law on the Legal Form of Mutual Guarantee

Companies (*Ley sobre el Régimen Jurídico de las Sociedades de Garantía Recíproca*), likewise requires registration with the Mercantile Registry.

The concept of joint ventures, however, is not new in Spain. Under provisions of a royal decree contained in the Commercial Code of 1885, individuals as well as companies have been able to act jointly under a system of joint accounts (*cuentas en participación*) where one participant conducts business under his own name and liability, but with the addition of capital from others.

12.9 Foundations (*fundaciones*)

In addition to the standard forms of business described above there are over 2,700 registered foundations (*fundaciones*) in Spain dedicated to a wide range of cultural, medical, educational and social activities. These enjoy the benefits of a favourable tax status and they were reformed and given further encouragement by the 1994 Law on Foundations and Tax Incentives and Private Participation in Activities of a General Interest (*Ley de Fundaciones y de Incentivos Fiscales a la Participación Privada en Actividades de Interés General*). Many undertakings use this type of institution as a way of developing particular non-commercial aspects of their work. Thus, for example, the Spanish Organisation for the Blind (*Organización Nacional de Ciegos Españoles/ONCE*) which is a highly organised institution providing some 32,000 jobs for blind and handicapped people largely through its very successful promotion of a nation-wide lottery scheme, controls two important foundations, one for promoting the integration of the blind into the workforce (*Fundación ONCE*), and the other for training guide dogs (*Fundación ONCE del Perro-Guía*). The parent institution is organised as a group company (*Corporación Empresarial ONCE*) which includes a number of subsidiaries involved in property, construction and hotels.

In recent years, foundations have also been set up at other levels of government and administration, as witness those already referred to in 8.3.3.2.

12.10 Professional associations (*colegios profesionales*)

The position of these associations is formally recognised in article 36 of the Constitution which states that the special characteristics of the professional associations will be regulated by law and that their internal structure and operation must be democratic in nature. (Examples of these associations are provided in table 12.1.)

Over 700,000 professionals belonging to the *colegios*, with about half being in health-related professions and some 20,000 in the Lawyers' Association alone. The Professional Union (*Unión Profesional*) was established in 1980 in order to provide a central body to represent such professional associations and it currently has some thirty-three constituent members out of some seventy-five associations.

The basic legislation covering professional associations is the Law of 1974 modified by that of December 1978 which stipulates that in order to exercise a particular profession it is necessary to belong to the local branch of the relevant association,

Table 12.1 *Examples of professional associations, 1995*

Title of association	Profession
Colegio Nacional de Administradores de Fincas	Estate managers
Colegio Oficial de Físicos	Physicists
Colegio Oficial de Ingenieros de Construcción	Construction engineers
Colegio de Oficiales de la Marina Mercante	Merchant navy officers
Colegio de Abogados	Lawyers
Colegio de Economistas	Economists
Colegio de Médicos	Doctors
Colegio Oficial de Arquitectos	Architects
Colegio Oficial de Agentes de Cambio y Bolsa	Stockbrokers and exchange dealers
Instituto de Censores Jurados de Cuentas de España	Auditors

eligibility for membership in the first instance being based on the appropriate academic qualification. The *colegios* are empowered to regulate their own affairs in accordance with their statutes, which have to be approved by the particular ministry to which their profession pertains. Thus, for example, the Lawyers' Association (*Colegio de Abogados*) comes under the auspices of the Ministry of Justice to which any subsequent modifications of statutes have to be submitted. While internal structures vary from association to association, each normally includes a general council (*consejo general*) and a chairperson (*presidente*) who is likely to represent the association nationally and internationally. The major associations are organised on a regional basis as well as having a national headquarters.

In general the professional associations act to protect the interests of their members, serving both as pressure groups and as advisory bodies. They safeguard professional standards and the observation of professional etiquette, and anyone found failing in these respects may be struck off the register and disqualified from exercising the profession. The associations are also responsible for officially certifying documentation issued by their members. This is one of the ways, in addition to compulsory membership subscriptions, in which they raise income, since they make a percentage charge on the certification. The associations also have a legal right to be informed of any legislation which is likely to affect their profession, and in this respect they will be consulted on draft legislation within their ambit. Furthermore, they keep their members up-to-date through their own courses, conferences and publications.

However, in recent years the power exercised by these bodies has not been regarded very favourably by the PSOE government and legislative moves to weaken their position are in the pipeline in the form of a draft bill which, *inter alia*, would cease to make membership compulsory for health service professionals.

12.11 Employers' associations (*asociaciones empresariales*)

Article 7 of the Constitution recognises the significance of employers' associations and their right to defend and promote the interests of their members. The basic

Table 12.2 *Examples of membership of Spanish Employers' Confederation, 1995*

Ambit	Name of organisation	Sector
National	Confederación Española de Pequeñas y Medianas Empresas (CEPYME)	Small and medium-sized firms
	Confederación Española de Mujeres Empresarias (CEME)	Women employers
Regional	Confederación de Empresarios de Andalucía (CEA)	Andalusia
	Fomento del Trabajo Nacional	Catalonia
Sectoral	Asociación Empresarial de Agencias de Viajes (AEDAVE)	Travel agencies
	Asociación Española de Banca (AEB)	Banks
	Asociación Empresarial de Publicidad Exterior (AEPE)	Advertising
	Asociación Nacional de Fabricantes de Automóviles Camiones, Tractores y sus Motores (ANFAC)	Car manufacture
	Asociación de Navieros Españoles (ANAVE)	Shipbuilding
	Confederación Empresarial de Metal (CONFEMETAL)	Iron and steel
	Confederación Nacional de la Construcción (CNC)	Construction

constitutional requirement is that their structure and operation must be democratic and they must be properly registered (article 22). Allusion, if not specific reference, is also made to them in article 37 in the context of the representation of employers in the collective bargaining process, and in article 131.2 regarding their involvement in economic planning.

The Spanish Confederation of Employers' Organisations (*Confederación Española de Organizaciones Empresariales/CEOE*) was formed in 1977 to replace the three organisations which had represented employers' interests during the transition from dictatorship to democracy in the two previous years: *Confederación Empresarial Española* (*CEE*), *Confederación General de Empresarios* (*CGE*) and *Agrupación Empresarial Independiente* (*AEI*). Since then, the CEOE has grown into an effective body incorporating some 184 employers' federations drawn from 2,000 individual employers' associations which, in turn, represent nearly a million employers. This latter number is particularly high in view of the fact that the Spanish economy is characterised by small and medium-sized firms with over 99 per cent of undertakings employing fewer than 500 employees. The special significance of this is recognised by the presence of the Spanish Confederation of Small and Medium-Sized Firms (*Confederación Española de Pequeñas y Medianas Empresas/CEPYME*), itself a national and regional organisation made up of seventy-three associations, as a constituent member of the CEOE since 1980. It preserves a special status within the Employers' Confederation and appears as a separate signatory to social and economic agreements made with the government and unions (11.8). The CEOE is made up of seventeen confederations representing the autonomous communities, thirty-seven of a provincial nature, with the remaining 130 being sectoral, representing activities such as banking, iron and steel, advertising and construction, organised on a national or regional basis (table 12.2).

Representation is conducted through the principal policy-making body of the CEOE, the general assembly (*asamblea general*), which comprises 700 delegates elected by the 184 constituent associations. Every four years this assembly elects the chairman (*presidente*), currently José María Cuevas who in 1992 was re-elected for his third term of office, and a board of management (*junta directiva*) of some 72 board members (*vocales*) which in turn appoints the twenty-four-strong executive committee (*comité ejecutivo*). There are also a number of internal departments and specialised commissions, supported by the full-time secretariat, which study and report on issues such as economic policy, labour relations, overseas trade, legislative proposals, education and training and international affairs. The general assembly draws its financial resources largely from membership fees but, as with the political parties and the trade unions, it receives subsidies from the government in recognition of its special role within the Constitution.

The fundamental role of the CEOE is to act as the representative organisation for employers in relation to the government, the unions, international bodies and public opinion. This position has been secured at the expense of two rival national bodies – the General Confederation of Small and Medium-Sized Firms of Spain (*Confederación General de las Pequeñas y Medianas Empresas del Estado Español/COPYME*) and the Union of Small and Medium-Sized Firms (*Unión de la Pequeña y Mediana Empresa/UNIPYME*), both of which have failed to gain sufficient significant support. The supremacy of the CEOE–CEPYME was clearly signalled when it secured the totality of employer representation on the Economic and Social Council (*Consejo Económico y Social/CES*) when it was set up in 1992 (5.8). It also represents employers on numerous other national and regional bodies in which provision is made for employer and worker participation, such as the social security institutions INSS, INSERSO and INSALUD (6.4). It has played an important part in negotiating general economic agreements with the government and the unions (11.9). The CEOE does not negotiate collective agreements (*convenios colectivos*) on behalf of local employers; rather, this is left to the individual associations. It does, however, provide instructions and guidelines and at national level it is involved with pay norms and working conditions which affect about 85 per cent of the total labour force.

It is the employers' voice at an international level, for example, *vis-à-vis* the International Labour Organisation (ILO), the European Union and the European Union Confederation of Employers' Organisations (UNICE). It has had a permanent office for relations with the European Union in Brussels since 1980 which monitors and advises on the implications of EU policy for employers. It has embarked upon a policy of extending its representation abroad and it now has overseas offices in, for example, Washington and Tokyo.

There are also a number of management associations which operate mainly as sources of information, debate and discussion or as pressure groups for particular interests. The Association for the Advancement of Management (*Asociación para el progreso de la Dirección/APD*) which dates from 1956, with 3,000 members, regularly organises conferences, seminars and courses on current management issues. The Institute of Directors (*Círculo de Empresarios*) established in 1977 is an influential group of some 150 senior executives particularly from among the larger companies. The Association of Family-run Enterprises (*Instituto de la Empresa Familiar*) consists of representatives of nearly ninety important privately owned firms, such as González Byas (sherry), Antonio Puig (perfumes), Planeta (publishing) and Catalana Occidente (Insurance), who seek to defend their own special interests. Two more recently created organisations which aim to promote the role of younger managers and women respectively are the Spanish Confederation of Associations of Young Managers (*Confederación Española de Asociaciones de Jóvenes Empresarios/AJE*) founded in 1991, and the Organisation of Businesswomen (*Organización de Mujeres Empresarias y Gerencia Activa/OMEGA*) created in 1989.

12.12 Chambers of commerce (*cámaras de comercio*)

Chambers of commerce, industry and navigation (*Cámaras oficiales de comercio, industria y navegación*) are officially recognised corporations (*corporaciones*) which depend on the Ministry of Commerce and Tourism for the approval and modification of their statutes. They were first created by royal decree as early as 1886 and their basic legal status had remained largely unchanged since 1911. However, in order to adapt the chambers to the fact of Spain's membership of the European Union and to accommodate them to the reality of Spain's autonomous communities, the Basic Law on Official Chambers of Commerce, Industry and Navigation (*Ley Básica de las Cámaras Oficiales de Comercio, Industria y Navegación*) was approved in 1993. The main impact of the law is on their system of funding. Unlike their counterparts in most EU countries, membership is not on a voluntary basis and all those engaged in the activities covered by the chamber are automatically members, either as individual traders or as firms. Traditionally their income has come in the form of tax surcharges. The Treasury informs the specific chamber of the tax position of the individual traders and firms, and the Chamber is responsible for collecting the surcharge. However emphasis is now being placed on self-financing with the Chambers generating up to 40 per cent of their funds through, for example, courses, publications and donations. This system is being phased in over four years as the 2 per cent surcharge is progressively reduced. Regional variations to the surcharges as determined by the autonomous communities are also now permitted.

In 1994 there were eighty-one Chambers located in all the major cities of Spain and including co-ordinating Chambers at provincial level, but the 1993 legislation envisages a reduction in this number through mergers on a regional basis, and the new funding arrangements are likely to exacerbate this trend. The specific title of each *Cámara* depends on the activities which it represents and therefore *navegación* is confined to those operating in coastal areas. Thus, for example, compare *Cámara de Comercio e Industria de Madrid* and *Cámara de Comercio, Industria y Navegación de Barcelona*. The National Council of Spanish Chambers of Commerce (*Consejo Superior de Cámaras de Comercio, Industria y Navegación de España*) located in Madrid, acts as a central co-ordinating body disseminating information to the others and representing the Chambers nationally and internationally. Regional tension within the Chambers has been noted, however, and the Basque Chamber has been complaining about centralisation.

Chambers are intended to defend the interests of the individuals and the firms which they represent by providing a variety of services. These generally include legal services, economic and financial advice, research and information, representation abroad and, in particular, help in export promotion, documentation and trade missions. At the same time, they act as consultative bodies at local, regional and central government level on matters pertaining to industry and commerce. Therefore, they are involved in discussions on matters ranging from local issues, such as markets and postal codes, to the consideration of draft legislation on trade regulations and changes in taxation.

Their internal organisation depends on their respective statutes, but normally they have a general meeting (*pleno*), elected on the basis of the different sectoral interests which the chamber represents, to decide policy, and an executive committee (*comité ejecutivo*) for management purposes.

The Ministry of Commerce and Tourism, through its Directorate General for Commercial Policy (*Dirección General de Política Comercial*) is responsible for the Spanish Chambers of Commerce abroad. These also operate in conjunction with the Ministry-run Institute for Overseas Trade (*Instituto de Comercio Exterior/ ICEX*).

12.13 Comment

There has clearly been a flurry of legislative activity in regard to business and professional organisations since Spain became a member of the European Union, and the formal harmonisation of Spanish company law with European directives has now placed undertakings in Spain on an equal legal footing with counterparts in other member states. This means that the major companies are likely to pursue the best business and financial practices that are common elsewhere and that foreign investors and business partners will be able to regard published financial statements with more confidence than ten years ago. The record number of purchases of Spanish firms, just over 150 in 1994, is perhaps some evidence of this, together with increased confidence in the economic structure as a whole. However, this does not necessarily mean that all ingrained attitudes have altered or that compliance is complete in all sectors, nor does it imply that all enterprises yet fulfil all the requirements that are now expected of them. Thus, while the Mercantile Registry offers the possibility of transparency, it is evident that not all firms are filing their accounts as is required. The authorities are therefore having to introduce penalties for non-compliance which, *inter alia*, will have the effect of suspending registration.

The image of business in recent years has been somewhat tarnished by a number of corruption scandals involving public figures, for example, *Filesa* (Alfonso Guerra), *KIO* (Javier de la Rosa), *Ibercorp* (Javier de la Rosa) and *Banesto* (Mario Conde). The bureaucratic nature of Spanish administration, the presence of the public sector with lucrative contracts and the pressure to finance political parties are all perhaps particular contributing factors. However, this does not mean that sleaze in Spain is necessarily any greater than elsewhere, but at least it is given a very high profile by a demanding investigative press and a somewhat laborious legal system.

Business and professional organisations have become much more conscious of the regional dimensions of their activities. They have to be watchful of the implications of laws and policies emanating from the autonomous communities as well as those from the central administration and from Brussels. This more complex pattern has led to the need for more emphasis on regional offices and more sophisticated consultative processes which are not always easy to produce. The CEOE is certainly one organisation which has increased in status and made great strides in confronting the realities of Spain of the later 1990s. It has developed improved links with central and regional government and, at a time of frustration in 1995–96 with the impasse in political activity caused by the aura of scandal, it has even found unlikely allies in the trade unions.

Chapter 13

Financial institutions

13.1 Introduction

Spain's financial institutions have been subject to considerable modification as a result of the process of harmonisation with the European Union and with the development of the Single Market in particular. Banking and other financial institutions were brought into line with those of other EU countries by the 1994 Law on the Adaptation of Spain's Financial Institutions to the Second Directive on Banking (*Ley por la que se adapta la Legislación Española en materia de Entidades de Crédito a la Segunda Directiva de Coordinación Bancaria*).

Spain's traditionally rigid financial system had already begun to experience a much needed overhaul prior to EU membership in the late 1970s. The 1978 legislation permitting the establishment of foreign banks in Spain for the first time since the Spanish Civil War helped to introduce new financial instruments and techniques as well as new institutions. Reforms also saw the beginning of the gradual phasing out of the obligatory investment ratios for financial institutions in specific areas of the economy and for privileged clients in both the public and private sectors. The 1978 report of the *Comisión para el Estudio del Mercado de Valores* heralded a series of technical reforms in the securities markets which have come to fruition in the 1990s and which have helped to produce a more open system which is more capable of generating the resources needed to sustain economic growth.

The Spanish authorities enthusiastically embraced the concept of the free movement of capital with the removal of exchange controls in February 1992, in advance of the deadline established by the European Union. Although they subsequently had to suspend this provision for a short time, it is nevertheless now firmly embodied in current legislation and practice. This was principally through a series of royal decrees and resolutions of the Directorate General for Foreign Transactions (*Dirección General de Transacciones Exteriores/DGTE*) between 1991 and 1993. This was paralleled with dramatic impact by the almost complete liberalisation of foreign investment by non-Spanish residents in Spain, as well as investment abroad by Spanish residents. The main provisions are contained in the law and royal decree of 1992 on Foreign Investment in Spain (*Ley y Real Decreto sobre Inversiones Extranjeras en España*) and the DGTE's resolution of 1992 on the Procedure and Registration of Foreign Investment in Spain (*Resolución sobre Procedimiento de Tramitación y Registro de las Inversiones en España*). There are still a limited number of restrictions and safeguards, which apply mainly to non-EU residents, whereby

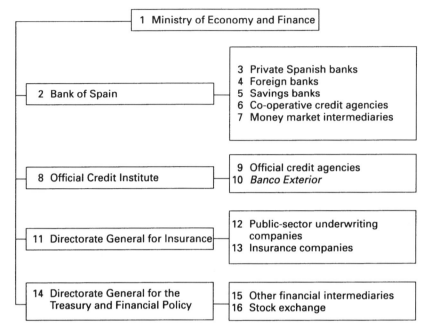

Figure 13.1 *Structure of Spain's financial institutions, 1995*

legal verification of residence or prior government clearance is required for certain large investments (this is especially the case where the investment is in over 50 per cent of a firm's share capital or totals more than 500 million pesetas), if the investment comes from a tax haven (*paraíso fiscal*) or if it is in sensitive areas such as gaming, radio and TV, defence-related industries or telecommunications. In any event foreign investment has to be recorded for statistical purposes in the Foreign Investment Register (*Registro de Inversiones*).

While overall control over financial institutions is in the hands of the Ministry of Economy and Finance, day-to-day control and regulation of the multiplicity of public and private sector entities is vested in a number of different bodies: the Bank of Spain (*Banco de España*), the National Securities Commission (*Comisión Nacional del Mercado de Valores/CNMV*), the Directorate General for the Treasury and Financial Policy (*Dirección General del Tesoro y Política Financiera*) and the Directorate General for Insurance (*Dirección General de Seguros*). These bodies and the principal financial institutions for which they are responsible are shown in figure 13.1 and described in more detail below.

It should be noted that the governments of the autonomous communities may now also exercise a degree of control over certain institutions of a regional character within their territory, namely over stock exchanges, savings banks and co-operative credit institutions.

13.2 Ministry of Economy and Finance (*Ministerio de Economía y Hacienda*)

Responsibility for overseeing financial institutions rests with the Ministry of Economy and Finance. It embraces all aspects of the economy from fiscal and monetary policy to economic planning and domestic and overseas trade. Its general co-ordinating and inspection role is, of course, particularly important and to this end it is sub-divided into a large number of departments which look after specific responsibilities. The long-established and formerly separate Ministry of Finance (*Ministerio de Hacienda*) also maintains provincial offices (*delegaciones provinciales*) as part of the system of delegated administration (6.5) but some of the functions of these offices are now devolved to the autonomous communities.

13.3 Bank of Spain (*Banco de España*)

The Bank of Spain is the nation's central bank and as such it needs to be distinguished from the commercial bank which bears the name *Banco Central Hispano*. It owes its origin to an eighteenth-century bank, the *Banco de San Carlos*. However, it was given the name *Banco de España* in 1856 and from that time onwards it assumed the role of central bank, although it remained nominally in private hands until it was nationalised in 1962. However, in line with EU policy in regard to the role of central banks and the creation of European monetary union it was converted into an autonomous body in 1994 through the Law on the Autonomy of the Bank of Spain (*Ley de Autonomía del Banco de España*).

13.3.1 Functions of the Bank of Spain

The main charge introduced by the 1994 Law was to establish the Bank's independence in regard to the definition and execution of monetary policy with the prime aim of combating inflation. However, any such monetary policy must support the government's general economic policy. Its other functions, as stated in the 1994 legislation, are as follows:

(i)   To be responsible for managing the nation's foreign currency reserves and exchange control policy.

(ii)   To promote the operation and stability of the financial system and to manage the bank clearing system (*cámara de compensación*). It is responsible for supervising the institutions within the system, although this may be done in conjunction with the autonomous communities in respect of certain institutions (13.1). The Bank of Spain has power to impose sanctions on those institutions which do not comply with its demands.

(iii)   To be responsible for determining the amount of currency in circulation and for the issue of notes and coins of legal tender.

(iv)   To act as bank to both the central government and the autonomous communities in regard to their income and expenditure and other normal banking functions, at home and abroad. Under the terms of the European Union Treaty of 1992 it may not, however, lend money to the state, the autonomous communities or local corporations.

(v)   To advise the government, to carry out appropriate studies and to draw up reports and statistics. The *Annual Report* and other publications of the Bank of Spain make an important contribution to the study of economic policy and development in Spain. At the same time the Bank's centralised data base of company balance sheets (*Central de Balances*) is a useful source of information on non-financial public and private sector enterprises. Although this is on a voluntary basis, some 30 per cent of firms which file their accounts with the Mercantile Registry (12.1) do so with the Bank of Spain.

(vi)   To establish relations with other central banks and international monetary and financial institutions and represent Spain on these bodies.

13.3.2 Governing bodies

There are four principal sources of authority within the Bank of Spain itself:

(i)   The governor (*gobernador*) who is appointed by the government for a period of six years and whose post is not renewable.

(ii)   The deputy governor (*subgobernador*) who likewise is appointed for the same term of office.

(iii)   A governing council (*consejo de gobierno*) which in addition to the two senior appointments referred to above, consists of six directors (*consejeros*) proposed by the Ministry of Economy and Finance following consultation with the governor of the Bank, who serve for a period of six years, renewable for a further term; the director general of the Directorate General for the Treasury and Financial Policy (*Dirección del Tesoro y Política Financiera*); and the vice-chairman of the Spanish Securities Market Commission (*Comisión Nacional del Mercado de Valores*). The directors general of the Bank's departments and an employee representative are also non-voting members.

(iv)   An executive committee (*comisión ejecutiva*) which is made up of the governor, the deputy governor and two of the directors.

Perhaps not surprisingly, after the publicity given to the alleged activities of the former governor of the bank, Mariano Rubio (1.1.5), the 1994 legislation imposes very stringent conditions on the financial activities of the members of these bodies both during and after their terms of office.

13.3.3 Control and supervision of financial institutions

The Bank of Spain is responsible for a significant number of institutions which are described separately below (13.4–13.11).

Control over all these institutions has been progressively increased as the system has become more sophisticated. The Bank of Spain has established limits to the risks which various types of banking institutions are authorised to bear and it has strengthened its inspection and financial reporting procedures. It issues circulars advising institutions on the interrelationship which it wishes them to secure between items on their balance sheets and profit and loss accounts. Since 1978 it has had power to appoint temporary boards of management to assume responsibility for a bank's operations.

In 1977 the Bank of Spain was instrumental in setting up the Deposit Guarantee Fund (*Fondo de Garantía de Depósitos/FGD*) to cope with the bank failures and to give depositors some protection at a time when increasing strains were appearing within the financial system. The Fund consists of compulsory deposits from the banks together with an equal contribution from the Bank of Spain. It is run by its own board of management consisting of four representatives from the Bank of Spain and four from the banks themselves. There are similar funds for the savings and co-operative banks (13.9). The importance and effectiveness of the Deposit Guarantee Fund has been highlighted at various times in recent years (13.6.4).

The Bank's powers to intervene at an earlier stage in potential crisis situations were considerably strengthened by the 1988 Law on Control and Intervention in Banking and Other Lending Institutions (*Ley sobre Disciplina e Intervención de las Entidades de Crédito/LDIEC*). This gave the Bank of Spain wide powers of inspection and control, backed up with heavy penalties, and the power to appoint temporary boards of management to assume responsibility for a bank's operations if an entity was believed to be in dire straits. This was put to the test in 1993 in the case of one of the country's most important banks, *Banesto* (13.6.4).

The 1988 legislation was given an additional boost by the changes resulting from the harmonisation of Spanish financial institutions with those of the European Union in 1994. Anyone contemplating increasing their holding beyond certain levels or acquiring a significant influence of 5 per cent or more in a bank or lending institution has to inform the Bank of Spain accordingly. The Bank then has three months in which to accept or reject such a proposal.

The Bank of Spain has traditionally had responsibility for the public sector banking institutions. These were reorganised in 1991 under two main bodies, the Official Credit Institute (13.4) and the Spanish Banking Corporation (13.5) which are described below.

13.4 Official Credit Institute (*Instituto Crédito Oficial/ICO*)

The ICO was an autonomous administrative body (6.3) under the jurisdiction of the Ministry of Economy and Finance until 1989, when it became a state company with formal ownership of the shares of the various official credit agencies which it had previously controlled and co-ordinated. This situation, however, was short-lived and in 1991 a royal decree created the Spanish Banking Corporation, removing the four official credit agencies (*entidades oficiales de crédito/EOC*) from the auspices of the ICO (13.5.1–4) and thus effectively reducing the significance of this institution. The Official Credit Institute is now seen as the government financial agency (*agencia financiera del estado*) with its board (*consejo general*) appointed by the Council of Ministers on the recommendation of the Ministry of Economy and Finance. It provides financial assistance in specific economic crisis situations and disaster aid compensation programmes at the behest of the government. It also has some degree of autonomy in funding medium and long-term investment through the issue of various types of government securities.

13.5 Spanish Banking Corporation (*Corporación Bancaria Española SA/CBE*)

The creation of the CBE as a state financial holding company under the auspices of the *Dirección General del Patrimonio del Estado* (*DGPE*) (9.4.2.1) in 1991 marked an important change in public sector banking in Spain. The government, having encouraged the private sector banks to merge into bigger units, decided to follow the same course of action in regard to those institutions within its own remit. It therefore amalgamated a number of disparate institutions into this single group which would trade under the name *Argentaria*. This brought together six organisations: the four former ICO-run official credit agencies (13.5.1–4) three of which now operate with the status of fully-fledged banks, the Spanish Overseas Trade Bank (13.5.5) and the Post Office Savings Bank (13.5.6). While each member has preserved its own identity and continued to operate in its own particular segment of the market, the parent company, *Argentaria*, has adopted a high profile market-oriented approach. Although it failed to acquire *Banesto* (13.6.4), it has been involved in a number of take-overs and has been negotiating for a stake in the telecommunications industry. In 1993 the government brought in private capital, selling off just under 50 per cent of *Argentaria's* share capital. This process was taken even further in subsequent years and culminated in 1996 when the government, with the support of the *Banco de España*, took steps to privatise the 25 per cent holding that remained in the hands of the state. The principal companies within the CBE group are as follows:

13.5.1 Agricultural Credit Bank (*Banco de Crédito Agrícola/BCA*)

This provides credit for agriculture directly as well as indirectly through the *cajas rurales* (13.9).

13.5.2 Mortgage Bank of Spain (*Banco Hipotecario de España*)

This provides credit for housing. Previously, in 1982, it had absorbed the Construction Credit Bank (*Banco de Crédito a la Construcción*).

13.5.3 Local Authorities' Credit Bank (*Banco de Crédito Local*)

This provides credit for local authority projects.

13.5.4 Industrial Credit Bank (*Banco de Crédito Industrial*)

This provides credit for new firms and growth industries. This bank had previously assumed responsibility for the operations of the autonomous Fisheries' Credit Institution (*Instituto de Crédito Social Pesquero*) which provided funds for the purchase, improvement and repair of fishing vessels, and it had also taken over loans to the ship-building industry previously carried out by the *Banco de Crédito a la Construcción*. The Industrial Credit Bank, however, was immediately merged in 1991 into the Spanish Overseas Trade Bank (13.5.5) which likewise became part of this new group.

13.5.5 The Spanish Overseas Trade Bank (*Banco Exterior de España*)

This, as its name suggests, specialises in export-related activities. It was, however, very much a hybrid organisation, belonging administratively to the *Dirección General del Patrimonio del Estado* (9.4.2.1) with 40 per cent of its capital in the hands of private shareholders who included the bank's employees.

13.5.6 The Post Office Savings Bank (*Caja Postal de Ahorros*)

This is the other public sector institution which was brought into the CBE conglomerate. This lost its savings bank status and became a bank in all but name.

13.6 Private Spanish banks

13.6.1 Classification

Traditionally there were a number of separate legal classifications used when referring to private sector Spanish banks, such as national, regional, local industrial and commercial. In practice there is clearly still some degree of specialisation and the industrial banks (*bancos de negocios*), for example, perhaps influenced by foreign banking, concentrate more on corporate finance for larger clients and tend to deal in more business-oriented financial instruments. However, these distinctions, like the body which used to enumerate them, the National Banking Council (*Consejo Superior Bancario/CSB*), have now disappeared. The Spanish Banking Association (*Asociación Española de Banca Privada/AEB*) which formally replaced the CSB in 1994 as the representative forum for the banking sector, publishes monthly and annual statistics which at the beginning of 1995 classified and totalled the banks as shown in table 13.1.

The term 'Spanish private banks' refers to the fact that they are constituted under Spanish law and not to their ownership, as a significant number are in fact subsidiaries of foreign-owned banks. However, because of the significance of the role of foreign banks they are treated separately in this chapter (13.7). All the private banks are public limited companies regulated by the company law of 1989, the *Texto*

Table 13.1 *Classification of banks in Spain, 1995*

By area		By function	
National	37	Commercial	74
Regional	13	Industrial	24
Local	48		
Total	98	Total	98

Source: *Consejo Supérior Bancario.*

Refundido de la Ley de Sociedades Anónimas (12.1) with authority vested in a board of directors answerable to the shareholders through shareholders' meetings. However, over and above the requirements of this law, banks and other financial institutions are subject to strict supervision by the Bank of Spain and notification of any changes in shareholdings and other basic data, such as name, address and status, have to be submitted for registration in the Bank's Official Registry of Institutions (*Registros Oficiales de Entidades*). New banks have to comply with special requirements with regard, among other details, to their minimum share capital which according to the royal decree of 1988 had to be at least 1.5 billion pesetas.

13.6.2 Services

There is definitely no shortage of banks in Spain and, in fact, with over 17,000 branches and more than 150,000 employees, Spain has the highest ratio of banks to customers in Europe. Spanish banks, in general, offer a similar range of services to their EU counterparts. Their opening hours are generally from 9.00 a.m. to 2.00 p.m. on weekdays and from 9.30 a.m. until 1.30 p.m. on Saturdays. Cash dispensers known as 'automatic' or 'permanent cashiers' (*cajero automático* or *cajero permanente*) are very common and are generally shared on a network basis by several banks. In addition to current accounts (*cuentas corrientes* or *cuentas a la vista*), there are ordinary savings or deposit accounts (*cuentas de ahorros*), fixed-term savings accounts (*imposiciones a plazo*) and, more recently, special savings accounts (*supercuentas*) which combine current accounts and high interest rate savings facilities. The discounting of trade bills or bills of exchange (*letras de cambio*) is also very common, as this is still a major way of doing business in Spain.

13.6.3 Concentration

Despite failures and mergers, at the beginning of 1994 there were still some eighty private Spanish-owned banks. Although this number appears to be very high, there is, in fact, a high degree of concentration of resources and customers in the five banks which are designated as 'large banks' (*grandes bancos*) in Bank of Spain statistics. These five private banks in order of importance are: *Banco Central Hispano* (*BCH*), *Banco Bilbao Vizcaya* (*BBV*), *Banco de Santander, Banco Español de Crédito*

(*Banesto*) and *Banco Popular Español*. At the same time they control over twenty-five of the other banks which belong to their groups and this has been one way in which they have extended their representation on a regional basis. Thus the BBV owns the *Banca Catalana* and the *Banco de Crédito Canario*, while the *Banco Popular* controls the *Banco de Andalucía*, the *Banco de Castilla* and the *Banco de Galicia*. This is in addition, of course, to their branch network. Together these banks own over 80 per cent of the total assets of the private Spanish banking system. However, the Spanish banks are relatively small in world terms and the largest Spanish bank, the *Banco Central Hispano*, was only sixty-fifth in world rankings by assets in 1994. A further reason for the fall in the overall number of banks in recent years is due to their acquisition by foreign banks as a means of acquiring established outlets (13.7) and the merger of banks as a result of the banking crisis.

13.6.4 Banking crisis

The banking crisis of 1978–83 affected fifty-one of the 110 Spanish banks which existed in 1977. It was caused by a number of factors which included the restrictive monetary policy being pursued by the authorities in the light of the prevailing economic difficulties, the oil crises and the wage push inflation of the early days of political transition. The situation of these banks was exacerbated by the increased competition to obtain business and the downward spiral of fortune resulting from their close ties with industry. At the same time, the authorities were endeavouring to secure more authentic declarations of assets and liabilities, while the Bank of Spain itself was insisting on the closer scrutiny of accounts. The net result was the revelation in several instances of poor financial management and of a substantial number of banks in an official state of crisis. It was in these circumstances that the *Fondo de Garantía de Depósitos* (13.3.3) came into its own. A number of factors, ranging from the consequences of the economic crisis to defective banking practices and weak management, led to over fifty banks finding themselves in a state of crisis during this period. Twenty-six of these were assisted by the Deposit Guarantee Fund, while another four were taken over by other banks and one was dissolved. The problem was compounded by the RUMASA affair when the government expropriated the holdings of this conglomerate, which included some twenty banks. The Deposit Guarantee Fund administered the RUMASA group banks until their somewhat controversial disposal by the *Dirección General del Patrimonio del Estado* (9.4.2.1).

In December 1993 the Bank of Spain detected serious deficiencies in the assets and reserves of one of Spain's major banks, *Banesto*, and in accordance with its powers it replaced the entire board of directors with members of each of the other leading banks. At the same the Deposit Guarantee Fund set about carrying out a major rescue act, writing off bad debts and injecting fresh capital, to the point that it was able to sell the bank to the highest bidder, the *Banco de Santander*, in April 1994. The *Banco de Santander*, which had succeeded in becoming the majority shareholder in the face of competition from two other major banks, the BBV and *Argentaria*, has subsequently reduced its holding, which in December 1995 stood at some 48 per cent. *Santander* may or may not wish to continue controlling *Banesto*, but at least the continuity and separate identity of the latter is guaranteed at least until 1998 as one of the conditions of the take-over. Meanwhile the former chairman of *Banesto*, Mario Conde, is facing charges of fraud in one of a number of highly publicised scandals to hit the headlines in the 1990s.

13.7 Foreign banks

While foreign banks are now firmly established within the framework of the financial structure, it was not until the royal decree of 24 June 1978 that they were permitted to enter the Spanish system for the first time since the Spanish Civil War. This legislation, however, imposed significant restrictions on the foreign banks and appeared designed, at least in the short term, to protect the interests of the existing financial oligarchy enabling substantial consolidation to take place prior to eventual harmonisation with the European Union. Thus, there were limits to the funds these banks could raise, they were not permitted to open more than three branches, including their head office, and their securities portfolio had to consist exclusively of public sector stock. Nevertheless, by November 1985 there were thirty-seven foreign banks engaged in branch-banking in Spain which, despite the restrictions placed upon them, had managed to secure a significant 14 per cent of total banking business. As they could not take deposits from customers, they had to obtain their resources on the interbank market and consequently a much more sophisticated interbank market developed than had existed previously. Their main area of activity was in the field of corporate finance and they used their resources and their know-how to provide specialised services, such as foreign exchange dealing, export finance and leasing facilities. They played a very significant part in introducing new financial instruments, such as commercial paper (*pagarés de empresa*), and also new financial intermediaries, such as vehicle finance companies. The nature of these activities over a period of some fifteen years prior to the removal of restrictions in 1993 helps to explain the particular orientation of many foreign banks in Spain today.

Other foreign banks chose to go in for retail banking by taking over ailing Spanish banks and the RUMASA crisis provided an ideal opportunity for foreign investors (13.6.4). The Arab Banking Corporation secured the most viable RUMASA bank, the *Banco Atlántico*, and in April 1981 Barclays, which has progressed from representative office to branch-banking following the 1978 legislation, purchased the *Banco de Valladolid* from the Deposit Guarantee Fund. A year later the name was changed to *Barclays Sociedad Anónima Española* (*SAE*), i.e. Barclays Spanish Public Limited Liability Company, to distinguish it from the branch known as *Barclays PLC Sucursal en España*.

However, as from 1 January 1993, the introduction of the Single Market, the unrestricted provision of services and harmonisation with EU banking directives brought an end to the restrictions placed on the activities of foreign banks in Spain. Foreign banks are now subject to the same regulations as Spanish banks. This freedom also extends to non-EU banks provided that reciprocity is extended to Spanish banks in the relevant country. At the beginning of 1995 there were some eighty foreign banks operating permanently in Spain, of which twenty-six were sub-sidiaries (*filiales*) and fifty-three were branches (*surcursales*). Branches are simply treated as an extension of the parent bank and as such do not have separate legal status in Spain. Subsidiaries, on the other hand, are constituted as legal entities and come within the full ambit of Spanish company law with the same reporting and registration requirements as other SA companies within the financial sector (13.6.1). Banking statistics now generally do not distinguish between subsidiaries and Spanish banks but it is thought that the combined market share of the subsidi-aries and the branches is in the region of 20 per cent. In addition, more than twenty banks had by the same date chosen not to set up in Spain separately but simply to take advantage of the provisions of EU regulations to offer services in Spain. At the same time Spanish banks have taken advantage of the greater flexibility which is now permitted in order to establish their own branches and subsidiaries abroad.

13.8 Savings banks (*cajas de ahorros*)

Although the savings bank have in theory been able to undertake the same range of activities as private banks since 1977, it is not until relatively recently that this has become a reality. The savings banks have progressively increased their market share to over 40 per cent of total deposits and to just over 30 per cent of total investments. Traditionally they were seen as sources of finance for specific sectors, such as the INI (9.4.2.2), the public sector, small-sized firms and particularly house purchas-ing; now, however, as their obligatory investment ratios have disappeared, they have become much more broadly-based lenders. They still tend to draw the majority of their funds, however, from domestic savers, emigrants and small businesses and to command a strong element of regional loyalty.

Nowadays the main difference between savings banks and ordinary banks lies in their legal status. While the banks are profit-making SA companies (12.3) answer-able to their shareholders who benefit in the form of dividends, the savings banks are non-profit-making institutions. Surplus funds arising from operations go into reserves and into their social welfare fund (*obra benéfico-social*). These funds can be used to finance local welfare projects, cultural activities, research grants and so on, according to proposals drawn up by the welfare committee (*comisión de obras sociales*). Authority for approving such proposals, as well as for their overall banking business is vested in the general council (*asamblea general*). In turn, the general council, which consists of representatives of savers, local interests, found-ers and employees nominates the board of management and appoints the director general. A supervisory board (*comisión de control*) is responsible for watching over the management function of the board and is empowered to recommend the suspension of any of its decisions which it considers to be beyond its powers or prejudicial to its aims. Unlike SA companies which can always consider raising additional capital through share issues, the savings banks are limited to ploughing back profits as their means of expansion. They are normally obliged to retain 50 per cent of their surpluses for this purpose. They do, however, have power to issue non-voting bonds (*cuotas participativas de asociación*) but so far only the CECA (13.8.1) has taken advantage of this possibility. So far they have not adopted the approach followed in some other EU countries where savings banks have converted themselves into fully-fledged banks. Instead, their response to the need to expand has largely been through mergers which have led to a reduction in the number of separate entities from eighty in 1983 to fifty-one at the beginning of 1995. Thus, for example, the Andalusian *cajas* of Ronda, Cádiz, Almería, Málaga and Antequera amalgamated into UNICAJA while the merger of the two most important Catalan savings banks in 1991 resulted in the formation of the *Caixa d'Estalvis i Pensions de Barcelona*, the *Caixa*, which ranks alongside the top five largest banks in Spain.

The regional nature of their origin has remained an important feature. Originally they were tied to the province from which they drew their finance and where they were obliged to place a certain percentage of their investments. Their names tend to indicate their highly localised nature: *Caja de Ahorros de Murcia, Caja de Ahorros Provincial de Guadalajara, Caja de Ahorros Popular de Valladolid*. Sometimes their names retain indication of their origins in pawnship-beneficent societies (*montes de piedad*) as in the case of the *Caja de Ahorros y Monte de Piedad del Círculo Católico de Obreros de Burgos*. Now, however, they operate on a national scale, particularly in the case of the larger ones which are likely to have branches in major cities outside their home region, as for example with the Basque BBK (*Bilbao Bizkaia Kutxa*). While the degree of regional control has been subject to considerable debate and even litigation at the level of the Constitutional Court (2.5), the current division of authority appears to give central government, via the Bank of Spain, power over their activities as financial institutions, leaving organisational and institutional matters within the competence of the autonomous communities. The autonomous communities may also have a non-voting member on the supervisory board of those *cajas* which have their head offices in their region.

13.8.1 Spanish Confederation of Savings Banks (*Confederación Española de Cajas de Ahorros/CECA*)

The CECA is a savings bank in its own right with customers which include important public sector accounts such as ISFAS (6.4.3.2), MUFACE (6.4.3.2), SENPA (9.3) and UNED (6.3). This body provides advisory, representation and statistical services on behalf of the constituent savings banks, as well as acting as a clearing house for savings banks which have offices in Madrid and for some forty-four *cajas* in their dealings with the ordinary banks. It plays an important role in training, research and publications and it co-ordinates the extensive network of over 14,000 cash machines operated by the savings banks as well as managing their credit card operations. It has a branch in London which enables it to promote the services of the *cajas* in the City and to engage in stock market operations on behalf of clients and other savings banks. It ensures that the traditionally conservative savings bank movement is now engaging in a wide variety of financial operations including derivatives and off-balance sheet finance, options and swaps. At the same, however, this branch and the representative offices in Germany, France and the Benelux countries together with agreements with other institutions in Latin America continues to ensure the important flow of migrants' funds to the savings banks and the Spanish economy in general.

The internal organisation of the Confederation reflects the regional dimension of the savings bank movement with representation on the board of management (*consejo de administración*) being on the basis of one representative per autonomous community with additional representation for those regions whose *cajas* exceed certain percentages of the total deposits held by the savings banks as a whole.

13.9 Co-operative banks (*sociedades cooperativas de crédito*)

The basic function of these institutions is to provide finance for the co-operatives and their members which are associated with them. Because of their co-operative nature, while they can accept deposits from members and non-members, they may only lend to the members themselves. In general terms they are regulated by the same central and regional legislation as the non-banking co-operatives (12.7). However, like other financial institutions they are subject to strict supervisory control by the Bank of Spain.

They are basically two types: agricultural savings banks (*cajas rurales*) and general co-operative banks (*cooperativas no agrarias*). The rural savings banks, which are by far the most numerous are, in general, extremely small and localised. Although the percentage of total credit provided by all the credit banks is very small in comparison to the ordinary banks and the savings banks, they do, nevertheless, provide almost a third of the total bank credit for agriculture. However, this concentration has made them vulnerable to risk because of the particular vicissitudes of the agricultural sector and many of them have had to have recourse to the Co-operative Deposit Guarantee Fund (*Fondo de Garantía de Depósitos de Cooperativas*). In order to reduce their risks a number have become formally linked with the Agricultural Credit Bank (*Banco de Crédito Agrícola/BCA*), creating an associated group (*Grupo Asociado BCA–Cajas Rurales*). This provides a bridge for them with the official credit institutions and gives them the benefit of priority access to credit facilities. The arrangement also helps to decentralise the BCA (13.5.1).

On the other hand, the general co-operative banks operate in sectors such as construction, housing, commerce or the professions. The Workers' Co-operative Bank (*Caja Laboral Popular*) in Mondragón (12.7) provides a particularly important example, being by far the largest of all the co-operative banks with over 18 per cent of the total assets.

Like the other financial institutions described in this chapter, the co-operative banks in recent years have been subject to harmonisation with EU banking directives and structure reform in accordance with the wishes of different autonomous communities. Many of them have not been able to survive the changing economic and financial climate and have been forced to dissolve or have been taken over by the savings banks. Thus, of the total of 151 which existed in 1983, only seventy-four had survived by the beginning of 1995 and over 80 per cent of total assets were concentrated in some twenty of these.

13.10 Specialised credit companies (*entidades de crédito de ámbito operativo limitado/ECAOL*)

Under the terms of the 1994 legislation harmonising Spanish financial institutions with those of the European Union (13.1), a number of changes were made to the regulations under which certain specialised bodies would operate in the future. These bodies, which were relatively new in Spain, had been functioning under similar circumstances to the other borrowing and lending institutions which have been described above, although their credit operations were related to certain types of activity such as leasing and mortgaging. Now, however, they have to convert themselves into credit establishments (*establecimientos financieros de crédito*) indicated by the letters *EFC*, no later than 1 January 1997 when their sphere of operations as well as their sources of finance will be more specifically defined and restricted. These institutions are as follows:

13.10.1 Money market intermediaries (*sociedades mediadoras en el mercado de dinero/SMMD*)

These were introduced in 1981 on an experimental basis to give greater liquidity to the Spanish financial system as, until this time, there had not been a true secondary market for treasury bills, certificates of deposits and bills of exchange. The growth of the interbank market, following the entry of the foreign banks into Spain from 1978 onwards indicated the important role that these intermediaries could play. They take and place deposits from and with banks, savings banks and co-operative credit agencies, and they buy and sell short-term financial instruments such as treasury bills, certificates of deposit and bills of exchange.

The SMMDs are constituted as SA companies and they are strictly regulated by the Bank of Spain. They are intended to be independent of the banking institutions and for this reason no bank is allowed to hold more than 10 per cent of the capital of one of these companies.

13.10.2 Finance companies (*entidades de financiación*)

These are companies which provide hire-purchase finance for the sale and purchase of all classes of goods as well as being responsible for the operation of certain credit cards.

13.10.3 Leasing companies (*entidades de arrendamiento financiero/entidades de leasing*) **and factoring companies** (*entidades de factoring*)

They are involved in leasing capital equipment or factoring debts, as the case may be.

13.10.4 Mortgage companies (*sociedades de crédito hipotecario*)

They are concerned with granting credit for the construction industry and they are part of the attempt to create a wider mortgage market.

13.11 Financial guarantee companies

These are mainly institutions providing guarantee and underwriting facilities particularly for small and medium-sized businesses. They include the mutual guarantee companies (*sociedades de garantia recíproca/SGR*) (12.8) and refinancing companies (*sociedades de reafianzamiento*). There are a number of specialised underwriting operations supported by companies which operate under the auspices of DGPE (9.4.2.1). These are as follows:

13.11.1 Spanish Export Insurance Company (*Compañia Española de Seguros a la Exportación/CESCE*)

This is legally constituted to act as an insurance company in any field other than life assurance but has exclusively responsibility for underwriting exporting finance for state enterprises. The DGPE (9.4.2.1) directly and indirectly holds a 62 per cent stake in this company.

13.11.2 National Guarantees for Commerce Company (*Sociedad Nacional de Avales al Comercio SGR/SONAVALCO*)

This is empowered to underwrite and guarantee activities for any companies which become associated with it. The DGPE owns 78 per cent of this company.

13.11.3 National Agricultural Guarantees Company (*Sociedad Anónima Estatal de Caución Agraria/SAECA*)

This has a broad remit to assist agriculture, fishing and the food industry in general through the provision of guarantees and deposits. 80 per cent of this company is in the hands of the DGPE.

13.11.4 Joint Underwriting Company (*Sociedad Mixta de Segundo Aval*)

The DEGPE is a minority shareholder with a 38 per cent stake in this underwriting company.

13.12 National Securities Market Commission (*Comisión Nacional de Mercado de Valores/CNMV*)

The CNMV was established in 1988 when the securities market was formally reorganised by the Securities Market Law (*Ley del Mercado de Valores*). The CNMV was made responsible for the supervision of the various discrete but interconnected components of the financial markets: the stock exchanges (13.13), the public debt market (13.14), the futures and options market (13.15), the fixed rate market (13.16) and the collective investment institutions (13.17). It looks after the authorisation and regulation of the broking companies and agencies (13.13.2) and the admission and suspension of listed companies and securities. In particular it is empowered to protect investors by ensuring the transparency of the market and safeguarding against insider dealing (*uso de información privilegiada*). It demands a regular flow of information including audited accounts from quoted companies and insists on strict compliance with the submission of appropriate details and the approval of prospectuses before admitting companies on to the stock market for the first time. It maintains a data base of all listed companies and publishes annual statistics which include details of companies which have failed to comply with any of its requirements. It is run by a management board which consists of a chairperson and vice-chairperson appointed by the government, the director general of the Directorate General for the Treasury and Financial Policy (13.21), the deputy governor of the Bank of Spain (13.3) and three other directors appointed by the Ministry of Economy and Finance. The board is assisted by a consultative committee (*comisión consultiva*) which includes representatives of the four autonomous communities with stock exchanges (13.13) as well as broking firms (13.13.2) and investors.

13.13 Stock exchanges (*bolsas de valores*)

While the trend in most other countries has been towards the concentration of stock market activity into one central exchange, this has not been the case in Spain. The growth of regional autonomy has perhaps made such a move inopportune and indeed it has even resulted in the formal recognition of the exchange in Valencia (1980), in addition to the established exchanges in Madrid (1831), Bilbao (1890) and Barcelona (1915). The autonomous governments have administrative powers in regard to the exchanges within their territories. However, market forces are not always in accord with political considerations and there has been an increasing concentration of business in the Madrid Exchange which is now responsible for over 90 per cent of all transactions. The regional exchanges deal in a very limited number of locally-based companies such as *Asland Catalunya* in Barcelona, *Bankoa* in Bilbao and *Aguas Valencia* in Valencia.

13.13.1 Stock exchange regulating associations (*sociedades rectoras de la bolsa*)

Each exchange is run by an association, constituted as a public limited SA company, in which the shareholders are the members of the respective exchange. They regulate trading and admission or suspension to their specific exchange on a daily basis in conjunction with the CNMV and any regional regulations introduced by the relevant autonomous government.

13.13.2 Broking companies and securities agencies (*sociedades y agencias de valores*)

The members of each stock exchange who own and run the regulating associations now consist of broking companies (*sociedades de valores y bolsa*) and securities agencies (*agencias de valores y bolsa*). They are the only authorised dealers on the exchanges. The former are dealer and broker firms on their own account as well as on behalf of third parties. They can underwrite issues and provide credit facilities for investors, functions which are not open to the agencies which are primarily concerned with buying and selling on behalf of clients. At the beginning of 1995 there were thirty-two companies, mainly subsidiaries of banks and savings banks, for example, *Argentaria Bolsa BCH Bolsa*, and fifteen agencies. Since 1988 they have replaced the individual dealers and brokers (*agentes de cambio y bolsa*) who operated on the market prior to the reform law but who were permitted to be members as individuals until their retirement. These organisations are both distinguished from a further seventy companies and agencies, which deal in securities but which are not stock exchange members, by the use of the additional words *y bolsa* in their name. All the broking companies and agencies may also carry out a full range of investment and portfolio management activities across different areas of the other financial markets which are described below (13.14, 13.15 and 13.16).

13.13.3 Other stock market intermediaries (*otros intermediarios bursátiles*)

While the companies and agencies which are members of the exchanges are the only authorised dealers on the market itself, there are several intermediaries involved in investment which may act in their own name or on behalf of third parties. These include banks, savings banks, credit cooperatives and money market intermediaries (13.10.1), collective investment institutions and funds (13.17) and brokers (*corredores de comercio*) who belong to the professional association of brokers (*colegio de corredores*). There are some 650 officially registered members of the association who validate financial documents. In 1995 they were strongly resisting attempts to merge their role with that of the notaries (*notarios*).

13.13.4 Trading (*contratación*)

Only a tiny percentage of trading on the Madrid Exchange is now carried out on the floor (*parquet*) of the actual exchange during the normal hours of business from 10 a.m. to 12 noon. Ten minutes is given over to dealing in securities in specific sectors by groups (*corros*) of dealers before a bell then sounds to indicate the turn of another sector. Since 1988, the continuous market (*mercado continuo*) has progressively become the main method of trading, electronically linking, as it does, dealers on all four Spanish exchanges. The continuous market which operates from 11 a.m. until 5 p.m. is formally called the *sistema de interconexión bancaria* and is organised by a separate company, *Sociedad de Bolsas SA*, set up by the four exchanges to facilitate simultaneous trading on a national level. This in practice is the most important segment of the market with some 130 major companies being quoted and with its own index, IBEX-35, based on the thirty-five most important companies. In general, deals no longer require the physical transfer of share certificates since the recent implementation of the computer-assisted clearing and settlement system (*servicio de compensación y liquidación de valores*) envisaged in the 1988 reform law. This also functions as a company in its own right in which the Madrid Exchange is the major shareholder, together with the other three exchanges, broking companies and agencies and other financial intermediaries. However, it is in the process of being replaced by a more sophisticated system for recording data regarding fixed rate securities (*mercado electrónico de renta fija*) developed and used by the Madrid Exchange.

The Spanish stock exchange is still relatively small compared with those of other major EU member countries and not very representative of Spanish industry. Many companies in Spain are, of course, small in size and often strongly controlled by family interests and unwilling therefore to go public. At the same time, there has been a marked reluctance by companies to comply with the requirements of the CNMV to provide the necessary amount of information which would encourage investors. There are under 300 regularly quoted companies, compared to over 2,000 on the London Exchange and there is a very strong concentration of business in bank shares and in utilities, especially electricals. There has, however, been a considerable growth in foreign investment in the market which rose to become 44 per cent of the total invested in equities in 1993. There has also been a growth in institutional investment encouraged by more favourable tax treatment and by the increased significance of pension and investment funds. The number of investment funds quoted on the exchange had risen by 550 by mid-1995 (13.17.3–5).

13.14 Public debt market (*mercado de deuda pública*)

This is operated on behalf of the Bank of Spain by a computerised recording system (*Central de Anotaciones*) and it covers not only central government borrowing but also that of the regional governments as well as of public sector undertakings such as the INI (9.4.2.2), RTVE and the ICO (13.4).

13.15 Futures and options markets (*mercados de futuros y opciones*)

These derivatives markets are only newly operative in Spain, in practice since 1992 with the establishment of the Spanish Futures Market (*Mercado Español de Futuros Financieros/MEFF Sociedad Holding*). This co-ordinates two regulatory bodies for distinct sectors: for the fixed rate market, *MEFF Renta Fija* or *RF* in Madrid; for the variable rate market, *MEFF Renta Variable* or *RV* in Barcelona.

13.16 Privately administered fixed rate market (*Mercado de interés fijo de la Asociación de Intermediarios de Activos Financieros* or *Mercado AIAF*)

While the other securities markets described above are organised under the auspices of public administrative law, the market for institutional trading in fixed interest bearing bonds and debentures such as private sector issued promissory notes (*pagarés de empresa*), mortgage bonds (*cédulas hipotecarias*) and bonds in pesetas issued by non-residents in Spain (*bonos matador*), is privately administered by the Association of Intermediaries in Financial Assets (*Asociación de Intermediarios de Activos Financieros*). This began to function in 1991 following authorisation by the Ministry of Economy and Finance and it consists of some 130 financial intermediaries drawn from the banks and other institutions described above subject to compliance with minimum standards of liquidity. On the other hand, the retail trade in most of this type of asset as well as in public sector bonds is carried out on the stock exchange by the broking companies and agencies.

13.17 Collective investment institutions (*instituciones de inversión colectiva/IIC*)

In order to stimulate more institutional investment in Spain in addition to that carried out by the insurance and pension funds (13.20), the government has encouraged the creation of investment companies and funds since 1984 by the favourable tax treatment of savings and investments through these channels. This has led to the establishment of a number of institutions, the most important of which are usually owned by the banks and savings banks. They are subject to strict supervision and control by the Bank of Spain and the CNMV. The major types are listed below.

13.17.1 Investment companies (*sociedades de inversión mobiliaria/SIM*)

They invest and manage a minimum 90 per cent of their assets in stocks and shares.

13.17.2 Investment companies with variable capital to invest (*sociedades de inversión mobiliaria de capital variable/SIMCAV*)

These are more flexible types of investment company which can expand their share capital without the restrictions attributed to the standard form of SA company.

13.17.3 Investment funds (*fondos de inversión mobiliaria/FIM*)

The FIM are authorised to invest in any type of stocks and shares, short-, medium-, or long-term, private or public sector.

13.17.4 Short-term investment funds (*fondos de inversión en activos del mercado monetario/FIAMM*)

As the name implies the FIAMM are restricted to short-term investments (average eighteen months) usually in government bonds (*bonos del estado*) or company bonds (*pagarés de empresa*).

13.17.5 Gilt funds (*fondtesoros*)

These are simply variations of the FIM and FIAMM with a high level of obligatory investment in government securities.

These investment funds have become increasingly significant on the stock exchange itself and with over 600 of them in 1995 they are more numerous than ordinary quoted companies. The attractive rates of interest, particularly on public sector securities, have played a major part in stimulating this sector of the market, probably at the expense of direct investment in company equities.

There are also two other investment management companies which are not technically collective investment institutions, but which operate in a similar, albeit more general, way:

13.17.6 Collective investment management companies (*sociedades gestoras de instituciones de inversión/SGIIC*) and portfolio management companies (*sociedades gestoras de cartera/SGC*)

13.17.7 Mortgage fund management companies (*sociedades gestoras de FTH*) and mortage funds (*fondos de titulación hipotecaria/FTH*)

Another recent development has been the creation of mortgage market companies and funds following their authorisation in 1992. Mortgage funds (*fondos de titulación hipotecaria/FTH*) are managed by mortgage fund management companies (*sociedades gestoras de FTH*) approved by the Ministry of Economy and Finance on the recommendation of the CNMV.

13.18 Directorate General for Insurance (*Dirección General de Seguros*)

This Directorate General is the department within the Ministry of Economy and Finance responsible for the control and co-ordination of the insurance and pension sector. All insurance companies and pension fund management companies have to be officially registered with the Directorate General in the register of insurance entities (*registro especial de entidades aseguradoras*). They are also subject to regular inspection and they are required to submit their annual financial statements for scrutiny in order to ensure that proper regard is paid to the strict observance of minimum capital levels, investment and reserve ratios.

13.19 Insurance companies (*empresas aseguradoras/compañías de seguros*)

At present, the insurance sector plays a relatively small part in the Spanish economy in comparison with its importance in other major economies. For a variety of reasons there has not been a great volume of insurance business, particularly in the case of life assurance, where less than 15 per cent of the population are thought to be covered by voluntary schemes. On the other hand, however, with more than 500 registered insurers, Spain has far more companies than is normally the case. This means that most of the member companies of the National Insurance Association (*Unión Española de Entidades Aseguradoras, Reaseguradoras y de Capitalización/ UNESPA*) are small and localised with the exception of a limited number of national concerns such as *La Unión y el Fénix*, *Plus Ultra* and *La Estrella*. Many are organised in the form of mutual societies (*mutuas/mutualidades*) which can range from very small provident societies to substantial mutual insurance companies, such as the *Mutualidad de Seguros del Instituto Nacional de Industria* (*MUSINI*), responsible for providing cover for the employees in the INI and the INH state holding groups. The 1984 Private Insurance Law (*Ley de Ordenación de Seguro Privado*) revised in 1995, initiated a rationalisation process which has seen the disappearance of over 100 entities to date. More than 75 per cent of insurers now take the form of public limited SA companies with the largest national companies being organised on a group basis with separate provision for life, car household, general insurance, etc. This, for example, is the case with the *Corporación Mapfre*, Spain's largest insurance group in 1995. Harmonisation with the European Union and the prospects of a new and potentially lucrative market in insurance and pension schemes initially attracted a number of foreign companies into Spain such as the Zurich, Commercial Union and Royal Assurance which usually bought up national concerns as did Norwich Union in 1990 with the acquisition of the well known *Plus Ultra*. The interest of foreign insurers, however, has not been sustained and the banks and savings banks have become been the major participants in the sector. Thus, *Banesto* and *Banco Central Hispano* (*BCH*) both own two of the traditional flagship companies, *La Unión y el Fénix* and *La Estrella*, respectively. These large insurance companies have come to play an increasingly important role as institutional investors together with pension funds (13.20). There are also two public sector entities involved in certain aspects of insurance as follows:

13.19.1 Insurance Compensation Consortium (*Consorcio de Compensación de Seguros*)

This is an autonomous commercial body (9.3) with its own legal identity dating back to 1953 and reformed in 1981 when it was given responsibility for three other insurance underwriting bodies: the Insurance Guarantee Fund (*Fondo Nacional de Garantía de Riesgos de la Circulación*), the Road Vehicle Third Party Insurance Fund (*Comisaría del Seguro Obligatorio de Viajero*) and the Central Insurance Fund (*Caja Central de Seguros*). It covers the civil responsibility of all sectors of public administration in the event of accidents or losses concerning both their own personnel and members of the public. Insurance cover for natural disasters such as forest fires and floods form an important area of its work, particularly in the light of the extent of the damage in various parts of the country in recent years as a result of these phenomena. In the case of vehicle insurance, it provides cover where accidents have been caused by unknown persons or where the insurance company involved has collapsed.

13.19.2 State Agricultural Insurance Company (*Empresa Nacional de Seguros Agrarios/ENESA*)

This too is an autonomous commercial body which, because of its responsibility for agricultural insurance, is nominally under the jurisdiction of the Ministry of Agriculture, Fisheries and Food. Its board of management, however, is made up of an equal number of representatives from the Ministry of Agriculture and Fisheries, the Ministry of Economy and Finance and representatives of the farming sector. The high risks involved in this important sector of the economy have long posed a problem which private insurance has not been able to resolve fully. ENESA therefore co-ordinates and underwrites insurance in the sector and prepares an annual plan for consideration by the Directorate General for Insurance. It also draws up formal agreements with private insurers especially associated for the purpose in the Consortium of Insurance Entities (*Agrupación de Entidades Aseguradoras*).

13.20 Pension funds (*fondos de pensiones*)

Traditionally in Spain there has been heavy reliance on the state's social security provision which has given the highest state cover in western Europe with pensions at up to 90 per cent of wages on retirement. However, in recent years it has become very clear that the state can no longer sustain such a generously high level and the debate about the future of social security, together with generous tax concessions, has encouraged more than one in ten workers to make provision to supplement their future pensions. Thus private pension funds, which consist of the contributions made to pension plans (*planes de pensiones*) to provide benefits on retirement to participants, were regulated for the first time in Spain in 1987 and subject to modifications in 1994–95. While some large SA companies had already organised their own schemes, this legislation paved the way for other companies to promote schemes as well as for trade unions and professional bodies to follow suit for their members. It also made it possible for individuals to provide for themselves. The banks, savings banks and insurance companies have since emerged as the principal promotors (*entidades promotoras*) of such plans.

The funds have to be registered with the Directorate General for Insurance (13.18) in the pension funds register (*registro de fondos de pensiones*) and the Directorate General is responsible for inspection and the compliance with investment regulations. The funds have made an important contribution to the growth of institutional investment in Spain. Each fund is administered by a management company (*entidad gestora*) which is supervised by a board of trustees (*comisión de control*) consisting of representatives of the participants and the promoters. This is an attempt to protect the funds from being raided by companies seeking extra funds.

13.21 Directorate General for the Treasury and Financial Policy (*Dirección General del Tesoro y Política Financiera*)

Control over the finance, leasing and factoring companies for which this Directorate was previously responsible has now been transferred to the Bank of Spain. It does, however, have a broad range of functions in regard to the management of the national debt, the official records of financial institutions and oversight of legislation concerning banks and securities markets. The director general is a member of the National Securities Market Commission (13.12).

In terms of specific financial institutions, this department of the Ministry of Economy and Finance is now only responsible for keeping a register and supervising venture capital companies and funds.

13.22 Venture capital companies and funds (*sociedades y fondos de capital riesgo*)

These are important sources and ways of funding new companies and risky business projects. Together with other small and medium-sized businesses they may have recourse to the 'over the counter (OTC)' second market (*segundo mercado para pequeñas y medianas empresas*) as a way of raising the capital needed for expansion. The requirements for quotation on this market are much less stringent than for official quotation (*cotizacíon oficial*) on the stock exchange proper.

13.23 Comment

The Spanish authorities have taken pains to ensure the full harmonisation of Spanish legislation with European directives and consequently financial institutions have come a long way in the past ten years. Certainly in terms of their structure they are comparable to those of the other major EU countries, although many of the institutions and the financial instruments are still relatively new and the volume of activity is still in many instances comparatively low. However, there has been a notable increase in competition within the system with the emergence of new companies and larger groups. The most marked trend has been that of foreign interest in investment in Spain's financial markets. Although this has undoubtedly substantially increased the volume of activity, it has brought with it a significant degree of volatility as foreign investors have been quick to move funds as the international markets have gone through periods of major crises. This trend has also been exacerbated by the weakness of the peseta. Spain has been a member of the European Monetary System (EMS) since 1989 with its exchange rate subject to movements within the bands prescribed for members of the exchange rate mechanism (ERM), and the peseta, which operates within the broader 15 per cent band, was devalued four times between 1992 and mid-1995 (1.1.5).

The leading personalities in the financial world have always been the targets of media speculation in Spain and, because of the predominant position of the banks within the economy, they have been seen as its principal entrepreneurs. While rivalry between them was always seized upon, in recent times several of them have figured in the wave of scandals that rocked the González government in its later stages. It is perhaps not surprising that charges against Mariano Rubio, the former governor of the Bank of Spain, and Mario Conde, the chairman of one of Spain's leading private banks, should make headlines. However, it may also be a testimony to the efficacy of the regulatory bodies and procedures that corruption now comes more readily to light. Nevertheless, in today's computerised, global financial market, Spain is not alone in encountering such problems, as sagas such as BCCI and Barings well indicate.

One of the major debates that continues within the system is the extent to which the banks should be involved directly in industry. The crises of the late 1970s and early 1980s which affected the economy in general, and the banking sector in particular, were a salutary lesson for many bankers. The period signalled the beginning of an exodus from many sectors of industry as banks began to dispose of their shares on a large scale in attempts to reduce bad debts and high risks. The corollary of this, however, has been the expansion of foreign ownership of a substantial percentage of industry and commerce. This has highlighted differences within the ruling Socialist party in the mid-1990s. The Ministry of Economy and Finance, conscious of its responsibilities for safeguarding the solvency of the financial institutions, has encouraged the reduction of banking involvement in industry, while the Ministry of Industry and Energy has taken the opposite view. The banks themselves appear to have opted for a much more selective investment programme as they abandon some of their traditional strongholds, such as chemicals and construction, and instead look towards new high technology sectors such as telecommunications. In 1995 the impending privatisation of the DGPE's 35 per cent stake in *Telefónica* (9.4.2.1) triggered off intense debate about the future participation not only of the private sector banks, BBV and BCHO but also of the semi-publicly owned *Argentaria*. The resolution of this sale together with other privatisations may well reveal the direction in which the banking sector is heading. What is certain is that financial institutions will continue to be subject to considerable fluctuation and change as markets become increasingly more international in the future.

Chapter 14

The judiciary

Preliminary note

Since the Spanish and English judicial systems are in many ways very different, it is not always easy to find exact equivalents in English for some Spanish legal terms. For example, *juzgado, audiencia* and *tribunal* may all be translated as 'court', and the only distinction between them seems to be the level at which they operate, the *juzgados* always being at the lower end of the hierarchy (see figure 14.1, p. 294). Likewise, both the words *juez* and *magistrado* may be translated as 'judge' – although the latter is always senior to the former. Certainly *magistrado* does not equate to an English magistrate with all the connotations which the latter has for the involvement of non-professionals in the judicial system (something very rare in Spain). Thus, although the term 'magistrate' will be used in the course of this chapter to translate *magistrado*, the difference in meaning must be understood.

It should also be noted that in general terms the Spanish system is one based on civil law as opposed to the UK and American system of 'common law'. It is created by legislation and custom, applied by the judges rather than by jurisprudence – although with regard to the interpretation and application of the laws, the jurisprudence of the Supreme Court (14.5.1) is very significant.

14.1 Introduction

In all fully democratic systems, the judiciary acts as an independent power quite separate from the legislature and the executive; the judiciary, in fact, ensures that both of the latter conduct themselves in accordance with the law under the Constitution. Too often, however, in Spain's chequered history – and most recently during the Franco era – this 'separation' or 'division of powers' did not exist, as authoritarian regimes preferred to invest ultimate power with the executive, leaving the judiciary (and also Parliament) subordinated to it. Franco quite deliberately rejected the doctrine of the 'separation of powers' (to him synonymous with the liberal democratic systems he so vehemently detested) and instead promoted the theory of the 'unity of powers', which in practice meant the domination of the executive over both the legislature and the judiciary. Furthermore, the dictator established a parallel system of military courts and special 'public order' courts which acted quite independently of the ordinary courts; in fact, they were used by an all-powerful executive to try so-called 'political offenders,' i.e. opponents of his regime. As late as 1975, indeed, Franco continued to enact special legislation enabling him to bypass the normal judicial channels in order to pursue his own political ends.

After the death of the Caudillo, however, albeit slowly, the new democratic state made efforts to restore the independence, as well as the credibility, of the judiciary and to provide a judicial system that was, at least in theory, free from governmental interference. Only civilian courts would henceforth try civilian offences, with the military courts empowered to deal only with military affairs. Moreover, as early as 1976 Adolfo Suárez ensured that special courts like the infamous *tribunales de orden público* were swept away. Subsequently, after the first democratic election of 1977, there began the long process of democratising and modernising the whole complex structure of the Spanish judicial system. Clearly, the new structure would have to take into account Spain's new position within Europe and the new decentralised nature of the state (chapter 7).

14.2 Justice and the Constitution of 1978

Section VI of the Constitution is devoted entirely to justice. Articles 117–127 outline the main principles governing its operation and the administration of justice in Spain. Echoing article 2.1, and thus demonstrating that justice lies at the very heart of the Constitution, article 167 states:

> Justice derives from the people and is administered in the name of the king by judges and magistrates belonging to the judicial power; the latter are independent, cannot be removed from office, and they are accountable to and subject only to the law.

The concept of independence is reinforced in article 127 which states that judges (*jueces*) and magistrates (*magistrados*), as well as public prosecutors (*fiscales*), cannot, while in post, occupy any other public position or professional post (with the exception of teaching and research) nor belong to a political party (chapter 10) or trade union (chapter 11). A special law on incompatibilities attempts to reinforce this independence.

In addition to the basic principle of independence, the Constitution enshrines the concept of a unitary system of courts: article 127.3 and 127.5 explicitly pave the way for a single, unified system of courts, outside which no citizen can normally be tried. Article 127.4 limits their functions to the normal processes of law, thereby excluding their use for political ends.

A further principle embodied in the Constitution is that of publicity; article 120 requires that, with limited exceptions, all judicial proceedings shall be open to the public and that all sentences, reasons for which must be given, must be announced in public. Article 125 envisages the creation of a system of juries (*jurados*) in Spain (not traditional in the country) stating that this is one way in which the public will be able to participate in the judicial process. However, while popular opinion strongly favours such a development, the senior practitioners of justice have hitherto been largely hostile. None the less, Parliament approved a Jury Bill (*Ley del*

Jurado) in May 1995 in the hope of fulfilling this constitutional pledge – and in the course of 1996 the first juries began to function.

14.3 Basic legislation relating to the judiciary

Prior to 1985, the judicial system in Spain was subject to a labyrinth of laws and regulations, some of which dated back as far as 1870 and 1882. The most recent previous addition to this complex legislation was as long ago as 1944. Clearly, once democracy had returned to Spain and a new constitution had been approved, there was an urgent need to draw up comprehensive and detailed law that both enshrined the basic principles outlined above and updated the structures of what had become an antiquated and unwieldy system. In particular, it was essential that these new structures should take into account the new decentralised shape of the Spanish state.

14.3.1 Organic Law of the Judiciary (*Ley Orgánica del Poder Judicial/LOPJ*)

This law was first promulgated in June 1985, but in November 1995 was republished in an amended version which incorporated previous relevant legislation covering the period 1987–92. This law represents one of the most far-reaching and ambitious pieces of legislation enacted by the first government of Felipe González. It is divided into six 'books' (*libros*), each divided into several sections (*títulos*). The 'books' cover the following areas:

- *Book 1* refers to the scope and limit of jurisdiction, as well as to the staffing and organisation of the courts
- *Book 2* deals with the government of the judiciary
- *Book 3* covers the *modus operandi* of the courts
- *Book 4* is devoted to the role and functions of the judges and magistrates
- *Book 5* examines the Department of the Attorney General (*Ministerio Fiscal*), as well as other persons and institutions which work with the administrators of justice
- *Book 6* describes the nature and role of a wide range of personnel (for example, clerks of justice and forensic scientists) who are at the service of the administrators of justice.

14.3.2 Law of Staffing and Demarcation (*Ley de Planta y Demarcación*)

This law, approved by Parliament in December 1988, lays down what courts are to be established at various levels and what staffing each one is to be provided with. The first reference to this law was made in the preamble to the above organic law, which states that the establishment of a comprehensive network of judicial bodies (i.e. courts) is an essential ingredient of the implementation of article 24 of the Constitution (2.4.1.4).

14.4 Administration of justice

14.4.1 Overall structure

As outlined in book 1 of the LOPJ (preamble and article 30), justice is administered within an all-embracing, unitary system and is structured according to two criteria: the one territorial and the other functional. With regard to the first of these, the state is organised for judicial purposes into municipalities, *partidos judiciales* (two or more municipalities), provinces and autonomous communities, each level (including the state or national level) with its own corresponding judicial institutions. Regarding the second criterion, the system is divided according to five branches of justice or jurisdiction, each regulated by its own specific codes (*códigos*) or laws; these are:

- civil justice, which deals with matters of civil law under the Civil Code (*Código Civil*)
- criminal justice, which deals with criminal offences under the Penal Code (*Código Penal*)
- administrative justice, which deals with claims against the various branches of public administration; this is governed by the Law of Litigation and Administrative Jurisdiction (*Ley de Jurisdicción Contencioso-Administrativo*)
- social justice, which deals with employment and labour affairs
- military justice, which can (with very rare exceptions) only be applied to members of the armed forces, under the code of military justice (*código de justicia militar*).

Unlike the executive and legislative authorities, where many powers have been devolved to regional governments and parliaments, the judiciary remains largely a centralised, hierarchical system, since justice is not (and probably never will be) an area where regional variations are permitted or where power can be shared.

14.4.2 General Council of the Judiciary (*Consejo General del Poder Judicial/ CGPJ*)

This is the highest governing body of the judiciary, first envisaged in article 122 of the Constitution. Its current composition and powers (1995) are set out in book 2, section 2 of the LOPJ. It is composed of the president of the Supreme Court (14.5.1), who presides over its sessions, and twenty members (*vocales*) appointed by the Congress and the Senate, which each, by a three-fifths majority, must elect four members from 'lawyers and jurists of recognised competence who have exercised their profession for more than fifteen years', and six members from the body of practising judges and magistrates drawn from any section of the judiciary. Re-election is not allowed.

The method for election of members has recently become something of a political issue. Originally, when the Council was first set up in 1980, twelve out of the twenty were directly elected by the body of professional judges and magistrates. The

Popular Party (10.3.3), arguing that the system introduced by the Socialist government in 1985 gave too much say to politicians (albeit in their parliamentary capacity), stated that, if elected to power, it would restore the original system.

The powers of the CGPJ lie mainly in the area of appointments. For example, it has the right to propose, by a three-fifths majority, its own president, who is also that of the Supreme Court (14.5.1). It also recommends the appointment of two members of the Constitutional Court (2.5). In both these cases, it is the king who actually makes the appointments. In addition, the Council has the power to appoint magistrates serving in the Supreme Court, as well as the presidents of the regional high courts of justice (14.6.1) and of provincial courts (14.7.1). Moreover, it has responsibility for the training, location and promotion of judges and magistrates, as well as disciplinary affairs. This is done via that division of the Centre for Judicial Studies (*Centro de Estudios Judiciales*) which depends exclusively on the CGPJ. Inspection of the courts (*juzgados* and *tribunales*) also comes into the remit of the Council. Each year the CGPJ is expected to submit a report (*memoria*) to Parliament on its operation and activities, as well as those of the courts; this report may contain a list of what it considers to be the future requirements of the service in terms of staffing and resources. Additionally, the Council is the official publisher for all jurisprudence emanating from the Supreme Court.

The CGPJ functions in plenary session, but also has a standing committee (*comisión permanente*), which consists of the president and four members elected annually by the plenum by a three-fifths majority. The role of this committee is, among other duties, to prepare the meetings of the full Council, to ensure that the latter's decisions are implemented, and to approve the promotion structure (*escalafón*) of judges and magistrates. In addition, there is a disciplinary committee (*comisión disciplinaria*) which is also elected annually by a three-fifths majority. This consists of five Council members and its function is to take disciplinary action, when appropriate, against judges and magistrates. Finally, the Council also elects on the same basis an appointments committee (*comisión de calificación*), which consists of five members, and whose task is to advise the full Council in regard to the judicial appointments which fall within its remit.

14.4.3 Department of the Attorney General of the State (*Ministerio Fiscal*)

This important office, whose role is set out in article 124 of the Constitution and whose functions, structure and composition were established under a law of December 1981, has two basic functions. Firstly, it ensures that the system of justice functions in accordance with the law and to the benefit of the general public, whose interests it must protect; and secondly, it ensures that the courts are independent and serve the general good of society. In serving the interests of the public, the department is entrusted with the protection of the rights of citizens in the Constitution; thus, it is empowered with applying the appeal for protection (*recurso de amparo*) before the Constitutional Court (2.5.2.4). More particularly, this department – which must not be confused with the Ministry of Home Affairs (14.8) –

oversees the bureaucracy of the prosecution service and the whole career structure of the public prosecutors (*fiscales*) operating from national down to provincial level, which is quite separate from that applying to judges and magistrates.

The senior figure in the hierarchy is the attorney general of the state (*fiscal general del estado*); an alternative version in English – and indeed the literal translation – would be 'state public prosecutor', who is appointed by the king on the proposal of the Council of Ministers after consultation with the General Council of the Judiciary. He is responsible for the operation of the whole system and nominally in charge of the entire corps of *fiscales*. At the national level, he is assisted by the Prosecuting Council (*Consejo Fiscal*) and the Divisional Prosecutors' Council (*Junta de Fiscales de Sala*). There are also prosecutors' departments (*fiscalías*) attached to the Constitutional Court, the National Court (14.5.2) and the Audit Tribunal (9.9.3), as well as to the regional high courts and provincial courts. In April 1995, the Congress approved a bill to establish yet another *fiscalía*, called the *Fiscalía Anticorrupción*, although this was hotly opposed by opposition groups and the Association for Public Prosecutors (*Asociación de Fiscales*), who felt that this was yet another bureaucratic response to a serious problem (1.1.5).

14.5 National level courts

A simplified version of the court structure is given in figure 14.1. This does not include the National Court which, to a great extent, operates outside the normal hierarchy; the structure of this court is shown in figure 14.2.

14.5.1 Supreme Court (*Tribunal Supremo*)

The Supreme Court, located in the historic centre of Madrid, is the highest court of justice in the land for all matters, with the exception of constitutional guarantees which are, logically, dealt with by the Constitutional Court (2.5). It has jurisdiction throughout Spain, and is clearly an example of a central institution which, under current arrangements at least, could never devolve its powers to the new regional authorities. Only this court is allowed to bear the name *Supremo* (article 53, LOPJ).

The Supreme Court is composed of five divisions (*salas*), each headed by its own president, and consisting of magistrates whose number is fixed by law in each case. These are now dealt with separately.

14.5.1.1 Civil Division (Sala de lo Civil)

Under civil law (*derecho civil*), this division deals with various matters, including appeals of annulment (*casación*) and review (*revisión*). However, one of its major functions is to hear claims, in acts carried out while exercising their public office, against the prime minister, the presidents of both Houses of Parliament, the presidents of the Supreme Court and the General Council of the Judiciary, the president of the Constitutional Court, the president of the National Court, members of the

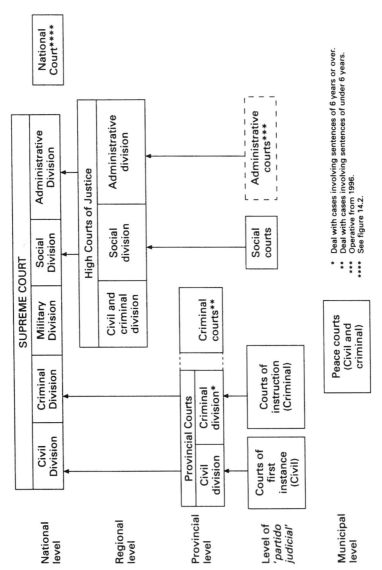

SUPREME COURT

| Civil Division | Criminal Division | Military Division | Social Division | Administrative Division |

National Court**

High Courts of Justice

| Civil and criminal division | Social division | Administrative division |

Social courts

Administrative courts***

Provincial Courts

| Civil division | Criminal division* |

Criminal courts**

Courts of first instance (Civil)

Courts of instruction (Criminal)

Peace courts (Civil and criminal)

National level

Regional level

Provincial level

Level of *'partido judicial'*

Municipal level

* Deal with cases involving sentences of 6 years or over.
** Deal with cases involving sentences of under 6 years.
*** Operative from 1996.
**** See figure 14.2.

Figure 14.1 *Simplified structure of courts, 1995*

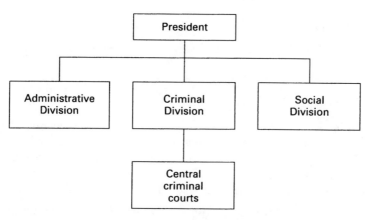

Figure 14.2 *Structure of National Court, 1995*

government, members of Parliament, presidents of autonomous communities, public prosecutors and other high ranking public servants. This division also deals with civil cases brought against magistrates of the National Court and of the regional high courts of justice.

14.5.1.2 Criminal Division (Sala de lo Penal)

Under criminal law (*derecho penal*), this division, as well as hearing annulment and revision appeals, deals with cases brought against a wide range of high ranking public persons. This list includes, in addition to those referred to in 14.5.1.1, the president and counsellors of the Council of State (5.7) and the ombudsman (2.6). As with the civil division, it can also deal with cases brought against magistrates in the National Court and in the regional high courts of justice.

14.5.1.3 Administrative Division (Sala de lo Contencioso-Administrativo)

Under the *Ley de Jurisdicción Contencioso-Administrativo*, this division, acting as a court of sole instance (*única instancia*), applies itself to cases of appeals against the actions and decisions of high ranking public bodies (as opposed to individuals). These include: the Council of Ministers (5.5) and its delegated committees (5.6); the General Council of the Judiciary (14.4.2); the Congress of Deputies (4.3.1); the Senate (4.3.2); the Constitutional Court (2.5); the Audit Tribunal (9.9.3); and the Office of the Ombudsman (2.6). This division also deals with annulment appeals against sentences passed in sole instance by the administrative divisions of the regional high courts of justice where there has been an appeal against actions and decisions of bodies forming part of state administration.

14.5.1.4 Social Division (Sala de lo Social)

Under labour law (*derecho laboral*), this division deals with annulment and review appeals.

14.5.1.5 Military Division (Sala de lo Militar)

This division is composed of a president and seven magistrates, four of whom are ordinary career judges, while the others belong to the legal corps of the armed forces. It deals with cases against high ranking officers in the forces, including captains general (*capitanes generales*) and hears appeals relating to disciplinary matters against sanctions imposed by the Ministry of Defence (*Ministerio de Defensa*).

In addition, the LOPJ alludes to the creation of another division (in the 1985 version of the law, this was referred to as the Revision Division (*Sala de Revisión*)), composed of the president of the Supreme Court, plus the presidents of each division and the longest serving and newest magistrate in each case. This is convened in cases where there is a challenge (*recusación*) to sentences passed by the president of the Supreme Court, by the presidents of division or by more than two magistrates from any division.

A point to stress is that the Supreme Court exercises a vital role in the interpretation of legislation and in thus building up a body of collective jurisprudence. Thus, it constitutes one of the major sources of law.

14.5.2 National Court (*Audiencia Nacional*)

The national court, though located in Madrid, has jurisdiction throughout Spain. To a large extent, it falls outside the basic court structure. It is divided into three divisions: criminal; administrative; and social affairs. Two or more sections (*secciones*) may be created within each division. In addition, attached to the National Court are five central courts of instruction (*juzgados centrales de instrucción*), each of which is headed by a judge (*juez*); these deal with criminal offences.

The Court is composed of a president, the presidents of each division and the magistrates. The president has the rank of a Supreme Court division president, and presidents of the divisions have the rank of supreme court judges. The criminal division is the court of last appeal in cases which fall into the following categories.

- crimes committed abroad when, in accordance with international agreements, it has been agreed to continue judicial procedures in Spain; thus, the Court is competent in matters of extradition
- crimes against the monarch, his/her consort, the successor to the throne, and high institutions of state
- crimes involving the forging of currency or relating to exchange control
- fraudulent activities designed to produce price changes and likely to have a wide-ranging, even national, impact

- drug-trafficking and frauds in the food, pharmaceutical and medicine industries.

In the last three cases, the National Court has jurisdiction provided that the impact of the alleged crime covers the territory of more than one *audiencia*, which in most cases will mean more than one province (14.7.1).

In addition, this division hears appeals against sentences passed by the central courts of instruction, which may be the first courts to hear cases in these categories.

The administration division, operating as a court of first instance, deals with appeals against actions and decisions of ministers and secretaries of state.

The social division, via special procedures, attempts to resolve challenges to the content of collective agreements (11.3.1.3) and conducts legal proceedings relating to collective disputes. In both the latter cases, the matters must apply to an area larger than an autonomous community. A recent example of the work of this division concerned the financial problems affecting the department store chain, the *Corte Inglés*.

In recent times, the National Court has been very much in the news. The criminal division has dealt with such high profile cases as the *Operación Nécora* (relating to the massive police operation to eradicate drug trafficking along the coast of Galicia) and the GAL affair (1.1.5), in which the investigating judge is Baltasar Garzón (14.9), a high profile judge of the National Court.

14.6 Regional level courts

Before the reform of 1985, sixteen so-called 'territorial courts' (*audiencias territoriales*) existed at the regional level – although their area of jurisdiction corresponded to no legally-constituted political or administrative entities at the regional level. With the creation and institutional development of the autonomous communities, there was a clear need to provide judicial bodies at that level, as already envisaged in the statutes of autonomy of the regional authorities (7.5.1 and 7.6.6).

14.6.1 High courts of justice (*tribunales superiores de justicia*)

In accordance with article 152 of the Constitution and with articles 70–79 of the LOPJ, a high court of justice has been established at the top of the pyramid of judicial organisation in each autonomous community, whose name is appended to the title. In addition to those in Ceuta and Melilla, there are, therefore, seventeen courts of this kind, corresponding to each of the autonomous communities established in Spain between 1980 and 1983 (7.6.6). While forming more properly part of the national structure of justice, they are also seen as representing one of the major institutions within the new regional entities.

In all the single-province communities, as well as in some of the multi-province regions, the high court of justice is normally located in the regional capital, along with the legislature and executive. In certain cases within the latter group, however, often for reasons of 'political fairness', the court has been located in a different provincial capital. One such case is that of Granada, the main seat of the high court of justice of Andalusia – though divisions of this court are also located in Seville, the regional capital, as well as in Málaga.

The high courts of justice are each composed of three divisions: a joint civil/criminal division, an administrative division dealing with complaints against the administration and a division concerned with social/labour affairs. Each high court consists of a president, who is also president of the joint division and has the rank of a magistrate of the Supreme Court, and the other divisional presidents, plus the magistrates.

Acting as a civil division, the joint court, among other functions, is a court of sole instance in claims against the president and ministers of the regional government and regional parliament. The administrative division, acting in sole instance, hears cases against administrative acts or decisions of the regional government, its president and ministers; it also acts as a court of appeal against decisions of the local administrative courts (*juzgados de lo contencioso-administrativo*) (14.7.5). The social court, acting in sole instance, deals with disputes affecting the interests of workers and employers on a scale no broader than that of the autonomous community; it also acts as a court of appeal against decisions made in local social courts (14.7.6).

Each high court, like the Supreme Court in Madrid, is endowed with a special division whose function is to hear complaints against the president, the division presidents, presidents of provincial courts (14.7.1) within the region concerned or against two or more magistrates of the high courts. This division is made up of the court and divisional presidents, plus the youngest serving magistrate in each division.

14.7 Local level courts

The term 'local' here, as in references to 'local administration' (chapter 8), is taken to mean all non-national and non-regional tiers within the administration of justice. These are the provincial, district/area (i.e. *partido*) and municipal levels, each treated separately below. As will be seen, the lower level courts or *juzgados* are not synonymous with a location at just the municipal or *partido* level: they are, in fact to be found at the provincial level and, as already seen (14.5.1), five central courts of instruction are located in Madrid.

14.7.1 Provincial courts (*Audiencias provinciales*)

These are located in provincial capitals, whose name they adopt, and have jurisdiction throughout each province. Sections of these courts may be located at a lower administrative level, in which case one or several *partidos* will be linked to them.

They normally consist of a president and two or more magistrates. However, where the number of cases is low, this may be reduced to two or even one magistrate, including the president. In such cases, it is the regional high court which decides the composition of the court. If two or more sections are created within the provincial court, these will have the same composition as the latter; the president will preside over the first of these.

The provincial courts deal only with civil and criminal matters, and the bulk of their work concerns the latter. The civil division deals largely with appeals against sentences passed by the courts of first instance (14.7.2) in the province, while the criminal division covers both serious criminal offences referred to it directly and appeals against sentences of the courts of instruction (14.7.3) located within the province. In addition, the provincial court hears appeals against decisions of prison surveillance courts (14.7.7) and the juvenile courts (14.7.8). Furthermore, these courts are entrusted with the task of arbitrating over disputes of competence between civil and criminal courts in the province.

It is in the section of the organic law dealing with the provincial courts that reference is made (article 83) to the establishment, role and function of the jury (*jurado*). As already observed, however, this provision of both the Constitution and of the organic law has only recently been fleshed out in detailed legislation (14.2). None the less, when juries are set up in Spain, it is at this provincial level that they will operate. Three other kinds of lower level court (*juzgado*) are also situated in the provincial capital. These are the criminal courts (14.7.4), the administrative courts (14.7.5) and the social courts (14.7.6). They are dealt with in the following section precisely because, in terms of hierarchy, they are of a lower level than the provincial court; in the case of the last two, these are, in any case, courts of first instance (not to be confused with the more specific use of this term in 14.7.2).

14.7.2 Courts of first instance (*juzgados de primera instancia*)

In each *partido judicial*, located in its main town, there are one or more courts of first instance, which deal with civil matters. One of their main tasks is to give a judgement in appeals submitted to them from the peace courts (14.7.9) and also to decide questions of jurisdiction (*competencia*) arising from these same courts within their *partido judicial*. These courts also normally hold the civil register (*registro civil*), unless this has been delegated to a peace court (14.7.9). In districts which have several courts of first instance, the Staffing and Demarcation Law (14.3.2) determines which shall hold this register.

14.7.3 Courts of instruction (*juzgados de instrucción*)

Most of these courts are also located at the level of the *partido judicial*. They deal with less serious criminal offences and prepare more serious cases which are to be heard either in the provincial courts or in the criminal courts (*juzgados de lo penal*) (14.7.4), located in the provincial capital. They, too, act as courts of appeal against judgements of the peace courts. They also have responsibility for dealing with *habeas corpus* matters within their area. Moreover, these are the courts with responsibility for granting authorisation for entry into private property, when this is requested by police officers or other public authorities. In Madrid, as we have seen (14.5.2) there are five central courts of instruction attached to the National Court.

It should be noted that, in the cities and larger towns, the courts of first instance and instruction are separate, while in the smaller towns they function as one under the same presiding judge. In the province of Málaga, for instance, there are three of each of these courts in Marbella (a town of over 86,000 inhabitants) and two each in the *cabezas de partido* of Vélez–Málaga, Antequera and Ronda, with populations respectively of 54,000, 40,000 and 34,500.

14.7.4 Criminal courts (*juzgados de lo penal*)

In each province, located in the provincial capital, there is one or more of these courts. In addition, it is possible to establish courts whose jurisdiction extends to one or more of the *partidos judiciales* of the province; such arrangements are set out in the Staffing and Demarcation Law mentioned above (14.3.2). The courts take the name of the town in which they are located. These courts were only established as recently as 1989 following a sentence the previous year of the Constitutional Court (2.5) which, wishing to bring Spanish practice in line with the dictates of the European Court of Human Rights, decided that the impartiality of judges was compromised when they acted as both examining and sentencing magistrates in criminal cases; previously in the *juzgados de instrucción* they had performed both functions.

14.7.5 Administrative courts (*juzgados de lo contencioso-administrativo*)

These courts have jurisdiction at provincial level, and there may be one or more of them in each provincial capital (regional capital in the case of the single-province communities). Depending on the volume of work to be transacted, such courts may also be established in smaller towns; in these cases, they will take the name of the municipality concerned, and their jurisdiction will extend to the whole of the *partido judicial* of which it is a part. It is also possible for such courts to be located with jurisdiction across provincial borders, provided that they fall within the same autonomous community. As their name implies, these courts, acting in sole or first instance, deal with complaints against the public authorities, which in most cases is likely to be the municipal councils, since higher level courts concern themselves with complaints against higher levels of administration.

14.7.6 Social courts (*juzgados de lo social*)

Like the administrative courts, these have jurisdiction at provincial level, and there may be one or more of them in each provincial capital. Likewise, it is possible, if geographical and professional reasons advise it, to situate additional courts in other centres. In exceptional circumstances, it is also possible to set up such a court with jurisdiction across two or more provinces belonging to the same autonomous community. These courts, acting in sole or first instance, deal largely with labour disputes which apply to an area no larger than a province.

14.7.7 Prison surveillance courts (*juzgados de vigilancia penitenciaria*)

There may be one or more of these courts, linked to the criminal justice system, in every province, their location depending on that of the prisons and detention centres. It is also possible to create such courts, whose jurisdiction extends to two or more provinces, within the same autonomous community. Conversely, in some cases jurisdiction will not extend to the whole of the province concerned. The central government determines the location of these courts, in consultation with the regional government concerned and with the General Council of the Judiciary (14.4.2). These courts, presided over by a surveillance judge (*juez de vigilancia*), oversee the internal regime of prisons, concerning themselves with security and disciplinary affairs, and ensuring that the rights and benefits of inmates are adequately protected and in accordance with the law.

14.7.8 Juvenile courts (*juzgados de menores*)

These are situated in provincial capitals and have jurisdiction at provincial level. There may be one or more of them in each province. Depending on the volume of work, it is possible to establish other courts whose jurisdiction extends to (i) a particular *partido judicial*; (ii) to a group of *partidos*; or (iii) across two or more provinces within the same autonomous community. They take the name of the town where they are located. As their name implies, these courts deal with offences committed by minors, which in the case of Spain means persons under the age of 18.

14.7.9 Peace courts (*juzgados de paz*)

These are located in every municipality, where there is not already a court of first instance and a court of instruction, and have jurisdiction only at municipal level. In practice, they are to be found in most municipalities with populations of under 6,000. A single secretariat (*secretariado*) may, in some cases, serve several courts. The peace courts deal with minor cases under both civil and criminal law. Under the latter, they may be delegated to take preventative measures. One of their functions under civil law is to maintain the civil register (*registro civil*) if this has been delegated to them by the appropriate court of first instance in the area (14.7.2).

The peace judges (*jueces de paz*), who preside over these courts for a period of four years, are appointed by the appropriate high court of justice, though the persons likely to be appointed will previously have been elected by an overall majority of the full council of the *ayuntamiento* concerned (8.3.2.1). In some ways, these figures are similar to English magistrates, since they do not have to have a degree in law –

though they must have qualifications that would permit them to embark on such a course. Peace judges receive a regular salary.

14.8 Ministry of Justice (*Ministerio de Justicia*)

14.8.1 Background

Historically, this has always been a separate Ministry. For a brief period, however, between 1994 and 1996, it was merged, for political reasons, with the Ministry of Home Affairs (*Ministerio del Interior*) (6.2.1) to form the Ministry of Justice and Home Affairs (*Ministerio de Justicia e Interior*). This was a situation which José María Aznar pledged, in his election manifesto in 1996, that he would reverse. The PP leader argued that such an arrangement did little to ensure a basic constitutional requirement that the judicial power and the executive be kept completely separate. On the other hand, such a criticism now carries less weight than it would have done during the Franco era when the whole of the court structure and administration of justice depended on the Ministry of Justice (tightly controlled by the executive) and not, as now, by an independent body like the General Council of the Judiciary. Thus, it should be realised that today, at least in theory, the Ministry of Justice is quite separate from the system of administering justice through the courts. This being the case, it is fair to ask what exactly is the role of this ministry and its major component parts.

14.8.2 Structure

Currently, matters relating to justice within this ministry are dealt with by the Secretariat of State for Justice (*Secretaría de Estado de Justicia*), which is responsible for liaising with the whole range of judicial bodies described above and with ensuring that all the legislation in this area serves the interest of protecting fundamental rights. It is also its responsibility to initiate legislation in the whole range of areas related to the administration of justice. This Secretariat includes the General Secretariat for Justice (*Secretaría General de Justicia*), which is concerned with providing human, financial and technological resources for the whole range of judicial bodies, including the Department of the Attorney General of the State or *Ministerio Fiscal* (14.4.3). In addition, it consists of various directorates general, including the Office for Religious Affairs (*Gabinete de Asuntos Religiosos*), the Directorate General for Registers (*Dirección General de los Registros*) (including those of properties and firms), the Directorate General for Conscientious Objection (*Dirección General de Objeción de Conciencia*) (which, among other matters, deals with alternatives to military service), and the Directorate General of the State Legal Service (*Dirección General del Servicio Jurídico del Estado*) (5.9). The latter is composed of several subdirectorates general, including that which provides a legal service relating to the European Commission (15.3.5) and the European Court of Human Rights. In addition, there is a further directorate general which is concerned with international co-operation and, in particular, deals with international agreements involving Spain and with ensuring that Spanish legislation conforms to international law.

Also dependent on the Secretariat of State for Justice is the Centre for Legal Studies of the Administration of Justice (*Centro de Estudios Jurídicos de la Administración de Justicia*). It is an autonomous body with the status of a public law entity (9.4.1). One of its main functions concerns the selection and initial training (both initial and continuous) of members of the public prosecuting corps (*carrera fiscal*), staff in the Secretariat of Justice as a whole and other personnel working within the area of the administration of justice. This Centre has links with appropriate bodies working in justice administration at the level of the autonomous communities.

14.9 Comment

In a wide-ranging survey published to coincide with the twentieth anniversary of the beginning of the democratic transition in November 1995, it is revealed that, of all the major institutions evaluated, the Spanish people hold the judiciary in the lowest esteem – even behind once very controversial institutions such as the armed forces and the Church. Given that, over the last decade at least, substantial reforms have been carried out in the structures and administration of justice, this finding is perhaps rather surprising. However, it has to be recognised that the traditional and apparently endemic slowness of the judicial process in Spain, far from being eradicated, has if anything only been compounded; democracy may have 'cleansed' the institutions of justice but in large measure has so far failed to make them more efficient. To many, the fact that the constitutional commitment to creating a jury system – and thus involving the citizenry in the judicial process – was honoured only seventeen years later was symptomatic of the government's basic indifference to the concept of public participation.

Moreover, in practice the administration of justice in recent years has by no means been free from controversy, thus giving the public further cause for disillusionment. At the lowest level, in the spring of 1995, in Madrid and Granada, groups of candidates entered for the competitive examinations (*oposiciones*) for junior legal assistants (*agentes auxiliares de la administración de justicia*) complained of serious irregularities in the conduct of examinations. A year earlier, the minister of justice was obliged to look into allegations of corruption involving the then vice-president of the General Council of the Judiciary (14.4.2). Most worrying, perhaps, in terms of what it seems to reveal about the Socialist government's attitude to justice is its clumsy attempts to use prominent judges to create a 'clean' image for its administration. Baltasar Garzón was persuaded to stand, albeit as an independent, in the PSOE list for Madrid in the general election of 1993. Within little over a year, however, he had abandoned his junior government post (in the Ministry of Home Affairs) to resume his post in the National Court (14.5.2) and, moreover, to lead the high profile investigation into the involvement of this same ministry in the GAL affair (1.1.5). In relation to this, the PP, with much public support, has promised, if elected, to prevent such a return to the courts within a period of two years. Yet, even the appointment as minister of justice and home affairs of the widely-respected Juan Alberto Belloch, also a judge by profession, was seen by many as a symbolic of a dangerous mingling of political and judicial affairs.*

* Belloch was appointed minister of justice after the election of 1993 and the following year was appointed minister of justice and home affairs when the two ministries were combined (6.2.1).

Chapter 15

Spain and Europe

15.1 Introduction

Economically, Spain has been inextricably bound up with Europe since the early 1960s as the policy of economic self-sufficiency, autarky, gave way to liberalisation and the country began to trade more freely with the outside world (1.1.3). Politically, however, integration was long delayed. Spain's 1962 application to join the then European Economic Community (EEC) as an associate member was ignored by countries which found Franco's political regime unacceptable. The maximum to which the country could aspire – and that albeit with conditions that barely favoured Spain – was a preferential trade agreement signed in 1970. After the dictator's death, however, economic and political integration could follow parallel paths. Pending the outcome of the protracted negotiations on EC entry following the elections of 1977, the country's new democratic credentials were endorsed by her acceptance, as early as October 1977, into the Council of Europe (15.3.9.1). Membership of NATO, while not of course a purely European organisation, also conferred a degree of additional political respectability on Spain and gave her the opportunity to become involved in dialogue with her European neighbours, most of whom were also members. The major economic and foreign policy objective of successive Spanish governments, however, became reality when on 12 June 1985 King Juan Carlos signed the Treaty of Accession in Madrid, thus paving the way for Spanish entry into the European Community (EC) as from 1 January 1986. This date marks an important watershed in the political, economic, social and cultural evolution of Spain.

Following a brief consideration of Spanish attitudes to Europe and official EU policy, this chapter aims to examine the extent of the country's involvement in its key institutions and to explore the range of government and other EU-linked institutions currently operating in Spain. Particular reference will be made to those Spanish institutions which are responsible for the management and distribution of community funding. An important section will briefly examine the financial flows between Spain and the European Union since 1986, and finally reference will be made to Spain's Presidency of the European Union between July and December 1995.

15.2 Attitudes and policy

15.2.1 Spanish attitudes to Europe

In Franco's time, democrats in Spain looked longingly northwards towards a Europe which to them embodied all the ideals which they were denied. Subsequently, this has had important implications for the country's attitude to EU membership. Political imperatives have often seemed to prevail over economic considerations, and may well have affected the terms on which Spain was able to join. Both at the official and popular level, there developed a generally enthusiastic consensus around the desirability of membership. Between 1977 and 1986, popular surveys revealed consistent majority support; all the major national and regional parties favoured integration. While, on the surface, this state of affairs seemed to be entirely desirable, in the long term (and this has already begun to happen) the development of a rather uncritical attitude to membership may well lead to a deeper level of disillusion, and even hostility, at the popular level as economic realities unfold. While monies have poured in from the three EU structural funds, and while Spain seems to have reaped considerable benefit, particularly in terms of infrastructure projects, criticism has tended so far to be muted. However, as transitional arrangements protecting Spanish industry and agriculture have steadily come to an end and as the country has had to compete on even terms with its neighbours, much of the euphoria generated in the 1980s has progressively begun to evaporate.

15.2.2 Spanish policy on Europe

Currently, in spite of severe internal economic and social problems, official policy is whole-hearted commitment to the Union. Under Felipe González, Spain was an enthusiastic signatory of the Single European Act (SEA) in February 1986 and the Treaty of European Union signed at Maastricht in February 1992, fully supporting the Social Chapter so mistrusted by the government of the United Kingdom. Although under intense pressure at times, the peseta has remained within the Exchange Rate Mechanism (ERM). More recently, in March 1995, Spain was one of only seven EU countries to remove all border restrictions under the Schengen Agreement. With regard to the future, the PSOE government supports the policy of economic and monetary union, believing that, although the country will face a painful struggle to meet the five criteria for convergence, a single currency will be in the best long-term interests of the Spanish economy. The PP, however, considers that a single currency is not feasible before 1999. Albeit with some reservations, the country's leaders favour a greater degree of political union, and are happy to see more convergence in matters of foreign policy and defence. Moreover, as one of the original promotors of the idea, Spain strongly supports the idea of European citizenship (*ciudadanía europea*), with a charter of European rights.

The only issue which has seriously divided Spain and her partners – an issue which in the spring of 1995 led to international friction (the dispute with Canada)

– has been the question of fishing rights. Indeed, opposition leaders feel that Spain's negotiators did not fight the case with sufficient vigour, so concerned were they not to 'rock the boat'. Otherwise, the only crack in the edifice of generalised solidarity with Europe appeared in 1994 when EU leaders were discussing arrangements for the inclusion of Austria, Finland and Sweden. Behind Spain's opposition to a change in the rule for majority voting lay a concern that, with the incorporation of these 'northern' members, the balance of power was slipping well away from the southern Mediterranean countries. Hence, too, Spain's determination to hold the Euro–Mediterranean Conference of November 1995 (15.6 and table 15.9, p. 342).

15.3 Spain in EU institutions

Following formal acceptance into the then European Community in January 1986, Spain was eligible for representation in a wide range of community institutions, including the Parliament, the Commission, the Council of Ministers, Court of Justice and Court of Auditors, as well as representation on the European Council which has a distinct status (15.3.3). Full representation in the European Parliament (EP), however, had to await the outcome of a special European level election held only in Spain on 10 June 1987 – although Spain was granted the right to send nominated parliamentary delegates to the European Parliament during the intervening period.

15.3.1 European elections in Spain

In the spring of 1987, the Spanish Parliament approved a bill for the reform of the 1985 General Electoral Law, the LOREG (4.3.1), thus enabling citizens to participate in European elections for the first time. In fact, the reform simply involved the addition of a section (*título*) to this law entitled 'Special arrangements for elections to the European Parliament' (*Disposiciones especiales para elecciones al Parlamento Europeo*). The preceding debate on this move involved little disagreement about the desirability of adopting proportional representation and the D'Hondt system as the method for allocating seats to parties; candidates would stand in blocked and closed lists, as in general, regional or local elections (4.3.1, 7.6.1 and 8.3.2.1). However, considerable divergence of opinion emerged over the question of the most appropriate constituency(ies), with the state level parties led by the PSOE advocating a single constituency (*circunscripción única*) for the whole country – a system, incidentally, also adopted by Denmark, France, Greece, Luxembourg, the Netherlands and Portugal – and the regionalist/nationalist parties like the CiU (10.4.5) favouring the autonomous community. Not surprisingly, the first option won the day.

As this system clearly favoured large parties, a number of small parties, especially regional ones, tended to group together in coalitions formed for the sole purpose of fighting these particular elections. In fact, while seven parties achieved some representation in 1987, this figure increased to eleven in 1989; yet in 1994 only five parties won seats (table 15.1). However, the general pattern has been for the two major

Table 15.1 *European elections in Spain, 1987–94*

Party	1987 Seats	% votes	1989 Seats	% votes	1994 Seats	% votes
PSOE	28	39.1	27	39.6	22	31.1
PP	17	24.2	15	21.4	28	40.6
IU–IC	3	5.2	4	6.1	9	13.0
CiU	3	4.4	2	4.2	3	4.7
Coalición Nacionalista (CN)[a]	1	1.7	1	1.9	2	2.8
Por la Europa de los Pueblos (PEP)[b]	–	–	1	1.5	0	1.3
Foro–CDS	7	10.3	5	7.2	0	1.0
HB	1	1.9	1	1.7	0	1.0
Poder Andaluz (PA/PAP)[c]	–	–	1	1.8	0	0.8
Izquierda de los Pueblos (IP)	–	–	1	1.8	–	–
Agrupación Electoral Ruiz Mateos[d]	–	–	2	3.8	0	0.4
BNG	–	–	0	0.3	0	0.8
Totals	60		60		64	

Notes:

[a] Includes PNV, CC, UV and PAR as well as other minor parties.
[b] Includes EA and ERC, as well as other minor parties.
[c] The 1989 result is for PA only.
[d] A right-wing grouping formed round the person of José-María Ruiz Mateos who was at the centre of the RUMASA scandal of the mid-1980s.
Source: Anuario El País (1995); *Elections to European Parliament 9–12 June 1994*, Eurostat (1994).

parties, the PSOE and the PP, to dominate the electoral scene on all occasions, garnering between them in June 1994 almost 71 per cent of the vote.

It is worth noting that the eligibility rules for MEPs have still not been fully harmonised. On the one hand, the European Parliament Act of 1976 permits them to remain as members of a national Parliament, yet prohibits their occupying other posts within certain EU institutions, such as the Commission and Court of Justice and a post within a national government. On the other hand, national law in many cases still governs eligibility for posts outside Parliament and government. In the case of Spain, for example, while it is not possible for members of the national and regional governments and parliaments to become Euro-MPs, there is nothing in the current legislation to prevent office holders elsewhere in the administration from standing. Indeed, one member of the Spanish Socialist group in Europe is Pedro Aparicio Sánchez who, following election to the European Parliament in June 1994, stayed on in his post as mayor of Málaga (8.3.2.2) until the local elections of May 1995. Ironically his successor, the conservative Celia Villalobos Talero, an MEP since June 1994, decided not to attempt to combine these two onerous duties – although legally she was not debarred from doing so in current Spanish legislation (see Law on Incompatibility in 5.4.6).

In general, the European election results in Spain have reflected the standing of the parties in domestic elections and, indeed, since the European Union did not constitute, until recently, an even remotely controversial issue, elections have tended to be fought on domestic issues, as has been the case in most other countries of the Union. Thus, in 1987, the victorious PSOE was riding the crest of a national wave and, because the newly formed PP had not had time to establish itself under its new leader, Aznar, in June 1989, it won a more convincing victory in the European than in the national elections, in which the ruling party lost its overall majority (1.1.5 and 10.3.1). June 1994, however, appeared to suggest a different voting tendency for Europe, for the PP won 40 per cent of the vote, ten points ahead of the PSOE; in fact, of course, the PSOE's victory of 1993 had been much narrower than any previous triumph, and subsequent scandals and allegations of corruption (1.1.5) had led to a rapid erosion in the standing of the ruling party. Although it might be argued that the increasingly critical attitude of *Izquierda Unida* (IU) (10.3.2) towards the European Union explains its encouraging showing of 13.5 per cent of the vote in 1994, in general it can be said that the European policy of the parties was not a relevant factor in the outcome of any of these elections.

The results of the three European elections hitherto held in Spain are given in table 15.1.

15.3.2 European Parliament (*Parlamento Europeo*)

15.3.2.1 Composition and role

As the Common Assembly of the Iron and Steel Community, the European Parliament traces its history back to 1952. However, direct elections to it were only agreed in 1976 and first implemented in 1979. Currently, leaving aside the delegates nominated by Austria, Finland and Sweden, the Parliament consists of 567 members who are elected by direct universal suffrage for a period of five years, most recently in June 1994. Although the main meeting place of the Parliament is in Strasbourg, members in fact divide their time between this city and Brussels and (to a much lesser extent) Luxembourg. Most plenary sessions are held in Strasbourg, one week out of four, though in recent times there has been a tendency to hold three-day *mini-plenos* in Brussels during certain months of the year. Most committee and political group meetings are held in the Belgian capital where much of the ground-work is completed before final votes are taken in Strasbourg.

The European Parliament is different from national parliaments in that it only shares legislative power with another EU institution, i.e. the Council (15.3.3). Up to the Treaty of Maastricht, its role in this field was largely consultative and, although under the procedure of co-operation it could make amendments to bills, in practice it had no power to block legislation. Since Maastricht, however, it has been able to extend its powers under the so-called assent procedure (*dictamen con-forme*) and, more significantly, under co-decision it has acquired the right to veto legislation in certain fields as well as the right to approve the appointment of the members of the Commission (15.3.5). Effectively, it also has the right to approve the appointment of its president since from a political point of view the opposition of the Parliament to a candidate would be very difficult to defy. These rights were first implemented with the appointment of Jacques Santer and his commissioners in January 1995. Previously the Parliament could only remove the Commission 'en bloc' by a vote of no-confidence.

In addition to legislative powers, the European Parliament has two other functions. Firstly, in budgetary matters, it has the final say over non-compulsory expenditure, which includes the weighty disbursements from the Structural Funds and the Cohesion Fund (15.5.3). Secondly, it exercises certain control powers: for example, the Maastricht Treaty formalised the practice of setting up temporary committees of enquiry to investigate alleged contravention or mismanagement in the institutions of the Union. A further example of control powers is that of the European ombudsman, organically linked to the European Parliament, which will be examined below (15.3.2.5).

15.3.2.2 Spanish representation in the Parliament

Following a transitional period when she was represented in the European Parliament by parliamentary delegates, Spain was first properly represented following the special election of 1987. As a medium to large-sized country, with a population of just under 40 million, she was first allocated sixty Euro-MPs (*eurodiputados*), a figure that was increased to sixty-four for the elections of June 1994. From an early stage, Spaniards have held important posts in the institutions of the European Union; the former Socialist minister, Enrique Barón Crespo, for example, held the post of president of the Parliament for two and a half years between 1989 and 1992. Currently, no less than three Spaniards, out of a total of fourteen, hold the rank of vice-president, including the distinguished lawyer, José María Gil-Robles Gil-Delgado.

A point worth noting is that of Spain's sixty-four MEPs twenty-one (32.8 per cent) are women, a statistic that puts Spain in fourth place after Luxembourg (50 per cent), Denmark (43.8 per cent) and Germany (34.3 per cent), and well ahead of the United Kingdom with 17.2 per cent. The highest percentage of Spanish women are to be found in the IU contingent (44.4 per cent).

15.3.2.3 European political groups

Currently, as can be seen in figure 15.1, following the elections in June 1994, the lion's share of Spain's sixty-four seats went to the PP (twenty-eight), with the PSOE in second place (twenty-two) and IU in third (nine). Ironically, the PSOE belongs to by far the largest group within Parliament, the Party of European Socialists (PSE) which has 221 members (including the three new member countries), while the PP, along with one *eurodiputado* each from CiU and CN, has joined the smaller European Popular Party (PPE), a christian democrat formation, which currently has 173 members. IU forms by far the largest group (nine) within the European Unitary Left (GUE), which has a total of twenty-eight members and consists mainly

Table 15.2 *European parliamentary groups, showing Spanish representation, 1995*

European Party	No. of seats	Spanish member(s)	No. of seats
Party of European Socialists (PSE)[a]	198	PSOE	22
European Popular Party (PPE)	157	PP	28
		CiU	1
		CN	1
European Liberal, Democratic and Reformist Party (ELDR)	43	PSOE	2
European Radical Alliance (ARE)	19	CN	1
European Unitary Left (GUE)	28	IU–IC	9
Forward for Europe (Forza Europa or FE)	27	–	–
European Democratic Alliance (ADE)	26	–	–
Green Party (V)	23	–	–
Europe of Nations (EDN)	19	–	–
Unattached (IN)	27	–	–
Totals	567	–	64

Note:
[a] The acronyms apply to the French names of the parties.
Source: Anuario El País 1995.

of members of European Communist parties. Table 15.2 gives an overall breakdown of all the parliamentary political groups of which Spanish parties are members.

Meetings of the political groups, both the European and national groups, tend to take place in Brussels in the first or second week of the month (except August) allocated for such meetings, but additional ones take place in Strasbourg immediately prior to the *pleno*. In June 1995, for example, the PPE and the PSE held nine individual meetings over a period of four weeks.

In recent times, there has been a tendency among both the PSOE and PP MEPs to vote against the wishes of their respective European groups in defence of certain national interests. This was the case over fishing rights, wine production and bills relating to food additives. It should be realised, however, that there is no 'natural' majority in the European Parliament and that majorities change according to the issue being debated. However, a considerable amount of 'group' discipline exists, particularly on ideological issues.

15.3.2.4 European parliamentary committees

Along with all other *eurodiputados*, the Spanish MEPs divide their time between Strasbourg, Brussels, and (to a lesser extent) Luxembourg, spending the most time in the Belgian capital where most meetings of the parliamentary committees (*comisiones parlamentarias*) are scheduled to take place. Most of their time is spent in meetings either of their own parliamentary (or Spanish) political group or in meetings of the one or more parliamentary committees (out of a total of twenty standing committees) to which they have been delegated. The process of delegation, which is by

Table 15.3 *European parliamentary committees, showing Spanish representation, 1995*

Committee	No. of members	No. of Spanish members
1 Foreign Affairs, Security and Defence Policy	53	4[a]
2 Agriculture and Rural Development	46	4
3 Budgets	34	4
4 Economic and Monetary Affairs and Industrial Policy	51	4[b]
5 Research, Technological Development and Energy	29	2
6 External Economic Relations	25	2
7 Legal Affairs and Citizens' Rights	25	4[b]
8 Social Affairs and Employment	43	3
9 Regional Policy	37	6[b]
10 Transport and Tourism	35	3
11 Environment, Public Health and Consumer Protection	44	3
12 Culture, Youth, Education and the Media	36	5[b]
13 Development and Co-operation	36	4
14 Civil Liberties and Internal Affairs	32	2
15 Budgetary Control	24	2
16 Institutional Affairs	40	6[a,b]
17 Fisheries	23	5
18 Rules of Procedure, Verification of Credentials and Immunities	23	2
19 Women's Rights	36	4
20 Petitions	27	4

Notes:
[a] Includes the Chair.
[b] Includes a Vice-Chair.
Source: Members of Committees and Subcommittees, European Parliament (1995).

no means mechanical, is expected to be 'equitable' and to take into account the relative strength in Parliament of the European political groups, as well as the balance of national groups – though the political complexion of members can in fact carry more weight than nationality in many cases.

In 1995, Spain was represented on all twenty committees, holding the chairs of four committees, including foreign affairs (Abel Matutes Juan – a former PP commissioner), institutional affairs (Fernando Morán López – the former PSOE foreign minister) and the crucial committee on fishing (Miguel Arias Cañete). In addition, six vice-chairs were allocated to Spain. The complete list of committees, giving the number of Spanish members, as well as the total number of members, is given in table 15.3.

In addition, Spanish *eurodiputados* can and do play an important international role as members of the twenty-two interparliamentary delegations (*delegaciones interparlamentarias*) which provide for dialogue between European parliamentarians and their counterparts in other individual or groups of countries outside the European Union (4.5.4). In 1995 Spain had three of the twenty-two chairs and six vice-chairs; not surprisingly, one of the chairs related to Latin America (South America) and two of the vice-chairs belonged to the Central and South American delegation. In recent years, these Latin American committees have acted as Hispanic-world pressure groups, attempting to secure more favourable trading arrangements, as well as EU development aid, for this region.

It is worth noting that since Spain's entry in January 1986, the European Union has made more strenuous efforts to forge stronger political and economic links with the countries of Latin America. The Parliament in particular has been very active in this field and has promoted a bi-annual conference of the European Parliament and the Latin American Parliament; the most recent of these took place in Brussels in June 1995. The latter was the 12th such conference, whose venue alternates between Europe and Latin America.

15.3.2.5 European Ombudsman (Defensor del Pueblo Europeo)

The creation of this post, with a role similar to that of the Spanish ombudsman (2.6), was first envisaged in the Maastricht Treaty of 1992, on the basis of a Spanish initiative. Under article 8d of this Treaty, 'every citizen of the Union may apply to the ombudsman in accordance with Article 138e' which states that 'the European Parliament shall appoint an ombudsman empowered to receive complaints from any citizen of the Union'. The statute of the ombudsman was adopted by the Parliament in March 1994, but disagreement about the method of appointment delayed the creation of this new office until the summer of 1995, when the Parliament voted for a former Finnish ombudsman. The distinguished Spanish jurist, Alvaro Gil-Robles, himself a former ombudsman in Spain, had been a very strong candidate.

The ombudsman serves for the same term as the Parliament, i.e. five years, but is eligible for re-appointment. He may be dismissed by the Court of Justice (15.3.6) at the request of the Parliament 'if he no longer fulfils the conditions required for the performance of his duties or if he is guilty of serious misconduct'.

15.3.3 European Council (*Consejo Europeo*)

In a sense, this body is merely the top tier of the Council of Ministers, out of which it has progressively grown and acquired an almost separate existence. It originated from the practice, started in 1974, of holding regular meetings of heads of state or government of member states; in recent times, the composition has varied: sometimes only the countries' leaders attend, while on other occasions (as in the Cannes summit of June 1995) the respective ministers of foreign and economic affairs are also present. These summits meet normally twice a year, usually in the capital or a major city of the country which at the time holds the presidency of the European Union (15.3.4.5). They are attended by either the president of the Commission or one of his deputies (15.3.5).

15.3.3.1 Role of the European Council

As the highest political body of the Union, the European Council is the sponsor of its major political initiatives. It has also become the principal organ for resolving controversial issues over which the Council of Ministers (15.3.4) has not been able to reach agreement. Moreover, it addresses current international issues through the procedure of European Political Co-operation, involving the diplomatic teams of member countries.

15.3.3.2 Spanish representation on the European Council

In the case of Spain, the representatives on the Council are normally the prime minister (from 1982 to April 1996 Felipe González) and his minister for foreign affairs (*ministro de asuntos exteriores*). In fact, the only countries whose head of state attends – a president with executive powers – are France and Finland.

15.3.4 Council of Ministers (*Consejo de Ministros*)

15.3.4.1 Role and nature of the Council

The European Council and the Council of Ministers are rather different from the Parliament and the Commission in that their principal members, the leaders and ministers of state, spend only a part of their time in the capital cities of the European Union. The government of each members state has only one seat on the Council of Ministers, but Council meetings can take several forms. Who occupies this seat depends entirely on the agenda of the meeting concerned; for example, only the ministers of economy and finance attend the Ecofin Council. By convention rather by statute, the so-called 'councils on general affairs' (*consejos de asuntos generales*), which are attended only by the foreign ministers of each country, tend to deal with the more weighty (often foreign policy and defence) issues and have come to enjoy rather higher *de facto* status. Council meetings are chaired by the minister concerned from the country which holds the presidency (15.3.4.5). For nine months of the year, meetings take place in Brussels, but in April, June and October they are held in Luxembourg. In addition to these normally monthly meetings, one or more Councils of Ministers may also be held in the country occupying the presidency (15.3.4.5; see also table 15.9). Any member state has the right to call a meeting if it considers it necessary. Meetings are always attended by a representative of the Commission (15.3.5).

The Council of Ministers is the principal decision-making body of the European Union and, after the European Council (to which it is organically linked), it constitutes the major political organ of the Community. It is in the Council where the particular interests of member countries are harmonised with those of the Union as a whole. Above all, however, the Council is the principal EU legislative institution, albeit sharing such powers, as we have seen (15.3.2) with the Parliament; it is the Council which decides to adopt or reject legislation emanating from the Commission (15.3.5).

15.3.4.2 Spanish Permanent Representation (Representación Permanente de España)

The permanent representations of the fifteen member countries, whose offices are located in Brussels, constitute (and in some cases are known as) their embassies in the European Union. Thus, all the high ranking staff are diplomats who, though based full-time in Europe, remain attached, organically and financially, to the ministry of foreign affairs of their home country. Each Representation is headed by either the ambassador (*embajador*) or by the permanent representative (*representante permanente*), who is assisted by a deputy permanent representative (*representante permanente adjunto*) and other high ranking diplomats, some of whom are known, rather pompously, as 'minister plenipotenciary' (*ministro plenipotenciario*). In addition to these employees of member governments, the Council has a General Secretariat (*Secretaría General*) which, as we shall see (15.3.4.4), consists of several hundred civil servants who are employees of the Community institutions.

Including the permanent representative and his deputy, also known as *ministro plenipotenciario*, the Spanish delegation currently comprises a total of fifty-nine diplomats. Of these, thirteen are attached to the Ministry of Foreign Affairs, including the two further plenipotenciary ministers, ten advisers (*consejeros*) and a first secretary (*primer secretario de embajada*). These constitute the diplomatic staff. The remaining staff belong to nine (formerly thirteen) departments and tend to be qualified and/or have expertise in specific areas; for example, there are departments of customs affairs (*asuntos aduaneros*), economic and commercial (*asuntos económicos y comerciales*) (the largest department), agricultural and fishing affairs (*asuntos agrícolas y pesqueros*) and industrial and energy affairs (*asuntos industriales y energéticos*). These departments are not to be confused with those of the General Secretariat to be examined below (15.3.4.4).

15.3.4.3 Council of Permanent Representatives (Comité de Representantes Permanentes/COREPER)

This committee works at two levels, COREPER II and COREPER I. The main function of both levels is to prepare the meetings for the Council of Ministers. The former consists of the ambassadors or permanent representatives of each member state and the latter of their deputies. COREPER II deals mainly with political and external affairs, economic and financial matters, as well as the 'new' areas covered by the Maastricht Treaty, namely home and justice affairs, and foreign and security policy. COREPER I, on the other hand, is concerned with the technical side of all the other Councils' work, such as agriculture, environment and trade. Both groups have set up a large number of ad hoc working parties with expertise in particular fields. Since Maastricht, for example, COREPER II has established two important sub-committees which prepare the work relating to justice and home affairs (the Political Committee) and foreign affairs and security (K4). At least 100 others, however, may exist at any one time.

15.3.4.4 General Secretariat of the Council (Secretaría General del Consejo)

This Secretariat, which comprises some 2000 Council officials who work for the Community, provides a permanent administrative, as well as advisory and consultancy service, to the Council of Ministers and in particular to the Presidency (15.3.4.5). It is presided over by the secretary general (*secretario general*), who is appointed by the Council. As well as the legal service (*servicio jurídico*) and translating department, it contains eight directorates general (*direcciones generales*) A–H, each divided into two, three or four sections. In 1995, Spain had two legal counsellors (*consejeros jurídicos*) and one director in DG–D dealing with research policy, as well as the European scientific and technical research programme, COST. In addition, there was an experienced Spanish diplomat, Francisco Fernández Fábregas, in charge of the directorate general with responsibility for inter-institutional affairs (relations with the European Parliament, for example), budgetary matters, staffing and information; the latter is the part of the directorate which deals with all the official publications of the Council.

15.3.4.5 Presidency (Presidencia)

The Presidency of the Council is held by each member state for six months on a rotational basis. The alphabetical order of rotation was reversed in 1993 to prevent one country from presiding over the Council during the same six-month period as its previous term. The Presidency's role is to determine the priorities of the Council, set the agenda for the six-month period of office and elect the necessary working groups. Hence, the country concerned can accrue considerable political influence at this time. Spain held the Presidency for the second half of 1995, having previously done so in the first half of 1989. There is little doubt that the main reason why Felipe González refused to bow to pressure to call early elections during this time was precisely because he did not wish to lose this prestigious opportunity to wield power at the European level.

The basic structure of the Council and its component parts is given in figure 15.1.

15.3.5 European Commission (*Comisión Europea*)

15.3.5.1 Nature and role

This executive and administrative arm of the Union is based in Brussels and Luxembourg. At the highest level, it consists of the commissioners (*comisarios*) nominated by each national government; these constitute the apex of a complex bureaucracy employing over 16,000 civil servants (*funcionarios*) who work exclusively for the Community. The Commission, by far the largest of the five EU institutions, is the source of all legislation relevant to the European Union. The initiation of legislation, a power which it exercises uniquely, is the principal function of the Commission – though it is also responsible for executing legislation and for super-

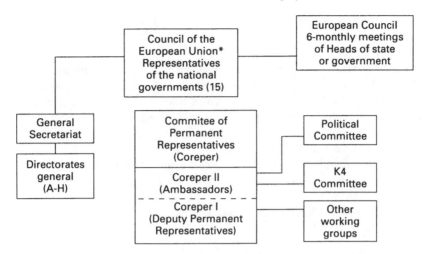

Figure 15.1 *Basic structure of European Council/Council of Ministers, 1995*

vising its implementation. In practice, legislation tends to originate from the commissioners, who request that the appropriate directorate general of the Commission (15.3.5.2) prepare a draft law, a process which involves consultation with all other relevant directorates. It should be stressed that the Commission is an independent and objective body working solely for the European Union and with no national axe to grind.

15.3.5.2 Commissioners (comisarios)

Although the Commission is the whole of the large organisation referred to above, the term is often used to refer solely to the executive tier. This consists of the twenty commissioners nominated by each of the fifteen national governments, who collectively make up what is sometimes called the College of Commissioners (*Colegio de Comisarios*). The number allocated to each country, as with the number of MEPs, is related to its population; each country has a minimum of one and a maximum of two. Member governments must nominate candidates according to internal political criteria, the main one being the balance between the parties in each national parliament.

Currently, Spain has two commissioners, Marcelino Oreja, a leading member of the PP, and Manuel Marín, of the PSOE, both of whom had previously played key roles in the long negotiations leading to Spanish entry. (Marín has now in fact been a commissioner for over a decade.) Like Marín, all the other commissioners hold two or more portfolios, each of which roughly corresponds to one of the directorates general or one of its departments. Currently, Spain's other commissioner, Marcelino Oreja, a former UCD foreign minister, is responsible for relations with the European Parliament, relations with member states (in matters concerning open government, information and communication), cultural and audio-visual affairs and institutional affairs (*asuntos institucionales*). Wearing the latter hat, Oreja is currently playing a vital role in the preparation of the all-important 1996 Intergovernmental Conference/(IGC).

Since the Treaty of Maastricht came into force in 1993, the Commission has been renewed every five years, within six months of the European elections, instead of the four years required previously. This change was introduced to allow the newly elected MEPs to have a say over the nominations for president and members of the Commission, one of the ways in which an attempt has recently been made to strengthen the role of the Parliament.

As we have already seen, co-ordination of the work of the Commission with that of other major institutions is attempted through the attendance of commissioners or representatives of the Commission at, for example, the Parliament (15.3.2), European Council (15.3.3) and the Council of Ministers (15.3.4).

15.3.5.3 President of the Commission

The Commission is headed by a president (*presidente*) who has to be acceptable to all the member governments and tends to rotate from one country to another, although this is not a requirement. He or she does not have to have served previously as a member of the Commission, but is normally a highly experienced, top-ranking present or former member of a national government with experience in European affairs. As already stated (15.3.2.1), the Parliament now effectively has the right to approve the appointment of the president, as well as the commissioners; likewise, the Parliament, to which the Commission leadership is ultimately responsible, has the right to force the latter to resign by approving a censure motion with an overall majority of members and two-thirds of the votes. Thus far, no Spaniard has held this high office, although Felipe González's name has in the past been mentioned on more than one occasion.

The president is assisted in his duties by two vice-presidents (*vicepresidentes*), both drawn from the group of commissioners. One of these is the PSOE veteran Manuel Marín, who also holds the portfolios of external relations with the Southern Mediterranean, the Middle and Far East, and Latin America (*relaciones exteriores con el Mediterráneo Sur, Medio y Extremo Oriente y América Latina*). Currently, the second vice-president is one of the two UK commissioners, Sir Leon Brittan.

The president and each of the commissioners are assisted by a small team of personal advisers, secretaries and administrators. Each of these offices (*gabinetes*) is headed by a chef de cabinet (*jefe de gabinete*) and tends to be staffed, though not exclusively, by people from the same country as the commissioner.

15.3.5.4 Basic structure

The structure of the European Commission is shown in a simplified form in figure 15.2. It is divided basically into the executive or policy-making arm which consists of the president and the commissioners aided by a General Secretariat (*Secretaría*

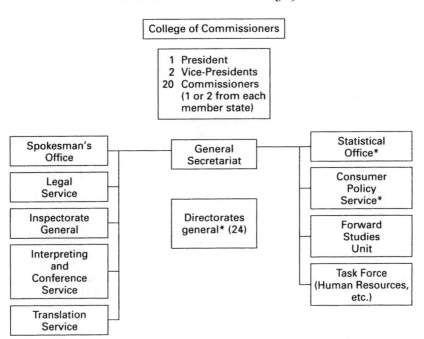

* Report to a specific Commissioner.

Figure 15.2 *Basic structure of European Commission, 1995*

General) (see below) and the administrative arm composed of the twenty-three directorates general (*direcciones generales*), each of which constitute what is effectively a government department, with its own staff of civil servants drawn from all the member countries and appointed principally on the basis of success in approved Community entrance examinations. In addition, the Commission has at its disposal a wide range of support services, some of which, like the legal service and the translating and interpreting department, actually employ more staff than some directorates general.

The directorates general vary considerably in size, but their internal structures tend to be similar. Each is headed by a director general (*director general*), who is effectively a political appointment, for which there is strong competition between the member states; he is assisted by one or more assistant director generals (*directores generales adjuntos*), which also tend to be political appointments, and advisers (*consejeros*), as well as by an administrative unit (*unidad administrativa*) providing technical and secretarial back-up. The major division of the directorate general, indicated by Roman numerals (I–XXIV) is the directorate (*dirección*), indicated by letters of the alphabet (A–F, for example). The number of these varies considerably, from the eleven in External Economic Relations (*Relaciones Económicas Exteriores*) to the three in Staffing and Administration (*Personal y Administración*). A

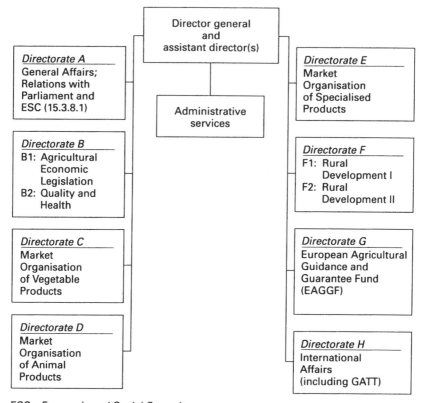

Director general
and
assistant director(s)

Administrative
services

Directorate A
General Affairs;
Relations with
Parliament and
ESC (15.3.8.1)

Directorate B
B1: Agricultural
Economic
Legislation
B2: Quality and
Health

Directorate C
Market
Organisation
of Vegetable
Products

Directorate D
Market
Organisation
of Animal
Products

Directorate E
Market
Organisation
of Specialised
Products

Directorate F
F1: Rural
Development I
F2: Rural
Development II

Directorate G
European Agricultural
Guidance and
Guarantee Fund
(EAGGF)

Directorate H
International
Affairs
(including GATT)

ESC = Economic and Social Commitee

Figure 15.3 *Directorate General of Agriculture, 1995*

breakdown of the structure of Directorate General VI, Agriculture, is given in figure 15.3.

In addition to the directorates general, the Commission includes a number of vital support services, some of which work exclusively for the president and his immediate staff, and others which are at the disposal of staff in all departments. The first group of Directorates includes:

- General Secretariat of the Commission (*Secretaría General de la Comisión*) which, as well as an executive group headed by the general secretary and an administrative unit, is divided into seven directorates (A–G), one of which, responsible for relations with the Council of Ministers, is headed by a Spaniard, Manuel Santarelli.
- Forward Studies Unit (*Célula de Prospectiva*)
- Inspectorate General (*Inspección General de Servicios*), headed by a Spaniard.

The second group includes:

- Legal Service (*Servicio Jurídico*)
- Statistical Office (*Oficina Estadística*), in which the directorate concerned with public relations and computerised statistics is headed by a Spaniard, as is that devoted to social/regional statistics and structural plans.
- Joint Interpreting and Conference Service (*Servicio Común de Interpretación y Conferencias*); this service has a general department which, among other things, offers advanced training in interpreting for graduates, one department which assists in the organisation of conferences, conventions, etc. and another which provides an interpreting service for staff of the Commission concerned with the organisation of conferences, conventions, etc. This is not to be confused with the (much larger) translation service (*servicio de traducción*), partly located in Brussels and partly in Luxembourg, which is offered, like the interpreting service, in the eleven official languages of the European Union; in this case, translators who specialise in a particular field or fields are grouped together in a total of seven directorates, including one for agriculture, fishing, regional policy and structural policies and another which deals with technology, energy, environment and consumer affairs.

15.3.5.5 Spanish representation in the Commission

Since January 1986, the Spanish presence within the bureaucracy of the Commission has been steadily increasing, as was to be expected. On the other hand, out of the total allocation granted to Spain as long ago as 1986, so far only some 900 posts have been taken up. Spaniards now currently hold over fifty posts at the level of head of unit upwards, including the posts of head of the Directorate General of Fishing, head of the Directorate General of Regional Policies and the directorates of Intervention in Underdeveloped Areas, National Economies, Competition Policies and Customs, and Relations with the Countries of non-EU Europe and the Commonwealth of Independent States (CIS). In addition, it is perhaps not surprising to find that there is a strong Spanish presence, including the director himself, in the department devoted to Latin America, within the Directorate General of External Economic Relations (*Relaciones Económicas Exteriores*) (table 15.4).

Some posts do not figure high up in the hierarchy but nevertheless represent very important functions within the Commission. One such post is that currently occupied by the Catalan Spaniard, Anna Melich, who is head of the unit in charge of monitoring public opinion (*seguimiento de tendencias de la opinión pública*), located within the Directorate General of Information, Communication and Culture (*Información, Comunicación y Cultura*). The findings of this unit – the result of on-the-spot surveys in member countries – are published in the influential six-monthly *Eurobarometer*. Following events like the result of the first Danish referendum on Maastricht and later the Norwegian rejection of integration, the Commission is determined not to be taken by surprise again; hence, it takes public opinion

Table 15.4 *Directorates General of European Commission, showing number of Spanish posts at senior levels, 1994*

DG	Name in English	Name in Spanish	Director generals	Directors	Heads of unit
1	External Economic Relations	*Relaciones Económicas Exteriors*	1[a]	1	3
1A	External Policies	*Políticas Exteriores*	0	0	1
2	Economic and Financial Affairs	*Asuntos Económicos y Financieros*		2	2
3	Industry	*Industria*	0	1	1
4	Competition	*Competencia*	0	2	1
5	Employment, Labour Relations and Social Affairs	*Empleo, Relaciones Laborales y Asuntos Sociales*	0	2	1
6	Agriculture	*Agricultura*	1[b]	2	3
7	Transport	*Transportes*	0	0	2
8	Development	*Desarrollo*	0	0	3
9	Personnel and Administration	*Personal y Administración*	0	0	2
10	Audio-Visual Affairs, Information, Communication and Culture	*Sector audio-visual, Información, Comunicación y Cultura*	0	0	1
11	Environment, Nuclear Safety and Civil Protection	*Medio Ambiente, Seguridad Nuclear y Protección Civil*	0	0	2
12	Science, Research and Development	*Ciencia, Investigación y Desarrollo*	0	1	1
13	Telecommunications, Information Industries and Innovation	*Telecomunicaciones, Industrias de Información e Innovación*	1[b]	0	4
14	Fishing	*Pesca*	1	1	0
15	Internal Market and Financial Services	*Mercado Interior y Servicios Financieros*	0	0	1
16	Regional Policies	*Políticas Regionales*	1	1	2
17	Energy	*Energía*	0	1	1
18	Credit and Investment	*Crédito e Inversiones*	0	0	1
19	Budgets	*Presupuestos*	0	0	1
20	Financial Control	*Control Financiero*	0	0	2[c]
21	Customs Union and Indirect Taxes	*Unión Aduanera e Impuestos Indirectos*		0	1
22	Business Policy, Commerce, Tourism and Social Economy	*Política Empresa, Comercio, Turismo y Economía Social*	0	0	0

Notes:
[a] Under the director general, Juan Prat has a special portfolio, with the rank of director general, responsible for North–South relations, Mediterranean policy and relations with Latin America and Asia.
[b] These are posts at the level of assistant director general (*director general adjunto*).
[c] This person is head of the unit which administers the EAGGF fund.
Source: Cargos en el Poder, Vol. III, Boletín Mensual, Madrid: Ediciones Carposa (1994).

throughout the European Union very seriously. Another function of this unit is to monitor the European press; as a result of such work, detailed monthly reports on the political situation in each member state are presented to Marcelino Oreja.

Another person who has a direct (and indeed much more frequent) line to Sr Oreja is Francisco Fonseca Morillo, one of only three expert advisers (*consejeros*) on the Task Force set up in the General Secretariat at the beginning of 1995 to co-ordinate negotiating positions prior to the Intergovernmental Conference (IGC) of 1996. Sr Fonseca, previously an adviser to Jacques Delors and a former director general of Budgetary Affairs, is an expert in Community law. He works under the Task Force director in collaboration with his two adviser colleagues and with the assistance of two civil servants also qualified in EU law.

Currently, however, the most influential Spaniard, apart from the two commissioners, is the former secretary of state for EU affairs, Carlos Westerndorp (subsequently Minister for Foreign Affairs), who is in charge of the fifteen-strong Reflexion Group (*Grupo de Reflexión*), whose task is to prepare the ground for the IGC.

Table 15.4 gives a list of all the directorates general of the Commission, with their names in Spanish, and indicates how many Spanish officials hold office at the level of head of unit or above.

15.3.6 Court of Justice of the European Union (*Tribunal de Justicia de la Unión Europea*)

This increasingly important institution of the Union, which is based in Luxembourg, is concerned to ensure the correct interpretation and application of the provisions of Community law. It has the right to consider the legal validity of acts of the Council and the Commission and may issue judgements on actions by these and by member states on, for example, grounds of incompetence or infringement of the Treaties. In addition, the Court has the right to give preliminary opinions on the applicability of draft international agreements with Community law. An individual citizen of the European Union may appeal against a Community decision that affects him; likewise, Community institutions, national courts and member states may bring cases before the Court. It should be noted that judgements of the Court are binding in each member state.

Currently, the Court of Justice, composed of one judge per member country (i.e. a total of fifteen) is presided over by an eminent Spanish jurist, Gil Carlos Rodríguez Iglesias. The judges are nominated by the respective national governments from among their most distinguished and experienced jurists. They are appointed in a staggered process every three years, seven or eight of the judges being appointed for six years for a renewable term of six years. The president is elected for a renewable term of three years from among the members of the Court.

The Single European Act (SEA) of 1986 provided for the creation of a European Court of First Instance. This Court, established the following year, also in Luxembourg, serves the purpose of relieving the Court of Justice of its increasing work-load and of improving the judicial protection of individual interests in the

Community. Each of the member states nominates a judge to serve for a term of six years, though membership is partially renewed every three years, as with the Court of Justice.

15.3.7 Court of Auditors of the European Union (*Tribunal de Cuentas de la Unión Europea*)

This Court is also situated in Luxembourg. It is an independent body consisting of fifteen auditors, one from each country, who are appointed for a six-year term by agreement of all member countries. Its principal task is to examine the accounts of the Community institutions as well as those of other administrations involved in the management of Community funds and to ensure that all revenue has been received and expenditure legally incurred. Since Maastricht, which raised its status from a body to an institution (see below), the Court has been required to provide the European Parliament and Council with an annual report conforming the reliability of all EU accounts and the legality of all related transactions.

As well as a secretariat, the Court is composed of three audit groups, each dealing with a different group of activities, areas or Community funds. Currently, the Spaniard Marcelino Cuesta de la Fuente occupies the important post of financial controller within the secretariat.

15.3.8 Other EU bodies

Technically, only the Parliament, Council, Commission, Court of Justice and the Court of Auditors comprise the institutions (*instituciones*) of the European Union. Other organisations may aspire to this status, but currently are regarded as no more than bodies or organs (*organismos*), most of which have only a consultative nature.

15.3.8.1 Economic and Social Committee (ESC) (Comité Económico y Social / CES)

This large organisation, located in Brussels, was established by the Treaty of Rome in 1957 as a consultative body for the EU institutions. Its influence has been strengthened over time, particularly by the SEA and the Maastricht Treaty. Its main task is to ensure that the major economic and social groups of all the member countries have a forum in which they can express their views to the Council, Commission and Parliament. In certain areas (whose scope has increased in recent years) consultation by the Council and Commission is mandatory (*preceptivo*); these include agricultural affairs, movement of labour, social policy, the European Social Fund, economic and social cohesion, vocational training, research and technological development. Since 1974, the ESC has also been able to issue Opinions on its own initiative; some recent examples of these are: growth, competitiveness and employment (October 1993) and supplier–consumer dialogue (November 1993). Currently, the ESC is pressing for institutional status, as well as an extension to the areas over which it is consulted.

The ESC is composed of 222 members from all member states proposed by the latter and approved by the Committee for a term of four years (renewable). The number allocated is related to the population of each country; Spain currently has twenty-one members. Committee members are drawn from a wide range of interest groups and in the ESC form three basic groups: (i) employers; (ii) unions; and (iii) various activities. The latter includes such sectors as agriculture, transport, the liberal professions, consumer groups and ecological interests. The Committee meets once a month in a plenary session that lasts two days. The president of the ESC, who serves for a term of two years, and is assisted by two vice-presidents, rotates from one group to another and (less formally) from one country to another. The current president, serving from October 1994 to October 1996, is the well-known Spanish entrepreneur, Carlos Ferrer Salat. The president, vice-presidents and thirty members elected by the Committee form the ESC Presiding Council or Bureau (*Mesa*); this constitutes the decision-making tier of the Committee, which is divided into nine sections and numerous ad hoc study groups. In addition, the ESC has a general secretariat headed by a general secretary; this represents the ESC's bureaucracy, which is divided into two directorates and employs over 500 permanent staff, half of whom are involved in some form of language work.

Of the twenty-one Spanish members of the Committee, there are three from the UGT trade union (11.4.1), one from *Comisiones Obreras* (11.4.2) and one from the SEAT car-manufacturing company based in Barcelona.

15.3.8.2 Committee of the Regions (Comité de las Regiones)

This is a relative newcomer to the scene, having been set up as recently as 1994 following a recommendation in the Maastricht Treaty (article 36) which urged a strengthening of the role of the regions in the Union. The initiative came largely from those member states which have a strongly regionalised structure (Belgium, Germany and Spain) and does not have the whole-hearted support of several other countries which do not want to see an erosion of the concept of the European Union as a 'community of member states'. Like the ESC, the Committee of the Regions, also based in Brussels, has only advisory status. Currently, the areas where it must be consulted are: economic and social cohesion; trans-European networks; public health; culture; education and training; regulations on the framework and co-ordination of structural funds; and the implementation of the European Regional Development Fund (ERDF). In addition, the Committee has a right to make its views known on any issue which it considers to have special regional implications. In April 1994, one of the first acts of the Committee was to adopt unanimously its first opinion on the proposal for a regulation establishing the Cohesion Fund.

Like the ESC, the Committee of the Regions is composed of 222 members, drawn from the member countries in the same proportions as the former. Members are delegated for a period of four years by member states, some of which, like the United Kingdom, insist that those nominated should already hold a democractic mandate within local government at the time of their nomination – though it is not a requirement of the European Union. In the case of Spain, seventeen of its twenty-one members are the presidents of the autonomous communities (7.6.2) who, as it happens, have also been democratically elected in regional elections. The other Spanish members are mayors of Madrid, Barcelona and two other large Spanish cities, who have been democratically elected in local elections (8.3.2.2). The Committee has a president, elected by the members for a period of two years, assisted by a vice-president, who is currently the high-profile mayor of Barcelona, Pasqual Maragall. Otherwise, the structure of the Committee is very similar to that of the ESC, with a Presiding Council (also elected for two years) and Permanent Secretariat.

Unlike the United Kingdom which (perhaps significantly) nominates mostly little-known local councillors to the Committee, Spain is an enthusiastic supporter. The regional presidents attend meetings of the Committee assiduously and, for other reasons, are frequent visitors to Brussels, where their interests are looked after by the Spanish Permanent Representation (15.3.4.2). One of the strongest Spanish voices in the Committee is the Catalan president, Jordi Pujol, who in fact has argued for the creation of two chambers of the Committee (one for the regions and one for the municipalities) in order to overcome existing disparities and divergence of interests.

15.3.8.3 European Investment Bank (EIB) (Banco Europeo de Inversiones/BEI)

This autonomous public financial body within the Union, based in Luxembourg, was created by the Treaty of Rome and its status was enhanced by the Treaty of Maastricht, which strengthened its role in promoting economic and social cohesion. In addition to providing aid to twelve Mediterranean countries and sixty-nine African, Caribbean and Pacific countries, the Bank's principal task is to 'contribute to the balanced development of the Community'. Operating on a non-profit basis, it makes long- and medium-term loans and guarantees to help finance investment projects which contribute to one or more of seven objectives. The latter include: the economic development of the Union's less privileged regions; improved transport and telecommunications infrastructure; urban development; environmental protection; and supporting the activities of small and medium-sized enterprises. In the period 1987–91, 94.4 per cent of disbursements involved loans within the European Union. The major divisions of the EIB are the Board of Governors (*Junta de Rectores*), the Board of Directors (*Consejo de Administración*), the Management Committee (*Comisión Rectora*) and the Audit Committee (*Comisión de Auditores*). The Board of Governors consists of fifteen ministers, usually the finance ministers, designated by the member states; its main tasks are to lay down general directives on credit policy, to approve the balance sheet and annual report, and to appoint members of the other three bodies. The Board of Directors has twenty-one members, one of whom is appointed by the Commission and the rest, on a proportional basis, by the member states; it has responsibility for deciding on loans and guarantees, raising funds and fixing lending rates. The Management Committee, which consists of a president and six vice-presidents, controls all current operations, recommends decisions to directors and is then responsible for carrying them out. The Audit Committee verifies that the operations of the Bank and the audit process have been conducted in the proper manner.

Currently, Spain's representation in the Bank is limited to the minister of economy and finance on the Board of Governors (Rodrigo Rato), two members of the Board of Directors, including the president of the Official Credit Institute (13.4), one member of the Management Committee (the present adviser to Sr Solbes) and one member of the Audit Committee.

A point that should be stressed is that the EIB deals with all reimbursable aid from the Union; it has become, in fact, the sole provider for loans (*préstamos*). All aid from the Commission, on the other hand, including disbursements from the three Structural Funds and the Cohesion Fund, is given in the form of grants (*subvenciones*).

15.3.9 Non-EU European institutions

15.3.9.1 Council of Europe (Consejo de Europa)

This institution, the first European-wide political organisation to be set up after the Second World War, was founded in 1949 with the aim of fostering greater unity among the peoples and nations of Europe. Its headquarters are in Strasbourg where it normally meets, but it also has an office in Brussels. Its aims are to promote greater European co-operation, to improve living conditions and develop human values, to uphold the principles of parliamentary democracy and to protect human rights. In fact, its activities cover all aspects of European affairs except defence. Currently, the Council consists of thirty-two member states, including Spain which was admitted in 1977. The main organs of the Council are the Committee of Ministers (*Comité de Ministros*) and the Parliamentary Assembly (*Asamblea Parlamentaria*). The former consists of the foreign ministers of the member states, each state holding the presidency for a period of six months. The Spanish representative held this post in the latter half of 1980. Sessions are held twice a year, although between these the ministers' deputies (permanent representatives to the Council) hold about twelve meetings a year. The Assembly comprises 248 representatives and 248 substitutes who are elected or appointed by their national parliaments. The number of national representatives is linked to the size of their respective populations. Meeting three times a year, it addresses only recommendations to the Committee of Ministers. The president is elected on a one-year renewable term (for a maximum of three years); the Spaniard Miguel Angel Martínez held this post between May 1992 and May 1993 and currently is once again the incumbent.

Human rights is an area in which the Council has been very active in recent years. Both the European Court of Human Rights (*Tribunal Europeo de Derechos Humanos*) and the European Commission of Human Rights (*Comisión Europea de Derechos Humanos*) were set up by the European Convention on Human Rights signed in

Rome in 1950. Spain subscribed to this Convention only after democracy had been restored, in October 1979.

On several occasions in recent years, Felipe González has used the meetings of the Council, notably the Assembly, to reach a wider European audience for conveying his views on such trans-national issues as drug-trafficking and political asylum.

15.3.9.2 Western European Union (WEU) (Unión de Europa Occidental/UEO)

The Western European Union was formed in 1954 as an inter-governmental organisation for European security co-operation. The Western European Union aims to maintain an ongoing dialogue among member countries in order to arrive at common positions on security–military issues. Currently, its members are: Belgium, France, Germany, Greece, Italy, Luxembourg, the Netherlands, Portugal, the United Kingdom and Spain, which was admitted in 1982. In 1992, Denmark and Ireland were admitted with observer status and Norway, Turkey and Iceland became associate members. At the Maastricht summit of December 1991, it was decided that the Western European Union would be developed as the defence element of the European Union and as the vehicle for strengthening the European pillar of the Atlantic Alliance.

In January 1993, the Intergovernmental Secretariat, previously based in London, was set up in Brussels with the main aim of providing closer links between the Western European Union and the European Union. This operates at two levels: (i) the Permanent Council consisting of ambassadors from all member states and (ii) the WEU Council consisting of the ministers of defence and foreign affairs of the countries concerned. The former meets with the Secretariat located in Brussels every three weeks and the Council meets twice a year. In addition, there is a Parliamentary Assembly consisting of 108 members and 108 substitute members from national parliamentary delegations to the Council of Europe (15.3.9.1) which meets in plenary session twice a year. Currently, there are twelve Spaniards in this Assembly; this compares with eighteen members each for the United Kingdom, France, Germany and Italy, and seven each for smaller states like Portugal, Belgium and Luxembourg.

15.4 EU-linked institutions in Spain

Well before Spain's official entry into the European Union, a wide range of public sector institutions were being set up in anticipation of full membership. These can be divided into two broad groups: (i) those located within departments of central and regional governments, as well as local administration; and (ii) those providing information about EU institutions, programmes and funding and sometimes representing the interests of EU institutions in Spain. In addition, one parliamentary body, the Joint Committee (15.4.1), plays an important role.

15.4.1 Joint Committee for the European Union (*Comisión Mixta para la Unión Europea*)

This committee is the successor to the Joint Committee for the European Communities, whose name (and, to some extent, its functions) was changed by a law published on 19 May 1994 following Spain's approval in Parliament of the Treaty of European Union (Maastricht). It is composed of an equal number of Congress deputies and senators, and also reflects the relative strength of the political groups within the two Chambers. This Committee is the only parliamentary body which has direct and regular links with the European Parliament (15.3.2), and hence it plays a vital role in ensuring that the *Cortes* are kept informed of activities and developments in the Parliament. Among the rights granted to the Committee are the following:

(i)   to receive, via the government, legislation proposals emanating from the European Parliament in sufficient time to be properly informed or to examine such proposals

(ii) to request a full debate on such proposals if it should consider them necessary

(iii) to request the appearance of a government member before the Committee to inform it of the outcome of bills approved by the European Council of Ministers

(iv) to be informed by the government about the general lines of its European policy

(v)   to draft reports on matters relating to the European Union, especially those under (ii) above

(vi) to establish links of co-operation with their counterparts in the parliaments of other members of the Union.

The Joint Committee also participates in the twice-yearly meetings of the Conference of Bodies specialising in European Community Affairs, known by its French acronym COSAC; these meetings are normally held in the country which holds the EU Presidency. COSAC first met in November 1989 and is convened by the parliament of that country to debate matters relating to European integration. Since 1981 there have also been regular meetings (every six months in practice) at the invitation of the country holding the Presidency between the president of the European Parliament and the presidents/speakers of the national parliaments. The purpose of these meetings is to review the network of relations among parliaments and to suggest ways in which links can be improved.

15.4.2 Central government departments

Although nearly all the ministries have areas or units (very often directorates general) dealing exclusively with European affairs, by far the greatest number in central government are located, perhaps not too surprisingly, within the Ministry of Foreign Affairs.

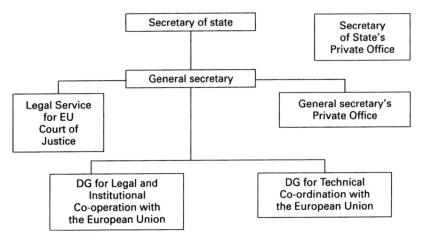

DG = Directorate General.

Figure 15.4 *Simplified structure of Secretariat of State for the European Union, 1995*

15.4.2.1 Ministry of Foreign Affairs (Ministerio de Asuntos Exteriores)

This Ministry formulates Spain's negotiating position *vis-à-vis* the European Union and, by holding meetings with other ministries, seeks to ensure that no single ministry defends its own interests rather than the interests of the country as a whole. The department within this Ministry dealing exclusively with European affairs is the Secretariat of State for the European Union (*Secretaría de Estado para la Unión Europea*) which in fact was established as long ago as February 1981, long before negotiations for entry had been concluded. A simplified structure diagram of this Secretariat is provided in figure 15.4. As can be seen, the secretary of state is assisted by a general secretary to whom in the first place the two directors general are responsible. Unusually for a government department (6.2.2), there is an extra tier between the general secretariat and the directorates general, thus reflecting the importance of this area of government: as well as the general secretary's private office (*gabinete*) of expert advisers, there is the State Legal Service for the Court of Justice of the European Union (*Servicio Jurídico del Estado ante el Tribunal de Justicia de la Unión Europea*) (15.3.6).

The Directorate General for Technical Co-ordination in European Affairs (*Dirección General de Coordinación Técnica Comunitaria*) deals with internal policy, including more technical, economic matters, while the Directorate General for EU Legal and Institutional Affairs (*Dirección General de Coordinación Jurídica e Institucional Comunitaria*) is concerned with external, more political affairs, including the interpretation of EU legislation.

15.4.2.2 Ministry of Economy and Finance (Ministerio de Economía y Hacienda)

After Foreign Affairs, this is the Ministry (13.2) which has most involvement in EU affairs. One of its main tasks is to prepare the draft state budget bill (*proyecto de ley de los presupuestos generales del estado*) in which are always included the flows of money from Spain to the European Union and vice-versa (15.5). This Ministry, moreover, is the general co-ordinating agency for all EU structural funds and initiatives. More specifically, it administers receipts from several (though by no means all) of these funds.

By far the most important of the latter is the European Regional Development Fund (ERDF), known in Spanish as *Fondo Europeo de Desarrollo Regional (FEDER)*. The department dealing with this fund is the Subdirectorate General for Management and Administration (*Subdirección General de Gestión y Administración*) which is a division of the Directorate General for Planning (*Dirección General de Planificación*). In turn, this Directorate is responsible to the General Secretariat for Planning and Budgets (*Secretaría General de Planificación y Presupuestos*).

Among the EU initiatives handled by this ministry are:

(i)   RECHAR: This initiative provides aid for the declining coal-mining areas of the Union. The areas to have benefited in Spain are Asturias, Catalonia, León–Valencia and Teruel–Zaragoza.
(ii)   STRIDE: This initiative is designed to increase capacity of innovation and technological development in less favoured areas or areas of industrial decline.
(iii) ENVIREG: This initiative aims to improve the environment and promote economic development. It is designed mainly for the less developed coastal areas of the European Union.
(iv)   PRISMA: The purpose of this initiative is to improve and extend infrastructures and services to firms in general and technical assistance to medium and small-sized firms in particular in less developed regions.

*15.4.2.3 Ministry of Labour and Social Security (Ministerio de Trabajo y Seguridad Social)**

The major EU-linked activity of this Ministry is its administration of the European Social Fund (ESF), known in Spanish as *Fondo Social Europeo (FSE)*. This is in fact managed by the European Social Fund Administration Unit (*Unidad Administradora del Fondo Social Europeo*) which is located within the Directorate General for Employment (*Dirección General de Empleo*).

Through the Fund for the Promotion of Employment (*Fondo de Promoción del Empleo*), the Ministry has also been promoting the EUROTECNET scheme which is designed to encourage innovation in professional training with the aim of adapting it to technological change. In this it collaborates with the INEM (11.9.5) and the Ministry of Education and Science (15.4.2.5).

* Now Ministry of Labour and Social Affairs (*Ministerio de Trabajo y Asuntos Sociales*).

15.4.2.4 Ministry of Agriculture, Fisheries and Food (Ministerio de Agricultura, Pesca y Alimentación/MAPA)

This Ministry, through various departments and autonomous administrative bodies (6.3), is responsible for the administration of the European Agricultural Guidance and Guarantee Fund (EAGGF), known in Spanish as *Fondo Europeo de Orientación y Garantía Agrícolas (FEOGA)*. The Guidance section of the fund is managed by the National Institute for Agrarian Reform and Development (*Instituto Nacional de Reforma y Desarrollo Agrario/IRYDA*). Within objective 5a of the EU structural fund policy, the Fund aims to accelerate the adaptation of agriculture in the light of changes to the EU's Common Agricultural Policy (CAP), known in Spanish as *Política Agrícola Común (PAC)*. More specifically, it aims to develop and extend production, to support young farmers, to promote professional training in this area and to sustain the income of farmers when affected by natural disasters. IRYDA is also responsible for administering in Spain bids and payments of the LEADER initiative (9.6.1), which is designed to promote integrated development in rural areas, including the development of rural tourism as a complementary income for farming families. In the period 1992–94 over fifty less developed areas of Spain benefited from the first phase of this scheme and the country is likely to profit even more from the six-year LEADER II, which covers the years 1994–99.

The Guarantee part of the EAGGF is administered by the Fund for the Organisation and Regulation of Agricultural Products and Prices (*Fondo de Ordenación y Regulación de Productos y Precios Agrarios/FORPPA*), whose aim is to guarantee a basic price for certain agricultural products. Actual payments under this scheme come from the National Service for Agricultural Products (*Servicio Nacional de Productos Agrarios/SENPA*). As we have already seen (9.3), both FORRPA and SENPA are autonomous commercial bodies. There is a separate fund for fish and marine products; this is the Fund for the Regulation and Market Organisation of Fish and Marine Products (*Fondo de Regulación y Organización del Mercado de Productos de la Pesca y Cultivos Marinos/FROM*).

15.4.2.5 Ministry of Education and Science (Ministerio de Educación y Ciencia/MEC)*

This Ministry plays a major role, sometimes in collaboration with other government departments, in the promotion of educational, training and exchange links with the countries of the European Union, with a particular emphasis on promoting transnational mobility of Spanish students and workers. Some of the departments of the ministry involved in EU initiatives are given below.

(i)   Department for the Organisation and Establishment of Professional Training (*Area de Ordenación e Implantación de la Formación Profesional*). This is the main department responsible for administering the EUROTECNET scheme in conjunction with the Ministry of Labour (15.4.2.3). This has recently been

* Now Ministry of Education and Culture.

incorporated into the wider LEONARDO programme which covers a wide range of higher education and training initiatives.

(ii)   Subdirectorate General for International Co-operation (*Subdireccin General de Cooperación Internacional*). As well as administering the LINGUA fund for the exchange of language students between the countries of the European Union, this department also promotes the exchange of language teachers and lecturers within the Community, collaborating, in the case of the United Kingdom, with the Central Bureau for Educational Visits and Exchanges. Recently, this scheme has been incorporated into the much wider SOCRATES programme.

This department also administers the TEMPUS fund, whose purpose is to support the development and improvement of higher education systems in eastern and central Europe. The second part of this scheme covers the period 1994–98.

(iii)   Secretariat General of the Universities Council (*Secretaría General del Consejo de Universidades*): Through the National Agency for ERASMUS Grants (*Agencia Nacional Española para becas ERASMUS*), thousands of Spanish University students have benefited from this now well-established fund for student mobility (other than language students). ERASMUS has now joined LINGUA in the new SOCRATES student mobility programme.

(iv)   Secretariat of State for Universities and Research (*Secretaría de Estado de Universidades e Investigación*). This major department of the Ministry, through a special office, deals with the COMETT initiative whose aim is to promote European-wide links and co-operation between higher education and the business world in member countries, with a special emphasis on new technologies. Under this scheme University students benefit from work experience in firms abroad. Like EUROTECNET, this scheme has recently been incorporated into the LEONARDO programme.

15.4.2.6 Ministry of Industry and Energy (Ministerio de Industria y Energía/MINER)

This Ministry is responsible, among other things, for administering EU support from research and development (R&D) in the area of biotechnology. This is done through the Centre for Industrial Technological Development (*Centro para el Desarrollo Tecnológico Industrial*). This is part of a wider R&D initiative involving a university research centre network across the countries of the European Union and is co-ordinated by the Interministerial Committee for Science and Technology (*Comisión Interministerial de Ciencia y Tecnología/CICYT*), which also acts as a monitoring agent for Spanish involvement in the programmes.

15.4.2.7 Ministry of Social Affairs (Ministerio de Asuntos Sociales/MAS)*

This Ministry is involved in a variety of EU programmes, particularly those involving young people and women. With regard to the first, the Institute for Young

* Now absorbed into the Ministry of Labour (15.4.2.3).

People's Affairs (INJUVE) (6.4.4.4) organises the programme entitled Youth Exchanges in the European Union (*Intercambios de Jóvenes en la Unión Europea*).

Through the Institute for Women's Affairs (6.4.4.3), it collaborates with the Ministry of Education and INEM to implement the IRIS network, which aims to promote professional training for women and to develop an equal opportunities policy. It also manages the NOW programme which aims to encourage women to rejoin the labour market and to found their own businesses or co-operatives.

INSERSO (6.4.4.1) runs the Spanish side of the EU HORIZON initiative, whose purpose is to facilitate the economic, professional and social integration of both people who are severely disabled and people who find such integration difficult.

15.4.2.8 Ministry of Public Works, Transport and the Environment (Ministerio de Obras Públicas, Transportes y Medio Ambiente/MOPTMA)*

This Ministry, though the Directorate General for Environmental Policy (*Dirección General de Política Ambiental*) manages the LIFE programme, which is developing an integrated approach to raising the quality of life, in both the environmental and socio–economic sense, within and beyond the countries of the European Union.

15.4.3 Regional government offices

Every one of the seventeen autonomous communities (chapter 7) has created a department which deals exclusively with EU affairs. These departments are situated in one of the regional ministries (*consejerías*) and will, of course, be located in the regional capital. The ministry concerned varies from one region to another, as does the status and title of the European department. In general, the department is a directorate general or service. In some of the larger regions, like Andalusia, these departments have established some offices at provincial level.

The ERDF regional office is normally located in the directorate general for planning (*dirección general de planificación*) of the regional ministry of economy and finance (*consejería de economía y hacienda*) of the regional government concerned, but in some cases (Aragón is an example), it is administered by a special Directorate General for Community Affairs (*Dirección General de Asuntos Comunitarios*).

The EAGGF regional office is usually to be found in the appropriate directorate general (figure 15.4, p. 300) of the regional ministry of agriculture (*consejería de agricultura*), although it may well be another ministry. In the case of Aragón, it is again the Directorate General for Community Affairs.

The European Structural Fund (ESF) regional office is most commonly located in either the regional employment agency (*agencia regional de empleo*), as is the case of Asturias, or in the regional labour ministry (*consejería de trabajo*).

Information on other Community funds or initiatives is usually available in the special Directorate General for Community Affairs or in the regional ministry for

---

* Now the Ministry of Promotion (Ministerio del Formento).

economy and finance. Otherwise, citizens can seek assistance in the information offices described in 15.4.

It is worthy of note that most of the regional governments, with the exception of the Balearics, La Rioja and Castile–La Mancha, have an office in Brussels and are thus able to keep up to date with the latest EU developments, particularly those affecting the regions.

15.4.4 Co-ordination

Co-ordination of policy between the central government ministries is organised by the Secretariat of State for the European Union (15.4.2.1), formerly headed by Carlos Westerndorp. Every fortnight there is a meeting of the Interministerial Conference for Community Affairs (*Conferencia Interministerial para Asuntos Comunitarios/CIAC*), which includes representatives of every ministry. The CIAC is used to resolve disagreement between ministries; however, if agreement cannot be reached here, the matter is submitted to the Committee for Economic Affairs (*Comisión de Asuntos Económicos*) (5.6.3). With regard to co-ordination of policy between Madrid and Brussels, this is achieved via regular contact between the Ministry of Foreign Affairs and the Spanish Permanent Representation to the European Union (15.3.4.2).

The autonomous communities, which have the right to be involved in national level debates on EU policy, have participated in this process since 1992 via the regular sectoral conferences which were examined in 7.7.5.2. Co-ordination between the major EU institutions and the regional departments dealing with Community affairs is arranged by the Secretariat of State in Madrid.

15.4.5 European Information Offices (*Oficinas de Información*)

This group consists of a variety of information centres ranging from EU institution representative offices to European documentation centres and business-oriented offices.

15.4.5.1 Office of the European Parliament

This is located in a building conveniently adjacent to the Congress of Deputies (4.3.1) in the centre of Madrid. It is headed by a director who is assisted by executive secretaries responsible for the following areas: administration; media and cultural affairs; and documentation. It plays an important role in informing public opinion in Spain about the role and activities of the European Parliament.

15.4.5.2 Office of the European Commission

This is also situated in the centre of Madrid. It is headed by a director, aided by an assistant director and executive secretaries responsible for the following areas:

Community competitive examinations and training (*concursos y formación comunitaria*); press information; audio-visual aids; communication and cultural affairs; documentation; administration; translating; and computing. The Office contains a well-stocked library of current EU publications and can also supply application forms for a range of Community examinations and grants. A similar Commission Office is located in the centre of Barcelona.

15.4.5.3 European Documentation Centres (Centros de Documentación Europea/CDE)

There are currently thirty-one of these centres, including a central office in Madrid, each headed by a director. There are no less than seven in the capital and two each in Barcelona and Bilbao. The majority of them are located in University faculties or departments, including the Open University (UNED) office in Madrid, but some can be found in business-related centres such as the chambers of commerce (*cámaras de comercio*), like the one in Alicante. In some cities – for example, Badajoz, Granada, Oviedo and San Sebastián – purpose-built centres have been established. In the last mentioned city, the local authority has set up a special European Studies Foundation Centre (*Fundación Centro Estudios Europeos*).

15.4.5.4 European Business Information Centres (Centros de Información Empresarial – Euroventanillas)

These business-oriented centres have so far been set up in only a few cities, including Barcelona, Bilbao, Madrid, Seville and Málaga. Their location varies from the Regional Ministry of Industry (*Consejería de Industria*) in the Catalán *Generalitat* (7.1) to the Confederation of Businessmen in Seville (*Confederación Sevillana de Empresarios*).

15.4.5.5 Business Cooperation Network (B C Net – Cooperación entre PYMES)

These centres, whose aim is to provide information on the European Union specifically for small and medium-sized firms, are arranged into groups (B1–6) according to zone of the country: north-west, north-east, Madrid, centre, east and south. There are thirty-eight of these centres in all, of which by far the largest group is the eastern one (fifteen), centred mainly on Barcelona and Valencia. Like the CDEs, they are located in a wide range of host organisations and have adopted a variety of legal personalities; for example, one in Asturias constitutes a Regional Development Institute (*Instituto de Fomento Regional*) and is located in the Technology Park (*Parque Tecnológico*) of Llanera, one in Bilbao is an association of engineering and consultancy firms known as *Asociación Vasca de Empresas de Ingeniería y Consultoria* (*AVIC*) and one of the ten in Barcelona is located within the offices of the multinational accountancy firm Price Waterhouse.

15.5 Financial flows, Spain–European Union and European Union–Spain

The aim of this section is briefly to explain the sources of EU finance and the purposes to which it is put, as well as both the contributions and payments applicable to Spain. Data will refer mainly to the budget for the year 1995–96, but figures for the years 1986–95 will also be given in order to show how the two-way funding process has evolved since Spain joined the Community in January 1986.

15.5.1 Budget of the European Union

It is not surprising that the methods for financing the Community and the various sources of revenue should have been modified over time, given that, if one dates its origins to the foundation of the European Coal and Steel Community (ECSC) in 1952, it has now been in existence for over four decades and given that the number of member states has been steadily expanding during that period of momentous economic and social change in Europe. Though a further reform of the method for financing the Union is likely to emerge in the near future, the current arrangements date back to a Decision of the European Council of June 1988. The different components of Community income are as follows:

(i)   A maximum levy of 1 per cent on iron and steel produced in members states, which was first introduced in 1952 at the time of the creation of the Coal and Steel Community. This figure can be increased only if the Commission obtains prior authorisation from the Council. In fact, as was the case in 1993 when the rate was fixed at 0.25 per cent, the maximum is often not applied. Until the reforms of 1970, this was the only source of Community resources Since 1988, this item has been included under customs duties (see (iii) below).

(ii) Levies on agricultural and sugar products.

(iii) Customs duties collected on the basis of the Common Customs Tariff (CCT) on imports to the Community.

(iv) The product of a maximum 1.4 per cent in value added tax (VAT or IVA) collected from a base harmonised throughout the Community. Between 1995 and 1999, this rate will be progressively reduced to 1 per cent.

(v)   Revenue resulting from the application of a rate related to the total gross national product (GNP) of each member state – a rate determined as part of the overall budgetary procedure after all other sources of revenue have been taken into account. A decision of the Edinburgh Summit of December 1992 allowed for an increase in the rate to be applied under this head, at the same time reducing the VAT referred to above. In fact, Spain, along with Greece, Ireland and Portugal, with GNP less than 50 per cent of the Community average, will benefit from a decision to apply a base rate of 50 instead of the 55 per cent of a state's GNP applied hitherto.

Table 15.5 *EU draft budget for 1995*

Head	1994 Amount	% of total	1995 Amount	% of total
1 Agriculture (EAGGF– Guarantee Section)	36,456.0	52.1	36,994.0	51.1
2 Structural actions[a]	21,304.1	30.4	22,507.0	31.1
3 Internal policies	3,952.4	5.6	4,226.4	5.8
4 External actions	3,143.7	4.5	3,711.6	5.1
5 Administrative costs	3,618.3	5.2	3,826.9	5.3
6 Reserves	1,535.0	2.2	1,146.0	1.6
Totals	70,013.5	100.0	72,411.9	100.0

[a] Over 90 per cent of these are accounted for by the three structural funds, the rest corresponding to the new Cohesion Fund.
Source: Proyecto de Presupuestos Generales del Estado 1995, Instituto de Estudios Fiscales (1995).

With regard to payments made by the Community to member states, these fall under the following headings:

(i)   Direct help to agriculture (EAGGF–Guarantee Section)
(ii)   Structural actions
(iii)   Internal policies
(iv)   External policies
(v)   Administrative expenditure
(vi)   Reserves.

As can be seen in table 15.5, by far the largest share of the 1995 draft budget is allocated to agriculture (51.1 per cent) and 'structural actions' (31.1 per cent), leaving only 17.8 per cent of the total budget for external aid, administrative costs and the reserve fund. The 'structural actions' include the three structural funds and the relatively new Cohesion Fund; in recent years, Spain has benefited considerably from these funds and stands to do so at least up to 1999.

15.5.2 Spain's contribution to the EU budget

As shown in table 15.6, Spain's contribution to the EU budget is divided into four sections. The heading 'traditional own resources' refers to sections (i)–(iii) indicated above, while the VAT and GNP headings are self-explanatory. The fourth section, however, covers development aid, which Spain began contributing to only in 1989 (this aid is provided over and above the total amounts in table 15.5). It is worth noting that under this heading Spain's contribution more than doubled between 1989 and 1993. Figures for the GNP contribution appear no earlier than 1989 since, as stated above, it was in the previous year that this new source of EU funding was implemented. As can be seen in table 15.6, the Spanish contribution under this heading rose by a factor of over five between 1989 and 1995.

Table 15.6 *Spain's contribution to EU budget, 1986–95*

Head	1986	1987	1988	1989	1990
Own resources	29,872.9	73,068.6	97,894.1	92,429.8	91,014.9
Net % of VAT	83,632.3	68,525.4	138,326.1	152,726.6	280,316.3
Net % of GDP	–	–	–	43,757.5	1,650.0
Sub-totals	113,502.2	141,594.0	236,220.2	288,913.9	372,981.2
Development Fund	–	–	–	7,711.8	10,757.2
Totals	113,502.2	141,594.0	236,220.2	296,625.7	383,738.4

Head	1991	1992	1993	1994	1995
Own resources	112,087.9	112,917.0	96,864.6	128,957.7	119,514.7
Net % of VAT	359,618.2	444,083.5	485,260.9	566,637.7	475,539.6
Net % of GDP	72,435.2	87,648.1	150,707.4	223,838.6	243,062.7
Sub-totals	544,141.3	644,648.6	732,832.9	919,434.0	838,117.0
Development Fund	12,954.4	14,431.5	15,620.5	18,500.0	18,880.0
Totals	557,095.7	659,080.1	748,453.4	937,934.0	856,997.0

Source: Proyecto de Presupuestos Generales del Estado 1995, Instituto de Estudios Fiscales (1995).

15.5.3 Transfers to Spain from the EU budget

Table 15.7 gives a breakdown of the receipts in Spain of financial assistance from the European Union. The EAGGF (Guarantee Section) makes direct payments to member states, while payments from the three structural funds and the Cohesion Fund are conditional upon matching funding being available from the fifteen countries concerned, either from central government or regional/local government. As can be seen, over the period in question, the EAGGF has consistently provided a very high percentage of the total receipts (57.5 per cent in 1995) and in overall terms these have increased by a factor of twenty-three during the period. Payments from the three structural funds have increased by a factor of eight and in 1995 represented 33.2 per cent of the total receipts. Moreover, the increase between 1994 and 1995 was 32.8 per cent. Clearly, the ERDF has made by far the largest contribution to Spanish coffers (double that of the ESF in 1995); on the other hand, the Guidance Section of the EAGGF, while remaining a relatively small percentage of all transfers from structural funds, has witnessed a dramatic increase since it was first applied in 1987.

The remaining 9.3 per cent of the total 1995 figures for transfers to Spain is accounted for by the Cohesion Fund, which was implemented for the first time in 1993. Over future years, this percentage is set to rise substantially (7.5.3.5).

As one of the poorer countries of the European Union, accentuated by the recent entry of Austria, Finland and Sweden, it is perhaps not surprising that Spain continues to be a net beneficiary of EU funds, receiving a total of 1,535,449 million pesetas in 1995, while contributing only 856,997 million to the Community budget.

Table 15.7 *Transfers to Spain from EU budget, 1986–95, million peseta*

Head	1986	1987	1988	1989	1990
1 EAGGF (Guarantee)	37,898.0	87,331.8	260,019.8	250,680.8	274,529.8
2 Structural Funds					
• ERDF	–40,457.5	–48,277.2	–69,596.4	–115,656.6	–138,184.4
• ESF	–23,918.4	–37,592.6	–38,655.0	–64,328.1	–53,078.5
• EAGGF (Guidance)	–	–2,849.8	–9,568.0	–36,353.2	–26,627.2
Sub-total Structural Fund	164,375.9	88,719.6	117,819.4	216,340.9	217,890.1
3 Cohesion Fund	–	–	–	–	–
4 Other transfers[a]	2,826.0	4,442.7	20,378.9	16,971.1	17,705.3
Totals	105,099.9	180,494.1	398,218.1	483,992.8	510,125.2

Head	1991	1991	1993	1994	1995
1 EAGGF (Guarantee)	428,725.3	462,670.5	602,077.4	700,000.0	872,979.0
2 Structural Funds					
• ERDF	–283,234.7	–313,371.2	–279,988.4	–175,000.0	–285,000.0
• ESF	–134,292.8	–106,965.4	–105,544.8	–120,000.0	–130,169.0
• EAGGF (Guidance)	–82,055.4	–84,642.5	–111,662.8	–89,000.0	–89,000.0
Sub-total Structural Funds	499,582.9	504,979.1	497,196.0	384,000.0	504,169.0
4 Cohesion Fund	–	–	32,448.9	131,000.0	142,000.0
5 Other transfers[a]	24,979.3	22,679.8	14,663.0	14,955.3	16,301.0
Totals	953,287.5	990,329.4	1,146,385.3	1,229,955.0	1,535,449.0

Note:
[a] This includes transfers related to payments from the EU Coal and Steel Community for restructuring these industries, as well as sundry grants related to tourism, culture and research.
Source: Proyecto de Presupuestos Generales del Estado 1995, Instituto de Estudios Fiscales (1995).

This is clearly shown in table 15.8, which brings together Spain's total payments and receipts since entry in 1986 and also indicates the percentage by which income exceeds expenditure for the period. In fact, the position is even more favourable for Spain in that ESF transfers made to INEM (6.4.3.3) and to regional and local administrations are shown in the separate budgets of these institutions and not in the general budgets of the state.

However, a word of caution should be added. In July 1995 the members of the Union warned Spain that, in line with the Community's convergence rules, if she did not substantially reduce her public deficit (currently standing at 6.6 per cent of GDP), she would stand to lose a significant proportion of the funds earmarked for Spain under the Cohesion Fund.

Table 15.8 *Statement of financial flows, Spain–European Union, European Union–Spain, 1986–95, million peseta*

Head	1986	1987	1988	1989	1990
Spain's EU contribution	113,505.2	141,594.0	236,220.2	296,625.7	383,738.4
EU transfers to Spain	105,099.9	180,494.1	398,218.1	483,992.8	510,125.2
Balance in real terms	−8,405.3	38,900.1	161,997.9	187,367.1	126,386.8
% loss/gain	−7	+27	+69	+63	+33
Head	1991	1992	1993	1994	1995
Spain's EU contribution	557,095.7	659,080.1	748,453.4	937,934.0	856,997.0
EU transfers to Spain	953,287.5	990,329.4	1,146,385.3	1,229,955.0	1,535,449.0
Balance in real terms	396,191.8	331,249.3	397,931.9	292,021.0	678,452.0
% loss/gain	+71	+50	+53	+31	+79

Source: Proyecto de Presupuestos Generales del Estado 1995, Instituto de Estudios Fiscales (1995).

15.6 Spanish presidency

Between July and December 1995 Spain – for the second time (the first was January–June 1989) – occupied the Presidency of the European Union. Given the internal political instability and the possibility that a general election could be called at any time, the omens for a strong Spanish performance were not good. However, both the Spanish government and Spanish officials in the Union put together an ambitious programme that combined general European (institutional) development and issues that were of particular interest to Spain.

Among the Euro-issues were the reform of the Maastricht Treaty, examined during 1995 by the Reflexion Group chaired by Carlos Westerndorp (15.3.5.5); this was to be the main item at the summit of heads of state and government in Formentor (Majorca) in September, though other matters, such as limitations to the veto rights of member countries and common foreign policy, were also debated. Another all-embracing issue was to be that of the single currency and the delicate question of the admissibility of a 'hard core' of states; this was tackled at the culminating Madrid summit in December. A European-wide issue, which had particular relevance in Spain (1.1.5), is the fight against unemployment, addressed at the October summit of EU employment ministers held in Córdoba.

An issue which, for both economic and political reasons, is of special interest to Spain is the European Union's relations with the countries of the Near East and North Africa; hence the importance attached to the Euro–Mediterranean summit in November held (at the request of the influential Jordi Pujol) in Barcelona. As well

Table 15.9 *Timetable for Spanish Presidency of European Union, July–December 1995*

Date(s)	Event	Location
1 July	Reflexion group to discuss institutional reform	Toledo
3 July	Meeting of Spanish government and European Commission	Madrid
8–9 July	Council of Ministers of Industry	Bilbao
15–16 July	Seminar for EU ministers of Transport	Palma de Mallorca
9–10 September	Council of Ministers of Foreign Affairs	Santander
17–18 September	Council of Ministers of Agriculture	Burgos
22–23 September	Meeting of European Council	Formentor, Mallorca
29–30 September	Council of Ministers of Economy and Finance	Valencia
14–15 October	Council of Ministers of Justice and Home Affairs	La Gomera
19–20 October	Council of Ministers of Culture	Madrid
21–22 October	Council of Ministers of Environment	Parque de Doñana, Huelva
28–29 October	Council of Ministers of Labour	Cordoba
13–14 November	Meeting of ministers of the Western European Union	Madrid
27–28 November	Euro-Mediterranean Conference	Barcelona
15–16 December	Meeting of European Council	Madrid

Source: *El País International* (3 July 1995).

as tilting the balance once more in favour of the 'southern axis' of the European Union, Felipe González attempted to raise awareness of the serious problems posed in the area (security and environment are only two examples) and to enhance Spain's role as an important interlocutor in this troubled region. There was also a generalised agreement among Spanish political leaders that the Presidency should be used as a platform to promote further and stronger links with the countries of Latin America, particularly through trade agreements giving favourable terms to such associations as *Mercosur* (Argentina, Brazil, Paraguay and Uruguay). The timetable for the Spanish presidency is shown in table 15.9.

While the aims of the PSOE are in broad terms acceptable to the PP, the IU is critical of what it regards as the government's tendency to hang uncritically on to the coat-tails of the most powerful EU members (like France and Germany), neither defending the best interests of Spain nor creating the more socially-oriented Community which they favour. Through its Federal Presidency (10.3.2.4), on 19 June 1995, it issued a detailed statement on how it considered that Spain could best use its privileged position. At the top of IU's agenda is the fight against unemployment (with an abandonment of neo-liberal policies for creating jobs), a greater emphasis on social policies, the inclusion of the environment in all other policies, the rejection of concepts like 'hard core' and 'two-track Europe', greater solidarity (expressed in tangible terms) with the countries of the Third World, more emphasis on human rights and a European rather than Atlanticist defence and security framework.

15.7 Comment

From the foregoing it should be apparent that, whatever the state of public opinion, public awareness and sense of identification with the European Union in the country, Spain is politically and institutionally committed to Europe. Whatever criticisms may currently be surfacing in certain quarters (notably in the agricultural and fishing communities), it is inconceivable that, at least in the short or medium term, any Spanish political party or important interest group would seriously advocate withdrawal. The well-organised group of British euro-sceptics, with probably not insubstantial support at the popular level, has so far no counterpart in Spain. None the less, it is probable that, in the coming years, while basically remaining a loyal member of the club, Spanish commitment will be qualified by an increasingly critical stance in certain areas as it strives, along with other countries, to defend its national interests.

An important test for Spain will come in the next few years if the 'two-track' model for implementation of Economic and Monetary Union (EMU) is adopted and if she, as current predictions for meeting the convergence criteria seem to suggest, is left in 'Division 2'. Such a development might be seen as a blow to national pride and exploited as such among the electorate by an anti-European political group committed to a radical change in the status quo. However, without a substantial realignment within the present political party system, it is difficult to see where such opposition would come from and, given the alternatives to continued membership of the European Union, it is unlikely that such an initiative would prosper.

Another crucial moment for Spain will come early in the next century – the predicted time of expansion towards the east; Spanish politicians are already voicing unease at the strong possibility that the 'cohesion' funding now benefiting poorer countries like Spain, Greece and Portugal, will then be directed towards the members of the former Eastern bloc. Spain would certainly be advised to take full advantage of the remaining years of the decade before the next enlargement and of the generous funding now flowing into the country, to ensure that strong foundations are laid for future 'autonomous' development and that once and for all the legacies of her backward past are eradicated.

Chapter 16

Conclusion

A comparison of this edition with that published in 1987 will show that the basic institutional structures established during the period 1978–83 are still in place and have remained largely unchanged. This is particularly the case in respect of what might be termed the 'bedrock' institutions, such as the monarchy, Parliament and central government and administration which, as well as the Constitution itself, have undergone the minimum of structural change. Where most updating has had to be carried out, as far as the public sector is concerned, is in relation to those two major developments which, over the last decade, have impinged most forcefully upon the country – the decentralisation of power to the regions and the accelerating process of European integration. With regard to the latter, chapter 15 has shown how this process has been reflected in a myriad new institutions created at all levels of national life, as well as in Spain's membership of the many already existing structures of the European Union. Chapters 12 and 13, which basically examine the private sector, reflect the considerable degree to which many of the institutions here have had to adapt to these two major transformations.

In general, it can be safely stated that those structures that have stood the test of time, while occasionally subjected to severe pressures, have been developed and consolidated. The liberal democratic system, which owes much of its strength and current legitimacy to the parliamentary monarchy at its apex, has stumbled on more than one occasion, especially when confronted by the twin scourges of terrorism and corruption, but cannot now be regarded as any less stable or effective than that of other states of western Europe.

In one respect, albeit at a high cost, Spain can perhaps claim to have surpassed a number of her neighbours, and that is in the bold manner in which she has addressed the question of centre–periphery tensions: devolution of real political power and resources from Madrid to the autonomous communities is a *fait accompli* and, whatever weaknesses it may display and whatever threats to it may still exist, must now be regarded as virtually irreversible. The establishment of some kind of federal state in Spain can now no longer be regarded as a remote possibility or utopian dream.

Equally irreversible is likely to be Spain's other major transformation, i.e. her progressive integration into the European Union. While at the popular level there is evidence that scepticism is on the increase (though probably less so that in some other member states), the commitment of nearly the whole of the political establishment and business/financial community to Europe, with the enthusiastic backing of the monarchy, is undisputed. As can be observed in many of the foregoing chapters, the European Union is now an increasingly relevant and important part of national life: whether it be in the public or private sector, in industry or education, in communications or sport, in tourism or the arts, the European dimension has become an inescapable reality.

In one sense, of course, political and economic institutions are only as good as the politicians, civil servants, economists and business people whose task it is to make them function, and there is little doubt that in recent times politicians and financiers in particular have sometimes fallen short of the standards expected of them by the public. There is little doubt that the cases of corruption alluded to in this volume bring considerable discredit not only on the persons concerned but also on the institutions which they represent. On the other hand, the hope is that via the institutions themselves – in particular those concerned with justice – corruption and other forms of infringements of the law by people in high office will be exposed and, hopefully, eradicated. However, preoccupation with the damage done in these recent high profile cases should not blind us to more mundane but equally harmful weaknesses in the Spanish institutional system, such as inefficiency, waste, excessive bureaucracy and lack of responsiveness to public feelings.

Currently, a short view of the scene might lead observers to a pessimistic analysis of the health of Spanish institutions. However, if a longer view is taken and if it is borne in mind how far Spain has travelled along the democratic road since 1975 and what positive gains have been achieved along the way, it is still possible to view the future in optimistic terms.

Appendix: elections in Spain, 1977–96

European elections

June 1987[a]	Won by PSOE (largest party)
June 1989	Won by PSOE (largest party)
June 1994	Won by PP (largest party)

General elections

June 1977	Won by UCD (largest party)
March 1979	Won by UCD (largest party)
October 1992	Won by PSOE (overall majority)
June 1986	Won by PSOE (overall majority)
October 1989	Won by PSOE (largest party)
June 1993	Won by PSOE (largest party)
March 1996	Won by PP (largest party)

Regional elections

ANDALUSIA

May 1982	Won by PSOE (overall majority)
June 1986	Won by PSOE (overall majority)
June 1990	Won by PSOE (overall majority)
June 1994	Won by PSOE (largest party)
March 1996	Won by PSOE (largest party)

BASQUE COUNTRY (EUSKADI)

March 1980	Won by PNV (largest party)
February 1984	Won by PNV (largest party)

[a] Elections called only in Spain following the latter's entry into EC in January 1986.

November 1986	Won by PSOE (largest party)[b]
October 1990	Won by PNV (largest party)
October 1994	Won by PNV (largest party)

CATALONIA (CATALUNYA)

March 1980	Won by CiU (largest party)
April 1984	Won by CiU (overall majority)
May 1988	Won by CiU (overall majority)
May 1992	Won by CiU (overall majority)
November 1995	Won by CiU (largest party)

GALICIA

October 1981	Won by AP (largest party)
November 1985	Won by AP (largest party)
December 1989	Won by PP (overall majority)
October 1993	Won by PP (overall majority)

OTHER REGIONS[c]

May 1983	Dominated by PSOE
June 1987	Dominated by PSOE
May 1991	Dominated by PSOE
May 1995	Dominated by PP

Local elections

April 1979	Dominated by UCD
May 1983	Dominated by PSOE
June 1987	Dominated by PSOE
May 1991	Dominated by PSOE[d]
May 1995	Dominated by PP

[b] In fact, a coalition government (PNV and PSOE) was formed which governed until October 1994; subsequently the PNV has led a three-party coalition government involving both the PSOE and EA (10.4.2).

[c] Since May 1983, at intervals of four years, there has been a common date for elections in the remaining thirteen autonomous communities and for the local elections.

[d] In these elections, the PP won several major cities from the PSOE, including Madrid, foreshadowing sweeping victories in May 1995 (10.6.3).

Select bibliography

Note: In addition to the following bibliographical sources, substantial use has been made of further primary documentation, including all the laws and decrees that are quoted in the text of the work and which can all be consulted in the *Boletín Oficial del Estado*.

1 Introduction

Political and economic background

Alonso Zaldívar, C. and Castells, M., 1992. *Spain beyond Myths*, Alianza Editorial
Anuario El País, 1982–95. *El País*
Arengo, E. R., 1995. *Spain: Democracy Regained* (2nd edn), Westview Press
Carr, R., 1982. *Spain 1808–1975*, Clarendon Press
Carr, R. and Fusi, J.P., 1979. *España: de la dictadura a la democracia*, Planeta
Díaz, E., 1987. *La transición a la democracia*, Eudema
Ellwood, S., 1994. *Franco*, Longman (Profiles in Power series)
García Delgado, J.L. (ed.), 1990. *España, vol. II: Economía*, Espasa Calpe
Gillespie, R., Rodrigo, F. and Story, J. (eds.) 1995. *Democratic Spain*, Routledge
Gilmour, D., 1985. *The Transformation of Spain*, Quartet Books
Giner, S. (coord.), 1990. *España, vol. I: Sociedad y política*, Espasa Calpe
González, M. 1979. *La economía política del franquismo (1940–70)*, Tecnos
Graham, H. (ed.) 1995. *Spanish Cultural Studies*, Oxford University Press
Gunther, R. (ed.), 1993. *Politics, Society and Democracy: the Case of Spain*, Westview Press
Harrison, J., 1985. *The Spanish Economy in the Twentieth Century*, Croom-Helm
Hooper, J., 1995. *The New Spaniards*, Penguin
Martínez Serrano, J.A. *et al.*, 1982. *Economía española: 1960–80*, Ediciones H. Blume
Pérez Henares, A. and Malo de Molina, C. 1995. *Así será España en 1996*, Temas de Hoy
Preston, P., 1986. *The Triumph of Democracy in Spain*, Methuen
Salmon, K., 1995. *The Modern Spanish Economy* (2nd edn.), Pinter
Wiarda, H. J., 1993. *Politics in Iberia*, HarperCollins

Institutions

Colomer, J., 1995. *Political Institutions in Europe*, Routledge
Heywood, P., 1995. *The Government and Politics of Spain*, Macmillan
Paloma, R. (ed.), 1995. *Sistema político español*, McGraw-Hill
Pérez de Lama, E., 1994. *Manual del estado español 1994*, Lama
Pérez Royo, J., 1994. *Curso de derecho constitucional*, Marcial Pons

Pombo, F., 1994. *Doing Business in Spain*, Mathew Bender
Secretaría General del Portavoz del Gobierno, 1995. *Agenda de la comunicación 1995*, Ministerio de la Presidencia
Spain, 1994. *Los cargos en el poder*, vols. I–III, Carposa
Zabalza Martí, A., 1992. *El sector público estatatal*, Ministerio de Economía y Hacienda

2 The Constitution of 1978

Aparicio, M., 1983. *Introducción al sistema político y constitucional español*, Ariel
Attard, E., 1983. *La Constitución por dentro*, Vergara
Bonime Blanc, A. R., 1988. 'The Spanish state structure: constitution-making and the creation of the new state' in Lancaster, T. (ed.), *Politics and Change*, Praeger pp. 11–34
Eibert, M. A., 1982. 'The Spanish constitutional tribunal in theory and practice', *Stanford Journal of International Law*, 18 (Summer), pp. 435–70
Esteban, J. de and López Guerra, L., 1982. *El régimen constitucional español*, vol. I, Labor
Figuerola Burrieza, A., 1993, 'La incidencia positiva del tribunal constitucional en el poder legislativo', *Revista de Estudios Políticos*, 81 (July–September) pp. 47–73
Peces-Barba, G., 1981. *La Constitución española de 1978*, Torres
Sánchez Agesta, L., 1980. *Sistema político de la Constitución española de 1978*, Editorial Nacional
Tamames, R., 1980. *Introducción a la Constitución española*, Alianza

3 The Monarchy

Areilza, J. M., 1977. *Diario de un ministro de la monarquía*, Planeta
Balansó, J., 1992. *La familia real y la famila irreal*, Planeta
Bayona, J. M., 1976. *Juan Carlos I*, Editorial Bruguera
Fuente, I., 1992. *Don Juan de Borbón, hijo de rey, padre de rey, nunca rey*, Prensa Ibérica
López Rodó, J., 1977. *La larga marcha de la monarquía*, Noguer
Palacio Atard, V., 1989. *Juan Carlos I y el advenimiento de la democracia*, Espasa Calpe
Papell, A., 1980. *La monarquía española y el derecho constitucional y europeo*, Espasa Calpe
Pérez Mateos, J. A., 1981. *El rey que vino del exilio*, Planeta
Powell, C. T., 1991. *El piloto del cambio: el rey, la monarquía y la transición a la democracia*, Planeta
1995. *Juan Carlos of Spain: Self-Made Monarch*, Macmillan Press
Vilallonga, J. L. de, 1994. *The King: a Life of King Juan Carlos*, Weidenfeld and Nicolson

4 Parliament

Aragón Reyes, M., 1980. *Legislación política española*, Centro de Estudios Constitucionales
1994. *Gobierno y Cortes*, Instituto de Estudios Económicos
Esteban, J. de and López Guerra, L., 1980. *El régimen constitucional español*, vol. II, Labor
Gonzalo, M., 1984. *Constitución española y reglamento del Congreso de los Diputados*, Congreso de los Diputados
Punsett Blanco, R. 1983. *Las Cortes Generales. Estudios de derecho constitucional español*, Centro de Estudios Constitucionales
Santamaría, J., 1994. 'El papel del Parlamento durante la consolidación de la democracia y después', *Revista de Estudios Políticos*, 84 (April–June), pp. 9–25

Santoalla López, F. 1982. *Constitución española y reglamento del Senado*, Publicaciones del Senado
1984. *Derecho parlamentario español*, Editorial Nacional
Secretaría General del Congreso, February 1995. *Boletín oficial de las Cortes Generales*, Congreso de los Diputados

5 Central government

Bar, A., 1988. 'Spain' in Blondel, J. and Muller-Rommel, F. (eds.), *Cabinets in Western Europe*, Macmillan pp. 102–19
Entrena Cuesta, R., 1994. *Curso de derecho administrativo*, vols. 1/2 (10th edn.), Tecnos
Heywood, P., 1991. 'Governing a new democracy: the power of the prime minister in Spain', *West European Politics*, 14, pp. 97–115
Martín Villa, R., 1984. *Al servicio del estado*, Planeta
Meliá, J., 1981. *Así cayó Adolfo Suárez*, Planeta
Osorio, A., 1980. *Trayectoria política de un ministro de la corona*, Planeta
Pérez Royo, J., 1994. *Curso de derecho constitucional*, Marcial Pons
Reviriego Márquez, R., 1982. *Felipe González, un estilo ético*, Planeta

6 Central administration

Beltrán, M., 1988. 'Spain' in Rowat, D. C. (ed.), *Public Administration in Developed Countries: a Comparative Study*, Marcel Dekker, pp. 255–72
Centro de Información Administrativa, 1995. *Organigramas de los ministerios*, Ministerio para las Administraciones Públicas
Entrena Cuesta, R. 1994. *Curso de derecho administrativo*, vols. 1/2, (10th edn), Tecnos
Gala Vallejo, C., 1980. *Gestión institucional de la seguridad social*, Ministerio de Sanidad y Seguridad Social
García de Enterría, E. (ed.), 1984. *España: un presente para el futuro*, vol. II, Instituto de Estudios Económicos
López Nieto, F., 1989. *La administración pública en España*, Ariel
Spain, 1994a. *Guía Laboral 1994*, Minsterio de Trabajo y Seguridad Social
1994b. *INSERSO 1994*, Ministerio de Asuntos Sociales

7 Regional government and administration

Acosta, R. *et al.*, 1984. *La España de las autonomías*, vols. I and II, Espasa Calpe
Agranoff, R., 1993. 'Intergovernmental politics and policy: building federal arrangements in Spain', *Regional Politics and Policy*, (2), pp. 1–28
Brassloff, A. 1989. 'Spain: the state of the autonomies', in Forsyth, M. (ed.), *Federalism and Nationalism*, Leicester University Press, pp. 24–50
1991. 'Spain: democracy and decentralisation', in Brassloff, A. and Brassloff, W. (eds.), *European Insights: Postwar Politics, Society, Culture*, Elsevier Science, pp. 57–68
García de Enterria, E., 1985. *Estudios sobre autonomías territoriales*, Civitas
González Navarro, F., 1993. *España, nación de naciones (el moderno federalismo)*, EUNSA
Grupo Editorial Mercado, 1991. *Manual de autonomías y ayuntamientos*, Banco de Crédito Local
Keating, M. 1988. 'Does regional government work? The experience of Italy, France and

Spain', *Governance: an International Journal in Policy Administration*, (2) (April) (whole volume)

Linz, J. J., 1989. 'Spanish democracy and the estado de las autonomías', in Goldwin, R. A. (ed.), *Forging Unity out of Diversity: the Approaches of Eight Nations*, American Enterprise Institute for Public Policy Research, pp. 260–303

Meillan Gil, J. L., 1988. *La ordenación jurídica de las autonomías*, Tecnos

Morata, F., 1992. 'Regions and the EC: a comparative analysis of four Spanish regions', *Regional Politics and Policy*, 2 (112), pp. 187–216

Rokkan, S. and Unwin, D. W. (eds.), 1982. The Politics of Territorial Identity (selected chapters), Sage Publications

Consejo de Política Fiscal y Financiera, 1992. *Acuerdo sobre el sistema de financiación autonómica en el período 1992–1996*, MAP

Ministerio de Administraciones Públicas, 1992. *Acuerdos autonómicos del 28 de febrero de 1992*, MAP

1994. *Informe económico–financiero de las administraciones territoriales en 1993*, MAP

Saavedra Acevedo, J., 1994. *Quince años de desarrollo autonómico: experiencias y enseñanzas*, MAP (unpublished)

8 Local administration

Bosch i Roca, N., 1988. 'Spanish local government: territorial organization and financing', *Planning and Administration*, 15 (1) (Spring), pp. 6–17

Centro de Estudios Municipales, 1980. *Provincia y diputaciones provinciales en el estado de las autonomías*, CEM

Clegg, T. 1987, 'Spain', in Page, E. C. and Goldsmith, M. J. (eds.), *Central and Local Government Relations: a Comparative Analysis of West European Unitary States*, Sage Publications, pp. 130–55

Ferrer Mateo, J., 1991. 'Improving access to administration in Spain' in Batley, R. and Stoker, G. (eds.), *Local Government in Europe*, Macmillan, pp. 146–54

García-Escudero Márquez, P., 1985. *Estudio sistemático de la Ley 7/1985 de 2 de abril reguladora de las bases de régimen local*, Editorial Praxis

Guía de Málaga, 1993. Ayuntamiento de Málaga

Memoria de actividades, 1993. Diputación Provincial de Málaga

Izquierda Unida, 1995. *Municipios y desarrollo sostenido en tiempos de crisis* (municipal election manifesto, May 1995), IU

Santigosa, A., 1992. 'The finance of Spanish local governments and its recent reform', *Local Government Studies*, 18 (4), pp. 136–57

Solé-Vilanova, J., 1989. 'Spain: regional and local government' in Bennett, R. J. (ed.), *Territory and Administration in Europe*, Pinter, pp. 205–29

9 Public enterprises

Casado González, M., 1993. 'El papel del sector público en el fomento de la competitividad, *Economía Industrial* (May/June)

Consejería de Economía y Hacienda, 1993. *El sector público empresarial de la comunidad autónoma de Andalucía*, Junta de Andalucía

Dirección General del Patrimonio del Estado, 1994. *Grupo Patrimonio: Memoria 1993*, Ministerio de Economía y Hacienda

Guía de Málaga, 1993. Ayuntamiento de Málaga

Instituto de Estudios Fiscales, 1994. *El sector público español: una panorámica estatal*, Ministerio de Economía y Hacienda

Instituto Nacional de Industria, 1993. *Grupo INI 1993*, INI

1993. Grupo *TENEO 1993*, INI

Martín Aceña, P. and Comín, F. 1988a. 'Una nota sobre los orígenes del Instituto Nacional de Industria', *Economía Industrial* (July/August), MINER

1988b. *INI: 50 años de industrialización en España*, Espasa Calpe

Repsol, 1995a. *Oferta pública de venta de acciones de Repsol SA*, Instituto Nacional de Hidrocarburos

1995b. *Informe Anual 1994*, Repsol SA

Secretaría de Estado de Hacienda, 1992. *El sector público estatal*, Ministerio de Economía y Hacienda

TENEO, 1995a. *Spain's leading industrial group*, INI

1995b. *Resultados 1994*, INI

10 Political parties

Amodia, J., 1990. 'Taxiconomía e inestabilidad del sistema de partidos en España', *ACIS*, 3 (Spring), (1), pp. 39–48

1993. 'Requiem for the PCE,' in Bell, D. (ed.), *Western European Communists and the Collapse of Communism*, Berg

Aznar, J. M., 1994. *España: la segunda transición*, Espasa Calpe

Bell, D. (ed.), 1983. *Democratic Politics in Spain*, chs. 1, 2 and 3, Pinter

Bruton, K., 1991. 'Political parties and trade unions in Spain', in Brassloff, A. and Brassloff, W. (eds.), *European Insights: Postwar Politics, Society, Culture*, Elsevier Science, pp. 81–95

Colomé, G. and López Nieto, L., 1993. 'The selection of party leaders in Spain: socialist cohesion and opposition turmoil', *Journal of Political Research*, 24, pp. 349–60

Esteban J. de and López Guerra, L., 1992. *Los partidos políticos en la España actual*, Planeta

Gillespie, R., 1989. *The Spanish Socialist Party: A History of Factionalism*, Clarendon Press

1993. 'Programa 2000: the appearance and reality of socialist renewal in Spain', in *West European Politics*, 16 (93) (January), pp. 78–96

Gilmour, J., 1987. 'From Francoism to democracy: Fraga and the Spanish right', *Iberian Studies*, 16, (1–2)

Guerra, A. and Tezanos, J. F., 1992. *La década del cambio: diez años de gobierno socialista 1982–92*, Sistema

Gunther, R., San, G. and Goldie, A., 1986. *Spain after Franco: the Making of a Competitive Party System*, University of California Press

Izquierda Unida, 1994. *Estatutos federales de Izquierda Unida*, IU

1995. *Municipios y desarrollo sostenible en tiempos de crisis* (municipal election manifesto, May 1995), IU

Partido Popular, 1993. *Estatutos XI Congreso Nacional*, PP

1994. *Fuertes en Europa. Programa de las Elecciones Europeas*, PP

Partido Socialista Obrero Español, 1988. *Programa 2000: aspectos y problemas de la vida política española*, Siglo XXI

1994. *Resoluciones del 33 Congreso Federal*, PSOE

Pérez Díaz, V., 1993. *The Return of Civil Society: the Emergence of Democratic Spain*, Harvard University Press

Share, D., 1989. *Dilemma of Social Democracy: the Spanish Socialist Workers' Party in the 1980s*, Greenwood Press

Walker, D. 1989. *Towards a Predominant Party System? Spain since 1977*, University of Strathclyde (*Occasional Papers in Government and Politics*)

Wiarda, H. J., 1993. *Politics in Iberia*, ch. 7, HarperCollins

11 Trade unions

Alarcón Cracuel, M. R., 1994. *La reforma laboral de 1994*, Marcial Pons

Bruton, K. 1991. 'Political parties and trade unions in Spain', in Brassloff, A. and Brassloff, W. (eds.), *European Insights: Postwar Politics, Society, Culture*, Elsevier Science

Confederación de Comisiones Obreras, 1992. *Estatutos aprobados en el V Congreso Federal*, CC.OO

Confederación de Comisiones Obreras y Unión General de Trabajadores, 1991. *Iniciativa Sindical de Progreso (ISP)*, CC.OO and UGT

FOESSA, 1994. *La situación social en España en 1994*, Euroamérica

García Delgado, J. L. 1990. *España, vol. II: Economía*, ch. 13, Espasa Calpe

Gillespie, R., 1990. 'The break-up of the "socialist family": party–union relations in Spain 1982–89', *West European Politics*, 13 pp. 47–62

Hawkesworth, R. I. and Fina, L., 1987. 'Trade unions and industrial relations in Spain: the response to the economic crisis' in Brierley, W. (ed.), *Trade Unions and the Economic Crisis of the 1980s*, pp. 64–83

Miguel, A. de 1994. *La sociedad española 1993–94*, Alianza

Miguélez, F., 1995. 'Modernisation of trade unions in Spain', *Quarterly of the European Trade Union Institute*, pp. 79–97

Ministerio de Trabajo y Seguridad Social, 1991. *Las elecciones sindicales de 1990: Resultados*, MTSS

Pombo, F., 1994. *Doing Business in Spain*, ch. 15, Mathew Bender

Secretaría de Organización Confederal, 1992. *UGT, afiliación y dirigentes*, UGT

1995. 'Spain', in Buxton, L. A. (ed.), *Employment Law in Europe: a Country by Country Guide* (2nd edn.), Gower

Subsecretaría de Trabajo y Seguridad Social, 1994. *Anuario de Estadísticas Laborales 1993*, MTSS

Tamames, R., 1993. *Estructura económica de España* (22nd edn.), ch. 31, Alianza Editorial

Unión General de Trabajadores, 1994. *Resoluciones del 36 Congreso Federal*, UGT

Zaragoza, A., 1988. *Pactos sociales, sindicatos y patronal en España*, Siglo XXI

12 Business and professional organisations

Anuario El País, 1994. *1995*, El País

Banco de España, 1994. *Central de balances 1993*

CECA, 1994. *Memoria 1993*

CEOE, 1994. *Memoria 1993*

Del Valle, V. and Gómez de Aguero, J. L., 1994. *Economía y organización de empresas*, MacGraw-Hill

Donaghy, P. J. and Laidler, J., 1994. *Understanding Spanish Accounts*, Pitman

Economist, various issues. *Surveys on Spain*

Financial Times, various issues. *Surveys on Spain*

González, J. A. and Gallizo, J. L., 1992. *European Financial Reporting: Spain*, Routledge
ICEX, 1990. *A Guide to Business in Spain*, ICEX
Iriarte Ibarguen, A., 1994. *Guía Duesto mercantil*, Duesto
Ministerio de Industria e Energía, 1993. *Las empresas industriales en 1992*, MINER
Miranda, S., 1993. *Spain: Practical Commercial Law*, Longman
Pombo, F., 1994. *Doing Business in Spain*, Mathew Bender
Salmon, K., 1995. *The Modern Spanish Economy* (2nd edn.), Pinter
Valle, V. del and Gómez de Aguero, J. L., 1994. *Economía y organización de empresas: una aproximación económica, jurídica y organizativa*, McGraw-Hill
Wright, V. (ed.), 1994. *Privatization in Western Europe*, Pinter

13 Financial institutions

AEB, 1994. *Annual Report 1993*, AEB
Amat, O., 1994. *La bolsa: funcionamiento y técnicas para invertir*, Duesto
Banco de España, 1995. *Annual Report 1994*
Cacho, J. M. C., 1994. *Un intruso en el laberinto de los elegidos*, Temas de Hoy
CEDA, 1994. *Guía del sistema financiero español*, Fareso
Conde, M., 1994. *El sistema: mi experiencia del poder*, Espasa Calpe
Economist, various issues. *Surveys on Spain*
Financial Times, various issues. *Surveys on Spain*
García Delgado, J. L. *et al.*, 1993. *Lecciones de economía española*, Civitas
González, J. A., 1992. *European Financial Reporting: Spain*, Routledge
Marton, S. J. and Brown, K., 1994. 'Argentaria: Branching out', *Morgan Stanley European Banking Commentary* (5 October)
Ontiveros, E. and Valero, F. J., 1994. *Introducción al sistema financiero español*, Civitas
Pringle, R., 1994. 'A new era for the Banco de España', *Central Banking*, 5 (2) (Autumn)
Warner, A., 1994. 'Disaster recovery (Banesto)', *The Banker* (October)

14 The Judiciary

Beltrán, M., 1988. 'Spain', in Rowatt, D. C. (ed.), *Public Administration in Developed Countries: A Comparative Study*, Dekker
Ministerio de Justicia e Interior, 1994. *Boletín de Información: Ley Orgánica del Poder Judicial*, MJI
Muñoz-Arguelles, L. and Fraticelli-Torres, M., 1985. 'Selection and training of judges in Spain, France, West Germany and England', *Boston College of International and Comparative Law Review*, 8 (1), pp. 1–37
Pérez Royo, J., 1994. *Curso de derecho constitucional*, ch. 22, Marcial Pons
Pombo, P., 1994. *Doing Business in Spain*, chs. 1 and 23 (postscript), Mathew Bender
Sánchez Goyanes, E. 1982. *Constitución española comentada*, ch. 13, Paraninfo
Vogler, R., 1989. *Spain: a guide to the Spanish Criminal Justice System*, Prisoners Abroad Handbook Series

15 Spain and Europe

Almarcha Barbado, M. A. (ed.)., 1993. *Spain and EC Membership Evaluated*, Pinter
Arnal, M., 1993. *España ante el reto europeo*, Diputación de Zaragoza

Comisión de las Comunidades Europeas, 1993. *Dígame: Guía de información europea en España*, Comisión de las Comunidades Europeas

Dirección General de Estudios, 1994. *De la Comunidad Europea del Carbón y del Acero a la Unión Europea*, Parlamento Europeo

Directorate General for Research, 1994. *Fact Sheets on the European Parliament and the Activities of the European Union*, European Parliament

European Commission, 1994. *Eurobarometer – Public Opinion in the European Union: Trends 1974–1993*, European Commission

European Commission, 1995. *European Reports (January–August 1995)*, European Commission

January–March, 1995. *Europinion: Results of Surveys of European opinion*, European Commission

Hudson, M. and Rudcenko, S., 1988. *Spain to 1992: Joining Europe's Mainstream*, Economist Intelligence Unit (*Special Report*, 11)

Morata, F., 1992. 'Regions and the EC: a comparative analysis of four Spanish regions', *Regional Politics and Policy*, 2 (1/2) (Spring/Summer), pp. 187–216

Parlamento Europeo, 1995. *Reglamento* (10th edn., June), Parlamento Europeo

Partido Socialista Obrero Español, 1995. *La conferencia intergubernamental de 1996: bases para una reflexión*, PSOE (Brussels)

Pombo, F., 1994. *Doing Business in Spain*, ch. 24, Mathew Bender

Yannopoulos, G. Y. (ed.), 1989. *European Integration and the Iberian Economies*, Macmillan

Critical studies

In addition to the above, mainly specific works, the following publications, which offer in-depth critiques of Spanish public life and institutions today, are recommended:

Díaz Herrera and Durán, I., 1994. *Los secretos del poder*, ediciones Temas de Hoy

Gutiérrez, J. L. and Miguel, A. de, 1989. *La ambición del César*, Ediciones Temas de Hoy

Ramírez, P. J., 1994. 'La triple crisis de la democracia española', *ACIS*, 7 (2) (Autumn), pp. 2–7

Sinova, J. and Tusell, J., 1992. *La década socialista: el ocaso de Felipe González*, Espasa Calpe

Tamames, R., 1993. *La España alternativa*, Espasa Calpe

Finally, one of the most valuable books available for consultation on almost any aspect of life past and present in Spain is the following publication (released in a new, expanded second edition in 1994):

Shields, G. 1994. *World Bibliographical Series, vol. 60: Spain*, Clio Press

Index of institutions and office holders

Spain

European Union

Note: Unlike the Spanish institutions, these are indexed in their English form, which is already likely to be familiar to the reader; Spanish equivalents and, where utilised, Spanish acronyms are given in brackets afterwards, as in the body of the text